European Antitrust Law

For Maria Rosario

European Antitrust Law

Prohibitions, Merger Control and Procedures

Lorenzo Federico Pace

Associate Professor of EU Law, University of Camerino
Attorney at Law, Rome

Edward Elgar

Cheltenham, UK • Northampton, MA, USA

Published by
Edward Elgar Publishing Limited
Glensanda House
Montpellier Parade
Cheltenham
Glos GL50 1UA
UK

Edward Elgar Publishing, Inc.
William Pratt House
9 Dewey Court
Northampton
Massachusetts 01060
USA

A catalogue record for this book
is available from the British Library

Library of Congress Control Number: 2006940075

ISBN 978 1 84542 695 8

Printed and bound in Great Britain by MPG Books Ltd, Bodmin, Cornwall

Contents

Preface

Since the end of the 1990s the Community antitrust system has undergone radical changes. The salient features of these changes have been both the alteration of the goals of Community antitrust law and the enactment of new implementing regulations.

Changing the goals of Community antitrust law has brought about a consequential change in the way in which Articles 81 and 82 are interpreted. In particular, the German influence which had marked it since its inception has gradually been abandoned.

The new rules implementing Articles 81 and 82 EC (Regulation 1/03) and those relating to merger control (Regulation 139/04) have brought about substantial changes in the procedures by which the relevant rules and prohibitions are enforced.

These changes have made it necessary to take a fresh look at this area of law. On this basis, I have endeavoured to organise the Community antitrust system in a new and coherent way, taking into account not merely the interpretation of Articles 81 and 82 EC, but also the procedural aspects of both Regulation 1/03 and of Regulation 139/04.

When writing this book, I have the good fortune to be able to move freely between Italy, Spain and Germany and in each of these three countries I have incurred debts of gratitude.

In Italy, I worked for a long time in the Section for International and European Law in the Law Faculty of the University of Rome 'La Sapienza'. I should like to thank Professor Paolo Picone, Professor Gian Luigi Tosato and Professor Ugo Villani for the help and intellectual stimulation that they have given me over the years.

In Spain, thanks to Professor Maria del Rosario Espinosa Calabuig, I was able to carry out research in the Law Faculty of the University of Valencia.

In Germany, I worked for a long time at the Max Planck Institut in Hamburg. I would like to thank Professor Jürgen Basedow, the Director of the Institute, for the time he was able to spare me and for having allowed me unlimited access to the Institute. I would also like to thank Professor Ernst-Joachim Mestmäcker for all the long but essential discussions that I had with him. Finally, I would like to thank Professor Heike Schweizer for the time that we spent together in convivial discussions about Community law.

Finally, warm thanks to Michael Wilderspin for his assistance in translating the text into English.

I hope that the reader will find this book interesting and useful. Like anything, it is certainly capable of further improvement. I would therefore invite anyone having comments to send me them at the following e-mail address: lfpace@competition-law.eu .

L.F.P.

PART I

CARTELS AND THE PROCESS OF EUROPEAN INTEGRATION

1. The Worldwide Industrialisation of the 19th Century and the 'Cartelisation' of the European Economy

In order to understand European antitrust law we do not need to identify the first laws in human history that outlawed agreements between undertakings fixing production quotas or prices of goods or those that forbade the creation of monopolies. That would take us back to the laws of ancient Egypt (Herlitzka, 1963, p. 121). In order to understand why European antitrust law originated and to understand the unification of the European economic area in the 20th century, we simply have to look at the process of industrialisation which took place in the western world in the 19th century.

1.1. THE WORLDWIDE INDUSTRIALISATION OF THE 19TH CENTURY AND THE BIRTH OF CARTELS IN THE USA AND IN EUROPE

Between 1815 and 1850 and again between 1870 and 1915, Europe enjoyed periods of peace. Those periods were marked by impressive economic growth, large numbers of important scientific inventions and the development of international competition between undertakings (Barbagallo, 1929, p. 283; Beaud, 2000, p. 177; see also Cameron and Neal, 2003). This era was known as 'Competitive Imperialism'. That expression was chosen in the light of the competition between the main industrialised countries (France, the United Kingdom, Germany and the United States of America) and to distinguish it from the first industrial revolution which took place at the end of the 18th century and which was characterised by British economic hegemony.

International competition gave rise to economic protectionism, despite which exports grew rapidly. In the 1870s and 1880s, exports between the main industrialised nations grew by 400% (500% in the USA, 220% in the UK and 180% in France) (Barbagallo, 1929, p. 250).

At the end of the 19th century, a second wave of colonisation by the industrialised nations took place against the background of the development of national capitalism on an international scale. One of the objectives of this colonisation was to establish new outlets for national products.

This period lasted until the outbreak of the First World War. So far as companies were concerned, its characteristic features were the constant growth in the size of the average firm and a considerable number of mergers (Beaud, 2000, p. 178).

The general increase in competition was also a consequence of the extension of the territory in which individual entrepreneurs could carry on their own activities. It led in its turn to the conclusion of agreements between competitors ('cartel agreements') aimed at getting rid of what the entrepreneurs regarded as 'ruinous competition'. Cartel agreements were agreements between competitors and their purpose was usually to fix prices and production quotas (De Novellis, 1931, p. 138).

Cartels began to be a problem in both Europe and the USA around the 1860s and 1870s.

1.1.1. Industrial Cartels in the USA

In the 19th century, the USA was an independent federal state which had expanded from the Atlantic seaboard to the Pacific coast. Around 1870, the Civil War between the industrialised North and the agricultural South had ended and significant industrialisation was taking place. The USA was already a 'common market' made up of a huge area without frontiers in which industrialisation and trade could develop freely (Dagnino, 1928, p. 131). Between 1878 and 1882, the rail network expanded from 4,300 kilometres to 18,600 kilometres. The growth of the rail network and the development of other means of transport gradually linked areas which had originally been cut off from one another. In its turn, this development encouraged trade and economic growth (De Novellis, 1931, p. 138).

In the second half of the 19th century the USA began to experience the establishment of industrial cartels in various sectors of the economy including the railways, gunpowder, tobacco, oil, steel, coal, gas and sugar (Beaud, 2000, p. 176).

The consequences of cartels in the USA (such as increases in the price of goods) gave rise to considerable protests from the entrepreneurs who were affected by the agreements and from the population at large. Mainly as a reaction to this, some states enacted antitrust laws in 1887. Those laws prohibited agreements limiting trade within the states and/or forbade conduct monopolising or attempting to monopolise trade (Hovenkamp, 1994, p. 670; see also Pace, 1999).

It was only in 1890 that Congress, following the pattern of the laws of the individual states, enacted the Sherman Act, which prohibited both cartels and conduct calculated to create monopolies. The purpose of the Sherman Act was not to replace the antitrust regimes in the individual states but rather to protect interstate commerce.

1.1.2. Industrial Cartels in Europe

Around 1870, when its main period of industrialisation began, Europe differed from the USA in not having a united 'common market'. It was divided into sovereign states and included three of the four main economic powers in the world (France, Germany and the UK). Since these states were sovereign, they could modify the trade flows between themselves as they wished through the use of 'levers' such as customs duties and taxes.

These countries shared an imperialist vision. They considered it in their interest to have economic growth with the objective of controlling new trade outlets for the benefit of their own companies and with a view to excluding companies from other countries (Beaud, 2000, p. 179). Industrial cartelisation began to take place in this context.

In Germany, due to more rapid economic development and industrialisation, cartelisation took place very quickly (Beaud, 2000, p. 159). The customs reform of 1879 gave the first push in that direction and subsequently the tendency towards cartelisation became more and more marked (Dagnino, 1928, p. 69).

The creation of cartels in Germany is documented as early as the 1820s (for example a cartel for the production of steel wire was concluded in 1822, see Kastl and Metzner, 1963, p. 461). However, it was not until the 1870s that cartels became a stock feature of the German Empire. Although there are no entirely precise statistics on the number of cartels in Germany, it has been calculated that there were around 345 between 1889 and 1899 (Vito, 1939, p. 5). Nevertheless, Germany did not enact any cartel legislation before 1923 and its first antitrust legislation dates only from 1957.

The fact that the approach towards cartels in Germany was so different from the American approach can only be explained by the principle of 'competitive imperialism' (Beaud, 2000, p. 187). As one author expresses it:

> Germany needed a powerful economy, which could not do without cartels. Cartels were one aspect of the new mercantilism. Without them, the state could not expand its own sphere of economic power. In the context of competition between Nations in the global marketplace, cartels played the role of industrial organisations to combat foreign competition and particularly the American trusts. It would have been unthinkable to combat cartels only on German territory. (Nörr, 1994, p. 29)

Similar reasons prevented any attention being paid to the negative effects of cartels on the population at large. Industrial cartels were useful ‘primarily for the state, the economy and large interest groups. The negative effect of cartels on all other persons who suffered because of them was secondary’ (ibid. p. 30). The situation did not even change in 1902 after consumers began to protest about the effects of cartelisation, as they had in the United States in the 1880s. In Germany, the protests led to the setting up of an enquiry into cartels, which lasted until 1906 (Vito, 1939, p. 199). The enquiry did not lead to any antitrust legislation or any means of controlling industrial cartels and, in fact, no such legislation was enacted until 1923.

Industrial cartels began to be established in other European countries before the First World War. The speed with which this took place varied from country to country and depended on local conditions. In France, the *comptoirs de vente* took root. Austria-Hungary and Belgium had the biggest number of cartels after Germany. Cartels and similar organisations for production and sale existed in the UK, Italy and Spain. However, ‘generally speaking, those agreements were far less significant and solid than the German cartels and German trusts’ (Dagnino, 1928, p. 75).

1.1.3. Cartels: The USA and Europe Compared

The above-mentioned factors explain why the dynamic of cartel regulation in Europe was so different from the United States.

In the United States, antitrust laws were initially enacted at the state level and were only later enacted at the federal level. In Europe, on the other hand, no national antitrust laws existed before the establishment of the antitrust regime in the Treaty of Rome (1957) (see Pace, 2000a).

In the 1870s, a common market already existed in the United States. It merely needed to be allowed to develop. The general objective, adopted first by the states and subsequently at the federal level, was to prohibit conduct by undertakings that were liable to impede the right of other undertakings to carry out their own activities and was harmful to consumers. However, the enactment of antitrust legislation was perceived in some quarters as an impediment to economic growth, and in the 1930s this led to some calls for it to be repealed (see Fetter, 1931).

In the Europe of the 1870s, on the other hand, there was no ‘common market’ but only national markets. The objective of individual states was not to create a European market. Quite the contrary, they were all competing with the others to control the European economy. The most extreme attempt to achieve this goal was made by Nazi Germany during the Second World War (Lador-Lederer, 1959, p. 4).

It is no coincidence that the first body of competition law on the European continent was ‘European’ (that is, the 1957 Treaty of Rome) and that the first national antitrust laws, enacted by the Federal Republic of Germany, came into force on the same day as the Treaty of Rome (1 January 1958).

1.1.4. Industrial Cartelisation and the First World War

In addition to cartelisation at the national level, international cartelisation also began to develop. By 1914, around one hundred cartels between similar industries in different countries aiming voluntarily to control competition between foreign markets had been concluded (ibid., De Novellis, 1931, p. 140).

During this period a proposal was made to establish a European customs union based on industrial cartels. In 1916, Friedrich Naumann proposed to link the gradual abolition of customs duties between European central powers to the establishment of cartels which would gradually cover all production (ibid.). That proposal was to be revived in a different guise in 1931 when France put it forward in the context of the Study Committee for the European Union (*infra*).

1.2. THE FIRST WORLD WAR AND THE CARTELISATION OF THE 1920S

The development of both national and international cartels after the First World War was closely connected with the extremely difficult economic and political situation. In the 1920s and 1930s, the economies of the main industrialised countries were extremely weak and had slowed down considerably by the end of the 1920s. At that time the European economics were already facing difficulties; the 1929 Wall Street crash and the subsequent Great Depression caused them to collapse. The collapse was also partly attributable to other factors: the international economic system had no means of controlling world trade (apart from industrial cartels) and there was no stable system of payment (Beaud, 2000).

The First World War had forced states to industrialise more. This had increased the tendency towards concentrations, which in turn increased the potential for production in Europe and the world (De Novellis, 1931, p. 140). In the period after the First World War, the cartels which had been dissolved were re-established except where this would have been expressly unlawful (Scott, 1932, p. 7). New cartels also developed extremely rapidly. The reasons for the growth of industrial cartels after the First World War were, *inter alia*:

1. *Overproduction.* The need to find a solution to the problem of

overproduction of goods caused by the cessation of hostilities led to agreements among competitors.

2. *Peace treaties*. Some countries lost parts of their territory as a result of the peace treaties. Consequently, some industries lost vital parts of their own structure and were not in a position to carry on operations unless they cooperated with companies in the countries which had taken over parts of their national territory. This was characteristic of the potassium and steel cartels.
3. *Autarchy (self-sufficiency)*. This form of economic policy was common until the end of the 1920s and had led to the establishment of customs barriers. In particular, the European and American efforts to attain autarchy considerably impeded the development of international trade. To solve this problem, the producers concluded international agreements (Vito, 1939, p. 214).

In order to have a clear idea of how widespread cartels were, it is useful to list, for each economic sector, the industrial cartels that were active in 1931 (De Novellis, 1931, p. 141; see also Werr, 1936, p. 151).

1.2.1. Chemical Cartels

- Carbide cartel.
- Chestnut extract cartel – Yugoslavia, Germany and Italy.
- Dyestuffs cartel – France and Germany.
- European glue cartel (for obtaining raw materials or the sale of the finished products) – UK, Italy, France, Germany, Austria, Belgium, Spain, the Netherlands, Hungary, Poland, Yugoslavia, Romania, Switzerland, Czechoslovakia, Denmark, Latvia and Sweden
- Iodine agreement – Chile, France, UK and Norway
- Potash syndicate – Germany and France.
- Quinine agreement – between Dutch, Javanese, British, German, French, Swiss, Japanese and American producers.
- Sulphuric acid cartel – Poland and Germany.
- Superphosphate cartel – Belgium, the Netherlands, UK, Germany, Czechoslovakia, Denmark, Finland, France, Norway, Poland, Sweden, French North Africa and the Union of South Africa.
- Cyanamid syndicate – between German, Belgian, French, Italian, Polish, Scandinavian, Swiss, Czechoslovak and Yugoslav producers.
- Glauber salt agreement – UK and Germany.
- Calcium carbide cartel – all producing countries.
- Aniline dye agreement – Germany, France and Switzerland.
- Bismuth agreement – Germany, UK, France and Italy.

- There were also international agreements on magnesite, borax, white lead and common salt.

1.2.2. Electricity Cartels

- International electric lamps syndicate – UK, Austria, Germany, Switzerland, the Netherlands, Hungary, Czechoslovakia, Sweden, Italy and Japan.
- Agreement on raw electrical materials – concluded by French and German producers, with the participation of Swiss producers.
- Canadian–European electrical agreement – established in 1930 with American Swiss and Italian capital.

1.2.3. Glass Production Cartels

- Bottle makers' cartel – UK, Germany, Austria, Hungary, Czechoslovakia, the Netherlands, Sweden, Norway and Denmark.
- International glass syndicate – Belgium, France, the Netherlands and Canada.
- Central European glass tableware cartel.
- Mirror cartel – Germany, Belgium and Czechoslovakia.

1.2.4. Iron and Steel Cartels

- European enamel cartel – Germany, Czechoslovakia, Poland, Austria and Hungary.
- International steel cartel – Belgium, France, Germany, Luxembourg, Saarland, Czechoslovakia, Austria and Hungary.
- International iron wire cartel – Germany, France, Belgium, the Netherlands and Luxembourg.
- International rail cartel – UK, France, Belgium, Luxembourg, Germany, Poland, Austria and Czechoslovakia.
- International iron and copper tubing cartel – France, Belgium, Germany, Luxembourg, Czechoslovakia, Poland and Hungary.
- International tinplate cartel – Germany, Austria, Saarland, Czechoslovakia and Hungary.
- Thomas slag cartel – Belgium, France, Germany, Luxembourg and Saarland.
- International wagon cartel – Belgium, France, Germany, Luxembourg, Saarland, Czechoslovakia, Austria, Hungary, Italy and Switzerland.

1.2.5. Metals and Minerals Cartels

- Aluminium cartel – France, Germany, UK, Italy, Austria and Switzerland.
- Copper cartel – UK, USA, Belgium, Spain and Yugoslavia. This cartel involved 95% of worldwide production.
- Ferromanganese cartel – UK, Germany, Norway and USA.
- Ferrosilicon cartel – Germany, Switzerland, Scandinavia and Austria.
- Magnesite cartel.
- Tin cartel – between British and American producers.
- Titanium cartel – Norway, France, Germany and USA.
- Nickel cartel – worldwide.
- International lead financial pool – predominantly Anglo-American.
- Uranium syndicate – Czechoslovakia and Belgium.
- White lead cartel – UK, Germany, Belgium, Italy, Austria and the Netherlands.
- Zinc cartel – Belgium, the Netherlands, France, Germany and Poland.
- Diamond syndicates – there were a number of such syndicates, the purpose of which was to maintain prices by limiting production. The South African government was involved.
- Bauxite cartel – Italy, Switzerland and Hungary.

1.2.6. Textiles Cartels

- Linen cartel – Central and Western European producers.
- Wool cartel – Belgian, French and British producers.
- Artificial silk cartel – between the Anglo-German group Glanzstoff Courtauld and the Italian Snia-Viscosa.

1.2.7. Cardboard and Cellulose Cartels

- Cellulose cartel – Czechoslovakia, Germany and other countries.
- Cardboard packaging agreement – Czechoslovakia, Austria, Hungary and Yugoslavia.

1.2.8. Miscellaneous Cartels

- International Hide Tanning Cartel – Belgium, France, Germany, UK, Italy, the Netherlands and Sweden.
- Timber Cartel – Finland and Sweden.
- Cement Cartel – France, Belgium, Poland, Germany, Scandinavia, the Netherlands and Luxembourg.

- Porcelain Agreement – Germany and Czechoslovakia.
- European Wood Screws Syndicate – producers from all European countries.
- International Nail Syndicate – Germany, the Netherlands and Denmark.
- International Tyre Agreement – UK, Germany, France, Belgium and USA
- Linoleum Cartel – Germany and central European states.
- Meat Cartel – Poker Konzern (Chicago) and Nestey Group (London).
- Margarine and Fatstuffs Cartel – worldwide.
- The Sugar Production Agreement which was concluded at the end of 1930 with the adoption of the Chadbourne reduction plan involved both cane-sugar (Cuba and Java) and beet-sugar producers (Central Europe, Poland and Belgium).

1.3. THE INTERNATIONAL STEEL CARTEL

A closer look at the international steel cartel is useful in order to have a better understanding of the relationship between industrial cartels and European integration. The steel sector, along with coal (an essential ingredient for producing steel) would later be the subject of the first stage of European integration through the European Coal and Steel Community (ECSC) Treaty.

The following factors played a role in the establishment of the steel cartel:

- The peculiar distribution of the relevant raw materials (that is, iron and coke). Eighty per cent of the European deposits of these two materials were located in an approximately square area 500 km long which covered parts of Belgium, France, Germany and Luxembourg. All the deposits in Europe, including those in Italy, Czechoslovakia, Austria and Hungary, were located in an approximately square area 1000 km long (Scagnetti, 1933, p. 109).
- Germany had considerable reserves of both iron and coal on its territory, whereas France had considerable reserves of iron but only limited coal reserves. Due to economies of scale, national production in both countries exceeded domestic demand and they therefore needed to find opportunities to sell their products abroad (Dagnino, 1928, p. 110).

France's need for coal reserves was temporarily resolved by two expedients:

- Certain specific provisions in the Treaty of Versailles (ibid., 1939, p. 212) to the detriment of Germany (however, those provisions caused considerable chaos throughout the entire steel industry in Central Europe) (Vito, 1939, p. 104); and

- France's military occupation of the Ruhr coalfields in 1923 (Dagnino, 1928, p. 83; Scagnetti, 1933, p. 107).

After the First World War, it became clear immediately that the economic situation in these sectors was unstable as regards both the distribution of coalfields and outlets for steel production. The problems of obtaining coal supplies and exporting the finished product were therefore closely connected. The only solution was an agreement:

> The bosses [in Germany] asked themselves whether they should persist in increasing ruinous competition, or whether they should instead attempt to control production by keeping it to a level which could be absorbed by the market. The French asked themselves whether they should continue to be plagued by the worry of obtaining coke supplies when they could easily obtain them through an agreement with Germany. The Germans asked themselves whether they should engage in a worldwide search for iron when it was on their doorstep. They therefore wondered whether they should pool their problems and resolve them jointly so as to rationalise the industry gradually and reduce costs in such a way as to allow outlets to be increased. (Dagnino, 1928, p. 103)

They therefore chose this course. Belgium, the Saarland and Luxembourg, which bordered both France and Germany and had reserves of the appropriate raw materials, also had to be involved (ibid., p. 102).

On 30 September 1926 these five countries established the steel cartel. The cartel's official name in German was *Rohstahlgemeinschaft* (ibid. p. 104), which translates as '*Steel Community*'. The name is striking since it brings to mind the completely different ECSC Treaty of 1952.

In 1927, companies in Czechoslovakia, Austria and Hungary also joined the agreement.

The Steel cartel's main objective was to protect internal markets (Kiersch, 1963, p. 345). It aimed to limit production through the establishment every three months of a tonnage programme which allowed a quota to be allocated to each national group on the basis of pre-determined coefficients (Lador-Lederer, 1959, p. 101). The agreement, as concluded in 1926, was dissolved in September 1930 (Vito, 1939, p. 163; Lador-Lederer, 1959, p. 123).

In 1933, the need to regulate competition (and thus the quantities and prices of products) breathed new life into the cartel. Within a few years all European countries, including the UK, and many non-European countries, including the USA, acceded to the agreement.

In order to be able to participate in the steel cartel, the United States had to circumvent the prohibitions established by the 1890 Sherman Act. To do this, it took advantage of certain provisions of the 1918 Webb–Pomerene Export Act, which allowed American firms to create export cartels provided that these did not have any effects on their national market.

Almost all firms in the industrialised countries acceded to the cartel. Germany, France, Belgium and Luxembourg were members from the establishment of the cartel in 1926 until it was finally wound up in 1939. Austria and Czechoslovakia joined in 1927. A number of firms in countries which were not members *stricto sensu* of the organisation cooperated with the system, sometimes only in specific cartels. Those countries were the USA (1929), Canada (1929), the Netherlands (1932), Denmark (1932), Sweden (1933), Norway (1934), Poland (1935), the UK, (1935), Italy (1937), and Romania, Spain, Finland and Yugoslavia (1939). Only Japan, which was probably prevented by the outbreak of the Second World War, did not accede to the cartel and restricted itself to cooperating with the international tubing cartel (Kiersch, 1963, p. 290).

At its greatest extent, the steel cartel covered 90% of worldwide exports of steel, which represented almost 5% of the export value of all goods. The agreement 'gave rise to the most formidable oligopolistic structure which the world had ever known' (Lador-Lederer, 1959, p. 24). It was wound up in 1939 because of the outbreak of the Second World War (ibid., p. 290; Kiersch, 1963, p. 349).

1.4. ATTEMPTS AT EUROPEAN UNIFICATION BASED ON CARTELS

Cartels became widespread and were significant economic actors because there was no national or international means of controlling them. The debate about their role in the international economy became especially relevant in the middle of the 1920s, *inter alia*, because of Europe's economic difficulties.

1.4.1. The 1927 Conference of the League of Nations

In both 1927 and 1930, the Economic Conference of the League of Nations was a forum for debate on some important economic questions. The issues discussed were the ongoing economic crisis, the development of a strategy to control cartels and ways of unifying Europe (Dagnino, 1928, p. 63; Del Marmol, 1959, p. 35).

In 1927, the League of Nations organised an International Economic Conference in Geneva. The two subjects that attracted most attention were industrial agreements and the issue of customs tariffs. During the general discussion on the worldwide situation, a number of subjects were debated. Among them were:

- the harm attributable to the existing systems of protectionism;
- the markets' poor capacity for absorption;
- Increased fiscal pressure;
- The permanent state of disorganisation which still existed in many economic sectors; and
- the diminishing importance of Europe in relation to other parts of the world and the need for countries to cooperate.

During the debate which took place in 1927 there was considerable opposition to the regulation of international cartels. Regulation, which was proposed primarily by France, in order to find ways of controlling cartels at the international level, was opposed mainly by the Germans, British and Norwegians.

The Conference concluded with an anodyne decision which accepted the German, British and Norwegian position and spelt failure for all of the French initiatives (Lador-Lederer, 1959, p. 187). In its final report, the Conference refrained from making any general judgement and recognised that, in certain circumstances and subject to guarantees, international agreements in the industrial sector would have a beneficial influence on the organisation of European production and trade (Dagnino, 1928, p. 63).

The member states of the League of Nations, which were predominantly European (von Puttkamer, 1965, p. 143), thus consciously preferred to favour their own national interests by allowing the establishment and growth of cartels. They did this in preference to seeking a solution which, given the scale of cartels, could have been exclusively European. The consequences of that choice played a role in bringing about, less than ten years later, what John Maynard Keynes described as the 'European Civil War', with 50 million dead throughout the world.

1.4.2. The Briand Plan of 1929 and the Failure of the 1931 Study Commission on European Union

Two years after the 1927 Conference, France once again proposed the establishment of a system to regulate the European economy. The details of the proposal were presented on 5 September 1929 at the 10th General Assembly of the League of Nations by Aristide Briand, the French Foreign Minister. The project consisted in creating links between the peoples of Europe through bodies of a federal nature (Albonetti, 1960, p. 28). Briand proposed *inter alia*:

- the establishment of economic relations, particularly in the light of the crisis existing at that time; and
- at a later stage, it would be possible to create ties of a political nature although they would have an effect on the sovereignty of individual states.

The original draft of the French proposal of 1929 was modified to a certain extent in the light of comments from various participating states. It was subsequently submitted as a memorandum addressed to the League of Nations and deposited on 1 May 1930. In contrast to the 1929 draft plan, the establishment of a political organisation was proposed. Any encroachment on the sovereignty of the participating states was excluded, as had been the case in 1929.

After the memorandum had been submitted, the 'Study Commission for the European Union' under the chairmanship of Briand was established. It followed a proposal from France and Yugoslavia which had been put forward within the framework of the United Nations. The Commission worked throughout 1932 but the proposals which it put forward were rejected by the Assembly of the League of Nations.

It is interesting to look in more detail at the proposals for the economic convergence of the states of Europe which were submitted to the Commission.

In the session of the Commission which took place between 15 and 21 May 1931, an attempt was made to establish a customs union (Mestmäcker, 1965, p. 350). As regards the issue of economic convergence, the Commission's draft was based on three principles:

- an economic system organised on the basis of international cartels;
- the abolition of customs duties through the cartels; and
- no encroachment by the organisation on the sovereignty of the Member States.

The proposal for a European Union based on economic cartels was not entirely new and bore some similarities with the proposal put forward by Naumann in 1916. Nevertheless, it was given serious consideration by some of the members of the League of Nations (Scagnetti, 1933, p. 32).

However, as mentioned above, the proposal of the Commission submitted in 1932 was rejected by the General Assembly of the League of Nations (Albonetti, 1960, p. 51).

Notwithstanding its ultimate failure, Briand's plan represented the first attempt to unify Europe through cooperation between European states that took account of the prevailing state of industrialisation in Europe.

1.5. THE BEGINNING OF NATIONAL LAWS ON CARTELS

Given the lack of any international bodies capable of regulating international trade and managing worldwide economic crises, industrial cartels continued to play a significant role in controlling trade. Partly as a consequence of the 1927 and 1930 conferences, in which states rejected any international form of control of cartels, control remained the prerogative of individual countries.

From the beginning of the 1920s, European countries began to enact laws to control cartels. However, they did not go as far as the Sherman Act. In other words, they did not enact a general prohibition on anticompetitive agreements between undertakings or on unilateral monopolistic behaviour.

The laws enacted in European countries were necessary to control the economic power held by the 'cartelised undertakings'. However, they aimed to protect only the economy of the country concerned. At that time, there was no notion of any 'general European interest', which was taken up only at a later stage by the European Economic Community (EEC).

Since the French and German experiences in regulating cartels were important when Articles 81 and 82 EC were drafted (*infra*), it is worth examining briefly the cartel laws enacted in those countries during this period.

1.5.1. Cartel Law in Germany

Germany developed an organised system of cartel control before other European countries. However, the German system took little account of the American antitrust laws (Vito, 1939, p. 198).

In Germany, the first legislation in the field was the *Verordnung gegen Missbrauch wirtschaftlicher Machtstellung* (Regulation against the Abuse of Economic Power) of 2 November 1923, known as the *Kartellverordnung*. The regulation stipulated that contractual terms inserted by members of a cartel as the result of the abuse of their economic power were null and void. Furthermore, the legislation established a special court, the *Kartellgericht* (Cartel Court), to enforce the law (Blum, 1932, p. 135). The objective of the legislation was simply to control cartels and not to eliminate them. Indeed, after its enactment, the number of cartels continued to increase, rising from 1500 in 1923/24 to 2100 in 1930 (De Novellis, 1931, p. 138; Vito, 1939, p. 5; Kronstein, 1962, p. 119).

On 26 July 1930 the 'Emergency Decree' (*Notverordnung*) was issued. This legislation, too, aimed to control rather than prohibit cartels. Its main function was to control prices which had risen sharply as a consequence of the period of German hyper-inflation.

In 1933, after the National Socialist government had come to power, the *Zwangkartellgesetz* (Compulsory Cartel law) was enacted. By virtue of that law, the Minister of the Economy had the ultimate power to regulate production and investments in the national economy, particularly with a view to creating compulsory cartels. The Minister could not only encourage negotiations for the purpose of concluding such agreements, but also regulate the rights and duties of the participants and prohibit statutory amendments. The Minister had the power to monitor and inspect cartels. This system was conceived as a way of rationalising the German economy and, some years later, of organising the Third Reich's war effort (Lador-Lederer, 1959, p. 5).

1.5.2. Cartel Law in France

France enacted specific legislation on agreements between undertakings as early as 1791. The '*Loi Le Chapelier*' of 14 June 1791 abolished professional guilds. The only interests recognised as worthy of protection were private interests and the general interest. Protection of group interests was thus excluded. The Law deemed that agreements to determine the prices of goods and services concluded between persons exercising the same economic activity were contrary to the interest of citizens. Such agreements were subject to criminal sanctions (Tchernoff and Lapie, 1932, p. 49).

Article 419 of the 1810 *Code pénal* established the crime of 'cornering the market'. The *actus reus* of this offence was 'association of holders of goods and public stock (industrialists, tradesmen, bankers) having the effect of interfering with prices as determined by free and natural trade competition' (Salandra, 1934, p. 28; Del Marmol, 1959, p. 79). The Law only struck at the exercise of particular influence on the market (that is, interfering with prices), and did not penalise all agreements limiting competition. Over time, this factor gave rise to case law, which drew a distinction between:

- bad agreements (*mauvaises unions*), which artificially fixed prices at a level different from what was deemed to be the 'normal' one; and
- good agreements (*bonnes unions*), which brought about an alteration in prices considered to be abnormal thereby bringing them to the level that was deemed to be 'normal'.

Article 419 of the *Code pénal* was amended by the Law of 3 December 1926. This law criminalized agreements and practices causing an alteration in prices with 'a view to gaining a profit which was not the result of the natural interplay between supply and demand' (Salandra, 1934, p. 29). The lack of any clear prohibition of cartels and the existence of the vague concept of 'artificial profit' made the law difficult to apply. It was amended in 1953 and replaced by the *délit de coalition*. This text was later taken into account when drafting the prohibition of anticompetitive agreements falling under Article 81 EC (*infra*).

2. The Dissolution of the Worldwide Steel Cartel and the Establishment of the ECSC System

At the end of the Second World War, attempts were made at the international level to control international cartels through the Havana Charter (Picone and Ligustro, 2003, p. 7). At the European level, after some attempts in the Council of Europe (1949) and the Economic Commission for Europe (1950; see Del Marmol, 1959, p. 37), cartel control became an important factor in the process of European integration.

The objective of European unification had to take a back seat to more pressing and concrete problems, in particular the need to draw up rules for European trade after the end of the Second World War. Before the war, the lack of any specific international regulations in the field had led to trade being regulated through international cartel agreements concluded by the undertakings themselves. After the war it was therefore necessary to decide whether or not cartels should continue to be used as a means of regulating international trade.

2.1. ATTEMPTS TO RE-ESTABLISH THE STEEL CARTEL

In Europe, the steel sector was one of the strategic industrial sectors which required rules to be enacted. Steel could not be treated in isolation from the issue of trade in coal, which was an essential factor in the production of steel (*supra*). The sheer size of the undertakings in the sector, linked with certain economic factors specific to the sector (such as fixed production costs, economic cycles) and the geographical distribution of the relevant raw materials (that is, iron and coke), had, from the middle of the 1920s, required the creation of the worldwide steel cartel which was dissolved in 1939.

After the war, various factors (including the dissolution of the cartel) led to the question of drawing up rules to regulate at least the intra-European steel trade. The need to draw up 'European' rules led to efforts to re-establish the same steel cartel. Towards the end of 1949 and the beginning of 1950 the representatives of the steel producers in Germany, France, Belgium, the Netherlands, Luxembourg, Sweden, Switzerland and probably the UK tried to establish agreements relating to the sale of various goods (Wells, 2002, p. 172).

2.2. THE SCHUMAN DECLARATION

The Benelux countries were behind the plan, put forward in 1950, to create an organisation that would provide for the joint management of the production of coal and steel, in particular as between France and Germany (Schulze and Hoeren, 2000, p. xxi).

The essential features of this objective were defined in the Schuman Declaration, named after the French Foreign Minister. Attainment of the objective would require the establishment of an organisation run by a supranational body, thereby ensuring independence from the influence of the participating states. The structure envisaged thus differed from the approach taken by the Briand Plan of the 1930s (*supra*).

The objective of the Schuman Declaration was to eliminate the reasons which had led to the Second World War and thereby prevent any possibility of a similar conflict occurring in the future (Del Marmol, 1959, p. 38). According to the intentions expressed by Schuman, an economic type of organisation was only the first step towards a more complete plan for European political union.

That said, as we have seen, the proposed organisation found a concrete solution to a fundamental problem of the European economy. At the end of the Second World War, the problems caused by the tension between the limited territorial reach of states compared with the huge size of companies and the international scale of their activities had still not been solved. Any state acting alone was no longer able to control companies that carried out economic activities outside its national territory.

2.3. THE PROBLEM OF CARTELS AND THE SCHUMAN DECLARATION

Initially, the Schuman Declaration of 9 May 1950 contained no express reference to cartel regulation (Wells, 2002, p. 163). Its only reference to cartels was the statement that 'unlike an international cartel, the planned organisation will guarantee the functioning of the market and the expansion of production'. These words were added by Jean Monnet on 28 April 1950 (Schulze and Hoeren, 2000, doc. 3). This reference was developed in a note annexed to the Schuman Declaration on 9 May 1950 (ibid., p. xxi).

The official documents show that Monnet himself wondered whether the organisation envisaged by the Schuman Declaration would not in fact be, to all intents and purposes, an industrial cartel. He argued 'We do not want a cartel, but we are in a cartel. Any decision on prices establishes a system similar to a cartel' (Schulze and Hoeren, 2000, p. xxi). Monnet's misgivings are understandable because the participation of member states in a cartel, as provided for by the Schuman plan, was not a novelty. The tin cartel, as modified in 1931, provided for the direct participation of Member States in the management of the agreement (Scagnetti, 1933, p. 204).

In a working document addressed to all the national delegations, Monnet explained that one of the objectives of the organisation would be to eliminate 'cartel practices'.

It has been claimed that the decisive push towards including antitrust rules in the ECSC Treaty was provided by the American government (Schulze and Hoeren, 2000. doc. 7; Wells, 2002, p. xxi; see also Gerber, 1998). It is certainly the case that, on 4 October 1950, Monnet himself gave a forthright warning to the heads of the delegation that, if there were no clear rules prohibiting cartels, the American government would not give any financial support to the coal and steel project (Schulze and Hoeren, 2000, p. xxi). Walter Hallstein, the German Foreign Minister, was also aware of this. The attitude of the United States was that a new cartelisation of the European, and in particular the German, economy should be prevented. The US position had been clearly expressed in an internal letter of 6 September 1944 sent by Franklin D. Roosevelt, the President of the United States, to the American Foreign Minister (Pace, 2005, p. 56).

For that reason Monnet not only made it clear that the ECSC was not a coal and steel cartel. He also undertook to take personal charge of drawing up the main principles of European antitrust law. In those principles it is stated that one of the aims of the ECSC Treaty was precisely to prohibit agreements between competitors.

2.4. THE ECSC TREATY AND COMPETITION LAW

On 18 April 1951, Belgium, France, Germany, Italy, Luxembourg and the Netherlands signed the Treaty establishing the European Coal and Steel Community (ECSC Treaty) in Paris. The Treaty entered into force on 23 July 1952 for a period of 50 years and thus expired on 23 July 2002.

The objectives of the ECSC Treaty, as expressed in its Article 2, were economic expansion, the growth of employment and a rising standard of living in the Member States. Article 3 provided that the actions which could be carried out to attain these objectives were the ensuring of an orderly and equal access to all the goods and markets which fell within the scope of the Treaty, the encouragement of the rational development of trade and increased production. In other words, the Treaty established a common market limited to the six signatory states and to the coal and steel sector. In the last analysis, this system was required due to the dissolution of the worldwide steel cartel in 1939.

Antitrust provisions were contained in Articles 65 and 66. Article 65 related to cartels, Article 66(1) regulated concentrations and Article 66(7) concerned the use of a dominant position for purposes contrary to the Treaty.

By the end of the ECSC Treaty's fifty-year period of validity in 2002, the steel market had developed, the scale of companies had increased and the market had been rationalised over the years. All these factors meant that it was no longer necessary to make the sector subject to a *lex specialis* such as the ECSC Treaty. The whole coal and steel sector was thus transferred under the umbrella of the EC Treaty and it is now governed by the rules on the common market.

2.5. THE FAILURE OF THE EUROPEAN DEFENCE COMMUNITY AND THE PROCESS OF EUROPEAN INTEGRATION

The next stage in the creation of a united Europe was to be the establishment of the European Defence Community (EDC). The purpose of the relevant agreement was to create a defence structure which would pool the military organisations of the participating states. Moreover, Article 38 of the Draft Treaty committed the signatories to study and plan a European Political Authority. In 1954 the project collapsed following France's failure to ratify it (Albonetti, 1960, p. 144).

It is important to bear this event in mind in order to understand the context of the later genesis of the EEC Treaty and the importance of the common market which that Treaty regulates. The failure of the EDC confirmed what the Briand Plan had already shown in 1930, that is, that the states of Europe were, at least at that time, incapable of making progress in organising the European Area on anything other than an economic basis.

3. The EEC and the Birth of European Competition Law

In 1955, the Benelux countries were once again behind an agreement whose purpose was to organise cooperation between the states of Europe on a lasting and peaceful basis (Schulze and Hoeren, 2000, p. xxv). The stillbirth of the EDC, like the failure of the plan for European Union of 1931, had shown that it was not possible to found such cooperation on a strictly political basis. A different strategy was thus required. The development and the growth of industry in Europe meant that the project needed to have an economic foundation.

3.1. THE MESSINA CONFERENCE AND THE SPAAK REPORT

The principles of the proposed plan were defined at the 1955 Messina conference and summarised in the Final Report (known as the Spaak Report). These principles were remarkable for being diametrically opposed to what had been formulated 25 years earlier at the International Conference which had taken place in 1930 (*supra*). In essence, the strategy of the organisation was to create a European area based on undistorted competition between undertakings. In stark contrast to the Briand Plan, its guiding principles were as follows:

- it was to be an international organisation;
- in order to attain the objectives of the Treaty, certain aspects of the sovereignty of the Member States would be limited; and
- economics would take precedence over politics.

More specifically, as regards the principles by which the economy would be regulated, the Spaak Report advocated a twin-track approach:

1. The first aspect was the creation of a customs union within which competition between undertakings would be safeguarded.

2. Both cartels and unilateral abuses of a dominant position enjoyed by an undertaking would be made illegal.

If we compare this plan with the French project dating from the early 1930s, we can appreciate how radically different its philosophy was. In particular, the basis of the economic system of the earlier project would have been the establishment of a customs union through cartels to promote economic convergence among its Member States (*supra*).

3.2. THE ESTABLISHMENT OF THE EEC TREATY

The six countries which were already signatories of the ECSC Treaty signed in Rome the EEC Treaty on 25 March 1957 and it, like the Euratom Treaty, came into force on 1 January 1958 for an unlimited period.

In addition to its ultimate objective of preserving peace, which was referred to in the recitals, the purposes of the Community were defined in Article 2 of the EEC Treaty. They were 'to promote throughout the Community a harmonious development of economic activities, a continuous and balanced expansion, an increase in stability, an accelerated raising of the standard of living and closer relations between the states belonging to it'. Article 3 (1957) listed the actions which were to be taken in order to attain the objectives provided for in Article 2.

3.2.1. The Common Market and the *Res Publica Comunitaria*

The common market referred to in Article 2 was established in order to allow companies to carry on their activities in competition with each other and without discrimination on the ground of nationality. In this sense, the common market brought about the birth of a *Res publica comunitaria* ('European Commonwealth'). For the first time, and in marked contrast to the events of the preceding decades, the states of Europe united to create an institution for the common good which genuinely belonged to everyone and which was also conceived as being for the benefit of the citizens of Member States. Thanks to the provisions guaranteeing the common market, these citizens had rights conferred directly on them (*infra*).

The common market, protected externally by the common customs union, had to be protected from its 'enemies', string pullers who wished, and indeed still wish, to push back the common market so that it is simply the sum of all the national markets. This would restrict competition within the common market and would ultimately have the aim of limiting its advantages for European citizens.

The first enemy was the 'enemy within' the common market, which can be both Member States and individuals. In order to protect the common market from the activities of Member States, the EEC Treaty provided for:

- The four fundamental Community freedoms, which consist essentially in prohibiting Member States from limiting the free movement of undertakings, the factors of production and workers on grounds of nationality.
- The power to approximate 'such provisions laid down by law, regulation or administrative action in the Member States as directly affect the establishment or functioning of the common market' (Article 100 EEC).
- The competition rules addressed to the Member States (Articles 86 and 87 EEC).
- In order to protect the common market from the behaviour of individuals, the EEC Treaty prohibited undertakings from restricting competition, which it achieved through Articles 85 and 86 EEC.

The common market was also protected from the second enemy, the 'enemy at the gate'. This expression refers in particular to agreements concluded by Member States and third countries or non-Community organisations which might jeopardise the unity of the common market. Such agreements could 'bring about discrimination, distortion of competition and the destabilisation of the Community market'.[1] Article 110 of the 1957 EEC Treaty established the common commercial policy to provide protection from that enemy.

The Court of Justice was later to make an important contribution to the realisation of the common market by developing the three fundamental principles which distinguish the Community from other international organisations, namely:

- *The principle of independence.*[2] This has guaranteed that the institutional structure of the Community is independent from the influence of the Member States.

---

[1] *Commission v. Kingdom of Denmark*, Case C-467/98, E.C.R. 2002 p. I–9519, § 46.

[2] See, *inter alia*, *Van Gend & Loos v. Netherlands Inland Revenue Administration*, Case 26/62, E.C.R. English special edition 1963, p. 1, p. 3; *Flaminio Costa v. ENEL*, Case 6/64, E.C.R. 1964, p. 1129; *Amministrazione delle finanze dello Stato v. SpA Simmenthal*, Case 106/77, E.C.R. 1978, p. 629; *Molkerei – Zentrale Westfalen/Lippe GmbH v. Hauptzollamt Paderborn*, Case 28/67, E.C.R. 1968, p. 192; *Andrea Francovich e Danila Bonifaci v. Italian Republic*, Joined Cases C-6/90, C-9/90 and.C.R. 1991, p. I–5357.

- *Direct effect.*[3] This principle, which must be distinguished from 'direct applicability' (*infra*), requires national courts to enforce certain rules of Community law which have particular characteristics. Rules are held to be directly effective if they are clear, unconditional and sufficiently precise.
- *The supremacy of Community law*,[4] which is closely linked to the principle of direct effect. It requires national courts to set aside national laws which conflict with provisions of Community law having direct effect. The purpose of this principle is to ensure the uniform and simultaneous application of Community law throughout the Member States.

3.2.2. The Provision of Antitrust Rules and the Transition from National Cartel Law to Community Competition Law

As mentioned, the antitrust provisions were regulated in the Treaty of Rome by Articles 85 and 86 (1957). They prohibited, respectively, anticompetitive agreements and the abuse of a dominant position. Unlike the ECSC Treaty, the EEC Treaty contained no specific rules regulating concentrations. Those rules were introduced by Regulation 4064/89,[5] later replaced by Regulation 139/04[6] (*infra*).

Establishing competition rules addressed to undertakings had important consequences for the system as a whole. Articles 85 and 86 were the first steps in creating a European competition law (*Wettbewerbsrecht*) as opposed to a national law on cartels (*Kartellrecht*) which had been seen in Europe in the 1920s and 1930s.

3.2.3. The Role of the Commission in the Community Legal Order

Within the institutional system of the EEC Treaty, the Commission played a fundamental role. It was supranational, and thus independent of the Member States, rather than simply an intergovernmental body. By being able to act independently, the Commission ensured the protection of the *res publica comunitaria* ('Community common good') as opposed to the specific interests of the Member States or of individuals. It ensured compliance with

---

[3] For the relevant case law, see *infra*.

[4] See, *inter alia*, *Flaminio Costa v. ENEL*, Case 6/64, E.C.R. 1964, p. 1129; *Amministrazione delle finanze dello Stato v. Simmenthal*, cit..

[5] Council Regulation 4064/89 of 21 December 1989 on the control of concentrations between undertakings, OJ L 395 of 30 December 1989, p. 1.

[6] Council Regulation 139/04 of 20 January 2004 on the control of concentrations between undertakings (the EC Merger Regulation).

the obligations imposed by the EEC Treaty:

- on Member States, through the mechanisms provided by Articles 169 (now Article 226) and following; and
- on individuals, through Articles 89 (now Article 85) and following (on this point, see extensively Mestmäcker, 1993, p. 1).

3.3. SOME OBSERVATIONS ON THE PROCESS OF EUROPEAN INTEGRATION

Both the purposes of the Community of 1957 and the way in which it is organised have undergone significant changes during the 'process of European integration'.[7] This process has been marked by three guiding principles.

The first guiding principle has been the development through the Community method and has been marked by two principal 'variables':

1. *An increase in the number of powers conferred on the Community.* The process of conferring more powers on the Community started in the 1970s. It has been responsible for five separate aspects of integration:

   - the modification of the objectives of the Community (Articles 2 and 3 EC);
   - the problem of the 'legitimation' of the EC;
   - the need to regulate the exercise of the Community's legislative powers (Article 5 EC);
   - the extension of majority voting in the Council; and
   - the development of flexible methods of further European integration.

2. *The increase in the number of Member States.* In 1957 the Community comprised six founding states. Over the years it has expanded gradually and, since 1 January 2007, has 27 Member States. Expansion has meant that the operation of the institutional system has progressively become more complex. This, in turn, has required structural amendments of the Community institutions which started with the Treaty of Amsterdam.

---

[7] In particular, through the Single European Act, which was signed on 17 February 1986 in Luxembourg and which entered into force on 1 July 1987; the Treaty on European Union, which was signed on 7 February 1992 in Maastricht (NL) and which entered into force on 1 November 1993; the Amsterdam Treaty, which was signed on 2 October 1997 and which entered into force on 1 May 1999; and the Treaty of Nice which was signed on 26 February 2001 and which entered into force on 1 February 2003.

The second guiding principle has been the development of methods of cooperation other than the Community method *stricto sensu*. This process started with the establishment of European Political Cooperation in the 1986 Single European Act. This became the Common Foreign and Security policy in the Maastricht Treaty. In the same Treaty, provisions on 'Cooperation in the fields of justice and home affairs' were added.

The third guiding principle, the protection of fundamental rights, has developed differently in the European Community from the way in which it has evolved in the European Union:

1. Within the European Community, fundamental rights have been protected thanks to the development of the relevant case law of the Court of Justice. This process culminated in the solemn proclamation of the Charter of Fundamental Rights in Nice.
2. Within the European Union, this process has followed two different lines:

   - Article 6 EU, which requires the Union to respect fundamental rights, as guaranteed by the ECHR and the constitutional traditions common to the Member States;
   - Article 7 EU, which requires Member States to respect fundamental rights and which provides for the possibility of sanctions in case of violations of those rights.

These three guiding principles of European integration were fused in the text of the 'Treaty establishing a Constitution for Europe' signed in Rome on 29 October 2004. The process of ratification in the Member States was placed in doubt after the 'No' votes in the French and Dutch referenda in 2005.

The Constitution should have a triple function:

- Part II, the Charter of Fundamental Rights, transposes into legal rules the common values of 25 Member States and more than 450 million people.
- Part III, The Politics and Functioning of the Union, establishes the rules of a complex institutional system involving 25 Member States.
- Part III, Title V, External Action of the Union, allows the Union to ensure greater coordination, no longer limited to commercial policy, in the way in which it conducts its foreign policy.

3.4. CARTELS AND THE PROCESS OF EUROPEAN INTEGRATION IN THE 20TH CENTURY: A HISTORICAL PERSPECTIVE

If we summarise the rise and fall of cartels (including the appearance of national cartel law and the subsequent transition to Community competition law) we can identify the reasons behind the establishment of the EEC and the process of European integration in the 20th century. It can be argued that the EEC is not an organisation established to facilitate the concentration of capital or to open the internal markets of the Member States. It resulted from the need in the post-war period to regulate the 'economic evolution', and started in the coal and steel sectors with the ECSC.

The birth of the Community can be traced to the crisis of the 'national state' in Europe. Originally the national state was treated as a legal order capable of regulating any socio-economic question. It found itself in a crisis because it was not capable of solving each and every economic problem. The scale of European industry and of the cartels which it had spawned had, in substance, prevented the state from being fully able to carry out this function (Lador-Lederer, 1959, p. 18).

Despite the profound changes to the original European Economic Community which have occurred in the last fifty years, the economic roots of the process have not disappeared.

The equality between the Member States established by the EC Treaty (and by Article 5 of the EU Constitution itself) is a result of the process of European integration. It is a consequence of the creation of a common market in which undertakings can carry on their activities without being discriminated against on the grounds of nationality, that is, on the basis of equality. The principle of equality of undertakings on the market required the Treaty of Rome to be based on the principle of equality of the individual Member States within the Community. Such equality had never been conferred in earlier types of European territorial union which were not based on the recognition and regulation of private economic initiative. (See for instance the process of 'European integration' which took place in the Roman period after the 3rd century BC.[8])

The principle of equality has been transformed into a general principle that

[8] The process of 'European integration' during the Roman period after the 3rd century BC can be compared with the integration of the 20th century AD, but the comparison is limited to the size of the territory which was subject to the sway of each of the legal orders concerned. Under the Roman Empire there was no industrial structure allowing a supranational legal organisation to be created for such a vast territory and the consequence was that Rome assumed control over its provinces on the basis of 'domination' rather than equality between the parties. On this point, see Talamanca (1989, p. 111) and Pekàry (2003, p. 195).

is not limited to undertakings. The principle of equality between undertakings has subsequently evolved into a general principle of equality among citizens of different Member States, now recognised in the status of European citizenship. Article 10 of the EU Constitution itself provides that citizens of the Member States 'enjoy the rights and are subject to the duties provided for in the Constitution'. In this way, it differs from other historical experiences such as 'European unification' in the time of the Romans.[9]

To sum up, the history of cartels in Europe shows that the process of European unification has been – and still is – based on the capacity of individuals to exercise their right of economic initiative. The future of the European Union, and whether it will prosper or decline, will depend *inter alia* on how that right is regulated as well as on the capacity of the 'European economic system' to compete with both old and new common markets (such as the United States, China and India) in the broader global market.

[9] Such as the 'European unification' which occurred under the Romans. At that time, the Roman legal system was not based on any principle of equality in so far as it concerned relations between Rome and the conquered provinces. Consequently, the population of the conquered provinces was subordinate to Rome. It was only in 212 AD that the *Constitutio Antoniniana* officially recognised the population of the provincial territories as being equal to the Romans by granting them Roman citizenship.

PART II

EUROPEAN ANTITRUST POWERS

4. The Antitrust Powers of the EC Treaty and the Concept of Antitrust Law

The Spaak Report advocated two types of provision:

- the first related to the prohibition of industrial cartels; and
- the second concerned the prohibition of monopoly behaviour by undertakings (Schulze and Hoeren, 2000, p. xxiv, *supra*).

The fact that the EC Treaty contains rules combating anticompetitive behaviour which are addressed to undertakings is a consequence of the approach adopted by the Treaty of Rome. The creation of an internal market in which the undertakings of different states compete with one another:

- presupposes that undertakings have the right of economic initiative; and
- implies that there must be some limits to the exercise of that right.

Articles 81 and 82 are not the only provisions of the Treaty of Rome which contain the antitrust powers that the Member States have conferred on the European Community. The Council's power to adopt regulations and directives pursuant to Article 83 forms part of the Community's antitrust competence and those powers are set out in Articles 83 to 85.

Articles 81 and 82 contain the substantive prohibitions of antitrust law.

Regulations and directives adopted on the basis of Article 83 establish a system of antitrust law which replaces the provisional structure established by Articles 84 and 85 EC, the purpose of which is to implement Article 3(1)(g) EC[1] and to create a system establishing a common market.[2]

[1] *Am and S Europe Limited v. Commission*, Case 155/79, E.C.R. 1982, p. 1575, § 15.

[2] *Italian Republic v. Council and Commission*, Case 32/65, E.C.R. 1966, p. 296; *Walt Wilhelm v. Bundeskartellamt*, Case 14/68, E.C.R. 1969, p. 1, § 4; *Acf Chemiefarma Nv v. Commission*, Case 41/69, E.C.R. 1970, p. 661; *Anne Marty Sa v. Estee Lauder Sa*, Case 37/79, E.C.R. 1980, p. 2481; *Am and S Europe Limited v. Commission*, op. cit., p. 1575; *National Panasonic (UK) Limited v. Commission*, Case 136/79, E.C.R. 1980, p. 2033, § 20; *Ministère Public v. Lucas Asjes, Andrew Gray, Jacques Maillot, Leo Ludwig*, Joined Cases 209 and 213/84, E.C.R. 1986, p. 1425; *Hoechst AG v. Commission*, Joined Cases 46/87 and 227/88, E.C.R. 1989, p. 2859, § 25; *Dow Benelux Nv. v. Commission*, Case 85/87, E.C.R. 1989, p. 3137, § 36; *Dow Chemical Iberica Sa v. Commission*, Joined Cases 97/87, 98/87 and 99/87,

Articles 84 and 85 EC themselves form part of the powers that have been conferred in order to safeguard competition. In the absence of regulations or directives adopted on the basis of Article 83, they provide for a transitional system of antitrust enforcement.

4.1. THE ROLE OF ANTITRUST LAW IN THE EC TREATY

In order to identify and fully understand the role of antitrust law within the EC Treaty, the relationship between 'objectives, activities and means' in the Treaty has to be borne in mind:

- Article 2 EC sets out the 'objectives' or 'tasks' (described rather more graphically in the French text as the 'mission') of the Community. In Article 2, the establishment of the common market is described as one of the Community's fundamental objectives.
- Article 3 EC 'determines the fields and objectives to which the activities of the Community are to relate, lays down the general principles of the common market, which are to be applied in conjunction with the respective chapters of the Treaty devoted to their implementation'.[3] Article 3(1)(g) EC mentions as one of the 'activities' of the Community 'a system ensuring that competition in the internal market is not distorted'. According to the case law, this provision represents a general aim of the Treaty and is 'a part of the general principles of the common market which are applied in conjunction with the relevant chapters of the Treaty'.[4]

E.C.R. 1989, p. 3165, § 22; *Orkem Sa. v. Commission*, Case 374/87, E.C.R. 1989, p. 3283, § 19; *Procureur de la République v. Bruno Giry*, Joined cases 253/78 and 1 to 3/79, E.C.R. 1980, p. 2327; *French Republic v. Commission*, Case C-202/88, E.C.R. 1991 p. I–1223; *Tetra Pak Rausing Sa v. Commission*, Case T-51/89, E.C.R. 1990, p. II–309, § 22; *Automec Srl v. Commission*, Case T-24/90, E.C.R. 1992, p. II–2223; *Federal Republic of Germany v. Council*, Case C-426/93, E.C.R. 1995, p. I–3723. On the objective of Article 83 EC as compared with Article 95 EC, see *French Republic v. Commission*, Case C-202/88, E.C.R. 1991 p. I–1223, § 23.

[3] *Echirolles Distribution SA v. Association du Dauphiné*, C-9/99, E.C.R. 2000, p. I–8207, § 22.

[4] *Henri Cullet v. Centre Leclerc*, Case 231/83, E.C.R. 1985 p. 305, § 10; *Compagnie commerciale de l'ouest v. Receveur principal des Douanes de la Pallice port*, Joined Cases C-78/90, C-79/90, C-80/90, C-81/90, C-82/90 and C-83/90, E.C.R. 1992, p. I–1847, § 18.

- Articles 81 and 82 EC constitute the 'means' by which Article 3(1)(g) of the Treaty is implemented. They are fundamental provisions which are essential 'for the accomplishment of the tasks entrusted to the Community and, in particular, for the functioning of the internal market'.[5]

4.2. THE CONCEPT OF ANTITRUST LAW

Two factors enable us to distinguish antitrust law from other laws regulating competition.

4.2.1. The Purpose of the Law

The general purpose of antitrust law is to prevent the behaviour of individuals from eliminating competition and establishing private monopolies in its stead. This distinguishes antitrust law from other types of market regulation (such as laws on unfair competition). This point applies irrespective of the fact that different schools of thought have developed various theories to explain the precise goals of antitrust prohibitions. However, whatever purpose one wishes to ascribe to antitrust law (for example, the right of initiative of individual economic operators or ensuring the efficient allocation of resources), all schools of thought recognise that a common objective of antitrust law is to prevent the exercise of the right of economic initiative from leading to a monopoly.

4.2.2. The Scope of the Rules

Antitrust law applies generally to every economic sector and to all undertakings (subject to certain specific exceptions, such as Agriculture in Article 32 EC). Antitrust law is a general system of regulation with which undertakings must comply. To that extent, there is no 'special antitrust law'.

This allows us to draw a distinction between antitrust law and other general sets of rules regulating market behaviour (that is, laws regulating the authorisation needed in order to carry out a specific activity in a particular economic sector, the ways in which undertakings may or must exercise their right of economic initiative, and the relations between undertakings *inter se* or between undertakings and public bodies).

The Commission defines antitrust law as being 'for the protection of

---

[5] *Eco Swiss China Time Ltd v. Benetton International NV*, Case C-126/97, E.C.R. 1999, p. I–3055, § 36; *Courage Ltd v. Bernard Crehan*, Case C-453/99, E.C.R. 2001 p. I–6297, § 20.

competition on the market' and regards it as distinct from legislation 'which protects other legitimate interests' (see Recital 9 of the Preamble to Regulation 1/03 and paragraph 39 of the Commission Notice on Cooperation within the Network).

In the European experience, antitrust law means the system established in 1958 by Articles 81 and 82 EC and national laws having the same objectives. These laws (beginning with the German *GWB*, which entered into force at the same time as the Treaty of Rome, on 1 January 1958) have all been enacted since the end of the Second World War. One point that they have in common is that they have definitively abandoned controlling – as opposed to prohibiting – cartels, which was the approach that characterised the previous laws enacted in the 1920s and 1930s (*supra*).

From a practical point of view, distinguishing antitrust laws from other market regulations is comparatively straightforward in the EC Member States, since the 'communitarisation' of national antitrust laws has led to almost all of the relevant national laws being worded similarly to Articles 81 and 82 EC (*infra*).

Certain provisions of the EC Treaty give examples which clarify the distinction between laws safeguarding competition (that is, antitrust law, *diritto di tutela della concorrenza*, *derecho de defensa de la competencia*) and general rules regulating competition (*disciplina della concorrenza*; *derecho de la libre competencia*).

In particular, within Part 3, Title VI, Chapter 1, entitled 'Rules on Competition' and comprising Articles 81 to 89, Articles 81 and 82 are provisions safeguarding competition.

Articles 86 and 87 EC are also rules 'regulating competition', but they are not laws 'safeguarding competition'. They are rules, subject to certain express exceptions, which require Member States not to intervene in the economy in a way which could distort competition in the common market. This is a consequence of the fact that the objective of the common market is to create an area in which undertakings from different Member States may be active without being discriminated against on the basis of their nationality by other Member States.

The Treaty provisions establishing the four freedoms also constitute market regulation but they are not rules 'safeguarding competition'. By prohibiting Member States from enacting rules which discriminate against undertakings on the grounds of nationality, those provisions permit competition on an equal footing between undertakings established in different Member States.

5. The Goals of European Antitrust Law

It is extremely important to define the goal of antitrust law since it, in turn, determines the scope of the right of economic initiative. The content of this right is dependent on whether the goal of antitrust law is seen as being to safeguard the right of initiative of individual economic operators or as being to protect the efficiency of undertakings (*infra*).

5.1. THE EVOLUTION OF THE GOAL OF EUROPEAN ANTITRUST LAW

One of the activities of the Community is to realise 'a system ensuring that competition in the internal market is not distorted' (Article 3(1)(g) of the Treaty). Since the Treaty at no point defines what is meant by undistorted competition, the determination of the goal of Community antitrust law is left to the discretion of the Commission which, by virtue of Article 211 EC, has the exclusive power to determine the orientation of Community antitrust policy, subject to the *ex post* review exercised by the Court of Justice (*infra*).

In order to determine what the goal of EC antitrust law is, we must therefore examine how the Commission has determined competition policy over time and how the Community judicature has reacted to this.

In this regard, we can identify three separate periods.

5.1.1. The First Period: The 1960s

In the 1960s there were no decisions applying Article 82 and so the goal of antitrust law was defined only with reference to Article 81. According to the case law, the aim of antitrust law was to maintain the 'unity of the market' and to prevent the creation of 'barriers between states' through the behaviour of private parties.[1] This goal can be explained by the need for Community antitrust law to tackle the strategies by which companies seek to use

[1] See *Italian Republic v. Council and Commission*, Case 32/65, E.C.R. 1966, p. 296; *Nv International Fruit Company v. Commission*, Joined Cases 41 and 44/70, E.C.R. 1971, p. 411, § 6; *Continental Can v.Commission*, Case 6/72, E.C.R. 1973, p. 215, § 25.

agreements to maintain the barriers partitioning the common market and which, prior to the entry into force of the EC Treaty, had been erected by state measures.

5.1.2. The Second Period: The 1970s to the 1990s

From the 1970s to the 1990s, the aim of Community antitrust law can be summarised by referring to what the Commission itself wrote in its Report on competition for 1985. In that Report, the Commission stated:

> The Member States of the European Community share a common commitment to individual rights, to democratic values and to free institutions. It is those rights, values and institutions at the European and national levels that provide necessary checks and balances in our political systems. Effective competition provides a set of similar checks and balances in the market economy system. It preserves the freedom and right of initiative of the individual economic operator and it fosters the spirit of enterprise. It creates an environment within which European industry can grow and develop in the most efficient manner and at the same time take account of social goals. *Competition policy should ensure that abusive use of market power by a few does not undermine the rights of the many*; it should prevent artificial distortions and enable the market to stimulate European enterprise to innovate and to remain competitive on a global scale. (Emphasis added)[2]

This approach gave rise to a considerable body of case law in which the aim of antitrust law was variously described as being the maintenance of workable competition, effective competition,[3] the prevention of the impairment of an effective structure of competition,[4] the maintenance of normal competition[5] or to prevent competition from being distorted 'to the detriment of the public interest, individual undertakings and consumers'.[6] (On this point and on the relationship between antitrust law and economic models, see van den Bergh and Camesasca, 2001, p. 21.)

---

[2] XV Report on competition policy, p. 11.

[3] *Metro SB – Grossmaerkte GmbH et Co. KG v. Commission*, Case 26/76, E.C.R. 1977, p. 1875, § 21; *Continental Can v. Commission*, op. cit., p. 215, § 25.

[4] See *Akzo Chemie Bv v. Commission*, Case C-62/86, E.C.R. 1991, p. I–3359, §§ 64 and 69; *Continental Can v. Commission*, op. cit., p. 215, § 21; *United Brands v. Commission*, Case 27/76, E.C.R. 1978, p. 207, § 86.

[5] *Tetra Pak Rausing Sa v. Commission*, Case T-51/89, E.C.R. 1990, p. II–309, § 23.

[6] *Hoechst AG v. Commission*, Joined Cases 46/87 and 227/88, E.C.R. 1989, p. 2859, § 25; *Dow Benelux Nv v. Commission*, Case 85/87, E.C.R. 1989, p. 3137, § 36; *Dow Chemical Iberica Sa v. Commission*, Joined Cases 97/87, 98/87 and 99/87, E.C.R. 1989, p. 3165, § 22; *Orkem Sa v. Commission*, Case 374/87, E.C.R. 1989, p. 3283, § 19.

- With regard to Article 81 EC, that approach, which 'maintains the freedom and the right of initiative of individual economic operators', led in the direction of an automatic prohibition of all agreements between competitors. This approach followed the approach provided for in German antitrust legislation, albeit the relevant provision is worded differently (*supra*).
- With reference to Article 82 the goal of antitrust law, as 'the protector of the freedom and the right of initiative of individual economic operators', is manifested in different ways, although its goal, like that of Article 81, is inspired by the Freiburg Ordoliberal School. According to the Commission's practice until the end of the 1990s, Article 82 EC covered 'abuse which may directly prejudice consumers as well as abuse which indirectly prejudices them by impairing the effective competition structure as envisaged by Article 3(f) of the Treaty'.[7] In other words, the detriment suffered by consumers who are victims of practices prohibited by Community competition law 'is not simply direct financial damage ... but also the indirect prejudice resulting from the impairment of the competitive structure'.[8]

5.1.3. The Third Period: From the 1990s to the Present Day

In the third period, the goal of EC antitrust law has been and continues to be the efficient allocation of resources in the market rather than the protection of the structure of the market (which implies protection not only of consumers but also of competitors).

This change of approach was made clear both in the Guidelines on the application of Article 81(3) and the Discussion Paper on the application of Article 82 which was published in December 2005.

In the Discussion Paper, the Commission maintained that 'the Community competition rules protect competition on the market as a means of enhancing consumer welfare and of ensuring an efficient allocation of resources' (§ 88).

However, this change of approach had been foreshadowed as early as 2002 in a statement of Philip Lowe, the Director General of DG Competition. Speaking in front of an American audience, he stated: 'Enforcement action aims at protecting competition ... The interest for consumers in the broad sense – individuals and businesses – is the primary concern. *The concerns of*

---

[7] *Istituto Chemioterapico Italiano SpA e Commercial Solvents Corporation v. Commission*, Joined Cases 6 and 7/73, E.C.R. 1974, p. 223, §§ 32–33.

[8] *Dunlop Slazenger International LTD v. Commission*, Case T-43/92, E.C.R. 1994 p. II–441, § 171; *Continental Can v. Commission*, op. cit., p. 215, § 12; *Tetra Pak Rausing Sa v. Commission*, op. cit. p. II–309, § 23; *Hoffmann-La Roche et Co. AG v. Commission*, Case 85/76, E.C.R. 1979, p. 461, § 38.

competitors are relevant to the extent and only to the extent that they provide evidence of actual or potential harm to competition and consumer interests' (Lowe, 2002).

Although the Commission has not given any express justification for having changed the goal of antitrust law, the reason can apparently be discerned from the 2001 Guidelines on the applicability of Article 81 EC to horizontal cooperation agreements (*infra*). It is there stated, at paragraph 3, that: 'companies need to respond to increasing competitive pressure and a changing market place driven by globalisation, the speed of technological progress and the generally more dynamic nature of markets'. In other words, the Commission seems to be stating implicitly that if it had maintained its previous approach regarding the goal of EC antitrust law, this might have protected the right of economic initiative of individual undertakings within the European market, but would at the same time have threatened the existence of undertakings operating on that market because of the competition from other undertakings which are also active in other parts of the world.

1. *Article 81 EC.* With reference to Article 81, the 2004 Guidelines on the application of Article 81(3) point out at paragraph 47 that 'the purpose of Article 81 is to protect effective competition by ensuring that markets remain open and competitive'. They then go on to maintain, at paragraphs 13 and 33, that 'the aim of the Community competition rules is to protect competition on the market as a means of enhancing customer welfare and of ensuring an efficient allocation of resources'. In other words, as stated in paragraph 105, 'the ultimate aim of Article 81 is to protect the competitive process' which in the Commission's view means winning 'customers by offering better products or better prices than those offered by rivals' (paragraphs 21 and 33).

   According to this approach the key criterion for evaluating both restrictions of competition attributable to an agreement and the existence of a dominant position is some degree of 'market power' (paragraphs 25 and 26).

   This change of approach to Article 81 is the result of a gradual shift in thinking which has taken place since 1998. It has gradually abandoned the foundations of the philosophy, heavily influenced by German thinking, that was prevalent during the second period. This development has involved:

   - abandoning the interpretation of Article 81(1) which entailed a virtually automatic presumption that every agreement constitutes an infringement. This presumption was definitively abandoned after the

1998 *European Night Services*[9] judgment (see also 1999 White Paper, § 78);

- the tendency, foreseen in the 2001 Guidelines on horizontal; agreements between competitors, towards adopting a positive approach to certain agreements between competitors[10] and
- a change in attitude towards the interpretation of Article 81(3), which started with the block regulation on vertical agreements and which was made more general in the Guidelines on the application of Article 81(3) (see in particular paragraph 7).

2. *Article 82 EC.* The Commission has not yet given a formal view on how the new goal of Community antitrust law has had an impact on the interpretation of Article 82. It has merely drawn attention (in the Guidelines on the application of Article 81(3) of the Treaty) to the fact that the degree of market power required varies according to whether an infringement of Article 81 or Article 82 is alleged. More precisely, it stated that 'the degree of market power normally required for the finding of an infringement under Article 81(1) in the case of infringements that are restrictive of competition by effect is less than the degree of dominance required for a finding of dominance under Article 82' (§ 26).

In December 2005 the Commission gave an informal view of the way in which the new goal of Community antitrust law has affected the purpose of Article 82. In an effort to distinguish the new approach from the old, the Commission stated in the Discussion Paper that 'the purpose of Article 82 is not to protect competitors from dominant firms' genuine competition based on factors such as higher quality, novel products, opportune innovation or otherwise better performance, but to ensure that these competitors are also able to expand in or enter the market and compete therein on the merits, without facing competition conditions which are distorted or impaired by the dominant firm' (§ 54).

According to the Commission, both Articles 81 and 82 'with regard to exclusionary practices', have 'the aim of maintaining effective competition on the market'. Effective competition brings 'benefits to consumers, such as low prices, high quality products, a wide selection of goods and services, and innovation' (§ 4). Referring more specifically to the objective of Article 82, the Commission states that:

[9] *European Night Services v. Commission,* Joined Cases T-374/94, T-375/94, T-384/94 and T-388/94, E.C.R. 1998, p. II–3141, § 78.

[10] Commission Notice Guidelines on the applicability of Article 81 to horizontal cooperation agreements, 2001 OJ C 3, p. 2.

> With regard to exclusionary abuses the objective of Article 82, is the protection of competition on the market as a means of enhancing consumer welfare and of ensuring an efficient allocation of resources. Effective competition brings benefits to consumers, such as low prices, high quality products, a wide selection of goods and services, and innovation. Competition and market integration serve these ends since the creation and preservation of an open single market promotes an efficient allocation of resources throughout the Community for the benefit of consumers. (§ 4)
>
> The essential objective of Article 82 when analysing exclusionary conduct is the protection of competition on the market as a means of enhancing consumer welfare and of ensuring an efficient allocation of resources. (§ 54)

In determining the objective of Article 82, the Commission once again stresses the link between competition and the competitive process, which it defines as the attempt 'to win customers by offering better products or better prices than those offered by rivals' (§ 84). The Commission underlines that 'when competition is eliminated the competitive process is brought to an end and short-term efficiency gains are outweighed by longer-term losses stemming inter alia from expenditures incurred by the dominant company to maintain its position (rent seeking), misallocation of resources, reduced innovation and higher prices' (§ 91).

Market power also plays a key role in the new interpretation of the concept of the abuse of a dominant position. Hence, 'for dominance to exist the undertaking(s) concerned ... must have substantial market power' (§ 23). In particular, 'market power is the power to influence market prices, output, innovation, the variety or quality of goods and services, or other parameters of competition on the market for a significant period of time' (§ 24).

5.2. DIFFERENCES BETWEEN THE GOAL OF EUROPEAN ANTITRUST LAW AND THAT OF THE ANTITRUST LAW OF THE MEMBER STATES

The goals of Community antitrust law are not necessarily the same as those of Member States' antitrust law and, indeed, the Court of Justice itself has accepted that Community antitrust law may have a different purpose from that of the Member States:[11]

[11] *Walt Wilhelm v. Bundeskartellamt*, Case 14/68, E.C.R. 1969, p. 1, p. 3; *Direccion General de Defensa de la Competencia v. Asociacion Espanola de Banca privada*, Case C-67/91, E.C.R. 1992, p. I–4785, § 28.

- The goal of Community antitrust law is to protect competition in the internal market according to the objectives defined by Articles 2 and 3(1)(g) EC.
- The goal of national antitrust law is to achieve the aims which have been defined at national level (in Italy, for example, those aims are defined by Article 41 of the Italian Constitution, see Article 1(1) of the Italian antitrust law).

Equally, since the antitrust rules of the Member States may have different goals from Community antitrust law, they may lead to different results from those which would be reached by applying Articles 81 and 82, provided that the principle of effectiveness is complied with (*infra*).

In the light of these principles, the positions put forward both by the UK in the 1990s and by the Commission in the proposal for a regulation in 2000 are untenable: the UK, assuming that the aims of Community and national antitrust law were the same, maintained that the mere application of national antitrust law could directly protect the common market (see paragraph 191 of the XXIII Report on competition policy, 1993).

This argument cannot be correct since, if national bodies are to protect the common market pursuant to EC goals, they must apply Community antitrust law exclusively. If they are to apply national law to that end, simply ensuring that national law does not breach EC law (that is, does not come to a result which breaches the principle of the effectiveness of Community antitrust law) does not suffice. National law would, as the Commission argued in *BEMIM*,[12] need to reach precisely the same results as Community law. If application of national antitrust law did not come to the same result as applying Article 81 or 82, this would *ipso facto* mean that the enforcement of national law had aims which differed from the purpose of 'protecting the internal market'.

Similarly, the Commission's view expressed at part 2.C. of the 2000 Proposal for a Regulation is equally untenable. The Commission argues that 'parallel application of national and Community competition law should be avoided because it *leads to unnecessary parallel proceedings*' (emphasis added). This approach is at odds with the principles outlined above (*supra*) and approved by the Court itself since the *Walt Wilhelm* judgment (*supra*). The Court has accepted that it is legitimate for national law and Community competition law to have different aims. It is thus also acceptable for national law to reach different conclusions from Community law, provided that the principle of effectiveness is complied with.

[12] *BEMIM v. Commission*, Case T-114/92, E.C.R.1995, p. II–147.

The Commission's attitude is also flawed because it does not take account of the importance of Community antitrust federalism (*infra*). On this point, we should recall the following:

- The Community antitrust system is a two-tier system in which the national authorities participate by virtue of Article 84 EC. It is consequently necessary to maintain a form of 'external' control of the EC antitrust enforcement system by Member States (also through the parallel application of national law by the Member States) as opposed to 'internal' control carried out by virtue of Article 83(2)(e) EC (on the concept of 'external' and 'internal' controls, see *infra*).
- The application by Member States of national antitrust law creates a positive 'dialogue' between the Community and the Member State level. This dialogue contributes to defining Community competition policy. Since the national authorities can apply national antitrust competition law in parallel whit the Commission's application of Community law, they maintain the possibility of reacting to any antitrust policy decided on unilaterally by the Commission. This means that, when applying national antitrust law, they may come to conclusions which are stricter than those provided for by Community competition policy (except as regards the application of Article 81(3) EC).

6. The Characteristics of Articles 81 and 82 EC

The characteristic features of the prohibitions contained in Articles 81 and 82 EC have been defined in the case law of the Community courts which has revealed both similarities and differences between the two provisions.

6.1. SIMILARITIES BETWEEN THE TWO ARTICLES

According to the case law, both Articles 81 and 82 are addressed to undertakings.[1] The purpose of those Articles is to 'bring about the "activities" of the Community mentioned in Article 3' of the Treaty. This influences the way in which they are interpreted.[2] Since the prohibitions are 'an expression of the objective of Article 3(1)(g) of the Treaty', they should be interpreted in the light of both that provision and Article 2 EC.[3] In any case, 'Articles 81 and 82 cannot be interpreted in such a way that they contradict each other, because they serve to achieve the same aim'.[4] In particular, both articles must be interpreted in the context of the provisions of the preamble to the Treaty. Reference should particularly be made to the provisions relating to the 'elimination of barriers' and to 'fair competition', both of which are necessary for bringing about a single market.[5]

Articles 81(1) and 82 are formulated in a clear, unconditional and precise manner. This confers on them the character of rules having direct effect[6] (in other words they are directly effective).[7] They can therefore be directly

[1] See *Walt Wilhelm v. Bundeskartellamt*, Case 14/68, E.C.R. 1969, pp. 1, 5.

[2] *Italian Republicv. Council and Commission*, Case 32/65, E.C.R. 1966, p. 296; *Ahmed Saeed Flugreisen v. Zentrale Zur Bekaempfung Unlauteren Wettbewerbs*, Case 66/86, E.C.R. 1989, p. 803.

[3] *Hoffmann-La Roche et Co. AG v. Commission*, Case 85/76, E.C.R. 1979, p. 461.

[4] *Continental Can v. Commission*, Case 6/72, E.C.R. 1973 p. 215, § 25.

[5] See *Italian Republic v. Council and Commission*, op. cit., p. 296, paragraph 2.

[6] See *Bosch*, Case 13/61, ECR 1962, English special edition 45; *Belgische Radio en Televisie v. Sv Sabam e Nv Fonior*, Case 127/73, E.C.R. 1974, p. 51; *Anne Marty Sa v. Estee Lauder Sa*, Case 37/79, E.C.R. 1980, p. 2481.

[7] *Commission v. Italian Republic*, Case 48/71, E.C.R. 1972, p. 529, § 6.

applied by the national courts.[8] By contrast, Article 81(3) is not sufficiently precise to have a direct effect. Consequently, an agreement which is prohibited by virtue of Article 81(1) but which could be authorised under Article 81(3) cannot be directly evaluated by the national courts (on this point and the illegality of Article 6 of Regulation 1/03, see *infra*).

Furthermore, the European Court of Justice (ECJ) has held that Articles 81(1) and 82 confer on individuals rights which must be protected.[9] The right of economic initiative, as defined in the case law, has been put on a formal footing by Article 16 of the Charter of Fundamental Rights. That article, entitled 'Freedom to conduct a business', reads 'The freedom to conduct a business in accordance with Union law and national laws and practices is recognised'.

The fact that Articles 81 and 82 confer rights on individuals entails the important consequence that, if they are infringed by individuals[10] or by Member States,[11] the perpetrator has the obligation to make good any harm caused by the infringement.[12]

In the light of the role played by Articles 81 and 82,[13] national courts which, by virtue of their domestic procedural law, are required to apply, of their own motion, certain national law provisions are also required to do the same with Articles 81 and 82.[14]

6.2. THE DIFFERENCES BETWEEN THE TWO ARTICLES

According to the case law, Articles 81 and 82 are 'independent and complementary provisions designed ... to regulate distinct situations'.[15] This

---

[8] *Guérin automobiles v. Commission*, Case C-282/95 P, E.C.R. 1997, p. I–1503.

[9] *Jeroen van Schijndel v. Stichting Pensioenfonds voor Fysiotherapeuten*, Joined Cases C-430/93 and C-431/93, E.C.R. 1995 p. I–4705, § 14; *Brasserie du Pêcheur SA v. Bundesrepublik Deutschland* and *The Queen v. Secretary of State for Transport, ex parte: Factortame Ltd*, Joined Cases C-46/93 and C-48/93, E.C.R. 1996, p. I–1029; *Belgische Radio en Televisie v. Sv Sabam e Nv Fonior*, op. cit., p. 51, § 16. See. *Firma Sloman Neptun Schiffahrts AG v. Seebetriebsrat Bodo Ziesemer*, Joined Cases C-72/91 and C-73/91, E.C.R. 1993, p. I–887.

[10] See *Courage Ltd v. Bernard Crehan*, Case C-453/99, E.C.R. 2001, p. I–6297.

[11] See *Solred SA v. Administración General del Estado*, Case C-347/96, E.C.R. 1998, p. I–937.

[12] See *inter alia Andrea Francovich e Danila Bonifac v. Repubblica italiana*, Joined Cases C-6/90 and C-9/90, E.C.R. 1991, p. I–5357.

[13] *Eco Swiss China Time Ltd v. Benetton International NV*, Case C-126/97, E.C.R. 1999, p. I–3055, § 39; see also *Manfredi v. Lloyd Adriatico Assicurazioni*, Case C-295/04, E.C.R. 2006, *not yet reported*.

[14] *Jeroen van Schijndel v. Stichting Pensioenfonds voor Fysiotherapeuten*, Joined Cases C-430/93 e C-431/93, E.C.R. 1995 p. I–4705, § 14, § 14.

[15] *Tetra Pak Rausing Sa v. Commission*, Case T-51/89, E.C.R. 1990, p. II–309, § 25.

dictum is based not only on the fact that the two provisions address two distinct situations (that is, agreements involving two or more undertakings as opposed to unilateral conduct), but also reflect the point that they are applied in different ways. Application of Article 81 involves two stages:

- the first stage determines whether Article 81(1) has been infringed; and
- the second relates to exemption under Article 81(3) (according to whatever the detailed rules pursuant to Article 83 EC for the application of Article 81(3) provide).

Article 82, by contrast, involves only one operation, which is to determine whether a particular undertaking has abused a dominant position.[16]

Thanks to the way in which it is formulated, Article 82 has a direct effect. Thus, unlike Article 81(3), it is directly applicable by national courts without the need for any implementing measures adopted pursuant to Article 83(2)(b) EC. On the other hand, unless implementing measures under Article 83(2)(b) EC have been adopted, Article 81(1) may be applied, under Articles 84 and 85, by the Commission and the national authorities only. In the enforcement system governed by the Treaty of Rome (Articles 84 and 85), Article 81(3) may be applied by national courts only after the Commission or the national authorities have decided that it is applicable to a specific agreement.[17] In order to allow Article 81 to be applied by national courts in the enforcement system governed by Articles 84 and 85, the Member States should enact detailed rules for the application of Article 81(3) within the national legal system (that is, by specifying: whether it should be applied according to the principle of infringement or the principle of abuse; Member States should also identify the body which applies Community antitrust law and establish the proceedings and the penalties for infringement).

The Treaty regulates the issue of the nullity of agreements infringing Article 81 but does not contain any analogous provision applying to Article 82. Article 81(2) provides expressly that agreements which breach Article 81(1) are 'automatically void'. The Court has explained this rule on the basis that the importance of the prohibition of Article 81 led the framers of the Treaty to provide expressly in the Treaty that prohibited agreements are to be automatically void. The Court held that Article 81 was essential for the

[16] Ibid..

[17] See *Ahmed Saeed Flugreisen v. Zentrale Zur Bekaempfung Unlauteren Wettbewerbs*, op. cit., p. 803, § 32; *Ministere Public v. Lucas Asjes*, Joined Cases 209 and 213/84, E.C.R. 1986, p. 1425, § 88; *Italian Republic v. Council and Commission*, op. cit. p. 296; *Europemballage Corporation and Continental Can Company Inc. v. Commission Continental*, Case 6/72, E.C.R. 1973 p. 215 § 25.

functioning of the single market.[18] The consequences of making such agreements void are a matter for national courts.[19] The clarity of the sanction provided for by Article 81(2) entails a restriction on the Council's power to adopt directives or regulations under Article 83 EC. Such legislation may not modify what is provided for by Article 81(2).[20]

Although Articles 81 and 82 have different functions, the Court of Justice has held that they may be applied simultaneously to the same situation. Simultaneous application is possible if an 'undertaking in a dominant position has succeeded in having' agreements, which otherwise would not have been accepted, applied by other undertakings.[21]

The case law has also tackled the problem raised by the simultaneous application of Articles 81(3) and 82 EC to an agreement exempted by virtue of Article 81(3) but which, at the same time, constitutes an abuse of a dominant position.[22] In such a case, the agreement cannot infringe Article 81, but Article 82 nevertheless remains applicable to it. Had the Court decided that the abuse could be exempted by virtue of Article 81(3), this would have been tantamount to allowing Article 81 to determine whether Article 82 was applicable, despite the fact that the two articles fulfil a different function (albeit they are to be found in the same chapter of the Treaty).

---

[18] *Eco Swiss China Time Ltd v. Benetton International NV*, op. cit., p. I–3055, § 36.

[19] *Brasserie de Haecht v. Wilkin-Janssen*, Case 48/72, E.C.R. 1973, p. 77, § 4.

[20] Ibid., § 4/5.

[21] *Ahmed Saeed Flugreisen v. Zentrale Zur Bekaempfung Unlauteren Wettbewerbs*, op. cit., p. 803, § 37.

[22] See *Continental Can v. Commission*, op. cit., p. 215, § 25; *Tetra Pak Rausing Sa v. Commission*, op. cit., p. II–309, § 25.

7. The Scope of Articles 81 and 82 EC

7.1. PERSONAL SCOPE

It is clear from their wording that Articles 81 and 82 prohibit only conduct engaged in by 'undertakings'. However, the Treaty does not define the concept of an undertaking, and this task has thus been left to the Court of Justice. In a line of case law dating back to the early 1990s, the Court has determined how far this concept extends.

When it interpreted the concept of an 'undertaking' for the purposes of the ECSC Treaty, the Court gave a general and all-purpose definition.[1] However, for the purposes of the EC Treaty, the Court has held that two aspects are relevant in determining whether a person is deemed to be an undertaking.

7.1.1. A Subjective Element

The case law requires the presence of a subjective element, namely the existence of an entity to which the relevant economic behaviour can be imputed. More precisely, the Court has stated that 'in the context of competition law … the concept of an undertaking encompasses every entity …, regardless of the legal status of the entity and the way in which it is financed'. [2]

The scope of this concept is very broad and it is capable of embracing natural and legal persons, as well as public bodies.

---

[1] *Loeckner-Werke AG e Hoesch AT v. High Authority*, Joined Cases 17 and 20/61, E.C.R. 1962, English Special Edition, p. 325.

[2] *Klaus Hoefner e Fritz Elser v.Macrotron GmbH*, Case C-41/90, E.C.R.1991, p. I–1979, § 21; *Aéroports de Paris v. Commission*, Case C-82/01 P, E.C.R. 2002 p. I–9297, 75; *Poucet and Pistre*, Joined Cases C-159/91 and C-160/91, E.C.R. 1993, p. I–637, § 17; *Firma Ambulanz Glöckner v. Landkreis Südwestpfalz*, Case C-475/99, E.C.R. 2001, p. I–8089, 19; *Pavlov et al.*, Joined Cases C-180/98 – C-184/98, E.C.R. 2000, p. I–6451, § 74; *Fédération francaise des sociétés d'assurance and others v. Ministere de l'agriculture et de la pêche*, Case C-244/94, E.C.R. 1995, p. I–4013, § 14; *Albany International BV v. Stichting Bedrijfspensioenfonds Textielindustrie*, Case C-67/96, E.C.R. 1999 p. I–05751, § 77; *Job Centre coop. arl.*, Case C-55/96, E.C.R. 1997 p. I–7119, § 25.

7.1.2. An Objective Element

The test formulated by the Court also requires the presence of an objective element, which is that the activity in question must be an economic activity. The Court has also interpreted this aspect broadly, stating that 'any activity consisting in offering goods and services on a given market is an economic activity'.[3] Even a non-profit-making body may be engaged in an economic activity.[4]

Whenever the Court has held that a particular body is not an undertaking, the critical factor has been that that body is not engaged in an economic activity. In other words, the Court has decided that the objective element is lacking.

According to the case law, two categories of activity do not fulfil the requirements of the objective element, namely:

- activities connected with the 'exercise of the powers of a public authority';[5] and
- activities which fall outside the scope of economic activities.[6]

In order to determine whether a body is an undertaking, 'its nature, the rules to which it is subject and its objective must be examined'.[7]

7.2. TERRITORIAL SCOPE

Articles 81 and 82 apply to situations 'which may affect trade between Member States'. That expression defines 'the sphere of application of Community rules in relation to national laws'.[8]

---

[3] *Aéroports de Paris v. Commission,* Case C-82/01, E.C.R. 2002 p. I–9297, § 79; *Commission v. Italy,* Case C-35/96, E.C.R. p. I–3851, § 36; *Firma Ambulanz Glöckner v. Landkreis Südwestpfalz,* Case C-475/99, E.C.R. 2001 p. I–8089, § 19; *Pavlov and other,* Joined Cases C-180/98 - C-184/98, E.C.R. 2000 p. I–6451, § 75.

[4] *Fédération française des sociétés d'assurance v. Ministere de l'agriculture et de la peche,* Case C-244/94, E.C.R. 1995 p. I–4013, § 22.

[5] *SAT Fluggesellschaft mbH v. Eurocontrol,* Case-364/92, E.C.R. 1994 p. I–43, § 30; *Diego Calì & Figli Srl v. Servizi ecologici porto di Genova SpA (SEPG),* Case C-343/95, E.C.R. 1997 p. I–1547, § 23.

[6] *Poucet e Pistre,* op. cit., § 17; *Cisal di Battistello Venanzio & C. Sas v. INAIL,* Case C-218/00, E.C.R. 2002 p. I–691, 45; *Federation francaise des Societes d'assurance and others v. Ministere de l'agriculture et de la peche,* op.cit., § 22.

[7] *J. C. J. Wouters and others v. Algemene Raad van de Nederlandse Orde van Advocaten, con l'intervento di: Raad van de Balies van de Europese Gemeenschap,* Case C-309/99, E.C.R. 2002 p. I–1577, § 57

[8] *Istituto chemioterapico italiano S.p.A. e Commercial Solvents Corporation v. Commission,* Joined Cases C-6 and 7/73, E.C.R. 1974, p. 223, § 31.

Both practice and Community case law have conferred a very broad scope on Articles 81 and 82. This has been subject to criticism on the ground that the scope of these articles ought to be restricted (see the position of the UK, *infra*). In order to analyse whether such criticism is justified, we need to determine:

- first, whether the 'maturing' of the common market can reasonably be expected to lead to a reduction of the scope of Community antitrust law; and
- second, whether it is possible to argue that, for the purpose of protecting the common market, national law can replace Community antitrust law.

We have already answered the second question in the negative, stressing in this context that Community antitrust law does not have the same goal as national law (*supra*). We therefore need to examine only the first question. Since the scope of Community antitrust law is determined by whether a given factual situation 'may affect trade between Member States', it would be clearly unreasonable if the development of the European common market had shrunk, rather than broadened, it. Over time, the removal of legal barriers and the increase in size of individual undertakings in fact make it more likely that the behaviour of undertakings will more frequently affect trade between Member States. Consequently, the scope of Community antitrust law is certainly broadened rather than reduced as time goes on.

To that end, the Court of Justice has developed various criteria in order to define more precisely whether a particular antitrust case has Community relevance.[9]

7.2.1. Effect on Trade between Member States

Both Articles 81 and 82 apply only if the situation may 'affect trade between Member States'. As paragraphs 12 and 13 of the Guidelines on the effect on trade concept[10] express it, the effect on trade criterion 'is an autonomous Community law criterion ... which defines the scope of application of Community competition law'. It confines the scope of application of Articles 81 and 82 to agreements and practices that are capable of having a minimum level of cross-border effects within the Community.

With reference to Article 81, paragraph 13 of the Guidelines makes clear that the ability of the agreement or practice to affect trade must be

---

[9] *Carlo Bagnasco v. Banca Popolare di Novara,* Joined Cases C-215/96 and C-216/96, E.C.R. 1999, p. I–135, § 47.

[10] Commission Notice Guidelines on the effect on trade concept contained in Articles 81 and 82 of the Treaty, 2004 OJ C 101, p. 81.

'appreciable'. However, 'it is not required that each individual part of the agreement, including any restriction which may flow from the agreement, is capable of doing so'. It suffices that 'the agreement as a whole is capable of affecting trade between Member States' (paragraph 14). Furthermore,

> [It is] immaterial whether or not the participation of a particular undertaking in the agreement has an appreciable effect on trade between the Member States. An undertaking cannot escape Community law jurisdiction merely because of the fact that its own contribution to an agreement, which is itself capable of affecting trade between Member States, is insignificant. (paragraph 15)

Even agreements which do not infringe Article 81 may affect trade between Member States.

With reference to Article 82 the relevant principles are similar. As paragraph 17 of the Guidelines expresses it, 'it is the abuse that must affect trade between Member States. This does not imply, however, that each element of the behaviour must be assessed in isolation. Conduct that forms part of an overall strategy pursued by the dominant undertaking must be assessed in terms of its overall impact' (paragraph 17). Thus,

> [W]here a dominant undertaking adopts various practices in pursuit of the same aim, for instance practices that aim at eliminating or foreclosing competitors, in order for Article 82 to be applicable to all the practices forming part of this overall strategy, it is sufficient that at least one of these practices is capable of affecting trade between Member States. (paragraph 17)

The Notice gives precise guidelines on how to apply the concept of effect on trade to common types of agreements and, to that end, draws various distinctions between various categories:

- agreements and abuse concerning several Member States (section 3.1);
- agreements and abuses covering only one Member State or part thereof (section 3.2); and
- agreements and abuses concerning third countries (section 3.3).

These main categories are subdivided into further subcategories according to the nature of the agreement or abuse in question.

In order to determine whether there is an effect on trade between Member States, the Guidelines address the three elements which, according to the Community case law, constitute the concept.

The concept of 'trade between Member States'

The concept of 'trade' 'is not limited to traditional exchanges of goods and services across borders' (paragraph 19). It is a wider concept, which covers all cross-border economic activity, including establishment, consistently with the aims of the internal market. It also encompasses cases where agreements or practices affect the competitive structure of the market (for example, by eliminating or threatening to eliminate a competitor operating within the Community). This is the case because 'when an undertaking is or risks being eliminated, the competitive structure within the Community is affected and so are the economic activities in which the undertaking is affected' (paragraph 20).

For there to be an effect on trade 'between Member States' there must be an impact on cross-border economic activity involving at least two Member States. It is not required that the agreement or practice affect trade between the whole of one Member State and the whole of another Member State (paragraph 21). It may also affect simply part of a Member State, provided that the effect is appreciable. The effect is not determined by the size of the relevant market in which the agreement or unilateral conduct is implemented. Trade may be affected even where the relevant market is national or subnational (paragraph 22).

The notion 'may affect'

The expression 'may affect' serves to define the nature of the impact on trade between Member States that is required:

- On the pattern of trade. The expression 'may affect implies that it must be possible to foresee with a sufficient degree of probability on the basis of a set of objective factors of law or fact that the agreement or practice may have an influence, direct or indirect, actual or potential, on the pattern of trade between Member States' (paragraph 23).
- On the competitive structure. In determining whether the agreement or practice may affect trade it is also relevant to consider whether it affects the competitive structure inside the Community. If that is the case, Community law will apply (paragraph 23).

The standard test used to assess whether trade may be affected contains the following main elements:

1. *A sufficient degree of probability on the basis of a set of objective factors of law or fact.* This is an element which is based on objective factors, i.e. it does not (subject to certain exceptions, see paragraph 25) require subjective intent on the part of the parties. For Community law to be

applicable there does not need to be an actual effect on trade. It suffices if 'the agreement or practice is "capable" of having such an effect' (paragraph 23). For that purpose, there is no need 'to calculate the actual volume of trade between Member States affected by the agreement or practice' (paragraph 27). This is linked to the fact that 'Community law jurisdiction extends to categories of agreements and practices that are capable of having cross-border effects, irrespective of whether a particular agreement or practice actually has such effects' (paragraph 27).

The factors relevant to determining whether trade may be affected include:

- the nature of the agreement and practice (paragraph 29);
- the nature of the products covered by the agreements or practices (paragraph 30); and
- the significance of the undertakings concerned (paragraph 31).

In addition to these factors, it is necessary to take account of the legal and factual environment (paragraph 32).

2. *An influence on the pattern of trade between Member States.* Articles 81 and 82 apply when there is an influence on the 'pattern of trade between Member States'. Since this concept is used only to determine when Community law is applicable, the term 'pattern of trade' is neutral. It is not a condition that trade be restricted or reduced; patterns of trade may be affected even when an agreement or practice brings about an increase in trade (paragraph 34).
3. *A direct or indirect, actual or potential influence.* The Community case law has established that the influence of agreements and practices on patterns of trade between Member States can be direct or indirect, actual or potential (paragraph 36). Whereas 'direct effects on trade between Member States normally occur in relation to the products covered by an agreement or practice' (paragraph 37), indirect effects often occur in relation to products related to those covered by an agreement or practice (paragraph 38). This may be the case where an agreement relates to intermediate products which are not exported. If the final product is exported, interstate trade will thereby have been affected. To that extent, 'indirect effects on trade between Member States may also occur in relation to the products covered by the agreement or practice' (paragraph 39).

   Actual effects on trade between Member States 'are those that are produced by the agreement or practice once it is implemented'. Actual effects do not need to be demonstrated (paragraph 40). Potential effects are 'those that may occur in the future with a sufficient degree of probability.

In other words, foreseeable market developments must be taken into account' (paragraph 41). However, the inclusion of indirect or potential effects in the analysis of effects on trade between Member States does not mean that the analysis can be based on remote or hypothetical effects. Hypothetical or speculative effects are not sufficient for establishing Community law jurisdiction (paragraph 43).

The concept of 'appreciability'

The third element which must be present in order to apply Article 81 or 82 is that the agreement or practice must have an appreciable effect on trade. Agreements or practices 'fall outside the scope of application of Articles 81 and 82 when they affect the market only insignificantly having regard to the weak position of the undertakings concerned for the products in question' (paragraph 44).

A determination of whether agreements have an appreciable effect must be done on a case-by-case basis. In each individual case, various factors must be taken into account, in particular the following three:

- the nature of the agreement and practice;
- the nature of the products covered; and
- the market position of the undertakings concerned (paragraph 45).

Appreciability can be measured both in absolute terms (turnover) and in relative terms, comparing the position of the undertaking(s) concerned to that of other players on the market (market share) (paragraph 47). For that reason, 'the application of the appreciability test does not necessarily require that relevant markets be defined and market shares calculated'. For example, the sales of an undertaking in absolute terms may be sufficient to support a finding that the impact on trade is appreciable (paragraph 48). In any case, agreements and practices must always be considered in the economic and legal context in which they occur. For example, in the case of vertical agreements, it may be necessary to assess the cumulative effects of parallel networks (paragraph 49).

In order to determine whether an agreement has an appreciable effect on trade, the Commission draws a distinction between two different types of case:

1. *Cases in which trade is normally not capable of being appreciably affected* As the Commission stated at paragraph 3 of the *De minimis* Notice (*infra*), there is a rebuttable presumption that agreements between small and medium-sized enterprises (SMEs) are normally not capable of affecting trade between Member States (paragraph 50). SMEs are defined

as undertakings which have fewer than 250 employees and either an annual turnover not exceeding € 40 million or an annual balance-sheet total not exceeding € 27 million[11] (*De minimis Notice*, paragraph 3). The reason for this presumption is that the activities of most SMEs are normally local or at most regional in nature. The presumption does not apply where SMEs engage in cross-border activity.

2. *Generally applicable rules for determining whether or not there is an appreciable effect on trade between Member States* The Commission has drawn up various presumptions to help determine whether or not an agreement or practice has an appreciable effect on trade. The relevant turnover and market share thresholds are set out in paragraphs 54 to 57 of the Notice:

- *Negative rebuttable presumption.* The Commission has a standard defining the absence of an appreciable effect on trade, known as the NAAT rule (Not Appreciably Affecting Trade). This is a negative rebuttable presumption which defines the cases in which trade between Member States is normally not appreciably affected. As regards Article 81, the negative rebuttable presumption applies to all agreements within the meaning of Article 81(1) irrespective of the nature of the restrictions contained in the agreement, including restrictions that have been identified as hardcore restrictions in Commission block exemption regulations and Commission guidelines (paragraph 50).

  The presumption entails two consequences:

  - where it applies, the Commission will not normally institute proceedings either upon application or on its own initiative;
  - where the undertakings assume in good faith that an agreement is covered by the negative presumption, the Commission will not impose fines.

  Although a case-by-case assessment must be made, the presumption applies where two cumulative conditions are met. Those conditions relate to:

---

[11] Annex to Commission Recommendation 96/280/EC. See also Commission Recommendation on the Definition of Small and Medium-Sized Undertakings, 2003 OJ L 124/36.

- o the parties' market share. The presumption applies when the aggregate market share of the parties on any relevant market within the Community does not exceed 5%; and
- o the aggregate turnover of the undertakings concerned.

The way in which this condition applies depends on whether the agreement is horizontal or vertical:

- o In the case of horizontal agreements, the condition is that the aggregate annual Community turnover of the undertakings concerned in the products covered by the agreement does not exceed € 40 million.
- o In the case of vertical agreements, the condition is that the aggregate annual Community turnover of the supplier in the products covered by the agreement does not exceed € 40 million. In the case of licence agreements, the relevant turnover is the aggregate turnover of the licensees in the products incorporating the licensed technology and the licensor's own turnover in such products. In cases involving agreements concluded between a buyer and several suppliers, the relevant turnover is the buyer's combined purchases of the products covered by the agreements (paragraph 52).

The Notice also specifies the circumstances in which the presumption is applicable even where the turnover and market share thresholds have been exceeded. The Commission will apply the same presumption where during two successive calendar years the above turnover threshold is not exceeded by more than 10% and the above market threshold is not exceeded by more than 2 percentage points (paragraph 52).

The Notice also gives guidance as to how these tests are to be applied when the agreement concerns an emerging market or where the parties do not generate turnover or accumulate a relevant market share (paragraph 52).

The Commission intends to apply the negative presumption 'to all agreements, including agreements that by their very nature are capable of affecting trade between Member States as well as agreements that involve trade with undertakings located in third countries' (paragraph 58). Even where the agreement or practice falls outside the scope of the negative presumption, 'the Commission will take account of qualitative elements relating to the nature of the agreement or practice and the nature of the products that they concern' (paragraph 59).

- *Positive rebuttable presumption.* When these two thresholds are exceeded, there is a rebuttable presumption that the agreement does have an appreciable effect on trade. However, the presumption does not apply where the agreement covers only part of a Member State (paragraph 53).

7.2.2. *De Minimis* Agreements

Articles 81 and 82 of the EC Treaty provide explicitly that situations do not fall within the scope of Community antitrust law unless they affect trade between the Member States. The Court of Justice has added a further condition. By virtue of the case law, in order for those articles to apply, the impact of the relevant practice on competition must be appreciable.

Although this principle has been applied by the Court of Justice to both articles 81 and 82,[12] the Commission restricted the scope of the 2001 *de minimis* Notice[13] to agreements which do not appreciably affect competition. The Notice applies not only to agreements *stricto sensu* but also to decisions by associations of undertakings and to concerted practices (paragraph 5).

The principles of the *de minimis* Notice

In determining which agreements do not appreciably restrict competition, the Notice, like all Commission Communications adopted after 1999, operates on the basis of market shares. The Commission has thereby established a quantitative test for determining what does not constitute an appreciable restriction of competition under Article 81(1). To that end, the Notice sets out the relevant indicia, which are as follows:

- the method of calculating market shares (paragraph 10); and
- criteria for the determination of what are 'connected undertakings' for the purpose of assessing the market share of a given undertaking (paragraph 12).

---

[12] With regard to Article 81, see *Franz Voelk v. Vervaecke S.p.r.l.*, Case 5/69, E.C.R. 1969, pp. 295, 302; *Société anonyme Cadillon v. Firma Hoess, Maschinenbau KG*, Case 1/71, E.C.R. 1971, pp. 351, 356; *Distillers Company Limited v. Commission*, Case 30/78, E.C.R. 1980, pp. 2229, 3824; *Dansk pelsdyravlerforening v. Commission*, Case T-61/89, E.C.R. 1992, p. II–1931, 1986 ff. With regard to Article 82 EC, see *Nv l'Oreal e Sa l'Oreal v. PVBA*, Case 31/80, E.C.R. 1980, p. 3775, §§ 18, 28; *Greenwich film production v. SACEM*, Case 22/79, in E.C.R. 1979, pp. 3275, 3289.

[13] Commission Notice on agreements of minor importance which do not appreciably restrict competition under Article 81(1) of the Treaty establishing the European Community (*de minimis*), 2001 OJ C 368, p. 13.

The Commission notes that market share thresholds merely establish presumptions. Consequently, agreements between undertakings which exceed the thresholds set out in the notice do not necessarily restrict competition appreciably. Such agreements may still have only a negligible effect on competition and may therefore not be prohibited by Article 81(1) (paragraph 2).

If an agreement is covered by the Notice, the Commission will not institute proceedings either upon application or on its own initiative. Similarly, where undertakings assume in good faith that an agreement is covered by the Notice, the Commission will not impose fines (paragraph 4).

Application of the *de minimis* Notice

The Notice defines when the *de minimis* principles apply.

1. *Cases in which the* de minimis *principles apply.* The Notice draws a distinction between:

- *Agreements between competitors.* Agreements between competitors do not appreciably restrict competition if the aggregate market share held by the parties to the agreement does not exceed 10% on any of the relevant markets affected by the agreement, where the agreement is made between undertakings which are actual or potential competitors on any of the markets affected (paragraph 7.a).
- *Agreements between non-competitors.* Agreements between non-competitors are deemed not to restrict competition appreciably if the market share held by each of the parties to the agreement does not exceed 15% on any of the relevant markets affected by the agreement, where the agreement is made between undertakings which are not actual or potential competitors on any of these markets (paragraph 7.b).

In case of doubt as to which category an agreement falls into, the 10% threshold is applied.

The Commission has also established a rule relating to the appreciability of agreements in the case of the 'cumulative foreclosure effect of parallel networks of agreements having similar effects on the market' (paragraph 8). It has defined specific market shares for cases 'where in a relevant market competition is restricted by the cumulative effect of agreements for the sale of goods or services entered into by different suppliers or distributors'. In such cases, 'the market share thresholds … are reduced to 5%, both for agreements between competitors and for agreements between non-competitors. Individual suppliers or distributors are in general not considered to contribute significantly to a cumulative foreclosure effect'. The Commission also considers that 'a cumulative foreclosure effect is unlikely to exist if less than 30% of the relevant market is covered by parallel networks of agreements having similar effects' (paragraph 8).

As in the case of the Regulation on vertical agreements, the Commission explains how the assessment is to be made when the market shares fluctuate over time. It 'holds the view that agreements are not restrictive of competition if the market shares do not exceed the thresholds of respectively 10%, 15% and 5% set out in point 7 and 8 during two successive calendar years by more than 2 percentage points' (paragraph 9).

2. *Cases where the* de minimis *principles do not apply.* The Commission also explains that there are three categories of agreements to which the de minimis principle does not apply because they contain hardcore restrictions. They are as follows:

(a) Agreements between competitors. The *de minimis* principle does not apply to such agreements where they contain restrictions which 'directly or indirectly, in isolation or in combination with other factors under the control of the parties, have as their object:

- the fixing of prices when selling the products to third parties;
- the limitation of output or sales; and
- the allocation of markets or customers' (paragraph 11.1).

(b) Agreements between non-competitors. Nor does it apply to agreements between non-competitors containing restrictions which directly or indirectly, in isolation or in combination with other factors under the control of the parties, have as their object:

- the restriction of the buyer's ability to determine its sale price, without prejudice to the possibility of the supplier imposing a minimum sale price, provided that they do not amount to a fixed or minimum sale price as a result of pressure from, or incentives offered by, any of the parties; and
- the restriction of the territory into which, or of the customers to whom, the buyer may sell the contract goods or services, except the following restrictions which are not hardcore:
    - the restriction of active sales into the exclusive territory or to an exclusive customer group reserved to the supplier or allocated by the supplier to another buyer, where such a restriction does not limit sales by the customers of the buyer;

  - the restriction of sales to end users by a buyer operating at the wholesale level of the trade;
  - the restriction of sales to unauthorised distributors by the members of a selective distribution system; and
  - the restriction of the buyer's ability to sell components, supplied for the purposes of incorporation, to customers who would use them to manufacture the same type of goods as those produced by the supplier;

- the restriction of active or passive sales to end users by members of a selective distribution system operating at the retail level of trade, without prejudice to the possibility of prohibiting a member of the system from operating out of an unauthorised place of establishment;
- the restriction of cross-supplies between distributors within a selective distribution system, including between distributors operating at different levels of trade; and
- the restriction agreed between a supplier of components and a buyer who incorporates those components, which limits the supplier's ability to sell the components as spare parts to end users or to repairers or other service providers not entrusted by the buyer with the repair or servicing of its goods (paragraph 11.2).

(c) Agreements between competitors operating in different markets. The *de minimis* principle does not apply to agreements between competitors where the competitors operate, for the purposes of the agreement, at a different level of the production or distribution chain, any of the hardcore restrictions listed in paragraphs (1) and (2) (paragraph 11.2).

7.3. INTERNATIONAL ASPECTS OF COMMUNITY ANTITRUST LAW

Articles 81 and 82 also apply to agreements and unilateral behaviour implemented or taking place in territories outside the Community (this is referred to as the 'extraterritorial application' of Community antitrust law).

Extraterritorial application has its limits because antitrust law cannot, in the absence of international cooperation, be effectively applied on the territory of another state. For example, the use of powers of inspection against undertakings based in another state and the enforcement of antitrust decisions are clearly not feasible without international cooperation. This factor has led to attempts to find new means of safeguarding competition on an international basis, mostly through bilateral antitrust cooperation agreements.[14]

Recently, a further method of international antitrust cooperation consisting of discussion between the antitrust authorities of different states has emerged. The aim of such groups is to examine general problems of competition between states. To that end, the International Competition Network (ICN) was established in 2003. That body is an organisation in which both the European Community and the individual Member States with their respective competition authorities participate. This last type of international cooperation backs up, but does not replace, antitrust bilateral agreements.

---

[14] See, for example, the Agreement between the European Communities and the United States Regarding the Application of their Competition Laws, 1995 OJ L 96/45.

PART III

ARTICLE 81 EC

8. The Drafting of Article 81 EC

The drafting history of Article 81 EC at the end of the 1950s is interesting since it reveals how the cartel prohibition on cartels caused a clash between the legal cultures of France and of Germany.

8.1. THE SITUATION IN GERMANY

Germany had enacted cartel laws as early as 1920. Although those laws did not make cartels unlawful, they did prohibit the abuse of cartel agreements (*supra*). In the early 1940s, partly as a consequence of this economic policy choice, Germany's economy had been organised on the basis of cartels rather than competition (*supra*).

At the end of the Second World War, the Occupying Powers enacted a law on decartelisation (Rasch, 1955, p. 5). The German government subsequently established a Study Commission to draft laws to safeguard competition. The Study Commission finished its work just as the discussion on the antitrust rules of the Treaty of Rome was taking place. This caused certain difficulties for the German representatives in the Treaty drafting group. Those difficulties have only recently come to light following the publication of the relevant official documents (see Schulze and Hoeren, 2000).

In order to understand the position defended by the Federal Republic of Germany during the negotiations on the Treaty of Rome, one needs to bear in mind that there was a fierce debate in Germany on the issue of which cartel legislation model should be adopted. One school of thought advocated the *Verbotsprinzip* (principle of prohibition) whereas another favoured the *Missbrauchsprinzip* (principle of abuse).

The first group, influenced by the political and economic *débâcle* of Nazi Germany, maintained that in order to safeguard individuals' rights of economic initiative it was necessary to prohibit any kind of horizontal agreement between undertakings (that is, cartels). Furthermore, that school of thought contended that the dispersion of economic power and a generalised recognition of the right of economic initiative would promote social justice (see Heinemann, 1989). From a legal point of view, according to this approach, anticompetitive agreements between companies would have no legal force. They would acquire legal force only after the agreement had been notified to a particular regulatory body (Böhm, 1956, p. 173).

By contrast, the supporters of the principle of abuse advocated laws that would prohibit cartels and deprive them of legal effect only after it had been ascertained that the agreement was illegal (Isay, 1955, p. 339).

The principle that was adopted in the 1957 German Law on competition was the principle of prohibition, subject to certain specific exemptions (Rasch, 1955). Regulation of vertical agreements fell under a different law (Article 15 and following of the *GWB*) which was not based on the principle of prohibition. The German antitrust law was approved in 1957 and entered into force on 1 January 1958, the date of the entry into force of the Treaty of Rome including its antitrust provisions.

Consequently, during the drafting of the Treaty of Rome, the Federal Republic of Germany did not have a final version of its own antitrust laws at its disposal. It could not therefore put forward a clear competition policy regarding the assessment of agreements between undertakings.

8.2. THE SITUATION IN FRANCE

As early as the 1920s, France had enacted laws regulating agreements between undertakings (see Plaisant and Lassier, 1956). At the beginning of the 1950s, it established a committee to reform Article 419 of the 1926 Penal Code, which related to agreements among firms, since this provision had proved ineffective and difficult to enforce. The Draft Law of 10 July 1952 was probably influenced by the European model dating from the first half of the 20th century, which aimed to control cartels rather than prohibit them (Hamel and Lagarde, 1954, p. 280). That model presupposed that cartel agreements between companies were not necessarily harmful for competition and that a distinction therefore had to be made between good and bad agreements (Salandra, 1934, p. 28).

Article 1 of Draft Law 9951 provided that, in principle, agreements between companies aiming to improve production and distribution in the general interest were lawful (Del Marmol, 1959, p. 86). Article 2 of Draft Law 9951 prohibited only behaviour aimed at creating monopolies or 'coalitions' or limiting or eliminating unfair competition.

The proposal was radically amended.

In its final form, Article 59 *bis* of the Decree of 9 August 1953 regulated the '*délit de coalition*', thereby expressly prohibiting all agreements the object or effect of which was to distort competition. Only two categories of agreements falling within the scope of the prohibition provided for by Article 59 *bis* were exempted:[1]

- agreements provided for by laws or regulations;[2] and
- agreements which brought about specific advantages for competition.

This meant that as early as 1952, well before the antitrust provisions in the Treaty of Rome were negotiated, France had enacted laws regulating anticompetitive agreements. What is more, those laws expressed a clear policy choice as to how agreements between undertakings were to be legally appraised.

8.3. THE DRAFTING OF ARTICLE 81 EC

During the drafting of the antitrust rules of the Treaty of Rome, the French representatives proposed a rule on the prohibition of cartels which would harmonise the national laws on price discrimination (Schulze and Hoeren, 2000, doc. 51). As far as anticompetitive practices were concerned, the proposed rule would contain the same principles as Articles 59 *bis* and 59 *ter* of the French decree of 9 August 1953 (ibid. doc. 51). This aspect of the proposal drew a distinction between good and bad agreements. This meant that anticompetitive agreements were prohibited, but specific agreements which had a beneficial effect on competition could benefit from an exemption.

---

[1] In particular, Article 59 *bis* of the Decree of 9 August 1953 on the maintenance and re-establishment of free competition, which regulated the délit de coalition, provided as follows: 'Sont prohibées, sous réserve des dispositions de l'article 59 *ter*, toutes les actions concertées, conventions, ententes expresses ou tacites, ou coalitions sous quelque forme et pour quelque cause que ce soit, allant pour objet ou pouvant avoir pour effet d'entraver le plein exercice de la concurrence en faisant obstacle à l'abaissement des prix de revient ou de vente ou en favorisant une hausse artificielle des prix'.

'Tout engagement ou convention se rapportant à une pratique ainsi prohibée est nul de plein droit'.

'Cette nullité peut être invoquée par les parties et par les tiers, elle ne peut être opposée aux tiers par les orties; elle est éventuellement constatée par les tribunaux de droit commun à qui l'avis de la Commission, s'il en est intervenu un doit être communiqué'.

Article 59 *ter* provided as follows: 'Ne sont pas visées par les dispositions de l'article 59 *bis*, les actions concertées, conventions ou ententes':

'1. Qui résultent de l'application d'un texte législatif ou réglementaire';

'2. Dont les auteurs seront en mesure de justifier qu'elles ont pour effet d'améliorer et d'étendre les débouchés de la production, ou d'assurer le développement du progrès économique par la rationalisation et la spécialisation'.

[2] These became well known to EC law in that they were relevant to a number of judgments in the 1990s. See *Bureau National Interprofessionnel du Cognac v. Yves Aubert*, Case 136/86, E.C.R. 1987, p. 4789; *BNIC v. Clair*, Case 123/83, E.C.R. 1985, p. 391.

By contrast, the German representatives had difficulty in putting forward a clear proposal. Moreover, since it was not yet clear how their national law would be formulated, they feared that the drafting of the Community rules on cartels might conflict with it. It was in any event evident that the Treaty rules would have a considerable influence on their domestic law (ibid. doc. 62). After initial hesitation, the German representatives proposed that the principle of prohibition without exception should be accepted. They claimed that this was an indivisible proposal which could not be tampered with (ibid. p. xxvii).

When confronted with this proposal, the representatives of France and the other countries hardened their own positions, which led to a stalemate (ibid. p. xxvii). Official documents indicate that the German representatives themselves declared that 'it is impossible to impose at European level a principle (i.e. the principle of prohibition) which is the subject of discussions in Germany itself' (ibid., doc. 65).

The situation was resolved by Hans von der Groeben, the German chairman of the subgroup dealing with competition questions. He had been one of the authors of the Spaak Report, had close ties with the Freiburg Ordoliberal School and was later to become the first Director General for Competition in the Commission.

The compromise which von der Groeben proposed – and which was accepted by the parties – was a provision which prohibited anticompetitive agreements between undertakings (now Article 81(1)). It nevertheless provided for an exception to that principle and set out the conditions which must be met before the prohibition could be declared inapplicable (Article 81(3) EC) (ibid., doc. xxxi). Moreover, it was provided that 'any agreements or decisions prohibited pursuant to this Article shall be automatically void' (Article 81(2)), as was the case with Article 53 *bis* of the French decree of 1953 and the German *Notverordnung* of 1931.

In order to break the stalemate, Von der Groeben proposed to postpone the controversial decision as to how the exception provided for by Article 81(3) should be implemented. This decision would be taken in a regulation which would be enacted after the Treaty of Rome had been signed. To that end, on 28 November 1956 a draft article was prepared. After being redrafted a number of times, it became Article 83(2)(e) EC (ibid, p. xxxi).

By virtue of that compromise solution, Articles 84 and 85 EC provided that 'until the entry into force of the provisions adopted in pursuance of Article 83, the authorities of the Member States' would apply Article 81(1) and Article 81(3) EC 'in accordance with the law of their country'. In this way, the deployment of the national authorities was justified directly by provisions in the Treaty. Thus, by virtue of Article 84 EC the national authorities were competent to apply the exception provided for by Article 81(3) 'in accordance with the law of their country'. Under the terms of the compromise, the choice of whether to apply Article 81(3) according to the *Verbotsprinzip* of the *Missbrauchsprinzip* was temporarily left up to the Member States (see Spengler (1957) as to the positions taken by the Dutch government and the French and Italian parliaments in 1957).

9. The Implementation of Article 81 EC

Although Regulation 17/62, first Regulation implementing Articles 85 and 86 of the Treaty, is no longer in force, it is essential to grasp how that regulation implemented Article 81(3) in order properly to understand the *modus operandi* of Regulation 1/03.

9.1. IMPLEMENTATION OF ARTICLE 81 EC BY REGULATION 17/62

In 1961, the drafting of the text of the first regulation adopted pursuant to Article 83 EC proved to be the subject of lively discussions because, *inter alia*, the French and the Germans continued to apply different principles to the assessment of cartels.

Regarding the formulation of the rules applying Article 81(3) EC, the German representatives claimed that Article 81(3) should be applied according to the principle of prohibition which had been introduced in the *GWB* in 1957 (Deringer, 1965, p. 9).

The French representatives, in line with the decree of 1953, supported the application of Article 81(3) according to the principle of abuse. This would entail the validity of agreements concluded by the parties until such time as an infringement of Article 81 EC had been assessed (ibid., p. 9).

Arved Derringer, the German rapporteur of the regulation, helped with the difficult task of finding a compromise between the different positions.

Under the terms of the compromise, undertakings wishing to obtain an exemption pursuant to Article 81(3) EC were required to notify agreements to a single body. By virtue of Article 9(1) of the Regulation, that body was the Commission (ibid., p. 10). This is what had been requested by the Federal Republic of Germany. This provision was flanked by the consequence that, if the request for an exemption was rejected, the agreement would be unlawful *ab initio*.[1] However, even if the agreement turned out to be illegal, Article 15(5) Regulation 17/62 provided that notification prevented fines from being imposed with regard to the period between notification and the Commission's

[1] See *Brasserie de Haecht v. Wilkin-Janssen*, Case 48/72, E.C.R. 1973, p. 77, § 25.

decision on the substance.

Furthermore, Regulation 17/62 provided, as France had requested, that existing agreements were to benefit from temporary validity until the Commission had taken a decision, irrespective of whether or not they had been notified. However, if the agreement was not notified and was prohibited by virtue of Article 81(1) EC, it would be illegal *ex tunc*, without any possibility of its being evaluated under Article 81(3) EC.

The compromise solution struck a reasonable balance between the French and German principles on how to implement Article 81. Whether the final approach would be closer to the French or German system was thus dependent on the substantive application of Article 81(1) to determine.

A strict interpretation of the prohibition established by Article 81(1) would effectively require companies to notify agreements both in order to request an exemption under Article 81(3) and to ensure immunity from fines in case the exemption was refused. Such an interpretation would therefore be tantamount to acceptance of the German principle.

A less strict interpretation of the prohibition established by Article 81(1) would represent less of an incentive to notify agreements to the Commission and would hence give rise to a system more in line with the French principle of abuse.

In fact, the Commission's practice tended towards a strict interpretation of Article 81(1) which potentially prohibited all agreements. This, in turn, broadened the potential application of Article 81(3). This practice effectively transformed Article 81(1) into a rule embodying the principle of prohibition. This meant that during the first 40 years of application of Article 81(1) (that is, until the end of the 1990s) there was a practical need, albeit not a formal requirement, to notify agreements to the Commission. Notification at least ensured that agreements would be effective for a certain time and prevented fines being imposed if the request for an exemption was rejected and the agreement thus turned out to be void by virtue of Article 81(2) EC. This approach led, at Community level, to a system similar to what was provided for by the German antitrust system. This is not a coincidence, since the Commission's practice was indeed guided by German influence, in particular that of the Freiburg Ordoliberal School.

The main reason for this influence was that in 1960 Walter Hallstein, the then President of the Commission, had been instrumental in appointing Ernst-Joachim Mestmäcker as special competition adviser to the Commission. Professor Mestmäcker was a pupil of Franz Böhm, one of the joint founders with Walter Eucken of the Freiburg School. The appointment reflected the fact that the Commission needed to create a Community competition policy (Klug, 1963, p. 171). Professor Mestmäcker kept his position from 1960 to

1970 and brought the influence of the German school of thought to bear on the interpretation of both Articles 81 and 82 EC (Zacher, 1996, p. 24).

9.2. IMPLEMENTATION OF ARTICLE 81 EC AS PROPOSED IN THE WHITE PAPER ON MODERNISATION AND THE PROPOSAL FOR A REGULATION

With the exception of the amendment of Article 4(2) of Regulation 17/62, the enforcement of Article 81 EC by means of Regulation 17/62 remained substantially unchanged until the end of the 1990s.

As early as the beginning of the 1990s, the Commission's practice had shown the limitations of the Regulation 17/62 system.[2] In addition to an increase in the number of complaints of infringements made to the Commission, there was a chronic problem of overload caused by notifications of agreements made in order to obtain an exemption under Article 81(3) EC.

Faced with these problems, the Commission put forward in 1999 a White Paper on Modernisation of Antitrust Law in which it proposed a radical reform of Regulation 17/62.

In order to eliminate the workload caused by notifications for exemptions under Article 81(3), the Commission proposed to modify the authorisation system established by Regulation 17/62. The purpose was to 'adopt a directly applicable exception system allowing *ex post* supervision of restrictive practices'. In the Commission's view, the switch to such a system could be achieved by a Council Regulation, based on Article 83 of the Treaty, which would stipulate that all national authorities or courts before which the applicability of Article 81(1) of the Treaty was invoked would also consider the applicability of Article 81(3). This interpretation would have the effect of making restrictive practices which are prohibited by Article 81(1), but which meet the tests of Article 81(3), lawful as from the time they were concluded, without the need for any prior decision. Similarly, restrictive practices that restricted competition would be unlawful once the conditions of Article 81(3) were no longer fulfilled. This new framework would mean that restrictive practices would no longer have to be notified in order to be validated. The arrangements for implementing Article 81 as a whole would then be identical to those for Articles 81(1) and 82 (see paragraph 69 of the White Paper).

This approach was taken up by the proposal for a regulation adopted in

[2] See the Commission's practice as referred to in a number of judgments: *Stergios Delimitis v. Henninger Bräu AG*, Case C-234/89, E.C.R. 1991, p. I–935; *Automec Srl v. Commission.*, Case T-24/90, E.C.R. 1992, p. II–2223; *BEMIM v. Commission*, Case T-114/92, E.C.R.1995, p. II–147.

2000. Article 1 of the proposal, entitled 'Direct applicability', provided that 'agreements, decisions and concerted practices caught by Article 81(1) of the Treaty which do not satisfy the conditions of Article 81(3) ... shall be prohibited, no prior decision to that effect being required'.

9.3. IMPLEMENTATION OF ARTICLE 81 EC BY REGULATION 1/03

Regulation 1/03 deals not only with the application of Article 81(3) EC but also with the issue of the burden of proof and the obligation to apply Articles 81 and 82 EC.

Article 1 of the Regulation, entitled 'Application of Articles 81 and 82 of the Treaty', permits the application of Articles 81(1) and 81(3) by providing that no particular proceeding is required in order to benefit from an exemption under Article 81(3) (with reference to criticism of the Mestmäcker approach, see Pace, 2005, p. 108).

Article 1(1) provides that 'agreements, decisions and concerted practices caught by Article 81(1) of the Treaty which do not satisfy the conditions of Article 81(3) of the Treaty shall be prohibited, no prior decision to that effect being required'.

Article 1(2) deals with agreements prohibited by Article 81(1). It provides that 'agreements, decisions and concerted practices caught by Article 81(1) of the Treaty which satisfy the conditions of Article 81(3) of the Treaty shall not be prohibited, no prior decision to that effect being required'.

Article 2 deals with the burden of proving an infringement of Community antitrust law. Under Regulation 17/62, it was clear that the burden of proving a breach of Article 81(1) rested on the national authorities. Article 81(3) was applied exclusively by the Commission and a request to apply that provision had to be made by means of a notification by the undertakings involved in the agreement. The burden of proof for obtaining the exemption thus clearly lay on the undertakings notifying the agreement.

Under Regulation 1/03, by contrast, there is no longer a system of notifications for obtaining the exemption under Article 81(3). Had a specific rule not been provided for, this could have led to the conclusion that the national authorities bore the burden of proving that the conditions fixed by Article 81(3) were not satisfied. Had the application of Article 81(3) been raised before a national court, this would have implied that the party which had brought the action would have borne that burden. In the absence of any obligation on the part of the undertakings party to the relevant agreement to participate, that approach would have made it difficult, if not impossible, for the Commission, the national authorities or the plaintiffs in a case to prove that those conditions did not exist.

Article 3 defines the relationship between Community antitrust law and national law (paragraphs (2) and (3)). It also deals with the obligation of national courts and authorities to apply Articles 81 and 82 EC (*infra*).

10. The Content of Article 81 EC

Article 85 EC confers on the Commission the exclusive power to determine the orientation of Community competition policy, albeit the exercise of this power is subject to review by the Court of Justice. To that extent, the Commission can be said to define the content of the antitrust rules. In the last five years, since 1999, the Commission has radically altered the orientation of its policy. The change of approach has been 'codified' in a succession of Communications, Notices and Regulations that define the Community competition law currently in force.

Article 81(1) EC prohibits all agreements between undertakings, decisions by associations of undertakings and concerted practices which may affect trade between Member States and which have as their object or effect the prevention, restriction or distortion of competition.

Article 81(2) provides that any agreement prohibited pursuant to Article 81(1) is automatically void.

Article 81(3) provides for an exception to the prohibitions established by Article 81(1). It does so by making it possible for the provisions of paragraph (1) to be declared inapplicable in the case of agreements which contribute to improving the production or distribution of goods or to promoting technical or economic progress. Such improvements must also allow consumers a fair share of the resulting benefit. At the same time, they must not impose restrictions which are not indispensable to the attainment of the objectives and which do not afford those undertakings the possibility of eliminating competition in respect of a substantial part of the products in question. (See *supra* for the detailed rules on how Article 81(1) and (3) are applied pursuant to Regulation 1/03.)

The application of Article 81 comprises two stages:

1. In the first stage, it is assessed 'whether an agreement between undertakings, which is capable of affecting trade between Member States, has an anticompetitive object or actual or potential anticompetitive effects' (paragraph 11 of the Guidelines on the application of Article 81(3)).[1]

[1] Communication from the Commission guidelines on the application of Article 81(3) of

2. The second stage comes into play only if an agreement is restrictive of competition and thus infringes Article 81(1). At this stage the pro-competitive benefits produced by that agreement must be determined and it must be assessed whether these procompetitive effects outweigh the anticompetitive effects. The balancing of anticompetitive and pro-competitive effects is conducted exclusively within the framework laid down by Article 81(3) (paragraph 11 of the Guidelines on the application of Article 81(3).

The objective of Article 81 is to protect competition on the market as a means of enhancing consumer welfare and of ensuring an efficient allocation of resources. Competition and market integration serve these ends since the creation and preservation of an open single market promotes an efficient allocation of resources throughout the Community for the benefit of consumers (ibid., paragraph 13, see also *supra*).

10.1. THE PROHIBITION ESTABLISHED BY ARTICLE 81(1) EC

Article 81(1) EC prohibits agreements between undertakings in so far as they may affect trade between Member States and restrict competition.

This is a consequence of the basic principle of Community antitrust law that 'each economic operator must determine independently the policy which he intends to adopt on the market' (paragraph 14). Article 81 therefore prohibits agreements which, by distorting competition, do not comply with this principle.

In the Commission's view, the purpose of Article 81 is 'to protect effective competition by ensuring that markets remain open and effective' (Guidelines on the application of Article 81(3), paragraph 47). The ultimate objective is the protection of the competitive process (ibid., paragraph 105), which is defined as 'winning customers by offering better products or better prices than those offered by rivals' (ibid., paragraphs 21 and 33).

Article 81 applies to agreements, decisions and concerted practices.

The expression 'agreement' refers to the means whereby 'the undertakings in question ... have expressed their joint intention to conduct themselves on the market in a specific way'. [2]

A decision of an association of undertakings is a measure which,

---

the Treaty, 2004 OJ C 101, p. 97.

[2] *ACF Chemiefarma v. Commission*, Case 41/69, E.C.R. 1970. p. 661, § 112; *Heintz van Landewyck v. Commission*, Joined Cases 209/78 to 215/78 and 218/78, E.C.R. 1980. p. 3125, § 86; *SA Hercules Chemicals NV v. Commission*, Case T-7/89, E.C.R. 1991, p. II–1711, § 256.

'regardless of what its precise legal status might be, constitutes the faithful reflection of the (association's) resolve to coordinate the conduct of its members in accordance with the terms of the "decision".[3]

A concerted practice is 'a form of coordination of undertakings which, without having been taken to a stage where an agreement properly so-called has been concluded, knowingly substitutes for the risks of competition, practical cooperation between them'.[4]

The expressions 'agreement', 'decision' and 'concerted practices' are 'Community law concepts which allow a distinction to be made between the unilateral conduct of an undertaking and co-ordination of behaviour or collusion between undertakings' (paragraph 14). For this reason, it is only Article 82, which prohibits the abuse of a dominant position, and not Article 81, that applies to the unilateral conduct of undertakings.

The type of coordination of behaviour or collusion falling under Article 81 'is that where at least one undertaking *vis-à-vis* another undertaking undertakes to adopt a certain conduct on the market, or that as a result of contacts between them, uncertainty as to their conduct on the market is eliminated or at least substantially reduced' (paragraph 15).

Co-ordination may take the form of:

- obligations that 'regulate the market conduct of at least one of the parties'; and
- arrangements that 'influence the market conduct of at least one of the parties by causing a change in its incentives' (paragraph 15). Coordination need not be in the interest of all the undertakings concerned.

Coordination may be tacit or express. For an agreement to be able to be treated as having been tacitly concluded, 'there must be an invitation from an undertaking to another undertaking, whether express or implied, to fulfil a goal jointly' (paragraph 15).

In general, agreements are caught by Article 81(1) when they are likely to have an appreciable adverse impact on the parameters of competition on the market, such as:

- price;
- output; and

[3] *Verband der Sachversicherer e.V. v. Commission*, Case 45/85, E.C.R. 1987, p. 405, § 32.

[4] *Suiker Unie v. Commission*, Joined Cases 40/73–48/73, 50/73, 54/73–56/73, 111/73, 113/73 and 114/73, E.C.R. 1975, p. 1663, § 26; *HFB Holding für Fernwärmetechnik Beteiligungsgesellschaft mbH & Co. KG and others v. Commission*, Case T-9/99, E.C.R. 2002, p. II–1487, § 211.

- product quality, product variety and innovation.

Agreements can have this effect 'by appreciably reducing rivalry between the parties to the agreement or between them and third parties' (paragraph 16).

10.2. AGREEMENTS PROHIBITED BY ARTICLE 81(1) EC: AGREEMENTS HAVING AN ANTICOMPETITIVE OBJECT OR EFFECT

In order to assess whether an agreement infringes Article 81(1), it is necessary to take account of the 'actual context in which competition would occur in the absence of the agreement with its alleged restrictions' (paragraph 17). In making this assessment, the Commission considers that account must be taken of the likely impact of the agreement on both:

- inter-brand competition (that is, competition between suppliers of competing brands); and
- intra-brand competition (that is, competition between distributors of the same brand).

For the purpose of assessing 'whether an agreement or its individual parts may restrict inter-brand competition and/or intra-brand competition, it needs to be considered how and to what extent the agreement affects or is likely to affect competition on the market' (paragraph 18). Since Article 81 aims to protect both 'inter-brand' and 'intra-brand' competition, 'it may be necessary to analyse a restraint in light of both questions before it can be concluded whether or not competition is restricted within the meaning of Article 81(1)' (the test for assessing whether intra-brand or inter-brand competition is restricted is set out at paragraph 18).

In order to be struck at by Article 81 EC, an agreement must distort competition. Article 81 establishes what types of competition may be distorted. (See *supra* for the types of competition that are protected by Article 81.) An agreement or contractual restraint 'is only prohibited by Article 81(1) if its object or effect is to restrict inter-brand competition and/or intra-brand competition' (paragraph 19).

Although an agreement may fall under Article 81(1) whether it is its object or its effect which makes it anticompetitive, the distinction is nevertheless important for the purpose of:

- establishing whether the agreement is prohibited; and

- fixing the level of the fine.

Once it has been established 'that an agreement has as its object the restriction of competition, there is no need to take account of its concrete effects. In other words, for the purpose of applying Article 81(1) no actual anticompetitive effects need to be demonstrated where the agreement has a restriction of competition as its object (paragraph 20). By contrast, Article 81(3) applies to all agreements that fulfil the four conditions contained therein.

10.2.1. Agreements Having a Restriction of Competition as Their Object

The Commission takes the view that an agreement has an anticompetitive object when the restrictions

> by their very nature have the potential of restricting competition. These are restrictions which in light of the objectives pursued by the Community competition rules have such a high potential of negative effects on competition that it is unnecessary for the purposes of applying Article 81(1) to demonstrate any actual effects on the market. (paragraph 21)

Restrictions by object may be, for example:

- price fixing; and
- market sharing.

Such restrictions 'reduce output and raise prices, leading to a misallocation of resources, because goods and services demanded by consumers are not produced. They also lead to a reduction in consumer welfare, because consumers have to pay higher prices for the goods and services in question' (paragraph 21).

The assessment of whether an agreement has as its object the restriction of competition is based on a number of factors, in particular:

- the content of the agreement; and
- the objective aims pursued by it (paragraph 22).

It may also be necessary to consider:

- the context in which it is to be applied; and
- the actual conduct and behaviour of the parties on the market.

In the case of horizontal agreements, restrictions of competition by object include:

- price fixing;
- output limitation; and
- sharing of markets and customers (paragraph 23).

As regards vertical agreements, the category of restrictions by object includes, in particular:

- fixed and minimum resale price maintenance; and
- restrictions providing absolute territorial protection, including restrictions on passive sales (see paragraph 23, for an assessment of when horizontal and vertical agreements contain restrictions by object, v *infra*).

10.2.2. Agreements Having Restrictive Effects on Competition

If an agreement is not restrictive of competition by object, it is caught by Article 81(1) only if it has an anticompetitive effect. For an agreement to be restrictive by effect, 'it must affect actual or potential competition to such an extent that on the relevant market negative effects on prices, output, innovation or the variety or quality of goods and services can be expected with a reasonable degree of probability' (paragraph 24). Account must be taken of both actual and potential effects (paragraph 24).

Furthermore, the negative effects must be appreciable. The prohibition rule of Article 81(1) does not apply when the identified anticompetitive effects are insignificant (on the point, see *infra*).

The Commission maintains that an agreement has an anticompetitive effect 'when the parties individually or jointly have or obtain some degree of market power and the agreement contributes to the creation, maintenance or strengthening of that market power or allows the parties to exploit such market power' (paragraph 25). By the expression 'market power', the Commission is referring to 'the ability to maintain prices above competitive levels for a significant period of time or to maintain output in terms of product quantities, product quality and variety or innovation below competitive levels for a significant period of time' (paragraph 25). The creation, maintenance or strengthening of market power

> can result from a restriction of competition between the parties to the agreement. It can also result from a restriction of competition between any one of the parties and third parties, e.g. because the agreement leads to foreclosure of competitors or

because it raises competitors' costs, limiting their capacity to compete effectively with the contracting parties (paragraph 26).

Since the Commission considers that market power is a question of degree, it puts forward a test making a comparison between the degree of market power required to find an infringement of Article 81 in the case of an agreement having restrictive effects and the degree required to find dominance under Article 82. The Commission maintains that 'the degree of market power normally required for the finding of an infringement under Article 81(1) in the case of agreements that are restrictive of competition by effect is less than the degree of market power required for a finding of dominance under Article 82' (paragraph 26).

Normally, for the purposes of analysing whether an agreement has restrictive effects, it is necessary to define the relevant market (see *infra* for the detailed rules on how to define the relevant market). To that end, it is usually also necessary to examine and assess *inter alia*:

- the nature of the products;
- the market position of the parties;
- the market position of competitors;
- the market position of buyers;
- the existence of potential competitors; and
- the level of entry barriers (paragraph 27 of the Guidelines).

However, in some cases it may be possible to show competitive effects directly by analysing the conduct of the parties to an agreement on the market (on this point, see in particular paragraph 27).

With reference to an agreement that infringes Article 81, it is necessary:

- to verify that the main transaction foreseen by the agreement is not restrictive of competition; and
- to assess whether 'individual restraints contained in the agreement are also compatible with Article 81(1) because they are ancillary to the main non-restrictive transaction' (paragraph 28).

The concept of 'ancillary restraint' covers 'any alleged restriction of competition which is directly related and necessary to a main non-restrictive transaction and proportionate to it' (paragraph 29). For an ancillary restraint not to infringe Article 81(1), two conditions must be satisfied:

- it must be objectively necessary for the implementation of the main transaction and be proportionate to it; and

- it must be inseparably linked to it (paragraph 29).

The assessment of ancillary restraints

> is limited to determining whether, in the specific context of the main non-restrictive transaction or activity, a particular restriction is necessary for the implementation of that transaction or activity and proportionate to it. If on the basis of objective factors it can be concluded that without the restriction the main non-restrictive transaction would be difficult or impossible to implement, the restriction may be regarded as objectively necessary for its implementation and proportionate to it. (paragraph 31)

The assessment of an ancillary restraint must be distinguished from the application of Article 81(3):

> [The] defence under Article 81(3) ... relates to certain economic benefits produced by restrictive agreements and which are balanced against the restrictive effects of the agreements. The application of the ancillary restraint concept does not involve any weighing of pro-competitive and anticompetitive effects. Such balancing is reserved for Article 81(3). (paragraph 30)

10.3. THE EFFECT OF ARTICLE 81(2) EC

Where the agreement is prohibited by Article 81(1) and cannot be exempted by virtue of Article 81(3), Article 81(2) stipulates that it is void. Only the national courts may determine whether an agreement is void for this reason (*supra*).

If only part of the agreement is incompatible with Article 81, the 'automatic nullity only applies to those parts of the agreement that are incompatible ... provided that such parts are severable from the rest of the agreement as a whole' (paragraph 41). If only part of the agreement is void, 'it is for the applicable national law to determine the consequences thereof for the remaining part of the agreement' (paragraph 41).

10.4. THE EXCEPTION PROVIDED BY ARTICLE 81(3) EC

If an agreement falls within the scope of Article 81(1), the second possible stage of the application of Article 81 is triggered off. If an agreement is to be exempted from the prohibition contained in Article 81(1), paragraph 3 must be applied. According to the Commission's new approach, this phase consists in 'the assessment of the positive economic effects of restrictive agreements' (paragraph 32, for the new objectives of Community antitrust law, see *supra*). Agreements which 'restrict competition may at the same time have pro-competitive effects by way of efficiency gains. Efficiencies may create additional value by lowering the cost of creating an output, improving the quality of the product or creating a new product' (paragraph 33). In the Commission's view, 'when the pro-competitive effects of an agreement outweigh its anticompetitive effects the agreement is on balance pro-competitive and compatible with the objectives of the Community competition rules' (paragraph 33). The net effect of such agreements is to promote the very essence of the competitive process, namely to win customers by offering better products or better prices than those offered by rivals. This analytical framework is reflected in Articles 81(1) and 81(3). The latter provision expressly acknowledges that restrictive agreements may generate objective economic benefits so as to outweigh the negative effects of the restriction of competition (paragraph 33).

The application of Article 81(3) requires four conditions to be met. Two are positive and two are negative:

1. The agreement must contribute to improving the production or distribution of goods or contribute to promoting technical or economic progress.
2. Consumers must receive a fair share of the resulting benefits.
3. The restrictions must be indispensable to the attainment of those objectives.
4. The agreement must not afford the parties the possibility of elimination competition in respect of a substantial part of the products in question.

When these four conditions are satisfied, 'the agreement enhances competition within the relevant market, because it leads the undertakings concerned to offer cheaper or better products to consumers, compensating the latter for the adverse effects of the restrictions of competition' (paragraph 34).

Article 81(3) can be applied to:

- individual agreements (on this point, see *supra*); and
- categories of agreements by way of a block exemption regulation.

If an agreement is covered by a block exemption, the parties to the restrictive agreement are relieved of their burden of showing that their individual agreement satisfies each of the conditions of Article 81(3). They only have to prove that the restrictive agreement benefits from a block exemption (paragraph 35).

According to Article 29 of Regulation 1/03, both the Commission and the national authorities may withdraw the benefit of a block exemption. The Commission has this power 'when it finds that in a particular case an agreement covered by a block exemption regulation has certain effects which are incompatible with Article 81(3)' (paragraph 36).

The national authorities may, pursuant to Article 29 of Regulation 1/03,

> withdraw the benefit of a Commission block exemption regulation in respect of its territory (or part of its territory), if this territory has all the characteristics of a distinct geographic market. In the case of withdrawal, it is for the competition authorities concerned to demonstrate that the agreement infringes Article 81(1) and that it does not fulfil the conditions of Article 81(3). (paragraph 36)

National courts 'have no power to withdraw the benefit of block exemption regulations. Moreover, in their application of block exemption regulations, Member State courts may not modify their scope by extending their sphere of application to agreements not covered by the block exemption regulation in question' (paragraph 37). The Commission takes the view that, outside the scope of block exemption regulations, 'Member State courts have the power to apply Article 81 in full' by virtue of Article 6 of Regulation 1/03 (on the unlawfulness of Article 6, see *infra*).

10.5. THE APPLICATION OF THE FOUR CONDITIONS OF ARTICLE 81(3)

If an agreement is incompatible with Article 81(1) EC, Article 81(3) comes into play. In the case of non-restrictive agreements, there is no need to examine any benefits generated by the agreement (paragraph 40). By virtue of Article 2 of Regulation 1/03, the burden of proving that the conditions of Article 81(3) are satisfied lies on the undertakings seeking the exemption (*supra*).

The four conditions established 'by Article 81(3) are cumulative, i.e. they must all be fulfilled for the exception rule to be applicable. If they are not, the application of the exception rule of Article 81(3) must be refused. The four conditions of Article 81(3) are also exhaustive' (paragraph 42).

In the Commission's view, goals pursued by other Treaty provisions can be taken into account only to the extent that they can be subsumed under the four conditions of Article 81(3) (paragraph 42, on this point, see *infra*).

The assessment under Article 81(3) of the relevant benefits is 'in principle made within the confines of each relevant market to which the agreement relates' (paragraph 43). However, 'where two markets are related, efficiencies achieved on separate markets can be taken into account provided that the group of consumers affected by the restriction and benefiting from the efficiency gains are substantially the same' (paragraph 43).

In any event, 'the assessment of restrictive agreements under Article 81(3) is made within the actual context in which they occur and on the basis of the facts existing at any given point in time' (paragraph 44). It must therefore take account of any relevant changes in the facts. Should there be any material changes, 'the exception rule of Article 81(3) applies as long as the four conditions are fulfilled and ceases to apply when that is no longer the case' (paragraph 44).

No types of agreement are excluded *a priori* from being able to benefit from Article 81(3). If a restrictive agreement satisfies the four conditions it may in principle benefit from an exemption (paragraph 46). However, 'severe restrictions of competition are unlikely to fulfil the conditions of Article 81(3). Such restrictions are usually black-listed in block exemption regulations or identified as hardcore restrictions in Commission guidelines and notices' (paragraph 46).

The Commission does not accept that an exemption under Article 81(3) may be granted to ensure generally 'fair conditions of competition on the market'. It takes the view that any claim that restrictive agreements are justified because they aim at ensuring fair conditions of competition on the market is by nature unfounded and must be discarded. The purpose of Article 81 is to protect effective competition by ensuring that markets remain open and competitive. The protection of fair conditions of competition is a task for the legislator in compliance with Community law obligations and not for undertakings to regulate themselves (paragraph 47).

10.5.1. Efficiency Gains

The first condition of Article 81(3) is that the agreement promotes efficiency gains. Article 81(3) refers only to goods but it applies by analogy to services (paragraph 48).

In applying this first condition, only objective benefits can be taken into account. This means that efficiencies are not assessed from the subjective point of view of the parties (paragraph 49).

The purpose of the first condition 'is to define the types of efficiency gains that can be taken into account and be subject to the further tests of the second and third conditions of Article 81(3). The aim of the analysis is to ascertain what are the objective benefits created by the agreement and what is the economic importance of such efficiencies' (paragraph 50).

Since Article 81(3) does not apply unless the pro-competitive effects flowing from the agreement outweigh its anticompetitive effects, it is necessary to verify what is the link between the agreement and the claimed efficiencies and what is the value of those efficiencies (paragraph 50). To that end, all efficiency claims must be substantiated so that the following aspects can be verified:

- the nature of the claimed efficiencies;
- the link between the agreement and the efficiencies;
- the likelihood and magnitude of each claimed efficiency; and
- how and when each claimed efficiency would be achieved (paragraph 51).

The Commission emphasises that the types of efficiencies listed in Article 81(3) are broad categories which are intended to cover all objective economic efficiencies. It is therefore not appropriate to draw clear and firm distinctions between the various categories (paragraph 59). For the purposes of the Guidelines, the Commission draws a distinction between:

- cost efficiencies; and
- efficiencies of a qualitative nature whereby value is created in the form of new or improved products or greater product variety.

The Commission maintains that 'efficiencies stem from an integration of economic activities whereby undertakings combine their assets to achieve what they could not achieve as efficiently on their own or whereby they entrust another undertaking with tasks that can be performed more efficiently by the other undertaking' (paragraph 60). The process of research and development, production and distribution 'may be viewed as a value chain that can be divided into a number of stages. At each stage of this chain an undertaking must make a choice between performing the activity itself, performing it together with (an)other undertaking(s) or outsourcing the activity entirely to (an)other undertaking(s)' (paragraph 61). Both horizontal and vertical agreements may create efficiencies which allow them to benefit from an exemption under Article 81(3) (paragraph 62).

In the Notice, the Commission refers in particular to the following factors:

Cost efficiencies

The types of cost efficiencies which the Commission takes into account are as follows:

- efficiencies flowing from technological progress (paragraph 64);

- efficiencies resulting from synergies between undertakings (paragraph 65);
- efficiencies resulting from economies of scale (paragraph 66);
- efficiencies resulting from economies of scope (paragraph 67); and
- efficiencies resulting from better planning of production (paragraph 68).

Qualitative efficiencies
The types of qualitative efficiencies which the Commission takes into account are as follows:

- technical and technological advances and research and development agreements (paragraph 70);
- technical progress and joint production agreements (paragraph 71);
- technical progress and the combination of production assets (paragraphs 71 and 72); and
- technical progress and distribution agreements (paragraph 72).

10.5.2. A Fair Share of the Benefit for Consumers

The second condition imposed by Article 81(3) is that consumers must receive a fair share of the benefit resulting from the restrictive agreement.

The concept of consumers
Consumers are the customers of the parties to the agreement and subsequent purchasers. They may be:

- undertakings, as in the case of buyers of industrial machinery or an input for further processing; or
- final consumers, as in the case of buyers of impulse ice-cream or bicycles (paragraph 84).

The concept of a fair share
The concept of 'fair share' requires the passing-on of benefits to 'at least compensate consumers for any actual or likely negative impact caused to them by the restriction of competition found under Article 81(1)' (paragraph 85). In other words, 'in line with the overall objective of Article 81 to prevent anticompetitive agreements, the net effect of the agreement must at least be neutral from the point of view of those consumers directly or likely affected by the agreement' (paragraph 85). Consequently, 'if such consumers are worse off following the agreement, the second condition of Article 81(3) is not fulfilled' (paragraph 85). For consumers to receive a fair share of the benefits, it is not required that they 'receive a share of each and every

efficiency gain identified under the first condition' (paragraph 86). The decisive factor is 'the overall impact on consumers of the products within the relevant market and not the impact on individual members of this group of consumers' (paragraph 87). The Commission explains that

> if the agreement has both substantial anticompetitive effects and substantial pro-competitive effects a careful analysis is required. In the application of the balancing test in such cases it must be taken into account that competition is an important long-term driver of efficiency and innovation. Undertakings that are not subject to effective competitive constraints – such as for instance dominant firms – have less incentive to maintain or build on the efficiencies. The more substantial the impact of the agreement on competition, the more likely it is that consumers will suffer in the long run. (paragraph 92)

The analytical framework

When assessing consumer pass-on of efficiency gains, the Commission has special regard to the following aspects:

- cost efficiencies; and
- qualitative efficiencies.

There is a need to draw up an analytical framework for 'cases in which it is not immediately obvious that the competitive harms exceed the benefits to consumers or *vice versa*' (paragraph 93). The Commission accepts that 'in many cases it is difficult to accurately calculate the consumer pass-on rate and other types of consumer pass-on' (this shows once again that Article 81(3) does not have direct effect because it is not a precise provision. It cannot therefore be applied by national courts, *supra*). In that light, the Commission requests undertakings to substantiate their claims by providing estimates and other data to the extent reasonably possible, taking account of the circumstances of the individual case (paragraph 94).

Pass-on and balancing of cost efficiencies The Commission states that 'in assessing the extent to which cost efficiencies are likely to be passed on to consumers and the outcome of the balancing test under Article 81(3)', certain factors are taken into account, in particular:

- the characteristics and structure of the market;
- the nature and magnitude of the efficiency gains;
- the elasticity of demand; and
- the magnitude of the restriction of competition (paragraph 96).

With reference to this aspect, the Commission has set out the basic rules concerning the rational behaviour of an undertaking. It maintains that

> the nature of the efficiency gains also plays an important role. According to economic theory, undertakings maximise their profits by selling units of output until marginal revenue equals marginal cost. Marginal revenue is the change in total revenue resulting from selling an additional unit of output and marginal cost is the change in total cost resulting from producing the additional unit of output. It follows from this principle that as a general rule output and pricing decisions of a profit maximising undertaking are not determined by its fixed costs (i.e. costs that do not vary with the rate of production) but by its variable costs (i.e. costs that vary with the rate of production). After fixed costs are incurred and capacity is set, pricing and output decisions are determined by variable cost and demand conditions. (paragraph 98)

Pass-on and balancing of other types of efficiencies (qualitative efficiencies)
The Commission recognises that the assessment of the pass-on of qualitative efficiencies to consumers 'requires value judgment. It is difficult to assign precise values to dynamic efficiencies of this nature. However, the fundamental objective of the assessment remains the same, namely to ascertain the overall impact of the agreement on the consumers within the relevant market. Undertakings claiming the benefit of Article 81(3) must substantiate that consumers obtain countervailing benefits' (paragraph 103). In particular, the availability of new and improved products constitutes an important source of consumer welfare. As long as the increase in value stemming from such improvements exceeds any harm from a maintenance of an increase in price caused by the restrictive agreement, consumers are better off than without the agreement and the consumer pass-on requirement of Article 81(3) is normally fulfilled. In cases where the likely effect of the agreement is to increase prices for consumers within the relevant market it must be carefully assessed whether the claimed efficiencies create real value for consumers in that market so as to compensate for the adverse effects of the restriction of competition (paragraph 104).

10.5.3. Indispensability of the Restriction

The third condition of Article 81(3), relating to indispensability, is, logically enough, assessed by the Commission in the second place, before it examines the conditions relating to the passing on of a fair share to consumers.

This third condition is that 'the restrictive agreement must not impose restrictions, which are not indispensable to the attainment of the efficiencies created by the agreement' (paragraph 73). When assessing whether the third condition is satisfied,

> [The] decisive factor is whether or not the restrictive agreement and individual restrictions make it possible to perform the activity in question more efficiently than would likely have been the case in the absence of the agreement or the restriction concerned. The question is not whether in the absence of the restriction the agreement would not have been concluded, but whether more efficiencies are produced with the agreement or restriction than in the absence of the agreement or restriction. (paragraph 74)

This condition implies a twofold test as follows.

Reasonable necessity

The restrictive agreement as such must be reasonably necessary in order to achieve efficiencies. Furthermore, the individual restrictions of competition that flow from the agreement must also be reasonably necessary for the attainment of the efficiencies (paragraph 73).

> [The first test] requires that the efficiencies be specific to the agreement in question in the sense that there are no other economically practicable and less restrictive means of achieving the efficiencies. In making this latter assessment the market conditions and business realities facing the parties to the agreement must be taken into account. Undertakings invoking the benefit of Article 81(3) are not required to consider hypothetical or theoretical alternatives. The Commission will not second guess the business judgment of the parties. It will only intervene where it is reasonably clear that there are realistic alternatives available. (paragraph 75)

The parties to the agreement are only required to 'explain and demonstrate why such seemingly realistic and significantly less restrictive alternatives to the agreement would be significantly less efficient'. It is particularly important to examine whether, 'having due regard to the circumstances of the individual case, the parties could have achieved the efficiencies by means of another less restrictive type of agreement and, if so, when they would be likely to obtain the efficiencies' and whether 'the parties could have achieved the efficiencies on their own' (paragraph 76).

Indispensabilty of each restriction of competition

Once it has been ascertained that the agreement in question is necessary to produce the efficiencies, the indispensability of each restriction of competition flowing from the agreement must be evaluated. In that context, 'it must be assessed whether individual restrictions are reasonably necessary in order to produce the efficiencies' (paragraph 78). The parties bear the burden of substantiating their claim with regard to both:

- the nature of the restriction; and
- the intensity of the restriction.

A restriction is deemed

> indispensable if its absence would eliminate or significantly reduce the efficiencies that follow from the agreement or make it significantly less likely that they will materialise. The assessment of alternative solutions must take into account the actual and potential improvement in the field of competition by the elimination of a particular restriction or the application of a less restrictive alternative. (paragraph 79)

Regarding how indispensability is assessed, 'the more restrictive the restraint, the stricter the test under the third condition' (paragraph 79). In any event, it is unlikely that restrictions that are blacklisted in block exemption regulations or identified as hardcore restrictions in Commission guidelines will be considered indispensable (paragraph 79).

The assessment of indispensability is made within the actual context in which the agreement operates and must take account of, in particular:

- the structure of the market;
- the economic risks related to the agreement; and
- any incentives facing the parties.

The more uncertain the success of the product covered by the agreement, the more a restriction may be required to ensure that the efficiencies will materialise (paragraph 80).

10.5.4. No Elimination of Competition

The fourth condition of Article 81(3) is that the agreement may not give the undertakings concerned the possibility of eliminating competition in respect of a substantial part of the products concerned. In the Commission's view, this means that

> [The] protection of rivalry and the competitive process is given priority over potentially pro-competitive efficiency gains which could result from restrictive agreements. The last condition of Article 81(3) recognises the fact that rivalry between undertakings is an essential driver of economic efficiency, including

> dynamic efficiencies in the form of innovation. In other words, the ultimate aim of Article 81 is to protect the competitive process. When competition is eliminated, the competitive process is brought to an end and short-term efficiency gains are outweighed by longer-term losses stemming *inter alia* from expenditures incurred by the incumbent to maintain its position (rent seeking), misallocation of resources, reduced innovation and higher prices. (paragraph 105)

The concept of elimination of competition in respect of a substantial part of the products concerned is an autonomous Community law concept specific to Article 81(3) (paragraph 106).

Whether competition is being eliminated within the meaning of the last condition of Article 81(3) depends on the degree of competition existing prior to the agreement and on the impact of the restrictive agreement on competition, that is, the reduction in competition that the agreement brings about. The more competition is already weakened in the market concerned, the slighter the further reduction required for competition to be eliminated within the meaning of Article 81(3). Moreover, the greater the reduction of competition caused by the agreement, the greater the likelihood that competition in respect of a substantial part of the product concerned risks being eliminated (paragraph 107). To that end, there must be 'a realistic analysis of the various sources of competition in the market, the level of competitive constraint that they impose on the parties to the agreement and the impact of the agreement on this competitive constraint' (paragraph 108). Consequently, both actual and potential competition must be considered.

Actual competition

The parties' market shares are certainly a relevant factor in the assessment of the level of actual competition. However, 'the magnitude of remaining sources of actual competition cannot be assessed exclusively on the basis of market share. More extensive qualitative and quantitative analysis is normally called for' (paragraph 109).

In the assessment of the impact of the agreement on the market, 'it is also relevant to examine its influence on the various parameters of competition. The last condition for exemption under Article 81(3) is not fulfilled if the agreement eliminates competition in one of its most important expressions. This is particularly the case when an agreement eliminates price competition or competition in respect of innovation and development of new products' (paragraph 110).

Insights into the influence of the agreement on competition can also be provided by:

- the actual market conduct of the parties; and

- past competitive interaction. It may also provide an indication of the impact on the agreement on future competitive interaction.

Potential competition

In the context of the fourth condition, 'while sources of actual competition are usually the most important, as they are most easily verified, sources of potential competition must also be taken into account' (paragraph 114).

The assessment of potential competition requires an examination of entry barriers for undertakings that are not yet active on the relevant market. The Commission has provided a list of factors which must be taken into account in order to evaluate barriers to entry and the possibility for new entry on a significant scale. They are as follows:

- the regulatory framework;
- the cost of entry;
- the minimum efficient scale within the industry;
- the competitive strengths of potential entrants;
- the position of buyers and their ability to bring new sources of competition onto the market;
- the likely response of incumbents to attempted new entry;
- the economic outlook for the sector; and
- whether or not there has been past entry on a significant scale (paragraph 115).

If the parties claim that there are low barriers to entry, those claims 'must be supported by information identifying the sources of potential competition and the parties must also substantiate why these sources constitute a real competitive pressure on the parties' (paragraph 114).

11. Article 81 EC and Horizontal Agreements

Even before issuing its Guidelines on the application of Article 81(3) EC, the Commission had already adopted the Guidelines on the applicability of Article 81 EC to horizontal cooperation agreements,[1] in which it set out the principles governing the assessment of horizontal cooperation agreements in the light of Article 81. The purpose was to provide an analytical framework for the most common types of horizontal cooperation (paragraph 7).[2]

11.1. THE REASONS FOR THE NOTICE, ITS AIM AND THE TESTS WHICH IT ESTABLISHES

The expression 'horizontal agreement' means an 'agreement or concerted practice entered into between companies operating at the same level in the market' (paragraph 1). Such agreements are often types of cooperation between competitors, such as research and development (R&D), production, purchasing or commercialisation.[3]

The Commission felt it necessary to issue the Guidelines on horizontal cooperation agreements on the ground that:

> horizontal cooperation may lead to competition problems. This is for example the case if the parties to a cooperation agreement agree to fix prices or output, to share markets, or if the cooperation enables the parties to maintain, gain or increase

[1] Commission Notice Guidelines on the applicability of Article 81 of the EC Treaty to horizontal cooperation agreements, 2001 OJ C 3, p. 2.

[2] For the system of rules, on horizontal agreements, which is made up of regulations and communications, see, Council Regulation 2821/71 (Block exemption enabling regulation), 1971 OJ L 285/46; Regulation 2658/2000 on Specialization Agreements, 2000 OJ L 304/3, Regulation 2659/2000 on R&D Agreements, 2000 OJ L 304/7.

[3] For the system of rules, on vertical agreements, which is made up of regulations and communications, see Regulation 19/65 (Block exemption enabling regulation), 1965 OJ 533; Guidelines on Vertical Restraints, 2000 OJ C 291/1; Regulation 1400/2002 on Vertical Agreements in the Motor Vehicle Sector, 2002 OJ L 203/30; Regulation 772/2004 on Technology Transfer Agreements, 2004 OJ L 123/11; Guidelines on the Application of Article 81 to Technology Transfer Agreements, 2004 OJ C 101/2.

market power and thereby causes negative market effects with respect to prices, output, innovation or the variety and quality of products. (paragraph 2)

However, this does not rule out horizontal cooperation leading to 'substantial economic benefits' (paragraph 3).

Part of the thinking behind the Guidelines is that they can contribute to increasing the competitivity of small and medium-sized enterprises (*supra*). On this point, the Commission states that 'companies need to respond to increasing competitive pressure and a changing market place driven by globalisation, the speed of technological progress and the generally more dynamic nature of markets' (paragraph 3). Cooperation between undertakings 'can be a means to share risks, save costs, pool know-how and launch innovation faster' (paragraph 3). As regards small and medium-sized enterprises, 'cooperation is an important means to adapt to the changing market place' (paragraph 3). It adds that 'the Commission, while recognising the economic benefits that can be generated by cooperation, has to ensure that effective cooperation is maintained' (paragraph 4). In particular, 'Article 81 provides the legal framework for a balanced assessment taking into account both anticompetitive effects as well as economic benefits' (paragraph 4).

In the Guidelines, the Commission based its analysis on economic criteria such as the parties' market power and other factors relating to market structure. These 'form a key element of the assessment of the market impact likely to be caused by a cooperation and therefore for the assessment under Article 81' (paragraph 7).

11.2. COOPERATION AGREEMENTS FALLING UNDER ARTICLE 81(1) EC

The Guidelines only apply to types of cooperation that may generate efficiency gains. These are:

- agreements on R&D;
- production agreements (including specialisation agreements);
- purchasing agreements;
- commercialisation agreements;
- standardisation agreements; and
- environmental agreements (paragraphs 10 and 39 ff).

For each type of agreement, the Guidelines:

- provide a definition of the agreement;

- explain how the relevant markets are to be defined; and
- make an assessment in the light of both Article 81(1) and Article 81(3) EC.

The Guidelines also complement the research and development[4] and specialisation[5] block exemption regulations.

The Commission divides horizontal agreements into three separate categories as follows.

11.2.1. Agreements Which Do Not Fall Within the Scope of Article 81 EC

The Commission identifies agreements which almost never fall under Article 81(1) EC. This is normally the case for cooperation agreements which do not involve coordination of the parties' competitive behaviour in the market, such as:

- cooperation between non-competitors;
- cooperation between competing companies that cannot independently carry out the project or activity covered by the cooperation; and
- cooperation concerning an activity which does not influence the relevant parameters of competition.

These types of cooperation can fall within the scope of Article 81(1) only 'if they involve firms with significant market power and are likely to cause foreclosure problems vis-à-vis third parties' (paragraph 24).

11.2.2. Agreements that Fall Within the Scope of Article 81 EC

In the Commission's view, certain agreements almost always fall under Article 81 EC. Such agreements are, in particular, 'cooperation agreements that have the object to restrict competition by means of price-fixing, output limitation or sharing of markets or customers. These restrictions are considered to be the most harmful, because they directly interfere with the outcome of the competitive process' (paragraph 25).

As it did in the Guidelines on the application of Article 81(3), the Commission bases this view on the fact that:

---

[4] Commission Regulation (EC) 2659/2000 of 29 November 2000 on the application of Article 81(3) of the Treaty to categories of research and development agreements, 2000 OJ L 304, p. 7.

[5] Commission Regulation (EC) 2658/2000 of 29 November 2000 on the application of Article 81(3) of the Treaty to categories of specialisation agreements, 2000 OJ L 304, p. 3.

> price fixing and output limitation directly lead to customers paying higher prices or not receiving the desired quantities. The sharing of markets or customers reduces the choice available to customers and therefore also leads to higher prices or reduced output. It can therefore be presumed that these restrictions have negative market effects. They are therefore almost always prohibited. (paragraph 25)

11.2.3. Agreements that May Fall Under Article 81 EC

Agreements which do not fall into either of the above categories may fall under Article 81(1), but require further analysis to decide whether this is the case for a given agreement (paragraph 26).

For the purposes of this analysis, the Commission provides certain criteria. The starting point is the position of the parties in the markets affected by the cooperation:

> [This] determines whether or not they are likely to maintain, gain or increase market power through the cooperation, i.e. have the ability to cause negative market effects as to prices, output, innovation or the variety or quality of goods and services. To carry out this analysis the relevant market(s) have to be defined by using the methodology of the Commission's market definition notice. (paragraph 27, see *infra*)

If the parties 'have a low combined market share, a restrictive effect of the cooperation is unlikely and no further analysis normally is required'. If one of just two parties has only an insignificant market share and does not possess important resources, even a high combined market share does not normally indicate a restrictive effect on competition in the market (paragraph 28). The Commission does not establish a market share threshold above which it can be presumed that the parties have sufficient market power to cause restrictive effects. This is so because 'given the variety of cooperation types and the different effects they may cause in different market situations, it is impossible to give a general market share threshold' (paragraph 28).

In addition to market shares, the Commission considers that 'the market concentration, that is, the position and number of competitors, may have to be taken into account as an additional factor to assess the impact of the cooperation on market competition'. This may be done either:

- by means of the Herfindahl-Hirschman Index (HHI); or
- by means of the leading firm concentration ratio, which sums up the individual market shares of the leading competitors, usually indicated as 'CR' (paragraph 29).

Furthermore, 'depending on the market position of the parties and the concentration in the market, other factors' also have to be taken into account in assessing whether the agreement falls under Article 81(1). Those factors include:

- the stability of market shares over time;
- entry barriers;
- the likelihood of market entry;
- the countervailing power of buyers/suppliers; and
- the nature of the products (for example, homogeneity, maturity) (paragraph 30).

12. Article 81 EC and Vertical Agreements

In 1999 the Commission adopted the Block Exemption Regulation on Vertical Agreements.[1] The Regulation bears witness to a significant change of approach in the Commission's policy towards the assessment of this type of agreement. The earlier block exemption regulations in this field were made up of 'white-listed' and 'black-listed' contractual terms. For an agreement to be able to benefit from exemption under Article 81(3), it needed to contain white-listed terms. Not only was the content of the white and black lists controversial, the entire philosophy of the regulations was open to criticism on the ground that it unduly restricted the parties' freedom of contract. The fact that certain terms were obligatory whereas others were outlawed indirectly tended to harmonise the content of agreements concluded by undertakings doing business within the European Community.

This approach changed after the adoption of Regulation 2790/1999, which operates on the basis of tests taking market shares as their yardstick. If the tests are satisfied, the pro-competitive effects of the agreement are presumed to balance out the restriction of competition which it entails and the agreement therefore benefits from the Article 81(3) exemption. The Regulation therefore refers to 'a category of agreements which can be regarded as normally satisfying the conditions laid down in Article 81(3)' (Recital 2). That category includes:

1. Vertical agreements relating to the purchase or sale of goods or services, to the extent that those agreements are entered into by:

   - non-competing undertakings;
   - certain competing undertakings; or
   - certain associations of retailers of goods.

[1] Commission Regulation (EC) 2790/1999 of 22 December 1999 on the application of Article 81(3) of the Treaty to categories of vertical agreements and concerted practices, 1999 OJ L 336, p. 21.

2. Vertical agreements containing ancillary provisions relating to the assignment or the use of intellectual property rights.

The legal basis of Regulation 2790/1999 is Council Regulation 19/65/EEC of 2 March 1965 on the application of Article 85(3) of the Treaty to certain categories of agreements and concerted practices, as last amended by Regulation (EC) 1215/1999. Regulation 19/65 authorises the Commission to apply Article 81(3) EC to certain categories of vertical agreements and concerted practices falling within the scope of Article 81(1) EC.

After adopting Regulation 2790/1999, the Commission issued its Guidelines on Vertical Restraints.

12.1. THE SCOPE OF REGULATION 2790/1999

The expression 'vertical agreement' refers to an agreement between undertakings which operate at different stages of the production chain, such as an agreement between a producer of certain goods and a distributor of those goods. The Commission explains that the exemption is conferred on the agreements referred to in the Regulation because, in its view, such agreements 'can improve economic efficiency within a chain of production or distribution by facilitating better coordination between the participating undertakings'. In particular, they can lead to a reduction in the transaction and distribution costs of the parties and to an optimisation of their sales and investment levels (Recital 6 of the preamble to Regulation 2790/1999).

12.1.1. The Exemption Provided for by the Regulation Applies to Three Categories of Vertical Agreements

The general rule

The exemption applies to:

> agreements or concerted practices entered into between two or more undertakings each of which operates, for the purposes of the agreement, at a different level of the production or distribution chain, and relating to the conditions under which the parties may purchase, sell or resell certain goods or services ('vertical agreements'). The exemption shall apply to the extent that such agreements contain restrictions of competition falling within the scope of Article 81(1) ('vertical restraints'). (Article 2(1) of Regulation 2790/1999)

On the other hand, certain categories of agreements do not benefit from the exemption. They are as follows. Vertical agreements which have as their object:

- the restriction of the buyer's ability to determine its sale price;
- the restriction of the territory into which, or of the customers to whom, the buyer may sell the contract goods or services;
- the restriction of active or passive sales to end users by members of a selective distribution system operating at the retail level of trade;
- the restriction of cross-supplies between distributors within a selective distribution system, including between distributors operating at different levels of trade (regarding the definition of selective distribution system, see *infra*); and
- the restriction agreed between a supplier of components and a buyer who incorporates those components, which limits the supplier to selling the components as spare parts to end-users or to repairers or other service providers not entrusted by the buyer with the repair or servicing of those goods (Article 4 of the Regulation).

Vertical agreements between small and medium undertakings

Agreements concerning small and medium undertakings also benefit from the block exemption conferred by the Regulation. In particular, Article 2(2) provides that:

> [T]he exemption provided for in paragraph 1 shall apply to vertical agreements entered into between an association of undertakings and its members, or between such an association and its suppliers, only if all its members are retailers of goods and if no individual member of the association, together with its connected undertakings, has a total annual turnover exceeding EUR 50 million; vertical agreements entered into by such associations shall be covered by this regulation without prejudice to the application of Article 81 to horizontal agreements concluded between the members of the association or decisions adopted by the association.

Vertical agreements relating to the assignment or use of intellectual property rights

By virtue of Article 2(3) of the Regulation, the exemption also applies to vertical agreements containing provisions relating to the assignment to the buyer or use by the buyer of intellectual property rights. However, this is only the case where those provisions do not constitute the primary object of the agreements and are directly related to the use, sale or resale of goods or services by the buyer or its customers. The exemption is also further restricted by the condition that the provisions may not contain restrictions of competition having the same object or effect as vertical restraints which are not exempted under the Regulation.

12.1.2. The Exemption Provided for by the Regulation Does Not Apply to Two Categories of Vertical Agreements:

Vertical agreement between competing undertakings

By virtue of Article 2(4), the exemption does not apply to vertical agreements entered into between competing undertakings.

On the other hand, the exemption does apply where competing undertakings enter into a non-reciprocal vertical agreement provided the following conditions are satisfied:

- the buyer has a total annual turnover not exceeding €100 million; or
- the supplier is a manufacturer and a distributor of goods, while the buyer is a distributor not manufacturing goods competing with the contract goods; or
- the supplier is a provider of services at several levels of trade, while the buyer does not provide competing services at the level of trade where it purchases the contract services.

Vertical agreements covered by other block exemption regulations

By virtue of Article 2(5), the exemption provided for by Regulation 2790/99 does not apply to vertical agreements the subject matter of which falls under any other block exemption regulation.

The Guidelines on Vertical Restraints, which the Commission issued after enacting Regulation 2790/99, clarify the application of the Regulation to the following types of vertical agreement:

- single branding (paragraphs 138 ff. of Guidelines on Vertical Restraints);
- exclusive distribution (paragraphs161 ff. of Guidelines on Vertical Restraints);
- exclusive customer allocation (paragraphs 178 ff. of Guidelines on Vertical Restraints);
- selective distribution (paragraphs 184 ff. of Guidelines on Vertical Restraints);
- franchising (paragraphs 199 ff. of Guidelines on Vertical Restraints);
- exclusive supply (paragraphs 202 ff. of Guidelines on Vertical Restraints);
- tying (paragraphs 215 ff. of Guidelines on Vertical Restraints); and

- recommended and maximum resale price (paragraphs 225 ff. of Guidelines on Vertical Restraints).

12.2. THE GENERAL RULE RELATING TO THE APPLICATION OF ARTICLE 81(3)

Whether an agreement falls within the scope of Regulation 2790/99 depends largely on the market shares of the undertakings concerned. In the Commission's view, the market share criterion and the fact that certain vertical agreements are excluded mean that the participating undertakings are not able 'to eliminate competition in respect of a substantial part of the products in question' (Recital 12 of the preamble to the Regulation).

The Commission uses the market share test in order to determine the relevant undertakings' market power. This determines the degree of competition which those undertakings face from other suppliers of goods or services regarded by the buyer as interchangeable or substitutable from one another by reason of the products' characteristics, their prices and their intended use (Recital 7 of the preamble and Article 9(1) of the Regulation). The Commission assumes that there is an absence of market power where the 'share of the relevant market accounted for by the supplier does not exceed 30%' (Recital 8). In consequence, the exemption 'shall apply on condition that the market share held by the supplier does not exceed 30% of the relevant market on which it sells the contract goods or services' (Article 3(1). In that case, it can be presumed that 'vertical agreements which do not contain certain types of severely anticompetitive restraints generally lead to an improvement in production or distribution and allow consumers a fair share of the resulting benefits' (Recital 8).

In the specific case of vertical agreements containing exclusive supply obligations, 'it is the market share of the buyer which is relevant in determining the overall effects of such vertical agreements on the market' (Article 3(2)).

On the other hand, once the market share threshold of 30% is exceeded, it cannot be presumed that vertical agreements falling within the scope of Article 81(1) will usually give rise to objective advantages of such a character and size as to compensate for the disadvantages which they create for competition (Recital 9).

The Regulation provides for a precise method of calculating market share. In particular, the market share of 30% shall be calculated on the basis of the market sales value of the contract goods or services and other goods or services sold by the supplier, which are regarded as interchangeable or substitutable by the buyer, by reason of the products' characteristics, their prices and their intended use (Article 9(1)). For the purposes of Article 3(2), 'it is either the market purchase value or estimates thereof which shall be used to calculate the market share'. For the cases in which the Regulation requires annual turnover to be calculated (see Articles 2(2) and (4)), Article 10 sets out the appropriate methodology. Furthermore, Article 11 specifies that in certain cases undertakings may be treated as being connected for the purpose of the application of the Regulation.

The Regulation also stipulates the consequences of exceeding the market share threshold after the relevant agreement has been concluded. In particular, if the market share is initially not more than 30% but subsequently rises above that level without exceeding 35%, the exemption shall continue to apply for a period of two consecutive calendar years following the year in which the 30% market share threshold was first exceeded (Article 9(2)(c)). If the market share is initially not more than 30% but subsequently rises above 35%, the exemption shall continue to apply for one calendar year following the year in which the level of 35% was first exceeded (Article 9(2)(d)). Article 9(2)(e) provides that the benefits of points (c) and (d) may not be combined so as to exceed a period of two calendar years.

12.3. RESTRICTIONS EXCLUDING THE BENEFIT OF ARTICLE 81(3)

The Regulation also provides that certain types of restriction should preclude the agreement in question from benefiting from Article 81(3) EC. Recital 10 states that 'the Regulation should not exempt vertical agreements containing restrictions which are not indispensable to the attainment of the positive effects' contemplated by the Regulation. In particular, 'vertical agreements containing certain types of severely anticompetitive restraints such as minimum and fixed resale-prices, as well as certain types of territorial protection, should be excluded from the benefit of the block exemption established by this Regulation irrespective of the market share of the undertakings concerned'.

12.3.1. Restrictions Concerning the Imposition of a Minimum or Fixed Sale Price

The first basic limitation relates to terms determining prices. In particular, Article 4(a) of the Regulation stipulates that the exemption which it provides does not apply 'to vertical agreements which ... have as their object ... the restriction of the buyer's ability to determine its sale price, without prejudice to the possibility of the supplier's imposing a maximum sale price or recommending a sale price, provided that they do not amount to a fixed or minimum sale price as a result of pressure from, or incentives offered by, any of the parties'.

12.3.2. Restrictions Concerning any Form of Territorial Protection

A second fundamental type of limitation, the presence of which will entail the inapplicability of the block exemption, relates to the restriction of the territory into which, or of the customers to whom, the buyer may sell the contract goods or services, except:

- the restriction of active sales into the exclusive territory or to an exclusive customer group reserved to the supplier or allocated by the supplier to another buyer, where such a restriction does not limit sales by the customers of the buyer;
- the restriction of active sales to end users by a buyer operating at the wholesale level of trade;
- the restriction of sales to unauthorised distributors by the members of a selective distribution system; and
- the restriction of the buyer's ability to sell components, supplied for the purposes of incorporation, to customers who would use them to manufacture the same type of goods as those supplied by the supplier (Article 4(b)).

12.4. THE APPLICATION OF ARTICLE 81(3) EC TO NON-COMPETE OBLIGATIONS

The exemption provided for by the Regulation is also excluded with respect to certain types of non-compete obligations. Recital 11 states that 'the exemption of non-compete obligations should be limited to obligations which do not exceed a definite duration; for the same reasons, any direct or indirect obligation causing the members of a selective distribution system not to sell the brands of particular competing suppliers should be excluded from the benefit of this Regulation'.

12.4.1. Non-compete Obligations Exceeding Five Years

In particular, the exemption does not apply to any direct or indirect non-compete obligation, the duration of which is indefinite or which exceeds five years. A non-compete obligation which is tacitly renewable beyond a period of five years is to be deemed to have been concluded for an indefinite duration. However, the time limitation of five years shall not apply where the contract goods or services are sold by the buyer from premises and land owned by the supplier or leased by the supplier from third parties not connected with the buyer, provided that the duration of the non-compete obligation does not exceed the period of occupancy of the premises and land by the buyer (Article 5(a)).

12.4.2. Non-compete Obligations Persisting after the Termination of the Agreement

The exemption does not apply to certain agreements which contain non-compete obligations which continue after the termination of the agreement. In particular, Article 5(b) provides that it does not apply to 'any direct or indirect obligation causing the buyer, after termination of the agreement, not to manufacture, purchase, sell or resell goods or services', unless the obligation:

- relates to goods or services which compete with the contract goods services; and
- is limited to the premises and land from which the buyer has operated during the contract period; and
- is indispensable to protect know-how transferred by the supplier to the buyer and provided that the duration of such non-compete obligation is limited to a period of one year after termination of the agreement; this obligation is without prejudice to the possibility of imposing a restriction which is unlimited in time on the use and disclosure of know-how which has not entered the public domain.

12.4.3. Non-compete Obligations Concerning Selective Distribution Systems

The exemption does not apply to non-compete obligations connected with selective distribution systems. Article 1(d) defines the expression 'selective distribution system' as meaning 'a distribution system where the supplier undertakes to sell the contract goods or services, either directly or indirectly, only to distributors selected on the basis of specified criteria and where these distributors undertake not to sell such goods or services to unauthorised distributors'. By virtue of Article 5(c), the exemption does not apply to 'any direct or indirect obligation causing the members of a selective distribution system not to sell the brands of particular competing suppliers'.

12.5. WITHDRAWAL OF THE BENEFIT OF THE REGULATION BY THE COMMISSION OR THE NATIONAL AUTHORITIES

Article 6 defines the Commission's general power to withdraw the benefit of the exemption granted by the Regulation. It has this power 'in particular cases in which agreements falling under this Regulation nevertheless have effects incompatible with Article 81(3)'. Examples of this type of situation are given in Recital 13 of the preamble. It may occur 'when the buyer has significant market power in the relevant market in which it resells the goods or provides the services or where parallel networks of vertical agreements have similar effects which significantly restrict access to a relevant market or competition therein; such cumulative effects may for example arise in the case of selective distribution or non-compete obligations'.

Article 6 therefore grants the Commission the power to withdraw the benefit of the Regulation, pursuant to Article 7(1) of Regulation 19/65,

> where it finds in any particular case that vertical agreements to which this regulation applies nevertheless have effects which are incompatible with the conditions laid down in Article 81(3) of the Treaty, and in particular where access to the relevant market or competition therein is significantly restricted by the cumulative effect of parallel networks or similar vertical restraints implemented by competing suppliers or buyers.

If certain conditions are fulfilled, the national authorities are also permitted to withdraw the benefit of the Regulation. In order for them to be able to exercise this power, the following conditions, laid down by Article 7 of the Regulation, must be met:

- vertical agreements to which the exemption applies have effects incompatible with the conditions laid down in Article 81(3); and
- those effects are felt in the territory of a Member State, or part thereof, which has all the characteristics of a distinct geographic market.

In that case, the competent authority of the relevant Member State may withdraw the benefit of the Regulation on its territory under the same conditions as the Commission pursuant Article 6 of the Regulation. Finally, Recital 14 of the preamble states that the Member States 'should ensure that the exercise of this power of withdrawal does not prejudice the uniform application throughout the common market of the Community competition rules or the full effect of the measures adopted in implementation of those rules'.

PART IV

ARTICLE 82 EC

13. The Drafting of Article 82 EC

The Spaak Report foresaw that the EC Treaty would include a rule prohibiting monopolistic behaviour by undertakings. Official documents show that Article 82 EC proved less difficult to draft than Article 81. This is probably because, at that time, there were no corresponding rules in the legal systems of the six founding Member States. Germany was the only Member State that had felt it necessary to insert a provision on unilateral conduct by undertakings in the law on competition (Article 22 *GWB*).

During the drafting of this provision in the Treaty of Rome, discussion concentrated mainly on how the power of individual undertakings should be limited and on whether provision should be made for the control of concentrations, as had been done in the ECSC Treaty (see Schulze and Hoeren, 2000). In the Treaty of Rome, it was ultimately decided to insert a provision dealing with the prohibition of monopolistic behaviour by undertakings. Article 82 EC strikes at the unilateral behaviour of one or more undertakings in that it prohibits the abuse of a dominant position within the common market or in a substantial part of it in so far as the abuse may affect trade between the Member States.

This prohibition operated according to the principle of abuse and no specific provision was made for merger control (*infra*). In contrast to what was provided for with respect to Article 81 EC, the Treaty allowed no exemptions from the application of Article 82.

14. The Implementation of Article 82 EC

Unlike Article 81(3) EC, Article 82 does not require any implementing measures since, as the case law has recognised, it fulfils all the conditions necessary for it to have direct effect (*infra*). Given these factors, the provisions in Regulation 1/03 relating to Article 82 are similar to those in Regulation 17/62.

Article 1 of Regulation 17/62, entitled 'Basic provision', provides in pertinent part that 'the abuse of a dominant position in the market, as prohibited by Article 82 of the Treaty, shall be prohibited, no prior decision to that effect being required'.

Article 1(3) of Regulation 1/03 reads as follows: 'The abuse of a dominant position referred to in Article 82 of the Treaty shall be prohibited, no prior decision to that effect being required'.

Unlike Article 81(3) EC, Article 82 does not make any provision for granting exemption from the prohibition that it establishes. For that reason, the Community legislature has no competence to enact legislation exempting particular types of conduct from the application of Article 82.

15. The Content of Article 82 EC

The Commission has already set in train the process of adapting the interpretation of Article 82 to the new goals of Community antitrust law as it did at an earlier stage with regard to Article 81 (see *supra*). The first step in this process was the publication, in December 2005, of a discussion paper on exclusionary abuses, which is one of the categories of abuse of a dominant position (see *infra*). Purportedly, the 'discussion paper sets out possible principles for the Commission's application of Article 82 of the Treaty to exclusionary abuses'. However, it is clear from the content of the discussion paper that it goes further than the Commission indicated. It also deals with other aspects, for example by introducing significant changes to the very concept of a dominant position as it has been defined by the case law. One illustration of these proposed changes is that the Commission envisages eliminating the 'special responsibilities' incumbent on the undertaking holding the dominant position. Thanks to German influence (Mestmäcker and Schweizer, 2004, p. 392), the obligations flowing from these responsibilities represented one of the characteristic features connected with a dominant position.[1]

It is no coincidence that the innovative aspects of the discussion paper provoked such opposition from some of the Member States that as late as July 2006 the Commission had not been able to move on to the next stage of 'modernising' Article 82 by publishing a Communication on the interpretation of that article.

Despite the controversy that it has provoked, the discussion paper is an extremely significant document, albeit it represents only an informal exercise of the Commission's power to determine competition policy (Article 85 EC). By virtue of this power, the Commission will be able, at a later stage, to adopt formal acts, such as decisions, implementing the principles set out in the discussion paper, subject as always to the possibility of review by the Court of Justice.

However, even if the Commission does apply Article 82 according to the new approach that it appears to be advocating, the Member States will still be

---

[1] *Europemballage Corporation and Continental Can Company Inc. v. Commission* (*Continental Can*), Case 6/72, E.C.R. 1973, p. 215, § 25, § 27. As already noted, the principle applied by the Court in *Continental Can* had already been formulated by Mestmäcker (1966).

entitled to apply national antitrust law to abuses of a dominant position and this may be more stringent than Community law (see *supra*).

In the light of the above, we shall examine the content of the discussion paper, not merely in so far as it relates to exclusionary abuses, but also in relation to the determination of dominance. On the other hand, we shall examine exploitative and discriminatory abuses in the light of the existing case law.

15.1. THE DEFINITION OF A DOMINANT POSITION

The first paragraph of Article 82 EC provides as follows: 'Any abuse by one or more undertakings of a dominant position within the common market or in a substantial part of it shall be prohibited as incompatible with the common market in so far as it may affect trade between Member States'.

It is stated in the discussion paper, in terms similar to those employed in the Guidelines on the application of Article 81(3), that the objective of Article 82, at least as regards

> exclusionary abuses ..., is the protection of competition on the market as a means of enhancing consumer welfare and of ensuring an efficient allocation of resources. Effective competition brings benefits to consumers, such as low prices, high quality products, a wide selection of goods and services, and innovation. Competition and market integration serve these ends since the creation and preservation of an open single market promotes an efficient allocation of resources throughout the Community for the benefit of consumers. (Discussion paper on Article 82 EC, § 4)

An infringement of Article 82 requires the following conditions to be satisfied:

- one or more undertakings;
- which must have a dominant position on the relevant market; and
- which abuse the dominant position;
- this behaviour must affect trade between Member States.

Since we have already considered the concepts of an 'undertaking' and 'effect on trade between Member States' (see *supra*), we can now turn our attention, first, to the definition of a dominant position and, second, to the concept of an abuse of a dominant position.

In the discussion paper, the Commission, referring to the existing case law,[2] states that dominance is a position of 'economic strength enjoyed by an undertaking which enables it to prevent effective competition being maintained on the relevant market by affording it the power to behave to an appreciable extent independently of its competitors, its customers and ultimately of the consumers' (§ 20).

The dominant position may be held by a single undertaking or by more than one undertaking. In the latter case, it is referred to as collective dominance. For collective dominance to exist, 'the undertakings concerned must, from an economic point of view, present themselves or act together on a particular market as a collective entity' (§ 20).

Before an undertaking's position on the relevant market can be determined, it is first necessary to define the relevant market since 'the relevant market provides a framework for analysing whether the undertaking concerned holds a dominant position and, therefore, whether its conduct may be abusive within the meaning of Article 82' (§ 11). To put it more precisely, the purpose of defining the market is 'to identify in a systematic way the immediate competitive constraints faced by an undertaking. The objective of defining a market in both its product and geographic dimension is to identify all actual competitors of the undertaking concerned that are capable of constraining its behaviour' (§ 12).

15.2. THE DEFINITION OF THE RELEVANT MARKET

When the possible existence of a dominant position for the purposes of Article 82 is assessed or the future effects of a concentration are evaluated, it is of critical importance to define the relevant market. The fact that in the first case the assessment of the effect of the behaviour is *ex post* and in the second it is *ex ante* may lead to slightly different results. It is also necessary to define the relevant market for the purposes of Article 81 when assessing whether or not an agreement between undertakings has an anticompetitive effect (*supra*).

The Commission has stated in the Notice on the definition of relevant market[3] that market definition is a tool to identify and define the boundaries of competition between firms. The main purpose of market definition is to identify in a systematic way the competitive constraints that the undertakings involved face. The objective of defining a market in both its product and geographic dimension is to identify those actual competitors of the

---

[2] *United Brands v. Commission* (Chiquita Bananas), op.cit., p. 207, § 249

[3] Commission Notice on the definition of relevant market for the purposes of Community competition law, 1997 OJ C 372, p. 5.

undertakings involved that are capable of constraining those undertakings' behaviour and of preventing them from behaving independently of effective competitive pressure (paragraph 2).

The relevant market within which a given competition issue must be assessed is therefore established by the combination of the product and geographic markets (paragraph 9):

Relevant product market
The relevant product market 'comprises all those products and/or services which are regarded as interchangeable or substitutable by the consumer, by reason of the products' characteristics, their prices and their intended use' (paragraph 7).

Relevant geographic market
The relevant geographic market comprises 'the area in which the undertakings concerned are involved in the supply and demand of products or services, in which the conditions of competition are sufficiently homogeneous and which can be distinguished from neighbouring areas because the conditions of competition are appreciably different in those areas' (paragraph 8).

15.2.1. The Basic Principles for Market Definition

In the Commission's view, firms are subject to three main sources of competitive constraints, namely:

- demand substitutability;
- supply substitutability; and
- potential competition.

Demand substitutability
In the Commission's view, the principal criterion for defining 'all those products and/or services which are regarded as interchangeable or substitutable by the consumer' is demand substitutability. It states that 'from an economic point of view, for the definition of the relevant market, demand substitution constitutes the most immediate and effective disciplinary force on the suppliers of a given product, in particular in relation to their pricing decision' (paragraph 13).

The Commission adds that the competitive constraints arising from supply-side substitutability other than those described in paragraphs 20 to 23 (*infra*) and from potential competition are in general less immediate and in any case require an analysis of additional factors. As a result, such constraints are taken into account at the assessment stage of competition analysis (paragraph 14). A firm or group of firms cannot have a significant impact on the prevailing conditions of sale, such as prices, if its customers are in a position to switch easily to available substitute products or to suppliers located elsewhere. Basically, the exercise of market definition consists in identifying the effective alternative sources of supply for the customers of the undertakings involved, in terms both of products/services and of geographic location of suppliers (paragraph 13).

The Commission then indicates two ways of determining demand substitution.

The SSNIP Test The SSNIP (small but significant non-transitory increase in price) Test entails

> postulating a hypothetical small, lasting change in relative prices and evaluating the likely reactions of customers to that increase. The exercise of market definition focuses on prices for operational and practical purposes, and more precisely on demand substitution arising from small, permanent changes in relative prices. This concept can provide clear indications as to the evidence that is relevant in defining markets. (paragraph 15)

In substance the test entails answering the question

> whether the parties' customers would switch to readily available substitutes or to suppliers located elsewhere in response to a hypothetical small (in the range 5% to 10%) but permanent relative price increases in the products and areas being considered. If substitution were enough to make the price increase unprofitable because of the resulting losses of sales, additional substitutes and areas are included in the relevant market. This would be done until the set of products and geographical areas is such that small, permanent increases in relative prices would be profitable. (paragraph 17)

The equivalent analysis The second method is equivalent to the first and is used in cases concerning the concentration of buying power, where the starting point would then be the supplier and the price test serves to identify the alternative distribution channels or outlets for the supplier's products (paragraph 17).

In order to determine demand substitutability, the price to be taken into account, and which will then be increased by 5–10%, is the prevailing market price. The main problem arising in the application of the SSNIP Test is what is known as the 'Cellophane Fallacy'). This occurs when the price which is taken into account is not a competitive price but a price which is itself determined by anticompetitive behaviour. In that case, 'in particular for the investigation of abuses of dominant positions, the fact that the prevailing price might already have been substantially increased will be taken into account' (paragraph 19).

Supply substitution

The second source of competitive constraints is, in the Commission's view, supply substitutability. This means the possibility not for consumers to obtain a good or service different from the one whose price has been increased but for other undertakings to switch production to the relevant good or service. That possibility would neutralise the effect of the increase in price of the first product.

In the Commission's view:

> [S]upply-side substitutability may also be taken into account when defining markets in those situations in which its effects are equivalent to those of demand substitution in terms of effectiveness and immediacy. This means that suppliers are able to switch production to the relevant products and market them in the short term without incurring significant additional costs or risks in response to small and permanent changes in relative prices. When these conditions are met, the additional production that is put on the market will have a disciplinary effect on the competitive behaviour of the companies involved. Such an impact in terms of effectiveness and immediacy is equivalent to the demand substitution effect. (paragraph 20)

However, for the purpose of defining the relevant market, the Commission considers supply-side substitutability to be a less reliable test.

If the relevant undertakings do not have the possibility of changing their production in a relatively short period of time, the effects of supply-side substitutability and other forms of competition would not be examined until a later stage (paragraph 23).

Potential competition

The third source of competitive constraint is, in the Commission's view, potential competition. However, it is not taken into account when defining markets, since the conditions under which potential competition will actually represent an effective competitive constraint depend on the analysis of specific factors and circumstances related to the conditions of entry. If required, this analysis is only carried out at a subsequent stage, in general once the position of the companies involved in the relevant market has already been ascertained, and when such position gives rise to concerns from a competition point of view (paragraph 24).

15.2.2. Evidence Which is Material to Defining Relevant Markets

Applying such precise rules requires a lot of market information to be collected. The Commission has drawn up a non-exhaustive list of types of evidence which it considers relevant for the purpose of defining the product and geographic market.

Concerning the relevant product market
The evidence which the Commission will take into account when assessing the product market is as follows:

- actual substitution in the recent past (paragraph 38);
- various quantitative tests that have been specifically designed for the purposing of delineating markets (paragraph 39);
- views of customers and competitors (paragraph 40);
- consumer preferences (paragraph 41);
- barriers and costs associated with switching demand to potential substitutes (paragraph 42); and
- the existence of different categories of customers and price discrimination (paragraph 43).

Concerning the relevant geographic market
When defining the relevant geographic market, the Commission will take account of the following evidence:

- past evidence of diversion of orders to other areas (paragraph 45);
- basis demand characteristics (paragraph 46);
- views of customers and competitors (paragraph 47);
- current geographic pattern of purchases (paragraph 48);
- trade flows/patterns of shipments (paragraph 49); and
- barriers and switching costs associated to divert orders to companies located in other areas (paragraph 50).

15.2.3. Calculating an Undertaking's Market Share

Once the relevant market has been defined, it is possible to calculate the market share of the undertakings concerned. In particular, the definition of the relevant market in both its product and geographic dimensions allows the identification of the suppliers and the customers/consumers active on that market. A total market size and market shares for each supplier can be calculated on the basis of their sales of the relevant products in the relevant areas. In practice, the total market size and market shares are often available from market sources, that is, companies' estimates, studies commissioned from industry consultants and/or trade associations (paragraph 53).

15.3. DOMINANT POSITION

In the discussion paper, the Commission states that dominance consists of three closely linked elements:

- there must be a position of economic strength on a market;
- that enables the undertaking(s) in question to prevent effective competition being maintained on that market; and
- that affords the power to behave independently to an appreciable extent (§ 21).

The first element 'implies that dominance exists in relation to a market. It cannot exist in the abstract' (§ 22). Furthermore, 'it also implies that an undertaking either on its own or together with other undertakings must hold a leading position on that market compared to its rivals' (§ 22).

The second and third elements concern 'the link between the position of economic strength held by the undertaking concerned and the competitive process, i.e. the way in which the undertaking and other players act and interact on the market' (§ 23).

Dominance can be defined as the ability of an undertaking 'to prevent effective competition being maintained on the market and to act to an appreciable extent independently of other players' (§ 24). Independence, 'which is the special feature of dominance, is related to the level of competitive constraint facing the undertaking(s) in question' (§ 24).

In the Commission's view, 'for dominance to exist the undertaking(s) concerned must not be subject to effective competitive constraints' (§ 24). This is the case whenever the undertaking concerned has 'substantial market power' (§ 24). As already indicated in the Guidelines on the application of Article 81(3), market power means 'the power to influence market prices, output, innovation, the variety or quality of goods and services, or other parameters of competition on the market for a significant period of time' (§ 25).

Market power flows from the fact that the undertaking concerned is not subject to competitive restraints from other market players:

> Unlike undertakings in a market characterised by effective competition, a dominant undertaking not subject to effective competitive constraints is able to price above the competitive level. It can do so by reducing its own output or by

causing rivals to reduce their output. The foreclosure of competitors may therefore allow the dominant company to further raise price or keep prices high. (§ 25)

15.3.1. Determining the Existence of a Dominant Position

The Commission then draws up a list of factors which must be taken into account in determining whether an undertaking has a dominant position; in other words whether it is not subject to competitive restraints from other market players. The relevant factors are as follows:

- the market position of the allegedly dominant undertaking and of competitors;
- barriers to expansion and entry; and
- the market position of buyers (§ 28).

Once the relevant market has been defined, these factors play a role in determining whether, on that market, the allegedly dominant undertaking 'has the power to behave to an appreciable extent independently of its competitors, its customers and ultimately of the consumers, that is, whether it holds substantial market power' (§ 28).

The existence of a dominant position 'may derive from several factors which, taken separately, are not necessarily determinative' (§ 28).

Market position of allegedly dominant undertaking and its rivals

The analysis of the market position of the allegedly dominant undertaking and its rivals provides insight into the degree of actual competition on the market (§ 29).

The starting point for this analysis 'is the market shares of the various players. Market shares provide useful first indications of the market structure and of the competitive importance of various undertakings active on the market' (§ 29). In this sense, market shares represent 'a proxy for market power, which is the decisive factor' (§ 32).

Barriers to expansion and entry

In determining whether a dominant position exists, 'if the barriers to expansion faced by rivals and to entry faced by potential rivals are low, the fact that one undertaking has a high market share may not be indicative of dominance. Any attempt by an undertaking to increase prices above the competitive level would attract expansion or new entry by rivals thereby undermining the price increase' (§ 34).

Barriers to expansion and entry can have various causes, among which the Commission lists:

- legal barriers (special or exclusive rights, intellectual property rights and soon);
- sunk cost and capacity constraints;
- economies of scale and scope; and
- other strategic barriers to expansion or entry (training advantages or network effects, the use of long-term contracts with customers) (§ 40).

Market position of buyers
In determining the existence of a dominant position, the third significant factor is the market position of buyers. Like the other factors, this may indicate the extent to which buyers are likely to constrain the allegedly dominant undertaking (§ 41).

15.3.2. Collective Dominance

Article 82 also applies to collective dominance, which exists whenever two or more undertakings together hold a dominant position: 'For collective dominance to exist under Article 82, two or more undertakings must from an economic point of view present themselves or act together on a particular market as a collective entity' (§ 44). However, it is not necessary that 'the undertakings concerned adopt identical conduct on the market in every respect' (§ 44). What is important is that 'they are able to adopt a common policy on the market and act to a considerable extent independently of their competitors, their customers, and also of consumers' (§ 44).

The following may give rise to a common policy on the market:

- structural relations between the undertakings concerned which 'may flow from the nature and terms of an agreement between the undertakings in question or from the way in which it is implemented' (§ 45); and
- the structure of the market on which the undertakings carry out their activity since 'the existence of an agreement or of other links in law is not indispensable to a finding of a collective dominant position' (§ 46). In particular, undertakings in oligopolistic markets 'may sometimes be able to raise prices substantially above the competitive level without having recourse to any explicit agreement or concerted practice. Coordination is more likely to emerge in markets where it is relatively simple to reach a common understanding on the terms of coordination' (§ 47). In principle 'the simpler and more stable the economic environment, the easier it is for undertakings to reach a common understanding' (§ 47).

The ability to reach and sustain such a level of coordination depends on a number of factors relevant to the market and the undertakings operating on it, such as the following:

- each undertaking must be able to monitor whether or not the other undertakings are adhering to the common policy (§ 48);
- the implementation of the common policy must be sustainable over time (§ 49); and
- it must be established that competitive constraints do not jeopardise the implementation of the common strategy (§ 50).

15.4. ABUSE OF THE DOMINANT POSITION

The first paragraph of Article 82 establishes a general prohibition on undertakings abusing a dominant position. It provides that: 'Any abuse by one or more undertakings of a dominant position within the common market or a substantial part of it shall be prohibited as incompatible with the common market in so far as it may affect trade between Member States'.

The second paragraph goes on to list certain types of behaviour which may constitute such abuse. It reads as follows:

> Such abuse may, in particular, consist in:
> a) directly or indirectly imposing unfair purchase or selling prices or other unfair trading conditions;
> b) limiting production, markets or technical development to the prejudice of consumers;
> c) applying dissimilar conditions to equivalent transactions with other trading parties, thereby placing them at a competitive disadvantage;
> d) making the conclusion of contracts subject to acceptance by the other parties of supplementary obligations which, by their nature or according to commercial usage, have no connection with the subject of such contracts.

This is merely a list of examples of abuse and is not exhaustive.[4] As the wording of Article 82 indicates, such types of abuse consist mainly in attempts by the undertaking to abuse its dominant position in order to maximise its profits at the expense of its customers or suppliers. This is known as exploitative abuse.

The Community courts subsequently accepted that Article 82 could also apply to practices aiming to exclude from the market or marginalise a

[4] *United Brands v. Commission* (Chiquita Bananas), op.cit., p. 207, § 65.

competitor, thereby reducing the level of competition which still existed. (This type of abuse is known as exploitative abuse).[5]

A third category is discriminatory abuse. This consists in the dominant undertaking applying different conditions to contracting partners providing similar contractual performances.

A fourth category relates to structural abuses and is linked to the *Continental Can* line of case law.[6] In this type of case, the abuse consists in the dominant undertaking reinforcing its dominant position by taking over a competitor, thereby further reducing the level of competition existing on the market. This type of abuse was particularly significant before the Merger Regulation was enacted and reference is therefore made to Part X of this book for further discussion of it.

In the discussion paper, the Commission reclassifies the various types of prohibition established by Article 82 and, to this end, divides them into three separate categories:

- exclusionary abuses;
- exploitative abuses; and
- discriminatory abuses.

---

[5] *Europemballage Corporation and Continental Can Company Inc. v. Commission (Continental Can)*, op. cit., p. 215, § 25; *Giuseppe Sacchi*, Case 155/73, E.C.R. 1974, p. 409, § 74; *Hoffmann-La Roche et Co. AG v. Commission*, Case 85/76, E.C.R. 1979, p. 461, § 38; *Istituto Chemioterapico Italiano SpA and Commercial Solvents Corporation v. Commission*, Joined Cases 6 and 7/73, E.C.R. 1974, p. 223, § 25.

[6] *Europemballage Corporation and Continental Can Company Inc. v. Commission (Continental Can)*, op. cit., § 26.

16. Article 82 EC and Exclusionary Abuses

In the discussion paper on Article 82, the Commission 'sets out possible principles for the Commission's application of Article 82 of the Treaty to exclusionary abuses' (§ 1). In particular, the discussion paper considers not only the factors constituting dominance but also the characteristics of the principal types of exclusionary abuse (predatory pricing, single branding and rebates, tying and bundling, and refusal to supply).

16.1. EXCLUSIONARY ABUSES

By the expression 'exclusionary abuse', the Commission is referring to:

> behaviours by dominant firms which are likely to have a foreclosure effect on the market, i.e. which are likely to completely or partially deny profitable expansion in or access to a market to actual or potential competitors and which ultimately harm consumers. Foreclosure may discourage entry or expansion of rivals or encourage their exit. (§ 1)

16.1.1. The Ingredients of Exclusionary Abuse

In determining what constitutes exclusionary abuse, the Commission refers to the definition of abuse that the Court of Justice gave in *Hoffmann-La Roche*[1] in the context of exclusionary conduct. The Court held that abuse was:

> an objective concept relating to the behaviour of an undertaking in a dominant position which is such as to influence the structure of a market where, as a result of the very presence of the undertaking in question, the degree of competition is weakened and which, through recourse to methods different from those which condition normal competition in products or services on basis of the transaction of commercial operators, has the effect of hindering the maintenance of the degree of

[1] *Hoffmann-La Roche et Co. AG v. Commission*, Case 85/76, E.C.R. 1979, p. 461, § 38.

competition still existing in the market or the growth of that competition. (§ 57)

In the Commission's view, this definition implies two things:

- the conduct in question must have the capability, by its nature, to foreclose competitors from the market. To establish such capability it is in general sufficient to investigate the form and nature of the conduct in question (§ 58); and
- a likely market distorting foreclosure effect must be established in the specific market context.

Foreclosure is said to be market distorting if it likely hinders the maintenance of the degree of competition still existing in the market or the growth of that competition and thus have as a likely effect that prices will increase or remain at a supra-competitive level (§ 58).

As regards the question whether an 'anticompetitive foreclosure effect' exists, 'in general, the higher the capability of conduct to foreclose and the wider its application and the stronger the dominant position, the higher the likelihood that an anticompetitive foreclosure effect results' (§ 59).

These criteria (sliding scale) allow considerable leeway in determining whether or not particular behaviour constitutes an abuse. In its attempt to set out general principles for the application of Article 82, the Commission recalls that 'where a certain exclusionary conduct is clearly not competition on the merits, in particular conduct which clearly creates no efficiencies and which only raises obstacles to residual competition, such conduct is presumed to be an abuse' (§ 60).

The dominant company may rebut the presumption of abuse by proving that:

- the conduct does not and will not have the alleged likely exclusionary effect, or
- the conduct is objectively justified (§ 60).

The Commission divides exclusionary conduct into two categories as follows.

Non-price-based conduct

These conducts may be, for instance:

- contractual tying;
- single branding contracts; and
- 'naked' refusals to supply (§ 61).

Price-based conduct

The distinction is important since, where pricing behaviour is involved, the exclusionary effects of the conduct of the dominant company may depend on the efficiency of its rivals (§ 63). A very efficient rival 'may be able to thrive in a market where the dominant company prices in a certain way, while a less efficient rival may be excluded from the market' (§ 63).

The Commission bases its assessment of whether particular behaviour is anticompetitive on the premise that 'in general only conduct which would exclude a hypothetical "as efficient" competitor is abusive' (§ 63). The 'as efficient' competitor is 'a hypothetical competitor having the same costs as the dominant company. Foreclosure of an as efficient competitor can in general only result if the dominant company prices below its own costs' (§ 63).

On this point, the critical question is 'whether the dominant company itself would be able to survive the exclusionary conduct in the event that it would be the target' (§ 66).

If an 'as efficient competitor cannot compete with the dominant company, the Commission will consider the conduct to have the capability to foreclose competitors' (§ 68).

As an exception to the general principle, the Commission states that 'it may sometimes be necessary in the consumers' interest to also protect competitors that are not (yet) as efficient as the dominant company' (§ 68).

16.1.2. Objective Justifications

Even if it can be shown that the behaviour in question presumptively constitutes abuse, the undertaking concerned does not infringe Article 82 if it can prove that there is a justification for its behaviour.

In the discussion paper, the Commission identifies possible justifications for each of the different types of exclusionary abuse (see predatory pricing, 130; single branding obligation and rebate system, 176; tying and bundling 204; after-markets, 265).

The burden of proving an objective justification lies on the company invoking this defence (§ 77).

Objective necessity defence

The first type of justification is the so-called 'objective necessity defence', which applies 'where the dominant company is able to show that the otherwise abusive conduct is actually necessary conduct on the basis of objective factors external to the parties involved and in particular external to the dominant company' (§ 78). In this context, 'the dominant company must be able to show that without the conduct the products concerned can not or will not be produced or distributed in that market' (§ 80). However, 'it is considered not the task of a dominant company to take steps on its own initiative to eliminate products which it regards, rightly or wrongly, as dangerous or inferior to its own product' (§ 80).

Meeting competition defence

The second justification is the 'meeting competition defence', which applies 'where the dominant company is able to show that the otherwise abusive conduct is actually a loss minimising reaction to competition from others' (§ 78).

The 'meeting competition defence' is applicable only in relation to:

- 'pricing abuse'; and
- individual and not collective behaviour (§ 81).

For this second type of objective justification, a proportionality test is applied (§ 81).

An objective justification is not possible if 'the Commission, for instance through documents seized at the company, has been able to demonstrate that the objective aim of the conduct is to directly foreclose competitors' (§ 81).

The Commission also clarifies the other cases in which the 'meeting competition defence' can or cannot be applied:

- In case the conduct concerns pricing below average avoidable cost (AAC) the meeting competition defence can normally not be applied (§ 83). Pricing below average avoidable cost is in general neither suitable nor indispensable to minimise the dominant company's losses (§ 83).
- In case the abuse concerns pricing above average avoidable cost the meeting competition defence can be applied only if all the conditions of the proportionality test described in the previous paragraph are fulfilled, which in general is considered unlikely to be the case.

Efficiency defence

Another justification for conduct which is presumptively abusive is the 'efficiency defence', which is made out when the behaviour 'produces efficiencies which outweigh the negative effect on competition' (§ 77). With regard to the 'efficiency defence', 'the dominant company must be able to show that the efficiencies brought about by the conduct concerned outweigh the likely negative effects on competition resulting from the conduct and therewith the likely harm to consumers that the conduct might otherwise have' (§ 79).

For the 'efficiency defence' the Commission requires the dominant company to demonstrate that the following conditions are fulfilled:

- that efficiencies are realised or likely to be realised as a result of the conduct concerned (§ 85);
- that the conduct concerned is indispensable to realise these efficiencies (§ 86);
- that the efficiencies benefit consumers (§ 88); and
- that competition in respect of a substantial part of the products concerned is not eliminated (§ 91).

When all four conditions are fulfilled, the Commission takes the view that 'the net effect of such conduct is to promote the very essence of the competitive process, namely to win customers by offering better products or better prices than those offered by rivals' (§ 84).

16.2. PREDATORY PRICING

Predatory pricing is defined as:

> the practice where a dominant company lowers its price and thereby deliberately incurs losses or foregoes profits in the short run so as to enable it to eliminate or discipline one or more rivals or to prevent entry by one or more potential rivals thereby hindering the maintenance or the degree of competition still existing in the market or the growth of that competition. (§ 93)

From a competition point of view, 'predatory pricing is in practice often difficult to distinguish from normal price competition' (§ 94).[2] The characteristic feature of predatory pricing is lowering prices, but this is also a fundamental aspect of competition: 'By lowering its price and/or improving the quality of its products a company competes on the market. This is competition that benefits consumers and that a competition authority wants to defend and protect. Pricing is not predatory merely because a company is lowering its price' (§ 94).

> The predatory nature of charging lower prices to all or certain customers is found in the predator making a sacrifice by deliberately incurring short run losses with

[2] With regard to the current case law, especially with reference to the variable costs test see, *inter alia*, *Akzo Chemie BV v. Commissione*, Case C-62/86, E.C.R. 1991 p. I–3359; *Tetra Pak International SA v. Commission*, Case C-333/94 P, E.C.R. 1996 p. I–5951; *France Télécom SA v. Commission*, T-340/03, not yet published.

the intention to eliminate or discipline rivals or prevent their entry (§ 96).

> The company will make this sacrifice when it considers that it is likely to be able to recoup the losses or lost profits at a later stage after its actions have had the foreclosure effect. (§ 65)

> The exclusion should thus allow the predator to return to, maintain or obtain high prices afterwards. (§ 96)

The fact that predatory prices may result in lower prices does not represent an advantage for consumers since 'although consumers may have benefited from the lower predatory prices in the short term, in the longer term they will be worse off due to weakened competition resulting in higher prices, reduced quality and less choice' (§ 96).

> Such exclusionary strategy can normally only be effective and profitable if a company has already substantial market power on the market in question. In order for predation to be abusive under Article 82 the exclusion should be instrumental in protecting or strengthening the predator's dominant position and thereby allow the predator to return to or obtain high prices afterwards.(§ 97)

As regards the link between the dominant position and the market on which the predatory pricing takes place, the Commission points out that:

- in general predatory pricing will only be dealt with as an abuse under Article 82 if the dominant company applies it to protect or strengthen its dominant position. Usually it will do so by applying predatory pricing in the market where it has a dominant position.
- It may also do so by applying predatory pricing in another, for instance adjacent market, if it has the effect of protecting or strengthening its dominance in the dominated market. For the latter to happen, there is usually a certain degree of economic interdependence between the two markets, for instance because the products are complements or because demand on the separate antitrust markets is or is expected to become interrelated. (§ 101)

In assessing whether there is abuse, the Commission bases itself on certain cost benchmarks 'below which there is more reason to assume predation may take place and/or below which no additional proof may need to be brought by the authority because predation can be presumed' (§ 103, and for a list of possible cost benchmarks, see § 64). In the Commission's opinion, in general the appropriate cost benchmark is the one that most accurately justifies the presumption that pricing below that benchmark can be expected to be predatory. The relevant question in that context is whether the dominant company, by charging a lower price for all or a particular part of its output over the relevant time period, incurred or incurs losses that could have been avoided by not producing that (particular part of its) output. If such avoidable losses are incurred, the pricing can be presumed to be predatory. At the same time the benchmark must be practical enough to be implemented' (§ 106).

16.2.1. Pricing Below Average Avoidable Cost

The Commission considers that AAC is the appropriate cost benchmark since it is 'the appropriate and practical answer to the question about avoidable losses' (§ 108).

If 'the price charged by the dominant company is below AAC this means that the dominant company incurred a loss that it could have avoided. It is, at least in the short run, not minimising its losses. This is sufficient to presume that the dominant company made this sacrifice in order to exclude the targeted competitor'.

Since this is merely a rebuttable presumption, it is open to the undertaking concerned to prove that its behaviour is justified (§ 109).

16.2.2. Pricing Above Average Avoidable Cost but Below Average Total Cost

Where the dominant company prices 'above average avoidable cost but below average total cost', in order to prove that the pricing has a predatory intent, it must be shown on the basis of 'objective factors that the pricing of the dominant company has a predatory intent, that it objectively speaking is part of a strategy or plan to predate' (§ 112).

Intention to predate may be shown on the basis of certain factors taken together even if, taken individually, they would not prove a predatory strategy (§ 112).

The following elements may be important in proving the existence of a predatory strategy:

- direct evidence, such as documents from the dominant company; and
- indirect evidence: 'in case there is no direct evidence of a predatory strategy a case will have to be built on indirect evidence of such a strategy to predate' (see on this point § 114).

An important aspect of abuse by predatory pricing is 'recoupment', which concerns 'the question whether the negative effect on (the growth of) competition in the market makes the sacrifice of the temporarily incurred losses a good "investment" from the dominant company's perspective' (§ 122). In the Commission's view, 'for recoupment it is sufficient that the predation avoids or delays a decline in prices that would otherwise occur as a result of the increased competition that would have come from the companies that are now eliminated, disciplined or whose entry is prevented'.

It may often be impossible to exactly quantify the likely price and profit effects. It will in general be sufficient to show the likelihood of recoupment by investigating:

- the entry barriers to the market;
- the (strengthened) position of the company; and
- foreseeable changes to the future structure of the market.

As dominance is already established this normally means that entry barriers are sufficiently high to presume the possibility to recoup.

Therefore the Commission does not consider it is necessary to provide further separate proof of recoupment in order to find an abuse (§ 122).

Where the Commission argues a case of predatory abuse, the dominant company may rebut it by establishing that its conduct is wrongly assessed as predatory (§ 123).

16.2.3. Pricing Below Long-run Average Incremental Costs

In certain sectors the decisional practice of the Commission has deviated from the cost benchmark based on AAC and has chosen to use long-run average incremental costs (LAIC) as the benchmark.

In these cases the LAIC benchmark is used as the benchmark below which predation is presumed (§ 124).

It is presumed that pricing below LAIC is predatory in cases:

- concerning activities protected by a legal monopoly (§ 125); and
- concerning sectors which recently have been liberalised or which are undergoing liberalisation, such as the telecom sector (§ 126).

16.2.4. Pricing Above Average Total Cost

Where the price cuts result in prices above 'average total costs', they are in general, not considered to be predatory because such pricing can usually only exclude less efficient competitors. ... Where it thus can be established that the price, also after the price cuts, remains above average total cost the pricing will not be assessed as predatory, unless exceptional circumstances indicate that such price cuts have led or will lead to substantial harm to consumers. (§ 127)

16.3. SINGLE BRANDING AND REBATES

An attempt by a dominant company to increase its sales by making its product more attractive in terms of price/quality ratio is unobjectionable under Article 82. However, the following types of behaviour calculated to 'attract more of customers' demand' may constitute an abuse:

- *Single branding obligations.* Single branding obligations are obligations which require the buyer on a particular market to concentrate its purchases to a large extent with one supplier (§ 135).
- *Rebate system.* For example, 'the supplier may simply offer a rebate, in general from a list price, on an individual order of the buyer. Rebate systems can also be more complex where the supplier for instance offers a rebate on an aggregated number of orders of the buyer' (§ 136).

The main possible negative effect of single branding obligations and rebate systems is foreclosure of the market to competing suppliers and potential suppliers, which maintains or strengthens the dominant position by hindering the maintenance or growth of residual or potential competition (§ 139).[3]

Another possible negative effect of rebate systems is price discrimination between the different buyers (on this point, see *infra*).

Article 82 addresses single branding obligations and rebate systems to the extent that these:

- are methods different from those which condition normal competition; and
- have as effect to hinder the maintenance of the degree of competition still existing in the market or the growth of that competition (§ 144).

---

[3] With regard to the current case law see, *inter alia*, *Hoffmann-La Roche et Co. AG v. Commission*, Case 85/76, Racc. 1979 p. 461; *Michelin v. Commission*, Case 322/81, E.C.R. 1983 p. 3461; *Irish Sugar plc v. Commission*, Case T-228/97, E.C.R. 1999 p. II–2969; *British Airways plc v. Commission*, causa T-219/99, E.C.R. 2003 p. II–5917; *Manufacture française des pneumatiques Michelin v. Commission*, Case T-203/01, E.C.R. 2003 p. II–4071.

The incidence (that is, the extent that the dominant company is applying the single branding obligation or rebate system in the market) is the same as its tied market share (that is, that part of its market share sold under the single branding obligation or rebate system). The potential negative effects will in general depend on the size of the tied market share (§ 145).

16.3.1. Single Branding Obligations

Single branding obligations have by their nature the capability to foreclose because they require the buyer to purchase all or a significant part of its requirements from the dominant supplier.

Such an obligation may lead to market distorting anticompetitive effects even if only a modest part of market demand is affected by the obligation (§ 148).

Where the dominant company:

- applies a single branding obligation to a good part of its buyers, and
- this obligation therefore affects, if not most, at least a substantial part of market demand,

the Commission is likely to conclude that the obligation has a market distorting foreclosure effect and thus constitutes an abuse of the dominant position (§ 149).

In its assessment the Commission will, however, not only look at:

- the capability of the obligation,
- the degree of dominance and
- the level of the tied market share,

but will also take into account evidence why for particular reasons no market distorting foreclosure effect may result (§ 149).

The Commission will apply the same approach to so-called 'English clauses', that is, agreements requiring the buyer to report any better offer and allowing it only to accept such an offer when the supplier does not match it (§ 150).

16.3.2. Conditional Rebates System

Conditional rebates are granted to customers to reward a certain purchasing behaviour of these customers in a particular period of time.

The usual form is that the customer is rewarded if its purchases exceed a certain threshold during a defined reference period.

It makes an important difference for the assessment whether the rebate is granted:

- on all purchases during that period; or
- only on incremental purchases above the threshold (§ 151).

Conditional rebates on all purchases

Conditional rebates that are granted on all purchases in the reference period once a certain threshold is exceeded can have a strong foreclosure effect (§ 152):

> What is relevant for an assessment of the loyalty enhancing effect is ... the foreclosing effect of the rebate system on commercially viable amounts supplied by (potential) competitors of the dominant supplier. These competitors are smaller rivals already active in the market and potential entrants. The rebate system should not hinder efficient competitors to expand or enter. (§ 154)

If five conditions are met, 'the Commission is likely to conclude that the rebate system creates a market distorting foreclosure effect and thus constitutes an abuse of the dominant position':

- the dominant company applies a conditional rebate system where the rebates are granted on all purchases in a particular period once a certain threshold is exceeded;
- there is no indication that this threshold is set so low that for a good part of the dominant company's buyers it cannot prevent them from switching to and purchasing substantial additional amounts from other suppliers without losing the rebate (§ 152);
- the required share exceeds the commercially viable amount per customer (§ 154);
- the dominant company applies the rebate system to a good part of its buyers and this system therefore affects, if not most, at least a substantial part of market demand (§ 162); and
- there are no clear indications of a lack of foreclosure effect such as aggressive and significant entry and/or expansion by competitors and/or switching of customers (§ 163).

In case such a presumption of abuse is established, the dominant company may rebut the Commission's preliminary conclusion by showing that the rebate system none the less does not and will not have a foreclosure effect (§ 163).

Conditional rebates on incremental purchases above the threshold
In case the rebate is only available to incremental purchases, the dominant supplier, in order to create in a 'cost-efficient way a loyalty enhancing effect, will try to set the threshold at the level that the buyer would purchase in the absence of any loyalty enhancing obligation or rebate' (§ 166).

If the threshold is set at the amount that would anyhow be purchased, 'the rebate may induce the buyer to purchase extra units in order to be able to benefit from the rebate on these incremental purchases' (§ 166).

The strength of the inducement to purchase more from the dominant supplier (that is, the loyalty enhancing effect) will depend in the first place on the level of the rebate percentage: the higher this percentage, the lower the price for these additional purchases (§ 167).

To make this assessment, a distinction has to be made between two types of method for defining the purchasing threshold above which the discount is granted:

1. *Threshold set in terms of a percentage of total requirements of the buyer or individualised volume target.* In this case once it is established that:

   - the dominant company grants conditional rebates only on incremental purchases, and
   - where the threshold is set in terms of a percentage of total requirements of the buyer or an individualised volume target,

   the Commission will conclude that the rebate system constitutes an abuse only if the resulting price for these incremental purchases is a predatory price (§ 168).
2. *Threshold set in terms of rebates as a standardised volume target.* In case it is established that:

   - the dominant company grants conditional rebates on incremental purchases, and
   - that the threshold is set in terms of a standardised volume target,

   the Commission will apply the principles applying to predatory pricing.
   In such a case it is unlikely that the rebate system will have a loyalty enhancing effect (§ 169).

16.3.3. Rebates in Return for the Supply of a Service by the Buyer

In general, rebates conditional on the 'supply of a service by the customer, such as a rebate for payment in cash or payment upon delivery, will normally not be abusive' (§ 170). However, this principle does not apply to the types of conditional rebate described *supra.* They cannot be 'justified by claiming that the buyers are encouraged but not obliged to use the rebates obtained if they exceed a certain percentage of total requirements or an individualised volume target, for promotion or other activities' (§ 170).

16.3.4. Unconditional Rebates

Unconditional rebates are rebates which, 'while granted to certain customers and not to others, are granted for every purchase of these particular customers, independently of their purchasing behaviour. Unconditional rebates differentiate the purchase price between customers and may have exploitative effects' (§ 171).

However, unconditional rebates may have exclusionary effects, for example 'if a rebate is offered only to customers that might more easily switch to foreign suppliers because they are located in a border region' (§ 171).

To assess possible exclusionary effects, the Commission will apply the principles on predatory pricing to 'the resulting lower prices for certain customers' (§ 171).

In that case, the Commission will take into account that 'the exclusionary effect':

- may not only inhibit entry and competition for these customers that may more easily switch, but
- may also delay entry and competition that would benefit the other customers of the dominant company (§ 171).

16.4. TYING AND BUNDLING

Tying occurs when 'the supplier makes the sale of one product (the tying product) conditional upon the purchase of another distinct product (the tied product) from the supplier or someone designated by the latter. Only the tied product can be bought separately' (§ 177).

Bundling is the practice whereby 'a package of two or more goods is offered. Cases where only the bundle is available and not the components are referred to as pure bundling' (§ 177).

Cases where both the bundle and the components are available on the market are referred to as mixed bundling if the bundle is sold at a discount to the sum of the prices of the components (§ 177).[4]

Tying and bundling can lead to the following possible anticompetitive effects:

- Foreclosure,
- price discrimination, and
- higher prices (§ 179).

The discussion paper examines only the 'foreclosure effects of tying and bundling' (§ 179). In particular,

> a company that is dominant in the tying market can through tying or bundling foreclose the tied market and can indirectly also foreclose the tying market (horizontal foreclosure). By tying the dominant company reduces the number of potential customers that is available for its competitors in the tied market. This may cause existing competitors to be marginalised or exit from the tied market and create a barrier for new entrants. (§ 180)

Tying is mentioned by Article 82(d) as a possible abuse. It is abusive to make 'the conclusion of contracts subject to acceptance by the other parties of supplementary obligations which, by their nature or according to commercial usage, have no connection with the subject of such contracts'. In the Commission's view 'it may be abusive for a dominant company to tie sales of products even when this is in accordance with commercial usage in the market' (§ 182).

The possible abuse is a practice whereby the dominant company:

- imposes on customers the acquisition of one product or service conditional upon the purchase of another (tying); and
- forces or economically induces customers to only buy a bundle consisting of the two products (pure or mixed bundling) (§ 182).

For such practices to be prohibited under Article 82, the presence of the following elements is usually required:

16.4.1. The Company Concerned is Dominant in the Tying Market

For tying to be abusive the company concerned needs to be dominant in the

---

[4] With regard to the current case law see, *inter alia*, *Hoffmann-La Roche et Co. AG v. Commission*, Case 85/76, E.C.R. 1979 p. 461; *Tetra Pak International SA v. Commission*, Case C-333/94 P, E.C.R. 1996 p. I–5951.

tying market. It is not necessary that the company also is dominant in the tied market. However, dominance in also the tied market renders the finding of an abuse more likely. In order to assess this properly it is normally necessary to define the relevant market(s) in which both the tying and the tied product are sold (§ 184).

16.4.2. The Tying and Tied Goods are Two Distinct Products

What can be considered as distinct products is determined by the demand of the customers.

Two products are distinct if, in the absence of tying or bundling, from the customers' perspective, the products are or would be purchased separately.

It is, however, not necessary that the two products belong to two separate product markets. In a market with differentiated products, two products may be sufficiently differentiated that a company can be said to tie or bundle two distinct products (§ 185).

16.4.3. The Tying Practice is Likely to Have a Market Distorting Foreclosure Effect

The main direct anticompetitive effect of tying and bundling is possible foreclosure on the market of the tied product (§ 188).

In principle, the assessment of the foreclosure effect on the tied market can be considered to consist of two parts:

1. *To establish which customers are 'tied' in the sense that competitors to the dominant company cannot compete for their business* In the case of tying and pure bundling, the individual customers in question clearly are foreclosed to the competitors, at least until the expiry of contracts in the case of contractual tying (§ 189).

   In the case of mixed bundling this is less clear. 'Both products are available but may be priced in such a way that it would not be rational for customers to buy individual products from the bundle to match them with complementary products produced by a competitor' (§ 189). To this regard, 'competitors are foreclosed if the discount is so large that efficient competitors offering only some but not all of the components, cannot compete against the discounted bundle' (§ 189).

   The incremental price that customers pay for each of the dominant company's products in the bundle should therefore cover the long run incremental costs of the dominant company of including this product in the bundle. This would allow an equally efficient competitor with only one product to compete profitably against the bundle. Long run incremental

cost is used as the cost concept, since this captures the extra costs of the dominant company's activities in the market(s) in which it is not dominant. If a price charged by the dominant company covers its incremental costs, such a price cannot normally be considered exclusionary (§ 190).
However, it may exceptionally be concluded that although the price exceeds the long run incremental costs the mixed bundling none the less is considered exclusionary (§ 190).

2. *To establish whether these customers 'add up' to a sufficient part of the market being tied* 'The second part of the assessment is to establish whether the market as a whole can be considered to be foreclosed. The analysis of the foreclosure effect will take into account several factors (§ 196).

   In general, the higher the tied percentage of total sales on the tied market, the larger is normally the foreclosure effect. However, other factors are also relevant to determining whether the behaviour has 'an appreciable foreclosure effect' on the market (§ 196). Some of the more important are:
   - the overall strength of the dominant company on both the tying and the tied markets (§ 196);
   - the identity of the tied customers (§ 196);
   - a growing share of a market with network effects may also be problematic even if the share is still fairly low (§ 196);
   - the fact that other companies also tie may add to the foreclosure effect, since this can contribute to making entry more difficult (§ 197); and
   - the number of customers that buy both products (§ 198).

16.4.4. The Tying Practice is not Justified Objectively or by Efficiencies (§ 206)

16.5. REFUSAL TO SUPPLY

The analysis of refusal to supply focuses on 'situations where a dominant company denies a buyer access to an input in order to exclude that buyer from participating in an economic activity (vertical foreclosure)' (§ 209).

Generally undertakings are 'entitled to determine whom to supply and to decide not to continue to supply certain trading partners. This is also true for dominant companies' (§ 207). But 'refusals to supply or threats of refusals to supply by dominant companies may, however, be anticompetitive' (§ 208).

Although the excluded buyer could be only a customer, typically competition problems arise when it is also a rival to the dominant company in the economic activity for which the input is needed (§ 209). [5]

A refusal to supply may be classified as an exclusionary abuse when the dominant company prevents the requesting or terminated party from getting access to an input. As a result, this undertaking is either driven out of the market, marginalised or prevented from entering the market (§ 210).

In assessing this type of abuse 'it is useful to distinguish between an "upstream" market for access to the input and a "downstream" market for which the input is needed in order to manufacture a product or provide a service' (§ 212).

For a refusal to supply to be abusive, it must, however, have a likely anticompetitive effect on the market which is detrimental to consumer welfare (§ 210).

The doctrine of refusal to supply raises complex questions and two factors must be taken into account when applying it:

- First, 'the knowledge that [the dominant firms] may have a duty to supply against their will might lead companies not to invest in the first place or to invest less. Other companies may be tempted to free ride on the investment made by the dominant company instead of investing themselves' (§ 213).
- Second, 'access to the input may also lead other firms to increase investment in, for instance, follow-on research and development that would otherwise not be possible or profitable' (§ 213).

Consequently 'enforcement policy towards refusals to supply has to take into account both the effect of having more short-run competition and the possible long-run effects on investment incentives' (§ 213).

The concept refusal to supply covers a variety of practices and situations. Those covered in the discussion paper are:

- where one or more companies are terminating an existing supply relationship; and
- where one or more companies are refusing to start supplying an input, including where this input is covered by intellectual property rights (§ 215).

---

[5] With regard to the current case law see, *inter alia, Istituto Chemioterapico Italiano SpA e Commercial Solvents Corporation v. Commission*, Joined Cases 6 and 7/73, E.C.R. 1974 p. 223; *AB Volvo v. Erik Veng Ltd*, Case 238/87, E.C.R. 1988 p. 6211; *Radio Telefis Eireann (RTE) and Independent Television Publications Ltd (ITP) v. Commission*, Joined Cases C-241/91 P e C-242/91 P, E.C.R. 1995 p. I–743; *Oscar Bronner GmbH & Co. KG v. Mediaprint Zeitungs- und Zeitschriftenverlag GmbH & Co. KG*, Case C-7/97, E.C.R. 1998 p. I–7791; *IMS Health GmbH & Co. OHG contro NDC Health GmbH & Co. KG.*, Cases C-418/01, E.C.R. 2004 p. I–5039.

16.5.1. Termination of an Existing Supply Relationship

Four conditions have to be fulfilled in order to find that the termination of a supply relationship is abusive.

First, the behaviour can be properly characterised as termination. Although in some cases it is evident that a supply relationship is being terminated, 'in other situations it will have to be established that a certain type of behaviour in reality amounts to a termination' (§ 219). 'This can involve evaluating practices such as, for instance, delaying tactics in supplying, imposing unfair trading conditions, or charging excessive prices for the input' (§ 219). A particular type of behaviour that can amount to a termination is a 'margin squeeze' (§ 220)

Second, the refusing undertaking is dominant:

> A termination of a supply relationship can only raise competition problems if the undertaking refusing to supply has a dominant position on a defined market. This will often be an 'upstream' input market, but it may also be a distinct market where access is needed to link this market with another market, for example to interface information. (§ 221)

Third, the refusal is likely to have a negative effect on competition.

> The termination of one individual customer from the downstream market does not in itself constitute an abuse. An abuse may only arise when the termination is likely to have a negative effect on competition in the downstream market. This should however not be understood to mean the complete elimination of all competition. The extent to which the termination of one customer has an impact on the level of competition depends on the pre-existing competition on the downstream market. In some cases, the termination of one customer may have a detrimental effect on the level of competition; in other cases the impact may be small to insignificant'. (§ 222)

Fourth, the refusal is not justified objectively or by efficiencies (§ 224).

16.5.2. Refusal to Start Supplying an Input

Five conditions have to be fulfilled for a refusal to start supplying to be regarded as abusive.

First, the behaviour can be properly characterised as a refusal to supply. As in the case of termination of an existing supply relationship, it is only in certain cases that it is clear that particular behaviour amounts to a refusal to supply. 'In other situations it will have to be established that a certain type of behaviour in reality amounts to a refusal to supply. This can involve evaluating practices such as, for instance, delaying tactics in supplying, imposing unfair trading conditions, or charging excessive prices for the input' (§ 225).

Second, the refusing undertaking is dominant. A refusal to start supplying can be abusive only if the undertaking refusing to supply is dominant on a defined market. 'This will often be an "upstream" input market, but it may also be a distinct market where access is needed to link this market with another market, for example to interface information' (§ 226, to this regard see § 241). 'In some circumstances, there may not be an existing market for the input in question as it is used only by the owner in a captive market' (§ 227). For example, this is the case with intellectual property rights.

Third, the input is indispensable:

> To be an abuse the refusal to start supplying must concern an input, which is indispensable to carry on normal economic activity in the downstream market. Without this input companies cannot manufacture their products or provide their usual service levels. Therefore, when real or potential substitutes exist in the market, the input of the dominant company is not indispensable. The same holds if it would be legally and economically possible for other companies to produce the input in question themselves. (§ 228)

An 'input' is considered to be 'only when duplication of the existing facility is impossible or extremely difficult, either because it is physically or legally impossible to duplicate, or because a second facility is not economically viable in the sense that it would not generate enough revenues to cover its costs' (§ 229, for the specific case of intellectual property rights, see § 230)

Fourth, the refusal is likely to have a negative effect on competition:

> The likely exclusion of one individual competitor from the downstream market does not in itself constitute an abuse. An abuse only may arise when the exclusion of competitors is likely to have a negative effect on competition in the downstream market. This should however not be understood to mean the complete elimination of all competition. The extent to which the exclusion of one competitor has an impact on the level of competition depends on the pre-existing competition on the downstream market. (§ 231)

> The exclusion may also have a negative impact on competition in a new and not yet existing downstream market, if the owner of the indispensable input refuses access to a buyer that would use the input to manufacture a new product or provide a new service in such a not yet existing market. (§ 233)

Fifth, the refusal is not objectively justified. The undertaking may be able to show that there is a justification for the allegedly abusive behaviour (§ 234).

If an undertaking is obliged to grant access to an essential facility, it is entitled to appropriate compensation (§ 235).

16.5.3. Refusal to License Intellectual Property Rights

In the particular case of refusal to grant a licence for the exploitation of an intellectual property right (IPR), the Commission states that:

> there is no general obligation for the IPR holder to license the IPR, not even where the holder acquires a dominant position in the technology or product market. The very aim of the exclusive right is to prevent third parties from applying the IPR to produce and distribute products without the consent of the holder of the rights. This protection would be eroded if the holder of a successful IPR would be required to grant a licence to competitors from the moment the IPR or the product incorporating the IPR becomes dominant in the market. Imposing on the holder of the rights the obligation to grant to third parties a licence for the supply of products incorporating the IPR, even in return for a reasonable royalty, would lead to the holder being deprived of the substance of the exclusive right. (§ 238)

It follows that: 'the refusal to license an intellectual property therefore does not in itself constitute an abuse. Only under exceptional circumstances can the refusal to license an IPR be considered an abuse' (§ 239).

In the case of a refusal to license an IPR an additional condition may have to be met (§ 237):

> For example, the refusal by a dominant company to license access to the IPR could be considered abusive when the five conditions described above are all fulfilled and, furthermore, the refusal to grant a licence prevents the development of the market for which the licence is an indispensable input, to the detriment of consumers. (§ 239)

16.6. AFTERMARKETS

Aftermarkets or 'secondary markets' 'comprise complementary products (or "secondary products") that are purchased after the purchase of another product (the "primary product") to which it relates. Standard examples include after sales services and spare parts for durable goods, as well as consumables such as ink cartridges and toner for printers and photocopiers' (§ 243).[6]

Aftermarkets can cause competition problems when 'they are "proprietary", that is, when they are brand-specific in that secondary products that can be used with one brand of primary product cannot be used with another brand of primary product, although the primary products themselves are substitutes' (§ 244).

The competition problem flows from the fact that 'often patents or know-how will allow the supplier of the primary product to have a monopolistic position on the aftermarket' (§ 245). Consequently, 'the supplier of a primary product attempts to reserve the secondary market for itself' (§ 244).

Not every type of behaviour by the dominant company on the aftermarket will constitute an abuse since 'if the primary market is competitive, competition in the primary market may make price increases in the aftermarket unprofitable due to its impact on sales in the primary market, unless prices in the primary market are lowered to offset the higher aftermarket price' (§ 246).

16.6.1. Market Definition

In assessing whether behaviour on an aftermarket is abusive, the normal approach is applied at the market definition stage (see *supra*).

When defining the relevant market, only the aftermarket is taken into account. As the Commission puts it, 'the focus of the market definition exercise is on the aftermarket sales to customers who have already acquired the primary product and not on potential new future buyers of the primary product. The full effects of "bundle" or "systems" competition will thus be taken into account in the dominance analysis' (§ 247).

As regards the definition of the relevant market, 'an aftermarket consisting of the secondary products of one brand of primary product may not be a relevant product market in two situations' (§ 248):

- if it is possible to switch to the secondary products of other producers (§ 248); and
- if it may be possible to switch to another primary product and thus avoid the higher prices in the aftermarket (§ 249).

---

6 With regard to the current case law see, *inter alia*, *Hilti AG v. Commission*, Case T-30/89, E.C.R. 1991 p. II–1439.

16.6.2. Dominance

As regards finding that a dominant position exists, 'if an aftermarket consisting of the secondary products of one brand of primary product has been found to constitute a relevant product market, a dominant position on such a market can only be established after analysis of the competition on both the aftermarket and the primary market' (§ 251).

The general principle that the Commission uses in order to ascertain whether a dominant position exists on an aftermarket is that 'the stronger the competition on the primary market, and the weaker the position of the supplier in question on this market, the less likely it is that the supplier in question can be considered dominant on the aftermarket because of the link between the primary market and the aftermarket described above' (§ 260).

16.6.3. Abuse of a Dominant Position

Once it has been established that a company has a dominant position on an aftermarket, the Commission 'presumes that it is abusive for the dominant company to reserve the aftermarket for itself by excluding competitors from that market' (§ 264).

Such exclusion is normally realised through:

- tying;
- refusal to deal (for instance, a refusal to supply information needed to provide products or services in the aftermarket); and
- refusal to license intellectual property rights; or a refusal to supply spare parts needed in order to provide aftermarket services (§ 264).

17. Article 82 EC and Exploitative Abuses

Exploitative abuses occur when a dominant company 'has made use of the opportunities arising out of its dominant position in such a way as to reap trading benefits which it would not have reaped if there had been normal and sufficiently effective competition'.[1]

This type of behaviour generally corresponds to the examples of abuses listed in points (a) and (b) of Article 82, that is to say abuse consisting in:

- 'directly or indirectly imposing unfair purchase or selling prices or other unfair trading conditions'; and
- 'limiting production, markets or technical development to the prejudice of consumers'.

17.1. UNFAIR PRICES

Prices charged by a dominant company are considered to be abusive when they are 'excessive in relation to the economic value of the service provided'.[2] For this purpose, it must be shown not only that the profit margin deriving from the service is excessive but also that the price charged is 'either unfair in itself or when compared to competing products'.[3]

It is particularly difficult to find this type of infringement since it assumes that it is possible to define the point at which a price becomes abusive. The same difficulty persists even after the infringement of Article 82 has been found. Rather than defining what is a fair price, the Commission and the national authorities should simply provide for a range of prices outside which an abusive price can be presumed.[4]

---

[1] *United Brands v. Commission* (Chiquita Bananas), Case 27/76, E.C.R. 1978, p. 207, § 249.

[2] *General Motors v. Commission*, Case 26/75, E.C.R. 1975, p. 1367, § 12.

[3] *United Brands v. Commission* (Chiquita Bananas), op. cit..

[4] 76/353/CEE: Commission Decision of 17 December 1975, relating to a procedure under Article 86 of the EEC Treaty (VI/26.699 – Chiquita), in OJ L 095 of 9 April 1976, p. 1, § 76.

The Community case law and the practice of the Commission have tried to overcome the difficulties connected with determing unfair prices by formulating two tests, as follows.

17.1.1. Comparing Costs

Under this test, a price is abusive when the profit is excessive. In order to establish whether this is the case, it must be assessed whether the difference between the costs incurred and the price charged is excessive.[5] This relationship can be evaluated by taking the costs of production as a starting point; this will reveal the profit margin.[6] If prices are high in the absence of any objective justification, this is indicative of an abuse by the charging of excessive prices.[7] The costs themselves play a key role in determining whether especially high prices may be justified. In particular, the proportion of the undertaking's general costs that relate to the production of specific goods or services or the costs that are specific to a particular product or particular service.[8]

17.1.2. The Principle of Comparing Different Markets

This test involves comparing the prices charged on other markets in order to determine whether prices are unfair.[9] A price is deemed to be abusive when it is excessive in relation to the prices with which it is being compared.[10] Even in this case, the price resulting from the comparison is merely indicative since the undertaking has some freedom in deciding what prices to charge.

A comparison may be made on the basis of three different criteria:

1. *Territorial comparison* This involves assessing the same good or service on another geographic market where there is effective competition. In practice, this test plays an important role because it is based on prices actually charged in other Member States.[11]

---

[5] *United Brands v. Commission*, op. cit..

[6] *United Brands v. Commission*, op. cit., § 250; *General Motors v. Commission*, op. cit., § 12; *GT-link A/SV. de danske statsbaner (DSB)*, Case C-242/95, E.C.R. 1997, p. I–4449, §§ 39; *TNT Traco SpA v. Poste Italiane SpA and others*, Case C-340/99, E.C.R. 2001, p. I–4109, § 46.

[7] *Parke Davis v. Probel*, Case 24/67, E.C.R. 1968, p. 76, § 113; *Sirena v. EDA*, Case 40/70, E.C.R. 1971, p. 69, § 84; *Deutsche Grammophon v. Metro Grossmaerkte*, Case 78/70, E.C.R. 1971, pp. 487, 501; *Ministère Public v. Tournier*, Case 395/87, E.C.R. 1989, p. 2521, § 38.

[8] *United Brands v. Commission*, op. cit., § 305; *Ministère Public v. Tournier*, op. cit.; *Lucazeau v. SACEM*, Joined Cases 110/88, 241/88 and 242/88, E.C.R. 1989, pp. 2811, 2831.

[9] *Ministère Public v. Tournier, op. cit., § 34*; *Lucazeau v. SACEM*, op.cit..

[10] *General Motors v. Commission*, op. cit., § 15.

[11] *Parke Davis v. Probel*, op. cit., § 113; *Sirena v. EDA*, op. cit. § 84; *Deutsche*

The prices used to make the comparison may be either the prices charged by other companies,[12] or even those charged by the same dominant company on different markets.[13]

2. *Comparison over time* This test involves comparing the prices charged for a particular product by the dominant company during the reference period with those charged by the same company before it became dominant.
3. *Product comparison* This test involves making a comparison with the prices of goods or services which are similar to, but not interchangeable with, those of the dominant company. The Commission had recourse to comparison over time and product comparison particularly in the *British Leyland* case.[14]

17.2. UNFAIR TRADING CONDITIONS

Article 82 (a) cites the imposition, by the dominant company, of unfair trading conditions on its trading partners as an example of abuse.[15] The expression 'trading conditions' is not restricted to contractual terms *stricto sensu* but also refers to more general restrictions on the behaviour of the contracting partner imposed by the dominant company. Whether these conditions are held to be abusive depends not merely on how much they restrict the economic freedom of the undertakings, but also on the effect that they have on the market position of third parties.[16] Examples of practices having an indirectly restrictive effect are 'non-compete' obligations,[17] exclusive dealing obligations or preferential arrangements which operate to the detriment of the purchaser.[18]

The tests used to determine whether prices are abusive are also used to assess whether or not the conditions are unfair. Both types of abuse cause harm which can be evaluated economically.

Grammophon v. Metro Grossmaerkte, op. cit.; *Corinne Bodson v. Pompes funèbres des regions liberees*, Case 30/87, E.C.R. 1988, p. 2479, § 31; *Ministère Public v. Tournier*, op. cit., § 38; *Lucazeau contro SACEM*, op.cit., § 25.

[12] *Corinne Bodson v. Pompes funèbres des régions libérées*, op. cit., § 31.

[13] *Deutsche Grammophon v. Metro Grossmaerkte*, op. cit., 501; *United Brands v. Commission* (Chiquita Bananas), op. cit..

[14] *British Leyland v. Commission*, Case 226/84, E.C.R. 1986, p. 3263, § 25.

[15] *Giuseppe Sacchi*, Case 155/73, E.C.R. 1974, p. 409, § 17.

[16] *BRT v. SABAM*, Case 127/73, E.C.R. 1974, p. 313, § 12.

[17] *Suiker Unie v. Commission*, Joined Cases 40 and 48, 50, 54 n. 56, 111, 113 and 114/73, E.C.R. 1975, pp. 1663, 2016.

[18] *Hoffmann-La Roche et Co. AG v. Commission*, Case 85/76, E.C.R. 1979, pp. 461, 538; *AKZO v. Commission*, Case C-62/86, E.C.R. 1991, p. I–3359, § 149; *Comune di Almelo v. Energiebedrijf Ijsselmij*, Case-393/92, E.C.R. 1994, p. I–1477, § 44.

In order to determine whether trading conditions are abusive, two aspects have to be considered.

17.2.1. Balancing of Interests

Where it is unclear whether or not the conditions are unfair, a balance must be struck between the respective interests of the contracting parties. When evaluating its own interests, and thus its behaviour, the dominant firm must bear in mind the principle of proportionality.[19] Even if the contractual obligations are imposed for a purpose which is *per se* perfectly legitimate, those obligations may still constitute abuse if they impose an unreasonable restriction on the economic freedom of the contracting party.

17.2.2. The Objective of the Common Market

In assessing the fairness of trading conditions for the purposes of Article 82 EC, account must be taken not merely of the interests of the contracting parties but also of the objectives of the common market.[20]

17.3. LIMITING PRODUCTION, MARKETS OR TECHNICAL DEVELOPMENT TO THE PREJUDICE OF CONSUMERS

Article 82(b) prohibits abuse by a dominant company consisting in 'limiting production, markets or technical development to the prejudice of consumers'.

As in the case of abuses falling under point (a), identifying this type of abusive behaviour is particularly difficult since the task of determining the level at which limiting production, markets or technical developments becomes abusive within the meaning of Article 82 is a complex one. This difficulty is compounded by the fact that it may be possible to justify the behaviour of the dominant firm by reference to legitimate technical and economic reasons, such as adapting supply to demand.

The prohibition on limiting production applies not only to goods but also to services.[21] It can apply both to the production of the dominant company[22]

---

[19] *United Brands v. Commission*, op. cit., § 152; *Tetra Pak International v. Commission*, Case T-83/91, E.C.R. 1994, p. II–755, § 137.

[20] 71/224/EEC: Commission Decision of 2 June 1971, relating to a procedure under Article 86 of the EC Treaty (IV/26760 – 'GEMA'), OJ L 134 of 20 June 1971, p. 15.

[21] *Merci Convenzionali Porto di Genova v. Siderurgica Gabrielli*, Case C-179/90, E.C.R. 1991, p. I–5889, § 18.

[22] *Volvo v. Veng*, Case 238/87, E.C.R. 1988, p. 6211, § 9.

and also to that of other companies.[23]

Generally speaking, an abusive limitation of production or technical development occurs when the dominant company supplies a level of production or technological development which is substantially lower than the level which would be offered in a fully competitive market.[24]

[23] *Michelin v. Commission*, Case 322/81, E.C.R. p. 3461, § 71.

[24] *Merci Convenzionali Porto di Genova v. Siderurgica Gabrielli, op. cit., § 18; Klaus Hoefner and Fritz Elser v. Macrotron GmbH*, Case C-41/90, E.C.R. 1991, p. I–1979.

18. Article 82 EC and Discriminatory Abuses

Article 82(c) prohibits dominant undertakings from engaging in discriminatory practices by stipulating that 'applying dissimilar conditions to equivalent transactions with other trading parties, thereby placing them at a competitive disadvantage' constitutes abuse.

Depending on the form that it takes, this type of abuse may have either exclusionary (see Discussion paper § 140, 179) or exploitative effects (see Discussion paper, § 53).

Discriminatory abuses may take various forms, as follows.

18.1. DISCRIMINATION RELATED TO UNDERTAKINGS WHICH ARE NOT IN DIRECT COMPETION

Discrimination takes place when the dominant undertaking requires different consideration in respect of equivalent transactions which are performed at the same point in time.[1] Charging discriminatory prices constitutes abuse whether it takes the form of charging different prices in respect of the same transactions or of identical prices for different transactions.[2]

Abuse may take place when the undertaking, which is the victim of the discriminatory behaviour and which therefore suffers a competitive disadvantage, is active on a market different from the one in which the supplier engaging in the discriminatory behaviour holds a dominant position ('secondary line competition').[3] Thus, the type of infringement referred to in Article 82(c) does not concern cases where the abusive conduct of the dominant undertaking is performed against undertakings which are in

[1] 94/210/EC: Commission Decision of 29 March 1994 relating to a proceeding pursuant to Articles 85 and 86 of the EC Treaty (IV/33.941 HOV-SVZ/MCN), OJ L 104 of 23 April 1994, pp. 34, 47.

[2] *AKZO v. Commission*, Case C-62/86, E.C.R. 1991, p. I–3359, § 72; *Tetra Pak v. Commission*, Case C-333/94 P, E.C.R. 1996, p. I–5951, § 41.

[3] *BP and others v. Commission*, Case 77/77, E.C.R. 1978, p. 1513, § 29.

competition with it[4] ('primary line competition'). However, the discrimination may be excused if it is justified by objective factors.[5]

18.2. DISCRIMINATION AIMING AT DIVIDING UP MARKETS

The Court of Justice has stated that 'the responsibility for establishing the single ... market does not lie with' private parties.[6] For that reason, undertakings are entitled to adjust their behaviour according to the particular features of the various markets on which they are active. However, Article 82(c) prohibits a dominant company from charging different prices in the various Member States in which that company supplies its own goods or services. This type of behaviour is forbidden whenever its effect is to partition national markets artificially or is accompanied by actions calculated to have such an effect and appears to be aimed at maximising profits in relation to the profit margins which could have been attained in the absence of the objectionable behaviour.[7]

18.3. DISCRIMINATION ON THE GROUND OF NATIONALITY

Article 82(c) also prohibits discrimination based on the nationality of the undertaking.[8] This prohibition is closely linked to Article 12 EC, paragraph 1 of which stipulates that: 'Within the scope of application of this Treaty, and without prejudice to any special provisions container therein, any discrimination on grounds of nationality shall be prohibited'. However, the two rules have a different scope. Article 82 EC is of more restricted scope in that it is addressed only to undertakings in a dominant position. At the same time, Article 82(c) has a scope that is broader than that of Article 12 in that it refers to 'other trading parties' in general and its scope is not therefore limited to purchasers and distributors of different nationalities.

---

[4] *Irish Sugar v.Commission*, Case T-228/97, E.C.R. 1999, p. II–2969, p. 150.

[5] *United Brands v. Commission* (Chiquita Bananas), op. cit.

[6] Ibid., § 227.

[7] *United Brands v. Commission* (Chiquita Bananas), op. cit., § 231; *Tetra pak international v. Commission*, Case T-83/91, E.C.R. 1994, p. II–755, § 160; *British Leyland v. Commission*, Case 226/84, E.C.R. 1986, p. 3263, § 25; *Irish Sugar v. Commission*, Case T-228/97, E.C.R. 1999, p. II–2969, p. 125.

[8] *Société Corsica Ferries v. Direction generale des douanes francaises*, Case C-49/89, E.C.R. 1989, p. 4441; *GVL v. Commission*, Case 7/82, E.C.R. 1983, p. 483, § 56; *Deutsche Bahn v. Commission*, Case T-229/94, E.C.R. 1997, p. II–1689, § 93.

PART V

ARTICLES 81 AND 82 EC APPLIED TO THE MEMBER STATES

19. The Combined Effect of Articles 10 and 81 EC

Articles 81 and 82 relate only to the behaviour of undertaking and not to Member State measures (see *supra*). Nevertheless, in certain cases the Community antitrust rules can be applied directly to measures taken by the Member States. In this regard, the Court of Justice has taken the view that EC law precludes the Member States from enacting national measures which 'might deprive the competition rules addressed to undertakings of their effectiveness'.[1] This prohibition flows from Article 10 EC in conjunction with Article 81 EC and from Article 82 EC in conjunction with Article 86(1) EC.

Community case law stipulates that:

> although Article 81 of the Treaty is, in itself, concerned solely with the conduct of undertakings and not with measures adopted by the Member States by law or regulation, the fact remains that Article 81 of the Treaty, in conjunction with Article 10, requires the Member States not to introduce or maintain in force measures, even of a legislative nature, which may render ineffective the competition rules applicable to undertakings.[2]

We can identify four different types of case in which state measures have this effect. The first and second cases arise where a Member State requires or favours the adoption of agreements, decisions or concerted practices contrary to Article 81. The third case is when it reinforces the effects of such agreements and the fourth is when it deprives its own rules of the character of

[1] *S.A. G.B.- B.M. v. Association des détaillants en tabac* (ATAB), Case 13/77, E.C.R. 1977, p. 2115, § 33; *Eelliniki radiophonia tileorassi anonimi etairia e panellinia omospondia syllogon prossopikou ert v. dimotiki etairia pliroforissis e sotirios kouvelas e nicolaos avdellas and others*, Case C-260/89, E.C.R. 1991, p. I–2925, § 35; *Centro servizi Spediporto srl v. Spedizioni marittima del golfo Srl*, Case C-96/94, E.C.R. 1995, p. I–2883, § 20; *DIP spa v. Comune di Bassano del Grappa*, Joined Cases C-140/94, C-141/94 and C-142/94, E.C.R. 1995, p. I–3257, § 14; *Brentjens' Handelsonderneming BV v. Stichting Bedrijfspensioenfonds voor de Handel in Bouwmaterialen*, Joined Cases C-115/97 to C-117/97, E.C.R. 1999, p. I–6025, § 113; del 19 May 1993, *Criminal proceedings against Paul Corbeau*, Case C-320/91, E.C.R. 1993, p. I–2533 § 11.

[2] *Commission v. Italian Republic*, Case C-35/96, E.C.R. 1998, I–3851, § 53.

legislation by delegating to private economic operators responsibility for taking decisions affecting the economic sphere.[3]

The case law is classified in descending order by reference to the extent to which Article 81 EC may penalise the behaviour of undertakings. In the first line of cases, the behaviour of private persons may always be penalised by competition law, whereas in the fourth, the behaviour of individuals which is imposed by national rules may not be struck at by EC antitrust law, except in so far as the *CIF* case law is applicable (*see infra*).

19.1. NATIONAL MEASURES THAT REINFORCE THE EFFECTS OF AGREEMENTS CONTRARY TO ARTICLE 81

The first type of situation, which can be found in the *BNIC v Clair*[4] line of cases, arises when a national rule 'reinforces' the effect of an agreement prohibited by Article 81 EC. According to this case law, the national rule is illegal when two conditions are met:

- there must be an agreement which infringes Article 81 EC; and
- the national measure must subsequently make the agreement binding on the parties and/or must extend its binding nature to third parties.[5]

19.2. NATIONAL MEASURES THAT FAVOUR THE ADOPTION OF AGREEMENTS CONTRARY TO ARTICLE 81

The second type of situation, which can be found in the *Ahmed Saeed* line of cases,[6] arises when a national rule 'favours' the conclusion of agreements prohibited by Article 81 EC. A state measure is illegal when it creates conditions which facilitate the conclusion of agreements which infringe Article 81 EC. In this type of case, as in the above-mentioned *BNIC v Clair* line of cases, the anticompetitive agreement as such can be punished pursuant to EC antitrust law, irrespective of whether the national measure is illegal

---

[3] Ibid., § 54.

[4] *Bureau National Interprofessionnel du Cognac v. René Clair*, Case 123/83, E.C.R. 1983, p. 391.

[5] For a case in which the national law was unlawful because it extended the binding nature of an agreement prohibited by Article 81 EC to third parties, see *A.S.B.L. Vereniging van Vlaamse Resibureaus v. A.S.B.L.*, Case 311/85, E.C.R. 1987, p. 3801.

[6] *Ahmed Saeed Flugreisen v. Zentrale zur Bekämpfung unlauteren Wettbewerbs*, C-66/86, E.C.R. 1989, p. 803; *John Deere Ltd. v. Commission*, T-35/92, E.C.R. 1994, p. II–957.

pursuant to Article 10 in conjunction with Article 81 EC. The reason for this is that in both cases the anticompetitive agreements have been performed by undertakings whose freedom of action has not been constrained (*infra*).

19.3. NATIONAL MEASURES THAT REQUIRE THE ADOPTION OF AGREEMENTS CONTRARY TO ARTICLE 81

The third type of situation is to be found in the *CNSD*[7] line of cases. Here, a national rule requires undertakings to adopt agreements that are contrary to Article 81 EC. The undertakings are thus concluding those agreements as a consequence of the national measures themselves.[8] For this reason, provided that it has not 'gone beyond what is required by the law in force', the behaviour imposed by the Member State measure is not struck at by Article 81.

However, when the undertakings enjoy 'a margin of discretion in the implementation of the national legislation',[9] they must behave in a way which maintains 'the level of competition which could be left to exist after that legislation has been implemented'.[10] Should undertakings behave in a way which restricts competition more than the rule itself requires, that behaviour is struck at by Article 81.[11]

19.4. NATIONAL MEASURES THAT DEPRIVE MEMBER STATES' RULES OF THE CHARACTER OF LEGISLATION

The fourth type of case arises where a Member State 'deprives its own rules of the character of legislation by delegating to private operators responsibility for taking decisions affecting the economic sphere'. This type of situation, which can be found in the *Reiff* line of cases,[12] concerns laws which established a procedure for the enactment of a legal measure, during which various bodies are called on to give their views. The final measure should endeavour to represent the amalgam of the different interests of all those

---

[7] *Commission v. Italian Republic*, op. cit..

[8] Ibid., § 55.

[9] *Consiglio nazionale degli spedizionieri doganali v. Commission*, T-513/93, E.C.R. p. II–1807, § 71.

[10] Ibid., § 73.

[11] Ibid., § 74.

[12] *Bundesanstalt für den Güterfernverkehr v. Gebrüder Reiff GmbH*, Case C-185/91, E.C.R. 1993, p. I–5801.

bodies and, to that extent, express the public interest. In the procedure, the role of the undertakings is to formulate a proposal for an agreement. At the end of the procedure, a measure is adopted whereby the contributions of firms (that is, the agreements formulated by them) lose their autonomous character and are absorbed in the final legal measure. Pursuant to the procedure, the undertakings are also the addressees of the final measure.

For a national law to fall under the *Reiff* case law, two conditions are thus necessary:

1. Private individuals must participate in the procedure by proposing an 'agreement' within the meaning of Article 81. Those individuals must either be the firms that are the direct addressees of the final legal measure, or they must represent the interests of such firms (referred to as non-independent experts).
2. A state measure must be enacted at the end of the procedure. In the *Reiff* scenario, the participation of private individuals has no direct effect on the market; this factor distinguishes it from the *Italian Customs Agents* type of case. In *Reiff*, the procedure culminates in the adoption of a public measure, which constitutes the 'condition precedent'[13] to which the effectiveness of the participation of private individuals is subject.

A national law falling within the *Reiff* criteria infringes the combined provisions of Articles 10 and 81 EC in the following cases:

1. Where the content of the proposal is an agreement infringing Article 81 and has been drawn up by bodies which are not independent from the individuals who will be subject to the final measure (that is, there is an absence of independent experts). In that case, the final legal measure represents the interests only of the undertakings that have participated, directly or through 'non-independent expert', in the procedure.
2. Even if the proposal has not been drawn up by independent experts, and thus represents only the private interests of individuals rather than the general interest,[14] the final measure is none the less usually lawful if the Member State has not 'waived its power to make decisions of last resort or to review' implementation of the proposal adopted in the final measure.[15] The final measure would be unlawful where, for example, the public body which adopted the final measure was required simply to rubber stamp the proposal put forward by the individuals concerned and did not have the

[13] Opinion of Mr Advocate General Darmon, ibid., § 99.
[14] *Criminal proceedings v. Manuele Arduino*, Case C-35/99, E.C.R. 2002 p. I–1529, § 37.
[15] Ibid. § 40.

power to refuse to accept it. In those circumstances, the proposal could be said to be simply a cartel subject to the condition precedent of official approval.[16]

To sum up, pursuant to the *Reiff* case law, the national rule establishing the procedure is illegal if does not obviate 'the risk of a cartel'. That risk will exist if the measure adopted at the end of the procedure represents only the interest of the undertakings participating in the procedure.

Since the behaviour of the private individuals in the procedure (that is, the proposed agreement) is required by law and has no direct effect on the market, it cannot be struck at by Article 81 EC. That is possible only once the measure has been held to be illegal in the light of the *CIF* case law.

[16] On this point, see the Opinion of Advocate General Darmon in *Bundesanstalt für den Güterverkehr v Reiff*, op. cit., § 105.

20. The Combined Effect of Articles 82 and 86(1) EC

Two lines of case law establish how Article 82 EC applies to the Member States[1].The first line relates to Articles 82 in conjunction with Article 10 and the second to the combined effect of Article 82 and Article 86(1). However, the two lines of cases are in reality applying the same principle, which is that Member States are prohibited from adopting measures which frustrate the effectiveness of Article 82. In this regard, whether it is Article 10 or Article 86(1) that is to be applied in combination with Article 82 is irrelevant to the aim pursued by the case law since Article 86(1) is merely a specific provision implementing the general principles contained in Article 10.[2]

In the case law related to the prohibition of national measures which undermine the effectiveness of Article 82, the Court of Justice has stated: 'Article 82 applies only to anticompetitive conduct engaged in by undertakings on their own initiative, not to measures adopted by states'.[3] However, it goes on to point out that 'in the case of public undertakings and undertakings to which Member States grant special or exclusive rights, they are neither to enact nor to maintain in force any measure contrary to the rules contained in the Treaty',[4] in particular to the rules provided for in Article 12 (discrimination on the grounds of nationality) and Articles 81 to 89 (competition rules).

A national measure may frustrate the prohibition established by the combined effect of Articles 82 and 86(1) EC (by breaching the effectiveness of Article 82), when two conditions are met. Those conditions are that:

---

[1] *Centro servizi Spediporto srl v. Spedizioni marittima del Golfo*, op. cit., E.C.R. 1995, p. I–2883, § 20; *DIP v. Comune di Bassano del Grappa*, cit., §§ 14–24; *Corinne Bodson v. SA Pompes Funèbres des Régions Libérées*, Case 30/87, E.C.R. 1988, p. 2479, § 34; *Autotrasporti Librandi v. Cuttica spedizioni Srl*, Case C-38/97, E.C.R. 1998, p. I–5955, § 27.

[2] *Société civile agricole du centre d'insémination de la Crespelle v. Coopérative d'élevage et d'insémination artificielle du Département de la Mayenne*, Case C-323/93, E.C.R. 1994, p. I–5077, §15.

[3] *Regie des telegraphes et des telephones v. GB-Inno-BM*, Case 18/88, E.C.R. 1991, p. I–5941, § 20; see also *French Republic v. Commission*, Case C-202/88, E.C.R. 1991 p. I–1223.

[4] *Ex multis, Criminal proceedings against Paul Corbeau*, Case C-320/91, E.C.R. 1993, p. I–2533, § 12.

1. the national measure confers a dominant position on a specific firm. As regards the first condition, a national measure granting a special or exclusive right within the meaning of Article 86(1) may give rise to an individual[5] or collective[6] dominant position. That is not *ipso facto* contrary to Article 86(1); and [7]
2. the national measure is linked to the abuse by that specific firm of its dominant position. As regards the second condition, a Member State infringes the combined provisions of Article 82 and 86(1) EC 'only in two cases':[8]

- The first case is where 'the undertaking in question, merely by exercising the exclusive rights granted to it, is led to abuse its dominant position'.[9] In other words, the undertaking infringes Article 82 EC as a consequence of the very existence of the special or exclusive right which has been granted to it. The abuse of the dominant position is not a result of any behaviour of the undertaking. It is rather attributable to the national measure which does not allow the individual undertaking to behave in a way which does not infringe Article 82 EC.
- The second case is where the special or exclusive rights granted by the Member State 'are liable to create a situation in which the undertaking is led to commit such abuses'.[10] To the extent that the undertaking's behaviour constituting the 'abuse' is the only behaviour which could be

---

[5] *FFAD v. Københavns Kommune*, Case C-209/98, E.C.R. 2000, p. I–3743, § 65.

[6] *Centro servizi Spediporto srl v. Spedizioni marittima del Golfo*, op. cit., § 33; *Comune di Almelo and others v. NV Energiebedrijf Ijsselmij*, Case C-393/92, E.C.R. 1994, p. I–1477, § 42.

[7] *FFAD v. Københavns Kommune*, op. cit., § 66; *Brentjens' Handelsonderneming BV v. Stichting Bedrijfspensioenfonds voor de Handel in Bouwmaterialen*, op. cit., § 91; *Maatschappij Drijvende Bokken BV v. Stichting Pensioenfonds voor de Vervoer - en Havenbedrijven*, Case C-219/97, E.C.R. 1999, p. I–6121, § 83; *Corsica Ferries France SA v. Gruppo Antichi Ormeggiatori del porto di Genova Coop. arl*, Case C-266/96, E.C.R. 1998, p. I–3949, § 40.

[8] *Pavel Pavlov and others v. Stichting Pensioenfonds Medische Specialisten*, Joined Cases C-180/98 to C-184/98, E.C.R. 2000, p. I–6451; *FFAD v. Københavns Kommune*, op. cit.; *Brentjens' Handelsonderneming BV v. Stichting Bedrijfspensioenfonds voor de Handel in Bouwmaterialen*, op. cit.; *Maatschappij Drijvende Bokken BV v. Stichting Pensioenfonds voor de Vervoer- en Havenbedrijven*, Case C-219/97, E.C.R. 1999, p. I–6121; *Albany International BV v. Stichting Bedrijfspensioenfonds Textielindustrie*, Case C-67/96, E.C.R. 1999, p. I–5751.

[9] *Klaus Höfner and Fritz Elser v Macrotron GmbH*, Case C-41/90, E.C.R. 1991, p. I–1979, § 34; *Pavel Pavlov v. Stichting Pensioenfonds Medische Specialisten*, op. cit., § 127.

[10] *RTT v. GB-Inno-Bm SA*, Case 18/88, E.C.R. 1991, p. I–5941, § 20; *GT-link v. DSB*, Case C-242/95, E.C.R. 1997, p. I–4449, §§ 33–34; *Chemische Afvalstoffen Dusseldorp BV and others v. Minister van Volkshuisvesting, Ruimtelijke Ordening en Milieubeheer*, Case C-203/96, E.C.R. 1998, p. I–4075, § 61; *TNT Traco SpA v. Poste Italiane SpA and others*, Case C-340/99, E.C.R. 2001, p. I–4109, § 44; *Connect Austria Gesellschaft für Telekommunikation GmbH v. Telekom-Control-Kommission*, Case C-462/99, E.C.R. 2003, p. I–5197, § 80; *Brentjens' Handelsonderneming BV v. Stichting Bedrijfspensioenfonds voor de Handel in Bouwmaterialen*, op. cit., § 93.

performed by the undertaking, the infringement of Article 82 will be attributable solely to the Member State which has enacted the rule and not to the undertaking concerned.[11]

[11] *Criminal proceedings against Paul Corbeau*, op. cit., p. I–2533.

21. The Binding Nature of Unlawful National Measures and the Antitrust Liability of Private Persons and the Member States

Generally speaking, for an undertaking to be liable for conduct infringing Articles 81 and 82, it must have freedom of action; in other words it must be able to behave independently.[1] If Member States require undertakings to behave in an anticompetitive way or create a legal situation which gives no scope to undertakings' behaviour, the unlawful behaviour which ensues cannot be attributed to the relevant undertakings.[2] This is the case when a national law eliminates the application of Article 81 EC to the behaviour of individuals, as in the type of situation covered by the *Reiff*[3] case law and when the behaviour of undertakings, in the words of the *CNSD*[4] case law, has not 'gone beyond what is required by the law in force'. Similarly, as regards Article 82 EC, that is the case when the abusive behaviour of the firm which was granted a special or exclusive right is the only behaviour which could be performed by the undertaking, as illustrated by the *Macrotron* and *RTT* case law.

The possibility of not applying Community antitrust law to undertakings that are required to behave in an anticompetitive way should be interpreted narrowly.[5] It should only be accepted where the behaviour is a direct consequence of the national legal rules. Consequently, where the anticompetitive behaviour can be in some way attributed to the free will of an undertaking, that undertaking will not be relieved of *antitrust* liability in respect of that behaviour.[6] Thus, it is not relieved of liability in the types of

[1] *Commission v. Ladbroke Racing Ltd.*, Joined Cases C-359/95 P and C-379/95 P, E.C.R. 1997, p. I–6265, § 33.

[2] Ibid., § 33.

[3] *Bundesanstalt für den Güterfernverkehr v. Reiff*, op. cit., p. I–5801.

[4] *Commission v. Italian Republic*, Case C-35/96, E.C.R. 1998 p. I–3851.

[5] *Consiglio Nazionale degli Spedizionieri Doganali v. Commission*, Case T-513/93, E.C.R. 2000, p. II–1807, § 60; *CIF v. Autorità Garante della Concorrenza e del Mercato*, Case C-198/01, E.C.R. 2003, p. I–8055, §§ 67, 69.

[6] *Consiglio Nazionale degli Spedizionieri Doganali v. Commission*, op. cit., §§ 61, 62;

situation covered by the *BNIC v Clair*[7] and *Ahmed Saeed*[8] case law. Nor, as regards situations covered by the *CNSD* case law, is it relieved from liability in respect of behaviour which went beyond what was required by the rules in force.

On the other hand, for an undertaking that behaves in a way prohibited by Article 81 or 82, the possibility of being exempted from the application of Community antitrust law is ruled out in any case in which an individual is under an obligation not to apply the unlawful national rule. According to Community law, an individual is not required to disregard a national measure which he/she presumes to be in breach of the principle of the effectiveness of Community antitrust law (this point also applies to infringements of Article 3(2) of Regulation 1/03. See *infra* for discussion of the unlawful nature of that provision). In such cases, the individual may continue to apply that national legal rule, albeit it is not binding on individuals,[9] until such time as the relevant public authorities have formally ascertained its illegality.[10] In that situation, an individual who complies with a rule which may be unlawful (or which will later be declared unlawful) pursuant to Article 10 read in conjunction with Article 81 or pursuant to Article 82 read in conjunction with Article 86(1), and whose behaviour cannot be struck at by the EC antitrust prohibitions, does not infringe Community law. He/she is not, therefore, liable to pay compensation in respect of any harm that he/she has caused to other individuals.[11] On the other hand, if the conditions laid down by the Community case law are met,[12] the Member State which has enacted the measure will be liable to pay compensation.[13]

The Court of Justice has also indicated when, in such cases, an individual is required to disregard the national measure which breaches the principle of

---

CIF v. Autorità Garante della Concorrenza e del Mercato, op. cit., § 69.

[7] *Bnic v. Guy Clair*, Case 123/83, E.C.R. 1985, p. 391.

[8] *Ahmed Saeed Flugreisen v. Zentrale Zur Bekaempfung Unlauteren Wettbewerbs*, Case 66/86, E.C.R. 1989, p. 803.

[9] *CIF v. Autorità garante della Concorrenza e del Mercato*, op. cit..

[10] See ibid. On the contrast between that case law and the approach of the Commission and the Court of First Instance, *see infra*.

[11] Ibid.

[12] See, *ex multis*, *Andrea Francovich and Danila Bonifaci v. Italian Republic*, Joined Cases C-6/90 and C-9/90, E.C.R. 1991, p. I–5357, §§ 33–36; *Helen Marshall v. Southampton and South West Hampshire Area Health Authority*, Case C-271/91, E.C.R. 1993, p. I–4367, §§ 30, 34–35; *Brasserie du Pêcheur SA v. Bundesrepublik Deutschland and The Queen v. Secretary of State for Transport, ex parte: Factortame Ltd*, Joined Cases C-46/93 and C-48/93, E.C.R. 1996, p. I–1029; *The Queen v. H.M. Treasury, ex parte British Telecommunications plc*, Case C-392/93, E.C.R. 1996, p. I–1631, §§ 39–46; *Erich Dillenkofer v. Bundesrepublik Deutschland*, Joined Cases C-178/94, C-179/94, C-188/94, C-189/94 and C-190/94, E.C.R. 1996, p. I–4845, §§ 22, 26–72.

[13] *CIF v. Autorità garante della concorrenza e del marcato (AGCM)*, Case C-198/01, E.C.R. 2003, p. I–8055.

the effectiveness of Community antitrust law (the principles established by the Court are also applicable *mutatis mutandis* to measures which infringe Article 3(2) of Regulation 1/03, see *infra*). The Court has held that the individual must disregard the unlawful national measure once it has been formally ascertained that it is contrary to Community law. The national measure which must be disregarded because it is in breach of Community law does not need to be formally declared illegal in the context of infringement proceedings (under Article 226 EC). A decision of a national authority recording the illegality will suffice. This principle is applicable not only to Articles 10 and 81 but also to Articles 81 and 86(1). Once it has been ascertained that the measure is incompatible with EC law, if the individual addressees thereof continue to apply it, they may themselves be committing an infringement of Community antitrust law. This would give rise to the obligation to make good the damage caused to third parties, assuming that all the other conditions for such liability are satisfied.

PART VI

VERTICAL ASPECTS OF EUROPEAN ANTITRUST LAW

22. European Antitrust Powers and the Principles of Subsidiarity and Proportionality

In order to determine how Community antitrust competence is allocated between the Community and the Member States, we have first to examine whether Article 5 EC is applicable to it. Article 5 EC sets out how Community legislative competence should be applied. In this respect, three separate questions have to be answered:

- the first is whether Community antitrust rules are 'powers' within the meaning of the first paragraph of Article 5;
- the second is whether the principle of subsidiarity enunciated in the second paragraph of Article 5 is applicable; and
- the third is whether the principle of proportionality referred to in the third paragraph of Article 5 is applicable.

22.1. ARTICLES 81 TO 85 EC AS 'POWERS CONFERRED ON' THE COMMUNITY BY THE MEMBER STATES

Article 5 of the EC Treaty was inserted by the Maastricht Treaty (1992). It contains principles relating to the exercise of Community powers. In order to assess how far, if at all, Article 5 is applicable to Community antitrust law, we first need to ascertain whether antitrust law falls within the concept of 'powers conferred on' the Community by the Member States (first paragraph of Article 5).

That question must be answered in the affirmative. The 'Rules on competition applying to undertakings' are an integral part of the 'Rules on competition' (Part Three, Title VI; Chapter 1 EC). They contain a number of powers which have been conferred on the Community by the Member States and which correspondingly limit the powers of the Member States (*infra*). Community antitrust powers are made up of rules addressed to undertakings. The concrete form of those rules is partially remitted to regulations and directives enacted on the basis of Article 83 EC and to Articles 84 and 85 EC.

This position is confirmed by Article 13(1)(b) of the EU Constitution which lists 'the establishment of the competition rules necessary for the functioning of the internal market' as being an area where the Union has competence.

22.2. THE APPLICABILITY OF THE PRINCIPLE OF SUBSIDIARITY

The principle of subsidiarity (second paragraph of Article 5) was inserted as a reaction to the increase in the powers of the Community which began in the 1970s and to the disquiet which this phenomenon aroused in the Member States (as evidenced by pronouncements of the *Bundesverfassungsgericht*, the German Constitutional Court). The Member States aimed to put an end to the process by which powers were transferred surreptitiously to the Community without the appropriate constitutional procedures being complied with.

The second paragraph of Article 5 EC provides that:

> in areas which do not fall within its exclusive competence, the Community shall take action, in accordance with the principle of subsidiarity, only if and in so far as the objectives of the proposed action cannot be sufficiently achieved by the Member States and can therefore, by reason of the scale or effects of the proposed action, be better achieved by the Community.

The principle is thus applicable only to a shared competence which allows the Member States to take action at national level, such as competence in the area of the environment (*infra*).

However, with the exception of the powers conferred by Article 83 EC, Community antitrust law is not an exclusive competence of the Community. Nor is it the type of shared competence which, by virtue of Article 5 EC, could be exercised, depending on the circumstances, by either the Community or the Member States.

In fact (with the exception of Article 81(3) EC) it takes the form of prohibitions[1] having direct effect which are addressed to individuals and the implementation of which is partly dependent on directives and regulations adopted pursuant to Article 83 EC. For this reason, the principle of subsidiarity is not applicable to Articles 81 and 82 EC (see similarly Callies, 2002, § 27).

Member States retain competence, in parallel with the Community, to enact laws in the area falling within the scope of Articles 81 and 82 EC.

---

[1] *Commission v. Italian Republic*, Case 48/71, E.C.R. 1972, p. 529, § 9.

Provided that they comply with the principle of the effectiveness of Community antitrust law (*infra*), such laws may reach different results from EC antitrust law[2] (*supra*).

The fact that Article 5 EC is not applicable to Community antitrust law can also be explained on historical grounds. Community antitrust law, like the four fundamental freedoms, was established directly by the EC Treaty in 1957. The principle of subsidiarity, by contrast, was put on a formal footing only later in 1993. Most relevantly, the principle of subsidiarity was developed with reference to law-making powers which had been transferred to the Community and which did not comprise prohibitions having direct effect (that is, norms that could be applied by national courts). These powers applied in areas such as health or the environment which typically provide for a more or less well-defined objective that requires specific legislation for the implementation of the policies concerned.

Consequently, the Member States may not rely on subsidiarity to be able to exercise Community antitrust powers, and nor was subsidiarity developed in order to be applied to those powers.

Given the particular nature of Articles 81 and 82, determining whether antitrust law is to be exercised by the Community or the Member States simply entails deciding whether it is the Commission or the national authorities which should enforce the prohibitions which these articles establish. However, this question raises issues which are quite different from those raised by the issue of subsidiarity and it touches upon the decentralised enforcement by national bodies of those prohibitions (this question will be dealt with in Part IX of this book, *infra*).

The Commission has not been consistent with regard to the question whether the *antitrust* rules constitute an exclusive or shared competence.

First, on occasions, it has contended that Community antitrust competence is an exclusive competence.[3] According to that argument, the principle of subsidiarity cannot be applied in this area since it is not an area of shared competence (see *infra* for the opposite argument put forward by the Commission).

This position is not satisfactory. In the case of exclusive Community competence, the Member States are not entitled to enact any national legislation in the relevant area. If the Member States enact any rules in an area falling within an exclusive Community competence (such as the common commercial policy or the common fisheries policy) this would constitute an infringement of Community law and the national law would be illegal.

---

[2] See *Direccion General de Defensa de la Competencia v. Asociacion Espanola de Banca privada*, Case C-67/91, E.C.R. 1992, p. I-4785.

[3] See Commission, *The principle of subsidiarity – Communication of the Commission to the Council and the European Parliament*, SEC(92) 1990, def, p. 7.

However, in the *Walt Wilhelm* judgment the Court itself held that Member States were entitled to enact national antitrust laws. Provided that it did not frustrate the effectiveness of the Community antitrust rules, a Member State's antitrust law could be applied in parallel and would not therefore infringe Community law.[4]

Given that Community antitrust law is neither an exclusive nor a shared competence (*infra*), it is worthwhile examining how the relevant provisions of the Constitution for Europe deal with the issue of antitrust law. Article 13(1) of the Constitution lists 'the establishment of the competition rules necessary for the functioning of the internal market' as one of the Union's exclusive competences. However, it is clear that the Constitution does not treat competence in the area of competition (and hence antitrust) as being the same as, for example, 'the conservation of marine biological resources under the common fisheries policy' or the 'common commercial policy'. If that were the case, as mentioned *supra* in the case of the EC Treaty, all national antitrust rules would infringe EU law by virtue of Article 6 of the Constitution (principle of the primacy of Community law) in conjunction with Article 12(1) (elimination of the power of Member States to legislate in areas of exclusive Union competence). However, the Constitution does not purport to repeal national powers to enact antitrust legislation. It is no coincidence that in Article 163(2)(e) of the EU Constitution, just as in Article 83 EC, one of the purposes for which the Council may adopt regulations 'to give effect to the principles set out in' the antitrust prohibitions is to 'determine the relationship between Member States' laws and this Subsection as well as the European regulations adopted pursuant to this Article'. It is thus clear that Article 163 of the Constitution presupposes that antitrust prohibitions will continue to co-exist with national antitrust law. Closer examination of Article 13(1) of the EU Constitution reveals that only 'the establishing of the competition rules necessary for the functioning of the internal market' is defined as an 'exclusive competence'. This reference simply clarifies that 'the competition rules necessary for the functioning of the common market' are different from national competition rules, including antitrust rules, and that they have a different goal, which is peculiar to the Union. Rules to achieve the EU goal can be enacted only by the European Union, but this is without prejudice to the possibility of enacting national antitrust law. This principle is not a novelty given that it was established, as early as 1989, in the *Spanish Banks* judgment.[5]

---

[4] *Walt Wilhelm v. Bundeskartellamt*, Case 14/68, E.C.R. 1969, p. 1.

[5] *Direccion General de Defensa de la Competencia v. Asociacion Espanola de Banca privada*, Case C-67/91, E.C.R. 1992, p. I–4785.

This makes it clear that antitrust competence is not, technically speaking, an exclusive competence.

Second, on a number of occasions, the Commission has denied that Community antitrust competence is an exclusive competence. The Commission has also made the contradictory claim that the principle of subsidiarity is applicable to the enforcement of Articles 81 and 82 EC (see Recital 29 of the Preamble to the proposal for a regulation of 2000,[6] which was ultimately taken over as Recital 34 in the final version of Regulation 1/03). This would imply that Community antitrust competence is a shared competence.

However, the principle of subsidiarity is not applicable in the specific case of Articles 81 and 82 EC, unless the expression is understood in a non-technical sense, as meaning simply a means of dividing up the workload between the Commission and the national authorities (Brittan, 1993, p. 27). With the exception of Article 81(3), Articles 81 and 82 are prohibitions having direct effect and thus there is no possibility of invoking the principle of subsidiarity in order to assess whether it is the Community or the Member States which have the power to regulate this matter.

22.3. THE APPLICABILITY OF THE PRINCIPLE OF PROPORTIONALITY

The principle of proportionality is set out in the third paragraph of Article 5 EC which provides that 'any action by the Community shall not go beyond what is necessary to achieve the objectives of the Treaty'. This principle applies to Community antitrust competence and especially to regulations and directives adopted under Article 83 EC, which are measures which 'establish the powers of the Community antitrust system' (on this point, Article 3(2) of Regulation 1/03 is unlawful since, being a provision adopted on the basis of Article 83(3)(e) EC, it infringes the principle of proportionality. This point is examined, *infra*).

The principle enunciated in the third paragraph of Article 5 EC should not be confused with its homonym (that is, the general principle of proportionality). This latter principle applies not to the exercise of legislative powers but to individual implementing measures (that is, Commission decisions in the antitrust field).[7]

---

[6] *BEMIM v. Commission*, Case T-114/92, E.C.R.1995, p. II–147.

[7] *ITP v. Commission*, Case T-76/89, E.C.R. 1991 p. II–575, § 80.

23. Principles to Resolve the Conflict between European Antitrust Law and National Laws under the EC Treaty and Regulation 1/03

Since Community antitrust competence is not an exclusive competence (albeit it is not a shared competence either, *supra*), it does not prevent the Member States from enacting antitrust rules (or rules which apply to situations falling under Articles 81and 82 EC). This means that conflicts between Community antitrust law and national rules cannot be ruled out.

23.1. PRINCIPLES TO RESOLVE THE CONFLICT BETWEEN EUROPEAN ANTITRUST LAW AND NATIONAL LAWS

Community law provides for two ways of resolving this type of conflict:

- first, by recourse to general principles of Community law; and
- second, by means of directives or regulations adopted pursuant to Article 83(2)(e) EC.

For the purposes of the EC Treaty, the distinction between:

- conflicts between Community antitrust law and national law, and
- conflicts between Community antitrust law and laws which regulate situations falling within the scope of Articles 81 and 82 EC,

is unimportant. This point needs to be stressed at the outset.

It is clarified by Article 83(2)(e) EC which does not distinguish between the two situations but simply provides that 'the regulations or directives referred to in paragraph 1 shall be designed in particular: ... to determine the relationship between national laws and the provisions contained in this section or adopted pursuant to this article'. The specific relationship between

Community antitrust law and Member States' antitrust law is not relevant (compare, however, Article 3(3) of Regulation 1/03, *infra*). What is important is that Articles 81 and 82 EC should maintain their 'effectiveness'. This means that Member States should not enact rules which eliminate the effectiveness of those articles, whatever the objective of the national rules might be. Looked at from this angle, the antitrust laws of the Member States fall within the general category of national laws which apply to situations falling under Articles 81 and 82 EC.

The peculiarity of national antitrust law is that, to paraphrase Article 3(3) of the Regulation, it pursues an objective similar to that pursued by Articles 81 and 82 EC (on the differences between the respective goals of Community and national antitrust laws, see *supra*).

Regarding this problem, the case law on the conflicts between EC antitrust and national laws regulating situations falling under Articles 81 and 82 EC may suggest that there are two independent lines of case law:

- the first (the *Walt Wilhelm*[1] case law) concerns the relationship between Community antitrust law and national antitrust rules; and
- the second (the *INNO-ATAB*[2] case law) concerns the relationship between Community antitrust law and national rules applicable to situations falling within the scope of Articles 81 and 82 EC.

Both these apparently distinct lines of case law in fact have a bearing on precisely the same issue, namely measures which eliminate the effectiveness of Articles 81 and 82 EC.

The difference between the two lines of cases is that it is only in the *INNO-ATAB* line that the Court made it clear that the principle of effectiveness concerns all the competition rules in the EC Treaty (that is, Articles 81 to 89).

The lack of attention paid to the fact that both lines of case law pursue the same objective and are based on the same legal reasoning can probably be explained by two factors, as follows.

23.1.1. The Attitude of the Commission

Over the years, the Commission has maintained that two separate principles exist:

- the aim of the first is to resolve conflicts between Community antitrust law and national antitrust rules; and

---

[1] *Walt Wilhelm v. Bundeskartellamt*, Case 14/68, E.C.R. 1969, p. 1.

[2] *S.A. G.B.- B.M. v. ATAB*, Case 13/77, in E.C.R. 1977, p. 2115.

- the second is to resolve conflicts between Community antitrust law and laws which regulate situations falling within the scope of Articles 81 and 82 EC (*infra*). The 'discovery' of these two ostensibly separate principles was not based on the existence of two discrete principles of Community law but was connected with the policy of decentralising Community antitrust law.

23.1.2. The Effect which the German 'Two-hurdle' Theory (*Zweischrankentheorie*) Had on the Imagination of the Commentators

Until the end of the 1960s, when the Court gave its *Walt Wilhelm* judgment, proponents of the 'two-hurdle' theory tried to use it to define only the relation between Community and national antitrust law.

According to this theory, Community antitrust law and the law of the Member States pursued different objectives. National law only protected competition within Member States, whereas Community law only protected interstate competition. Consequently, so it was argued, there was no possibility of two sets of antitrust prohibitions being applied in parallel and thus conflicts between the two legal orders simply could not arise (Brinker, 2000, §12). The aim of this theory was to ensure that national antitrust law could be applied without any limitation being imposed by EC antitrust law.

In 1969, the Court rejected this theory in *Walt Wilhelm*. At paragraph 4 of the judgment, the Court stated that 'the national cartel authorities may take proceedings also with regard to situations likely to be the subject of a decision by the Commission'. Despite the Court's clear refusal to accept the 'two-hurdle theory', it continued to muddy the waters. Even more recent academic commentaries seem to show that the *Zweischrankentheorie* also prevented more attention being paid to the determination of the principles which really defined the relationship between Community and national antitrust law. Even now, some commentators consider that the principle which should be used to resolve conflicts between Community and national antitrust law is the 'modified two-hurdle theory' ('*modifizierte Zweischrankentheorie*') (Seitz, 2002, p. 83; Jung, 1995, p. 130). This presupposes, incorrectly, that the Court's approach to this problem in *Walt Wilhelm* was based on the *Zweischrankentheorie*. In reality, *Walt Wilhelm* is based on the clear principle that Member States may not enact laws which eliminate the effectiveness of Articles 81 and 82 (on this principle, see *supra*).

23.2. THE GENERAL PRINCIPLE FOR RESOLVING CONFLICTS BETWEEN COMMUNITY ANTITRUST LAW AND NATIONAL LAW

With regard to the general Community principles applicable to resolving conflicts between Community antitrust law and national law in cases falling under Articles 81 and 82 EC, we have to draw a distinction between principles which can be deduced from the case law and those that the Commission merely claims exist.

23.2.1. General Principles Deduced from the Case Law

The case law has made it clear that the Member States may not enact laws which 'prejudice the practical effectiveness of the competition rules applicable to undertakings'.[3] In other words, the Member States may not enact laws which allow undertakings to behave in a way which is prohibited by Articles 81(1) and 82 EC. Conversely, they may not prohibit agreements which are exempted by virtue of Article 81(3).

It would be contradictory, both legally and economically, for Member States, which have transferred powers to the Community in order to implement Articles 81 and 82, to enact laws which allowed undertakings to behave in a way prohibited by Community antitrust law. Such conflicting rules would simply negate the applicability of Community antitrust law and thus jeopardise the effectiveness of those prohibitions. However, this does not prevent national law from forbidding more than what is prohibited by Articles 81(1) and 82. A national rule forbidding an agreement which is not prohibited by Article 81(1) or conduct which is not prohibited by Article 82 does not cause any harm to the internal market.

In this context, the relationship between Article 81(3) EC and national laws has a special feature. Article 81(3) deals with exemptions from the prohibitions established by Article 81(1). To allow national laws to prohibit agreements exempted by Article 81(3) would, according to the reasoning in *Walt Wilhelm*[4] and *INNO-ATAB*,[5] infringe the principle of effectiveness.

---

[3] See *Walt Wilhelm v. Bundeskartellamt*, op. cit., p. 1; *Regie des Télégraphes et des Telephones v. Gb–Inno–Bm Sa*, Case 18/88, E.C.R. 1991 p. I–5941.

[4] *Walt Wilhelm v. Bundeskartellamt*, op. cit., p. 1; *Anne Marty Sa v. Estee Lauder Sa*, Case 37/79, E.C.R. 1980, p. 2481; *S.A. Saint Herblain Distribution v. Syndicat des Libraires de Loire-Ocean*, Case 299/83, E.C.R. 1985, p. 2515, § 14; *C.I.C.C.E. v. Commission*, Case 298/83, E.C.R. 1985, p. 1105; *Verband der Sachversicherer E. See v. Commission*, Case 45/85, E.C.R. 1987, p. 405, § 20; *Sotralentz Sa v. Commission*, Case T-149/89, E.C.R. 1995, p. II–1127; *Direccion General de Defensa de la Competencia v. Asociacion Espanola de Banca privada*, Case C-67/91, E.C.R. 1992, p. I–4785; *Oscar Bronner GmbH v. Mediaprint Zeitungs-und Zeitschriftenverlag*, Case C-7/97, E.C.R. 1998 p. I–7791; *Wouters v. Wouters*, Case C-309/99,

More precisely, the purpose of Article 81(3) EC, which is to promote 'a harmonious development of economic activities within the whole Community',[6] would be frustrated. It follows that agreements to which Article 81(3) is applicable, either through individual decisions or block exemption regulations, may not be prohibited by national rules.

The general principle of effectiveness of Community law is the key to resolving the conflict between Community and national law, and not merely when no implementing legislation has been adopted pursuant to Article 83(2)(e) EC. The principle continues to apply even if such legislation, such as Article 3 of Regulation 1/03, exists. If laws adopted on the basis of Article 83(2)(e) infringe this principle, the legality of those laws is tested by reference to that provision (*infra*).

23.2.2. General Principles Put Forward by the Commission

The Commission has adopted principles regarding the rules resolving conflicts between Community antitrust law and national law which are different from those set out above, with regard to both:

- the general principle; and;
- the prohibition on the Member States outlawing agreements falling under block exemption regulations applying Article 81(3).

General principles of Community law

Regarding the general principles of Community law resolving conflicts between Community antitrust law and national law, the Commission has maintained that 'it is inconsistent with the notion of a single market that agreements and practices capable of affecting cross-border trade should be subject to different standards and that an agreement which would be considered innocuous or beneficial under Community law can be prohibited under national competition law' (proposal for a regulation of 27 September 2000, section IV).

It is clear that the Commission's approach is in flagrant contradiction with the general principles applying to the relationship between Community antitrust law and national law in this field (*supra*). The Commission maintains

---

E.C.R. 2002, p. I–1577.

[5] *S.A. G.B.- B.M. v. ATAB*, op. cit., p. 2115, § 33. For the case law on Article 10 EC in conjunction with Article 82 EC, *see Dip Spa v. Comune di Bassano del Grappa*, Joined Cases C-140/94, C-141/94 and C-142/94, E.C.R. 1995 p. I–3257, § 24; *Centro Servizi Spediporto Srl v. Spedizioni Marittima del Golfo Srl*, Case C-96/94, E.C.R. 1995, p. I–2883, § 31; *Autotrasporti Librandi Snc di Librandi F. & C. v. Cuttica spedizioni e servizi internationali Srl.*, Case C-38/97, E.C.R. 1998, p. I–5955, § 27.

[6] *Walt Wilhelm v. Bundeskartellamt*, op. cit., p. 1, § 5.

that for national law to prohibit 'an agreement which would be considered innocuous' (that is, an agreement not prohibited by Article 81(1)) or 'beneficial' (that is, an agreement exempted by virtue of Article 81(3)) 'under Community law' is inconsistent with the notion of a single market. However, according to the general principles of Community law set out above (*supra*), in the first case, national legislation which is stricter than Articles 81(1) and 82 EC is lawful. In the second case, it is quite true that an agreement which fulfils the conditions for obtaining the exemption under Article 81(3) EC may not legitimately be prohibited by virtue of national antitrust law.

The principles which the Commission relies on are different from those defined in the *Walt Wilhelm* and *INNO-ATAB* case law because they have not been developed in order to define the relationship between Community and national antitrust law. The aim of those principles was linked to the policy of decentralising Community antitrust law.

The Commission's approach on this point began to take shape at the beginning of the 1990s. The Commission maintained the view, which it had put forward in 1992 in *BEMIM*, that if it closed proceedings for lack of Community interest, this required the national authorities to participate in the protection of the internal market. This policy, which was developed in an effort to limit its own direct enforcement of EC antitrust law, was used by the Commission in an effort to push the national authorities to make greater use of Articles 81 and 82. The Commission considered it either 'desirable that national authorities should themselves apply Community law directly or, failing that, obtain, by applying their domestic law, a result similar to that which would have been obtained had Community law been applied' (Paragraph 10 of the 1997 Notice on cooperation with national competition authorities). In this way, even if they applied only domestic antitrust law, the national authorities would safeguard the internal market.

In 2000, eight years after *BEMIM*, the Commission still formulated some provisions in the proposal for a regulation implementing Articles 81 and 82 with a view to reducing its own enforcement activity and requiring Member States always to apply Community antitrust law and thus to participate in the safeguarding of the internal market. Article 3 of the proposal stipulated that only Community antitrust law should be applied to cases having Community relevance. Had that proposal been accepted, both national authorities and courts would have been required to apply Community law alone to cases having Community relevance. However, the proposal was amended during the course of negotiations.

In order to come to this conclusion, it is clear that the Commission must treat the relationship between Community and national antitrust law as if Articles 81 and 82 were not prohibitions that follow the general principles of *Walt Wihelm* and *INNO-ATAB*. The Commission has treated the relationship between Community and national antitrust law as it does in the case of 'European market organisations' (Article 34 (1)(c) EC)[7] or Community 'common policies',[8] and thus treats Articles 81 and 82 as if they were an exclusive competence. It is no coincidence that, in justifying the exclusive application of Community antitrust law, put forward in Article 3 of the 2000 proposal for a regulation, the Commission claimed that:

> the ... proposal is thus fully in line with the principle enshrined in Article 5 of the Treaty, according to which action should be taken at the most efficient level. While promoting the Community interest *in a level playing field* throughout the single market, the proposal ensures that national competition authorities and courts can apply Articles 81 and 82 fully and effectively to all cases in respect of which intervention at national level is more efficient. (Emphasis added).

It can simply be retorted that, in the first place, the principle of subsidiarity cannot be applied to Articles 81 and 82 since these articles are not a shared competence (albeit, as illustrated *supra*, they do not represent an exclusive competence within the meaning of Article 5(2)).

In the second place, the aim of Articles 81 and 82 EC is to meet the objectives of Article 3 of the Treaty. In particular, 'Article 3 ... determines the fields and objectives to which the activities of the Community are to relate. It thus lays down the general principles of the internal market, which are to be applied in conjunction with the respective chapters of the Treaty devoted to their implementation'.[9] Contrary to what the Commission claims, 'the creation of a level playing field' is not one of the objectives set out in Article 3(1). As regards the field of competition, the objective is to create 'a system ensuring that competition in the internal market is not distorted', which is implemented by Articles 81 and 82.

Moreover, the Commission's approach has been rejected by the Court, which stated in *Spanish Banks* that national antitrust laws legitimately pursue different objectives from Community antitrust law.[10] The Court did not regard this as harmful to the internal market (*infra*).

Regarding the relationship with Article 81(3) EC

The Commission has found various ways to justify the rule that the Member

---

[7] *Filippo Galli (Pretura di Roma)*, Case 31/74, E.C.R. 1975, p. 47, §§ 29–32; *Nv International Fruit Company v. Commission*, Joined Cases 41 to 44/70, E.C.R. 1971, p. 411, §§ 23–26.

[8] *Ireland v. Commission*, Case 239/86, E.C.R. 1987, p. 5271, § 13.

[9] *Jean-Pierre Guimont*, Case C-448/98, E.C.R. 2000, p. I–10663, § 12.

[10] *Direccıon General de Defensa de la Competencia v. Asociacion Espanola de Banca prıvada*, op. cit., p. I–4785.

States may not prohibit agreements covered by block exemption regulations applying Article 81(3) EC.

Sometimes it claims that the aim of not allowing Member States to prohibit agreements exempted pursuant to Article 81(3) is to ensure the smooth functioning of the 'internal market' (see part IV of the proposal for a regulation of 2000, *infra*), which is an approach which we have already disputed (*supra*).

Sometimes the Commission justifies this approach by reference to the nature of the act implementing Article 81(3). For example, in Regulation 2790/99 on the application of article 81(3) of the Treaty to categories of vertical agreements,[11] it is stated in Recital 17: 'In accordance with the principle of the primacy of Community law, no measure taken pursuant to national laws on competition should prejudice the uniform application throughout the common market of the Community competition rules or the full effect of any measures adopted in implementation of those rules, including this Regulation'.

In reality, the requirement not to prohibit agreements exempted by virtue of Article 81(3) EC is not a consequence of the primacy of Community law which requires 'the full effect of any measures adopted in implementation' of the competition rules. Nor does it flow from the alleged 'uniform application throughout the common market of the Community competition rules' (on the non-existence of that principle and the unlawfulness of Article 3(2) of Regulation 1/03, see *infra*). Nor is it a consequence that, in general, an EC Regulation is directly applicable.

The real reason why Member States may not prohibit agreements exempted by virtue of Article 81(3) is that to do so would infringe the principle of the effectiveness of Community antitrust law (*supra*). Similarly, it is by virtue of that same principle that national measures which permit cartels prohibited by Article 81 EC or allow abuses of a dominant position prohibited by Article 82 EC are unlawful. It is thus the infringement of the principle of the effectiveness of Community antitrust law which triggers off the application of the principle of the supremacy of Community law.

[11] Commission Regulation (EC) No 2790/1999 of 22 December 1999 on the application of Article 81(3) of the Treaty to categories of vertical agreements and concerted practices, OJ L 333 of 29 December 1999, p. 21.

23.3. THE SYSTEM ESTABLISHED IN REGULATION 1/03 FOR RESOLVING CONFLICTS BETWEEN EUROPEAN ANTITRUST LAW AND NATIONAL LAW

The antitrust system established by the EC Treaty provides that Article 83(2)(e) is the only legal basis for enacting rules to resolve conflicts between Community antitrust law and national law. However, Regulation 17/62, the first Regulation implementing Articles 81 and 82, did not contain any rules implementing Article 83(2)(e). That power was exercised for the first time by means of Article 3 of Regulation 1/03, entitled 'Relationship between Articles 81 and 82 of the Treaty and national competition laws', which establishes three separate rules concerning the relationship between Community antitrust law and national rules:

- the requirement that national authorities and courts apply Community antitrust law when they decide cases of Community relevance falling within the scope of Article 81 or 82 EC (Article 3(1));
- the *de facto* exclusive application of Article 81 to agreements falling within its scope (Article 3(2)); and
- the exceptions to Articles 3(1) and 3(2) with regard to the application of national rules on mergers or of national provisions which pursue different objectives from Community antitrust law (Article 3(3)).

23.3.1. The Obligation Incumbent on National Authorities and National Courts to Apply Community Antitrust Law

Article 3(1) of the Regulation requires national bodies (both competition authorities and courts) to apply Articles 81 and 82 in proceedings in which national law is applied to a case of Community relevance (that is, a situation falling within the scope of Article 81 or Article 82 EC). Consequently – and contrary to what was foreseen in the proposal for a regulation of 2000 – the parallel application of Community and national law to the same case cannot be excluded. Recital 8 of the Preamble to the Regulation makes it clear that the aim of that provision is to 'ensure the effective enforcement of the Community competition rules and the proper functioning of the cooperation mechanisms contained in this Regulation'.

23.3.2. The Relationship between Community Antitrust Law and National Antitrust Law

Article 3(2) determines the relationship between Community and national antitrust law. The first sentence of Article 3(2) provides *de facto* that only Community law is to be applied to agreements falling within the scope of Article 81(1) EC. Although Regulation 1/03 allows for the possibility of parallel application of Community and national antitrust law, the effect of Article 3(2) is that 'the application of national competition rules may not produce an outcome which deviates from that resulting from the application of Article 81 of the EC Treaty' (Commission, at paragraph 17.4 of the XXXII Report on competition policy). Thus, Article 3(2) contains an exception to the principle of the effectiveness of Community law (*supra*). It prevents national laws from being stricter than Article 81 EC. By contrast, the general principle of effectiveness does not preclude national law from going further than Article 81(1) (except as regards agreements exempted by virtue of Article 81(3) EC).

The Regulation, quite correctly, draws a distinction between agreements 'which fulfil the conditions of Article 81(3) of the Treaty' and those which are covered by a regulation for the application of Article 81(3) of the Treaty. The distinction is important. According to the case law, while an agreement benefiting from an individual exemption granted pursuant to Article 81(3) EC is undoubtedly prohibited by virtue of Article 81(1), this is not necessarily the case with agreements covered by a block exemption regulation.[12]

The second sentence of Article 3(2) determines the relationship between Article 82 EC and national antitrust laws applicable to cases falling within the scope of that article. Consistently with the general principle of the effectiveness of Community antitrust law, Article 3(2) of the Regulation allows national law to be stricter than Article 82 EC.

The Council's justification for having adopted the first sentence of Article 3(2) of Regulation 1/03

The second sentence of Article 3(2) of the Regulation does not cause any problems because it leaves untouched the principle of the effectiveness of Community antitrust law. On the other hand, there are doubts as to the legality of the first sentence, which concerns the relationship between Article 81 EC and national cartel prohibitions.

The exclusive application of Community antitrust law to agreements falling within the scope of Article 81 EC is explained in Recital 8 of the preamble to the Regulation by the need to 'create a level playing field for agreements, decisions by associations of undertakings and concerted practices within the internal market'. For this reason, according to the recital, 'it is necessary to determine pursuant to Article 83(2)(e) of the Treaty the relationship between national laws and Community competition law'.

[12] *Italian Republic v. Council and Commission*, Case 32/65, E.C.R. 1966, p. 296.

Article 3(2) of Regulation 1/03 is unlawful because it infringes the principle of proportionality

In Recital 8 of the preamble, the Council posits a link between:

- the objective of the 'internal market' (Article 14 EC);
- regulations adopted on the basis of Article 83(2)(e) EC; and
- the enactment of rules, such as Article 3(2) of Regulation 1/03, which determine the relationship between Community antitrust rules and national law.

The existence of a relationship between the internal market and rules adopted pursuant to Article 83(2)(e) EC does not, however, resolve the problem of the proportionality of a rule such as Article 3(2) of the Regulation, which *de facto* provides for the exclusive application of Article 81 EC.

In order to 'establish whether a provision of Community law complies with the principle of proportionality', the Court of Justice has held that it 'must be ascertained whether the means which it employs are suitable for the purpose of achieving the desired objective and whether they do not go beyond what is necessary to achieve it'.[13]

To assess the proportionality of Article 3(2) we therefore need to examine whether or not:

- it is suitable for the purpose of achieving the objective for which it was adopted; and
- it goes beyond what is necessary to achieve that objective.

Article 3(2) of Regulation 1/03 is unsuitable for the purpose of achieving the objectives laid down by Article 3(1)(g) EC The case law shows that the purpose of provisions adopted pursuant to Article 83(2)(e) EC, such as Article 3(2) of the Regulation, must first be defined. The Court of Justice has consistently held that Regulations adopted pursuant to Article 83 EC aim to achieve the objectives set out in Article 3(1)(g) EC,[14] that is, establish a

---

[13] *Federal Republic of Germany v. Council*, Case C-426/93, E.C.R. 1995, p. I–3723, § 42; see also *United Kingdom of Great Britain and Northern Ireland v. Council*, Case C-84/94, E.C.R. 1996, p. I–5755, § 57.

[14] See *National Panasonic Limited v. Commission*, Case 136/79, E.C.R. 1980, p. 2033, § 20; *Am and S Europe Limited v. Commission*, Case 155/79, E.C.R. 1982, p. 1575, § 15; *Hoechst AG v. Commission*, Joined Cases 46/87 and 227/88, E.C.R. 1989, p. 2859, § 25; *Dow Benelux Nv v. Commission*, Case 85/87, E.C.R. 1989, p. 3137, § 36; *Dow Chemical Iberica Sa v. Commission*, Joined Cases 97/87, 98/87 and 99/87, E.C.R. 1989, p. 3165, § 22; *Orkem Sa v. Commission*, Case 374/87, E.C.R. 1989, p. 3283, § 19; *Tetra Pak Rausing Sa v. Commission*, Case T-51/89, E.C.R. 1990, p. II–309, § 22.

system ensuring that competition is not distorted in the internal market (*supra*). Consequently, the power to legislate pursuant to Article 83 must be used to determine the relationship between national and Community antitrust law to the extent that the application of the antitrust rules of the Member States prevents the objectives of Article 3(1)(g) EC from being met. It is therefore necessary to assess in which cases the application of the rules referred to in Article 3(2) prejudice the achievement of 'a system ensuring that competition in the internal market is not distorted'. In order to avoid implementing measures which would be inconsistent with such a system, Member States have to comply with the principle of effectiveness (*supra*). That means that the Member States must enact antitrust rules which outlaw agreements or practices forbidden by Articles 81 and 82 EC (except where Article 81(3) applies). However, it follows from this that the Member States retain the power to prohibit behaviour which does not contravene Articles 81(1) and 82 (*supra*).

It is easy to come to this clear conclusion because antitrust law takes the form of two prohibitions, namely Articles 81 and 82. Those prohibitions allow us to define precisely when the application of a national antitrust rule is harmful to the internal market (that is, except in the case of agreements exempted by Article 81(3) EC, only when national antitrust law prohibits less than does Community law). The situation is markedly different in the case of a legislative power whose implementation entails granting the Community institutions a great deal of discretion (such as EC environmental competence, see Krämer, 1987, p. 82).

Consequently, general principles suggest that it is unnecessary to enact a rule such as Article 3(2), which, in order to achieve the aims of Article 83(2)(e) EC, precludes the antitrust rules of the Member States from prohibiting more than Article 81(1) does. In other words, Article 3(2), which was adopted on the basis of Article 83(2)(e) EC, is not suitable to attain the objectives of Article 3(1)(g) EC. There is, in fact, no connection between the safeguarding of the internal market and the exclusive application of Community antitrust law, which is what Article 3(2) of the Regulation requires for agreements falling within the scope of Article 81 EC. Furthermore, as the first Recital of the Preamble to Regulation 1/03 recognises, 'in order to establish a system which ensures that competition in the common market is not distorted, Articles 81 and 82 of the Treaty must be applied effectively and uniformly in the Community'. Clearly, the attainment of a 'system which ensures that competition in the common market is not distorted', has nothing to do with the uniform application of national provisions applicable to anticompetitive agreements and Article 81, as required by Article 3(2).

However, this does not mean that the competence conferred by Article

83(2)(e) is not applicable. Quite the contrary, that competence has been properly exercised in the case of Article 3(3) of the Regulation.

Since the enactment of Regulation 1/03, the Commission has sought to justify Article 3(2). At paragraph 17.4 of the XXXII Report on competition policy, the Commission argued that:

> the resulting convergence of the rules applicable to transactions falling under Article 81, the so-called level playing field, will facilitate doing business in Europe and will be central to completion of the internal market and to consistent application of EU competition law once the Commission has given up its monopoly of granting exemptions under Article 81(3) of the Treaty.

With this statement, the Commission is endeavouring to make a novel application of the principles already disputed *supra.*

In reply, we can point out the following:

- first, the 'means employed' by Article 3(2) are not suitable for achieving the objective of measures adopted pursuant to Article 83(2)(e) EC. The aim of such measures is to achieve the objective laid down by Article 3(1)(g) EC. The objective of that Treaty provision is not to facilitate 'doing business' in Europe but, as argued *supra*, to establish 'a system ensuring that competition in the internal market is not distorted'. This is achieved through Articles 81 and 82 EC. Properly analysed, Article 3(2) of the Regulation tends to harmonise national antitrust rules. This is a power which is most certainly not conferred by Article 83(2)(e) EC;
- second, the internal market was already completed on 31 December 1992 (see Article 14(1) EC); and
- third, whether or not Member States' antitrust law is stricter than Article 81 EC has nothing whatsoever to do with the consistent application of Community competition law (*supra*).

For all these reasons, we can see that the Council infringed the principle of proportionality when it enacted Article 3(2). What that Article sets out to do is not 'suitable to achieve the objective pursued' by Article 3(1)(g) EC.

Article 3(2) of Regulation 1/03 exceeds what is necessary to achieve the objective laid down by Article 3(1)(g) of the EC Treaty In order to assess whether Article 3(2) of Regulation 1/03 is compatible with Article 5(3) EC, it is still necessary to determine whether it is proportionate to the objective that it pursues. That is the second limb of the test laid down by the case law. As we shall see, even if Article 3(2) were suitable to achieve the objective pursued by Article 3(1)(g) EC (*quod non, supra*), it is not proportionate to the aim pursued for the following five reasons.

First, even leaving to one side the relevance of Article 81(3) EC (*supra*), the antitrust rules of the Member States would reach a result conflicting with Community law if they prohibited less than did Articles 81(1) and 82. By providing for a system of control which precludes that possibility, Regulation 1/03 achieves what is really essential to avoid the application of national antitrust law which conflicts with the protection of the internal market, as indeed it is required to do by the EC Treaty. The proceedings established by Regulation 1/03 which entitle the Commission to monitor the Member States' competition authorities incidentally allow it to determine whether their enforcement of national law breaches Community law. One consequence of the requirement imposed by Regulation 1/03 on the national authorities and courts to apply Community antitrust law when they apply national antitrust law is that the Commission receives the draft decisions of the national authorities (pursuant to Article 11(4) *infra*) and the judgments of the national courts (pursuant to Article 15(2) *infra*), when Community law is being applied. In such measures there is, incidentally, a reference to any final measure applying national law to the case (*infra*). In this way, if the Commission takes the view that national measures infringe Community law, it can initiate control proceedings pursuant to Article 11(4) or Article 15(3) of Regulation 1/03 or it may even start infringement proceedings under Article 226 EC.

Second, the number of situations in which national antitrust law might conflict with Community law by prohibiting less than is required by Articles 81 and 82 EC or by outlawing agreements exempted by Article 81(3) has already been reduced by other proceedings established by Regulation 1/03. This point casts further doubt on the need for Article 3(2).

For example, the last sentence of Article 12(2) reduces the risk of the national authorities applying national and Community law differently. It does this in a way which is less constraining than Article 3(2) and consequently complies more fully with the principle of proportionality. It allows national authorities to use information obtained pursuant to the Regulation for the application of national competition law provided that two conditions are met. These are:

- national competition law must be 'applied in the same case and in parallel to Community competition law'; and
- the use of the information 'does not lead to a different outcome' from that reached by the application of Community law.

Article 12(2) thus provides for an incentive for national antitrust rules applied by the national authorities to lead to the same outcome as would be reached by applying Community law.

Third, the evolution of the Member States' antitrust systems, quite independently of Regulation 1/03, has radically reduced the probability of national antitrust laws leading to an outcome conflicting with the protection of the internal market. The national systems have evolved precisely with the objective of applying national antitrust law in such a way that it does not conflict with Community law. With regard to the prohibitions established by Articles 81 and 82 EC, the national antitrust systems have already been 'communitarised'. This means that the wording of the national antitrust prohibitions is substantially the same as that of Articles 81 and 82 EC (Dreher, 2000, p. 217; Schanze, 2003, p. 161). Furthermore, some Member States require domestic antitrust law to be interpreted according to the principles of Community antitrust law. Moreover, the Italian legislature has gone so far as to provide that national antitrust law has a merely residual scope which is, in the sense that applies only when Community law is not applicable (Article 1(1) of Law 287/90, for the text of the provision see *infra*).

The 'communitarisation' of national antitrust law is a voluntary development of the antitrust systems of the Member States and has nothing to do with Article 83(2)(e) EC. The 'communitarisation' prevents antitrust national laws from leading to an outcome which is in conflict with Community law. And, in fact, this type of 'voluntarily' harmonised national law not only prevents domestic antitrust rules from being stricter than Article 81 EC, as required by Article 3(2) of the Regulation, it also has the same result with respect to Article 82 EC, which is not required by Article 3(2). Thus, the problem which Article 3(2) sets out to resolve has already been dealt with directly by the Member States. However, this does not prevent the Member States from outlawing agreements which are not prohibited by Community law (except agreements exempted by Article 81(3) EC). This does not stop the objective laid down by Article 3(1)(g) EC from being achieved.

Fourth, we should recall that on 31 December 1992, when Regulation 17/62 was still in force, the internal market was completed (Article 14(1) EC). This was achieved without Regulation 17/62 providing for any rules regulating the relationship between Community and national antitrust law. Furthermore, when national law provided for antitrust laws, they were often formulated differently from the Community law provisions, which entailed a risk that their application would lead to a different outcome. Thus, if we look at what the Community legal system managed to achieve in 1992 without needing to have recourse to a provision such as Article 3(2), we can see that there is now even less need to enact this type of rule for the purposes of protecting the internal market.

Fifth, the Commission is not correct when it claims that a provision such as Article 3(2) needed to be adopted because the Court of Justice made a request to that effect in *Walt Wilhelm*. In part of the proposal for a regulation of 2000, the Commission maintained that 'to address this problem effectively it is necessary to adopt the solution alluded to by the Court of Justice in *Walt Wilhelm*,[15] namely to regulate the relationship between national law and Community competition law as provided for in Article 83(2)(e) of the EC Treaty'. However, in *Walt Wilhelm* the Court did not consider it necessary to determine the relationship between national and Community antitrust law. Quite the contrary, at paragraph 4 of the judgment the Court derives two different principles from the possibility of determining the relationship between national laws and the Community rules on competition. These principles are:

- the Treaty does not eliminate the antitrust powers of the Member States; and
- the 'supremacy of Community law' with respect to national law (paragraph 5).

Thus we can see that in 1969 the Court did not envisage 'determining the relationship between national laws and Community competition law'. In 1999 it went further when it expressly acknowledged that national antitrust laws may legitimately have a different goal from Community antitrust law.[16]

The Court thus adopted a line quite different from the Commission's 'uniform application of Community law' approach (*supra*). According to that incorrect approach, national antitrust rules (and in reality all rules applying to situations falling within the scope of Articles 81 and 82) may never reach results different from those reached by the application of Community law.

To conclude, the aspects which we have examined here, and which were not taken into consideration in drafting Article 3(2), show clearly that this provision manifestly 'goes beyond what is necessary to achieve' the desired objective[17] sought by regulations adopted under Article 83 EC. That is the establishment of 'a system ensuring that competition in the internal market is not distorted'.

Consequently, even if, *quod non*, Article 3(2) was 'suitable' to achieve the objective set out in Article 3(1)(g) EC (first test, *supra*), it infringes the second test of the proportionality of a Community act. This shows once more

[15] *Walt Wilhelm v. Bundeskartellamt*, op. cit., p. 1.

[16] *Direccion General de Defensa de la Competencia v. Asociacion Espanola de Banca privada*, op. cit., p. I–4785.

[17] *Federal Republic of Germany v. Councile*, op. cit., p. I–3723, § 42.

that that Article 3(2) is unlawful because it infringes Article 5(3) EC.

The fact that Regulation 1/03 was adopted unanimously by all the Member States does not 'save' it from being unlawful. Just like the Community institutions and individuals, Member States are bound by Community law as defined by the Court of Justice (regarding the role of the Court in safeguarding the legality of the EC legal order, see *infra*). The European Community 'is a community based on the rule of law, inasmuch as neither its member states not its institutions can avoid a review of the question whether the measures adopted by them are in conformity with the basic constitutional charter, the Treaty'.[18]

The illegality of Article 3(2) of the Regulation entails the 're-emergence' of the general principles governing the relationship between Community and national antitrust law (that is, the principle of the effectiveness of Community antitrust law).

23.3.3. The Exceptions to Articles 3(1) and 3(2) of Regulation 1/03

Article 3(3) allows certain exceptions to the principles established by Articles 3(1) and 3(2). It provides that 'without prejudice to general principles and other provisions of Community law, paragraphs 1 and 2':

- do not 'apply when the competition authorities and the courts of the Member States apply national merger control laws'; and
- do not 'preclude the application of provisions of national law that predominantly pursue an objective different from that pursued by Articles 81 and 82 of the Treaty'.

The relationship between Community antitrust law and national merger control law

The first part of Article 3(3) of Regulation 1/03 establishes an exception by providing that Articles 3(1) and (2) 'do not apply when the competition authorities and the courts of the Member States apply national merger control laws':

- This exception needed to be made because, by virtue of the *Philip Morris* and *Continental Can* case law (*infra*), mergers can be regarded as agreements between undertakings or practices and hence fall within the scope of Articles 81 or 82 EC (Recital 7 of the preamble to

[18] *Parti écologiste 'Les Verts' v. European Parliament*, Case 294/83, E.C.R.1986, p. 1339,§ 23.

Regulation 139/04).[19] Had this exception from the obligation imposed by Article 3(1) not been made, national authorities or courts assessing under national law a concentration not having a Community dimension (Article 21(3) of Regulation 139/04) would also have been required to initiate proceedings applying Articles 81 and 82 EC. To avoid multiple proceedings assessing the same concentration under both national and Community law, Regulation 1/03 establishes a derogation from Article 3(1). Consequently, in the above-mentioned cases, national authorities and courts are not required to initiate proceedings applying Articles 81 and 82 EC in parallel with proceedings assessing a concentration. However, although the provision is worded 'paragraphs 1 and 2 do not apply when the competition authorities and the courts of the Member States apply national merger control laws', the *Philip Morris* and *Continental Can* case law nevertheless allow Articles 81 and 82 to provide criteria to evaluate the legality of a merger not having a Community dimension.

- Article 3(2) Regulation 1/03 establishes an exception to the principle of the effectiveness of Community antitrust law, which normally resolves conflicts between Community and national antitrust laws (*supra*). By virtue of Article 3(3) Regulation 1/03, the normal principle re-emerges. In this context, the principle is that national antitrust law may not regard conduct prohibited by Article 81(1) or 82 EC as lawful (except in the cases exempted by Article 81(3) EC). Article 3(3) provides for 'an exception to the exception' established by Article 3(2) to the principle of the effectiveness of Community antitrust law (*supra*). Thus, national merger control laws may prohibit mergers which, pursuant to *Philip Morris* and *Continental Can*, are not prohibited by Article 81(1) EC or by Article 82 EC. National merger control law must prohibit mergers prohibited by virtue of Article 81(1) EC or Article 82. It may not prohibit mergers which are exempted by virtue of Article 81(3) EC.

23.3.4. The Relationship Between Community Antitrust Laws and Laws Which 'Predominantly Pursue an Objective Different from That Pursued by Articles 81 and 82 of the Treaty'

The second sentence of Article 3(3) provides for another exception to the rules established by Article 3(1) and (2). It stipulates that 'without prejudice to general principles and other provisions of Community law', paragraphs 1 and 2 do not 'preclude the application of provisions of national law that

[19] Council Regulation 139/04 of 20 January 2004 on the control of concentrations between undertakings (the EC Merger Regulation).

predominantly pursue an objective different from that pursued by Articles 81 and 82 of the Treaty' (with reference to the distinction between rules protecting competition and laws protecting other legitimate interests, see *supra*):

- If a law 'predominantly pursues an objective different from that pursued by Articles 81 and 82 of the Treaty' this has important consequences. In particular, if such a law is applied at national level, the national body is not required to initiate proceedings applying Articles 81 and 82 EC. Consequently, nothing precludes the initiation of proceedings to assess the compatibility of an agreement with this type of national law. It does not trigger off the obligation under Article 3(1) to open at the same time proceedings to assess whether the agreement infringes Article 81 EC. On the other hand, the competent national authorities are entitled, if they so wish, to open parallel proceedings assessing the legality of the agreement:

    - the first proceeding would apply the national law which pursues 'an objective different from Articles 81 and 82' EC; and
    - the second proceeding would apply Community antitrust law and, possibly, the Member State's antitrust law.

    The second sentence of Article 3(3) thus allows the application in parallel of two sets of rules, each of which has different aims but both of which apply to situations regulated by Articles 81 and 82 EC.
- Article 3(3) provides that national laws which 'pursue an objective different' from Articles 81 and 82 EC are not constrained by Article 3(2). This means that the relations between those laws and Community antitrust law are governed by the principle of effectiveness of Community antitrust law rather than by the system established by Article 3(2) (compare Recital 9 of the Preamble to Regulation 1/03). In this case, as in the case of merger control laws, Article 3(3) provides for an 'exception to the exception' imposed by Article 3(2) and thus revives the application of the principle of the effectiveness of Community antitrust law.

    Had this exception not been provided for, it might not have been possible for a national law having an aim different from that of Articles 81 and 82 EC to prohibit an agreement which was not prohibited by virtue of Article 81(1). Article 3(2) would have required the agreement, *ex hypothesi* falling within the scope of Article 81 EC, not to be prohibited by this type of national law unless it was also prohibited by virtue of Article 81(1) EC. In the last analysis, this would have precluded the application of national laws having objectives different from Articles 81 and 82 EC.

Consequently, the effect of Article 3(3) is that in the case of parallel proceedings, the limitations established by Article 3(2) (which in the author's view are illegal, *supra*) will apply to the first set of proceedings (that is, the proceedings in which national antitrust laws are being applied). On the other hand, the general principle of the effectiveness of Community antitrust law will pertain to the proceedings in which the laws protecting different interests are applied.

However, as Article 3(3) itself makes clear, this exception does not allow any derogation from the normal principles governing the relationship between Community antitrust law and national law (compare Recital 9 of the Preamble to Regulation 1/03). National laws protecting interests which are different from those protected by Articles 81 and 82 EC may not derogate from the principle of the effectiveness of Community antitrust law[20] (on this principle, see *supra*).

---

[20] *Tetra Pak Rausing Sa v. Commission*, op. cit., p. II–309, § 25.

PART VII

THE BODIES AND INSTITUTIONS OF THE EUROPEAN ANTITRUST ENFORCEMENT SYSTEM

24. The Commission

The Commission plays a central role in the operation of the Community antitrust system. Article 211 of the EC Treaty confers on it the role of 'custodian of Community legality'.[1] Because of the structure of the Community, this role requires it to be independent from the Member States or, to express it another way, to be 'supranational'.

Its supranational character gives the Commission a crucial role to play in the field of Community competition law, including antitrust law. The task conferred on the Commission 'by Articles 81 to 89 is to supervise the enforcement of the competition rules and thus to contribute to the institution of a system ensuring that competition in the common market is not distorted, as required by Article 3(2)(g) EC'.[2] By virtue of the EC Treaty, the Commission is 'responsible for the implementation and orientation of Community competition policy'.[3] In other words, it has the task of establishing concretely what type of competition should exist within the common market and how intense that competition should be. In the antitrust field the Commission, in the context of its 'general power of surveillance and control',[4] has 'the task of ensuring application of the principles laid down in Articles 81 and 82 of the EC Treaty'.[5]

---

[1] *Commission v Italian Republic*, Case C-35/96, E.C.R. 1998, p. I–3851, at paragraph 26.

[2] *Kingdom of the Netherlands v. Commission*, Joined cases C-48/90 and C-66/90, E.C.R. 1992, p. I–565, § 29.

[3] *Delimitis*, Case C-234/89, E.C.R. 1991, p. I–935; *Automec v Commission*, Case T-24/90, E.C.R. 1992, p. II–2223, § 73; *BEMIM v Commission*, Case T-114/92, E.C.R. 1995, p. II–147; *Masterfoods Ltd v. HB Ice Cream Ltd*, Case C-344/98, E.C.R. 2000 p. I–11369, § 73.

[4] *Bosch*, Case 13/61, E.C.R. 1962, English special edition 45.

[5] *Masterfoods Ltd v. HB Ice Cream Ltd*, op. cit., p. I–11369; *Automec Srl v. Commission*, *op. cit.*, p. II–2223, §§ 73–77.

25. National Antitrust Authorities

The expression 'national authorities' refers to the bodies which are empowered to apply national antitrust law in the respective Member States. By virtue of Articles 84 and 85 EC, those authorities are also actors within the Community antitrust system.[1]

Although national authorities are referred to in the EC Treaty, they are nevertheless still only authorities of the Member States and are not Community institutions.

Those bodies have a dual function (to apply both national and Community antitrust law) as a result of the negotiations on the drafting of the EC Treaty (*supra*). Pending the enactment of the first Regulation applying Articles 81 and 82 EC, the bodies in the Member States which would apply Community law had to be identified (*supra*). Even after the enactment of regulations, those bodies in the Member States have maintained this double role.

When they apply Community antitrust law, national authorities, like the Commission, safeguard the Community interest (see Commission Notice on the handling of Complaints, paragraph 1). However, the national authorities do not have the power to determine the orientation of Community antitrust policy. As Article 85 EC makes clear, this is exclusively a matter for the Commission. National authorities thus have a position within the Community antitrust system that is subordinate to that of the Commission.

The following provisions of Regulation 1/03 underline the point that national authorities are subordinate to the Commission:

1. The Commission's power to take over cases in which Community antitrust law is to be applied and thereby to relieve the national authorities of their power (Article 11(6) of Regulation 1/03, reiterating a power which already existed by virtue of Article 9(3) of Regulation 17/62).
2. The Commission's power to monitor forthcoming decisions of the national authorities acting under Articles 81 and 82 EC (Article 11(4) of Regulation 1/03).
3. The Commission's power to submit observations to national courts

[1] On the concept of 'Authorities in Member States', see paragraphs 54 and following of the judgment in *Ministère public v. Asjes*, Joined Cases 209 to 313/84, E.C.R. 1986, p. 571.

exclusively 'where the coherent application of Article 81 or Article 82 of the Treaty so requires' (Article 15(3) of Regulation 1/03);

4. The exclusive power of the Commission to issue guidance letters. By this means, the Commission can set out Community antitrust policy with respect to factual situations which have not been the subject of any decision or case law (see *infra*).

Because of their role within the Community antitrust system and their subordination to the Commission, the national authorities are appropriate bodies to cooperate with the Commission pursuant to Article 84 read in conjunction with Article 10 in order to promote the objective set out in Article 3(g) EC. Thanks to Articles 84 and 85 EC, the regulations and directives adopted under Article 83 EC can confer on them obligations and powers relating to the application of Articles 81 and 82 (relating, for example, to the structure and powers of the authorities and the exchange of information between them).

26. Antitrust Federalism

Although federalism is not expressly referred to in, or regulated by, the EC Treaty, it nevertheless constitutes an important aspect of the Community antitrust system.

'Antitrust federalism' is the means by which the Community legal system and the Member States can have a reciprocal influence on each other's antitrust system.

First, the Community legal system has an influence on the enforcement of the antitrust law of the Member States in two ways:

- By determining how conflicts between EC antitrust law and the Member States' antitrust law are to be resolved (this is achieved either by virtue of the general principle of effectiveness of Community law or by means of regulations and directives adopted under Article 83(2)(e) EC, *supra*).
- Through the procedures established by regulations adopted under Article 83 EC which ensure that national measures do not infringe Community antitrust law (see *infra*).

Second, Member States can exercise influence on Commission decisions applying Articles 81 and 82 EC through the means established by the EC Treaty (Articles 84 and 85) or implemented in Regulations (Regulation 17/62 and Regulation 1/03, see *infra*).

Antitrust federalism is important for several reasons.

First, antitrust federalism is a means of ensuring consistency in the application of EC competition law. Through the system of 'top-down' or 'descending vertical control', it ensures that Member States do not take measures which conflict with EC law and the common market (see *infra*).

Second, antitrust federalism is a counterweight to the Commission's power. Particularly for the Member States, antitrust federalism functions as a counterweight to the Commission's power to determine the orientation of antitrust policy. Community antitrust policy has an impact on all Member States and has direct effects on each of them and on their antitrust competence. It is therefore important for the Member States to have, in addition to the tools provided for by regulations adopted under Article 83(2)(c) EC some way of being able to express their own position, which may be different from the Commission's.

Community antitrust policy assumes concrete form through individual decisions and the practice of the Commission. Commission practice has an influence on the relevant bodies in the Member States and on the decisions which they may address to individuals irrespective of whether the national bodies are applying Community law (see Article 16 of Regulation 1/03) or national law (see Article 3(2) of the Regulation). When Member States apply national antitrust law, Article 10 EC, read in conjunction with Articles 81 and 82 EC (or, put another way, the principle of the effectiveness of Community law) precludes them from treating the same case less severely (when they apply Article 81(1) or Article 82 EC) or differently (where the application of Article 81(3) EC is in issue). It is therefore important for the Member States to have means at their disposal which allow them to express their own position, which may conflict with that of the Commission. Such means should not be limited to what is provided for in regulations adopted on the basis of Article 83(2) EC.

The Member States have the following ways to exercise influence on the Commission's power:

- Within the Community antitrust system, the Member States can use the procedures provided for by regulations or directives adopted under Article 83 EC in order to exercise influence.
- Outside the Community system, they may use their own antitrust law to prohibit cases which are not outlawed by Community antitrust law (except in the case of agreements exempted by virtue of Article 81(3)). This power was excluded in the proposal for a regulation of 2000, Article 3 of which envisaged the exclusive application of Community antitrust law to cases of Community relevance. This second means of formulating a national antitrust policy different from Community policy is particularly important for Member States. Without it, their only way to act as a counterweight to Community competition policy would be through the means established by regulations and directives adopted under Article 83 EC. On the other hand, the Member States' influence on the Community system is, quite properly, limited by the independence of the Commission, which is the supranational institution *par excellence.*

Third, antitrust federalism is a means of protecting individuals. Antitrust federalism is important as a means of protecting individuals. It may prevent the adoption of illegal decisions by the Commission and the national authorities applying Community law. This type of protection is provided for by regulations and directives adopted under Article 83 (in other words, within the Community system). These instruments allow the Member States to put forward views which may conflict with those of the Commission. Within the Community system, the role conferred on the national authorities, in particular by Article 14 of Regulation 1/03, is to make their decision-making procedure and that of the Commission more transparent (*infra*). This factor should allow any illegal aspects of draft decisions to be identified and removed before any unlawful measures are adopted. This is beneficial since, once measures have been adopted and have become binding, direct judicial intervention would be needed to eliminate their effects.

27. National Courts

The national courts play a vital role in the Community system. The Court of Justice has consistently held that 'pursuant to the principle of cooperation laid down in Article 10 of the Treaty, it is for national courts to ensure the legal protection which persons derive from the direct effect of provisions of Community law'[1] (see also paragraph 1 of the Notice on cooperation with the national courts). As the Commission itself has recalled, 'the Court has held that Article 81(1) of the Treaty and Article 82 of the EC Treaty produce direct effects in relations between individuals and create rights for individuals which the national courts must safeguard'[2] (see Commission Notice on the cooperation between the Commission and the courts of the EU Member States in the application of Articles 81 and 82 EC, hereinafter the 'Notice on cooperation with the national courts', paragraph 12).

It is pointed out at paragraph 9 of the Notice on cooperation with the national courts that the procedure 'for the enforcement of EC competition rules by national courts and the sanctions they can impose in case of an infringement of those rules are largely covered by national law'. However, national law must respect the general principles of Community law, such as effectiveness and equivalence.

The role that national courts play in the enforcement of Community antitrust law is different from the role played by the Commission and the national administrative authorities (see also Paragraph 16 of the Commission Notice on the handling of complaints by the Commission under Articles 81 and 82 of the EC Treaty, hereinafter the 'Notice on the handling of complaints'). For example, national courts can award damages to an individual who has been the victim of an infringement of Community antitrust law even if jurisdiction to that effect has not expressly been conferred on them. They can also award costs and issue interim measures (see paragraph 13 of the Notice on the handling of complaints and Recital 7 of the Preamble

[1] See, *inter alia*, *Aannemersbedrijf P.K. Kraaijeveld B.See v Commission*, Case C-72/95, E.C.R. 1996, p. I–5403, § 58; *Waterkeyn (Procureur de la République)*, Joined Cases 314 to 316/81 and 83/82, E.C.R. 1982, p. 4337.

[2] *Belgische Radio en Televisie v. Sv Sabam e Nv Fonior*, Case 127/73, E.C.R. 1974, p. 51, § 16; *Guérin automobiles v. Commission*, Case C-282/95 P, E.C.R. 1997, p. I–1503, § 39; *Courage Ltd v. Bernard Crehan*, Case C-453/99, E.C.R. 2001, p. I–6297, § 23; see also *Manfredi v. Lloyd Adriatico Assicurazioni*, Case C-295/04, E.C.R. 2006, not yet reported.

to Regulation 1/03).[3]

As regards the differences between the powers of the national courts and the other bodies that apply Articles 81 and 82 within the Community antitrust system, it is important to bear the following points in mind:

1. An important difference between the national courts and the Commission is that the former safeguard the individual rights of private persons, whereas the Commission is responsible for defining Community antitrust policy. Accordingly, when the Commission applies Articles 81 and 82 it acts in the public interest (see Article 85 EC and paragraph 27 of the Notice on the handling of complaints).[4] One consequence which flows from the Commission's power to define Community antitrust policy is that the national courts, notwithstanding their different role, are bound by the Commission's interpretation of Articles 81 and 82 EC (on this point, and particularly on the alleged general constitutional incompatibility of Article 16(1) of Regulation 1/03, see *infra*). More generally, as the Commission pointed out in paragraph 8 of the Notice on cooperation with the national courts, 'when applying EC competition rules, national courts are bound by the case law of the Community courts as well as by Commission regulations applying Article 81(3) EC to certain categories of agreements, decisions or concerted practices'.[5]
2. The national courts' role also differs from that of the national authorities, since the courts protect the 'interests of private parties' (or, to formulate their role more accurately, they safeguard the rights that Community law confers on those parties). By contrast, national authorities, like the Commission, act to safeguard the Community public interest.[6]

Since neither national courts nor national authorities have the power to determine Community antitrust policy, neither is hierarchically superior to the other. Unlike decisions taken by the Commission, decisions of national authorities applying Community antitrust law are not binding on national courts applying Articles 81 and 82.

---

[3] See *Courage*, ibid., §§ 26–27.

[4] See also *Masterfoods Ltd v. HB Ice Cream Ltd*, Case C-344/98, E.C.R. 2000 p. I–11369.

[5] On the relationship between the Commission and the national courts when applying Articles 81 and 82 EC, see *Stergios Delimitis v. Henninger Bräu AG*, Case C-234/89, E.C.R. 1991, p. I–935, and *Masterfoods Ltd v. HB Ice Cream Ltd*, op. cit.

[6] See *Automec Srl v. Commission*, Case T-24/90, E.C.R. 1992, p. II–2223.

PART VIII

THE ANTITRUST ENFORCEMENT SYSTEM ESTABLISHED BY THE EC TREATY

28. The Commission: Powers, Decisions and Penalties

In Articles 84 and 85, the EC Treaty contains a provisional antitrust enforcement system which applies quite adequately if no regulations or directives have been adopted pursuant to Article 83. It is not a coincidence that Articles 164 and 165 of the EU Constitution are worded virtually identically to Articles 84 and 85 EC (Pace, 2005).

Even after the enactment of the regulations adopted on the basis of Article 83,[1] Articles 84 and 85 EC still maintain certain effects today. These articles establish the basic roles and powers of the bodies within the system. Regulations adopted by virtue of Article 83 adhere to the structure of the system laid down by Articles 84 and 85 regarding the role of the Commission and national antitrust authorities, as indeed they are obliged to do.

28.1. POWERS AND DECISIONS

In the system established by Articles 84 and 85, EC the Commission's powers are severely restricted by the lack of any procedures to implement Articles 81 and 82 EC. Article 85(1) simply provides that 'the Commission shall ensure the application of the principles laid down in Articles 81 and 82'. In addition to conferring this power on the Commission, Article 85 also provides that it may be activated by an application from a Member State or by the Commission acting on its own initiative.

The EC Treaty also lays down the measures which the Commission is required to take when it has found that there has been an infringement of Articles 81 and 82. Article 85(1) EC provides that if 'it finds that there has been an infringement, it shall propose appropriate measures to bring it to an end'. At a later stage, if the undertaking does not bring the infringement to an end, 'the Commission shall record such infringement of the principles in a reasoned decision' (Article 85(2)).

[1] For the effects in the absence of legislation, see *Ministère public v Asjes*, Joined Cases 209 to 213/84, E.C.R. 1986, p. 1425, § 52 and *Ahmed Saeed Flugreisen v. Zentrale Zur Bekaempfung Unlauteren Wettbewerbs*, Case 66/86, E.C.R. 1989, p. 803, § 20.

Lastly, the EC Treaty gives the Commission power to 'authorise Member States to take the measures, the conditions and details of which it shall determine, needed to remedy the situation' flowing from the infringement. The intervention of the Member States to 'take the measures ... needed to remedy the situation' is required because no powers are conferred on the Commission to enforce the prohibitions established by Articles 81 and 82.

28.2. PENALTIES

Article 85(2) EC also makes provision for the penalties which may be imposed for infringements of the Community antitrust rules. By virtue of Article 85(2), 'if the infringement is not brought to an end, the Commission shall record such infringement of the principles in a reasoned decision. The Commission may publish its decision'. In this way, by establishing the consequences of an infringement, the Treaty identifies the Commission as the body that has the power to impose penalties on undertakings that infringe Community antitrust law. The penalties are then determined by legislation adopted under Article 83(2)(a) EC.

29. National Antitrust Authorities: Powers, Decisions and Penalties

29.1. POWERS AND DECISIONS

Article 84 EC, as already mentioned, refers to the 'authorities of the Member States' and thus identifies them as actors within the Community antitrust system. Bodies in the Member States were permitted to apply both Community antitrust law and national law as a result of the compromise reached during the drafting of the Treaty (*supra*). The fact that it was impossible to agree on whether the rules implementing Article 81(3) should be formulated according to the principle of abuse (as the French representatives advocated) or as a prohibition (as argued by Germany) had created an impasse. The compromise consisted in postponing the decision on the rules implementing Article 81(3) to a later stage, when a regulation under Article 83 would be adopted. Since it was important to make the antitrust prohibitions immediately operational, but provisionally impossible for the Commission to apply Article 81, the appropriate authorities (if any) in the Member States had to apply Articles 81 and 82 in place of the Commission. To that end, the Treaty conferred on them 'until the entry into force of the provisions adopted in pursuance of Article 83' the power to 'rule on the admissibility of agreements, decisions and concerted practices and on abuse of a dominant position in the common market'. This power was to be exercised not only 'in accordance with the law of their country' but also 'with the provisions of Article 81, in particular paragraph 3, and of Article 82'. Article 84 thus allowed Member States to continue to apply national law to agreements and abuses of a dominant position. Furthermore, pending the adoption of the first regulation to be adopted under Article 83 EC, Article 84 also gave them the discretion as to how, if at all, they would apply Article 81(3).

Member States wishing to exercise that power were required to identify:

- the body responsible for enforcing Articles 81 and 82;
- the procedures used to apply those articles; and

- the ways in which Article 81(3) was to be applied (these requirements are not very different from the system of designation provided for by Article 35 of Regulation 1/03, see *infra*).

So far as the Treaty is concerned, all that matters is that the Member States confer such power on a particular body. The structure, characteristics and legal nature of that body are left to the discretion of the Member States (compare Article 5 of Regulation 1/03, see *infra*).

Alongside the power of the national authorities to apply Articles 81 and 82, the EC Treaty confers power on the Commission to establish policy guidelines for the application of Community antitrust law. The Commission has the role of ensuring 'the application of the principles laid down in Articles 81 and 82'.

29.2. POWERS OF INVESTIGATION AND PENALTIES

The Treaty confers antitrust power but does not otherwise regulate how the national authorities are to apply Articles 81 and 82.

In consequence, the Treaty is silent on certain extremely important issues, such as the decisions which a national authority may adopt when it applies Articles 81 and 82, its powers to investigate infringements of those articles and the penalties which it may adopt for infringements of Community antitrust law.

In this respect, powers of investigation are particularly interesting.

The Treaty requires the Member States to collaborate with the Commission in cases which the Commission is investigating ('in cooperation with the competent authorities in the Member States, which shall give it their assistance'). However, the Treaty does not specify what investigative powers the Member States enjoy when they are engaged in the direct enforcement of Articles 81 and 82 and thus confers a broad margin of discretion as to the powers which the national authorities may exercise when, if at all, they apply Community antitrust law.

30. Mechanisms Allowing Cooperation between the Commission and National Antitrust Authorities

Articles 84 and 85 sketch out an embryonic structure which allows the Commission and the national authorities to cooperate with, and to monitor, each other.

The Treaty requires the national authorities to cooperate with the Commission in the investigation of infringements of Articles 81 and 82. It also sets out in summary form the powers which the Commission and national authorities have to investigate such infringements. Article 85(1) provides that 'the Commission shall investigate cases of suspected infringement of these principles' but Article 85(2) provides that 'the competent authorities of the Member States' are required to 'give it the assistance' necessary to investigate cases of alleged infringements of Community antitrust law. The cooperation of the national authorities with the Commission is required because, in the absence of any express regulation of its investigative powers, it is impossible for the Commission to carry out proceedings against undertakings.

31. Mechanisms Allowing the Commission and National Antitrust Authorities to Control Each Other

Articles 84 and 85 EC also specify how the Member States are to participate in investigations carried out by the Commission. Article 85(1) provides, *inter alia*, that 'in cooperation with the competent authorities of the Member States ... the Commission shall investigate cases of suspected infringement of these principles' laid down in Articles 81 and 82. Articles 84 and 85, which also require the competent authorities in the Member States to give the Commission their assistance in its investigation, underline that the national authorities have a twofold role. One is purely to implement antitrust procedures initiated by the Commission, while the other involves more active participation by providing for the cooperation of the national authorities.

In this way, these articles establish the principle of cooperation between the Commission and the national authorities at the stage of investigating presumed infringements and thus, indirectly, at the stage of adopting the decision (regarding the principle of cooperation between Commission and national authority in Regulation 1/03, see *infra*).

32. Judicial Enforcement of Antitrust Law

The system established by Articles 84 and 85 EC refers only to the Commission and 'the competent authorities in the Member States' as bodies applying Articles 81 and 82 EC. Unlike Regulation 1/03, those articles do not establish any specific rules relating to the role played by national courts within the Community antitrust system.

In the absence of directives or regulations adopted pursuant to Article 83 EC, national courts play a limited role in the system regulated by Articles 84 and 85 EC. This is because national courts apply and safeguard the rights conferred by Articles 81(1) and 82 EC by virtue of their direct effect. Although Article 82 EC has all the characteristics of a rule having direct effect, this is not the case with the prohibition of anticompetitive agreements.

In order to determine whether a particular agreement is automatically void by virtue of Article 81(2) EC, a national court must first examine whether the agreement is prohibited by virtue of Article 81(1). If it is, the court must also assess whether it can be exempted by virtue of Article 81(3).[1] Consequently, in order to determine in which cases the national courts may apply Article 81(3), the rules implementing that paragraph must have been adopted (according to the principle of prohibition or abuse) pursuant to Article 83(2)(b).[2]

In other words, until measures adopted pursuant to Article 83(1) EC have determined how Article 81(3) is to be adopted, Article 81(2) cannot be applied directly by national courts. In the absence of such a measure, they can avoid an agreement pursuant to Article 81(2) only where Article 81 has been applied by the Commission or the national authorities to a specific case. This means either that the Commission, acting under Article 85 EC, has assessed the agreement in the light of Article 81 or that the national authorities, acting under Article 84, have ruled on it and determined that it is prohibited by

---

[1] *Bosch*, Case 13/61, ECR 1962, English special edition 45; *Ahmed Saeed Flugreisen v. Zentrale Zur Bekaempfung Unlauteren Wettbewerbs*, Case 66/86, E.C.R. 1989, p. 803; *Brasserie de Haecht v. Wilkin-Janssen*, Case 48/72, E.C.R. 1973, p. 77.

[2] This issue is logically anterior to the different question whether national courts can apply a provision such as Article 81(3) EC inasmuch as it does not have a direct effect. For a discussion of the relationship between this statement and *Bosch*, see *infra*.

Article 81(1) and does not meet the requirements for exemption by virtue of Article 81(3).

PART IX

THE ANTITRUST ENFORCEMENT SYSTEM ESTABLISHED BY REGULATION 1/03

33. The Evolution of the Policy of Decentralising Antitrust Law

Before we examine Regulation 1/03 in detail, we need to look briefly at the events which led to its enactment. In particular, we shall consider:

- the objectives of Regulation 17/62, which was the first regulation implementing Articles 81 and 82;
- the development over the years of the antitrust system which made it necessary to amend Regulation 17/62;
- the development of the policy of decentralising Community antitrust law; and
- how this policy is implemented in Regulation 1/03.

33.1. THE ANTITRUST SYSTEM ESTABLISHED BY REGULATION 17/62

The first regulation implementing Articles 81 and 82 EC was adopted on 6 February 1962,[1] some five years after the signature of the Treaty of Rome and it entered into force on 13 March of the same year. It was repealed with effect from 30 April 2004. It had the following objectives:

1. to establish how Article 81(3) EC was to be applied;
2. to define powers within the Community antitrust system. Regulation 17/62 determined how Article 81(3) was to be applied (Article 1); the consequences of Commission decisions (Articles 2–8); and the bodies having power to apply Article 81(3) (Article 9).

In striking contrast to Regulation 1/03, relations between the Commission and the national authorities were not touched on in Regulation 17/62, The sole exception to this principle was Article 9 which regulated the powers of national authorities and the Commission's power to take over cases. This

[1] Council Regulation 17 of 6 February 1962, First Regulation implementing Articles 85 and 86 of the Treaty, 1962 OJ 13, 204 (English Special Edition 1959–1962, 87).

omission was understandable because at that time this relationship was unimportant. Moreover, some Member States had not even established a national competition authority which would apply Community law.

Regulation 17/62 gave rise to difficult negotiations at Council level despite the limited number of aspects that it dealt with (*infra*). It comprises only 24 articles and was thus very short in comparison with Regulation 1/03.

33.2. DEVELOPMENT OF THE COMMUNITY ANTITRUST SYSTEM FROM THE 1960S TO THE 1990S

Throughout the more than 40 years in which it was in force, Regulation 17/62 remained substantially unchanged (*supra*). At the same time, the Community system as a whole changed considerably. The changes were both legal and factual. The numerous amendments of the treaties bear witness to the legal changes, which were partly attributable to the increase in the number of Member States. An example of a practical change was the increasing number of cases which fell within the scope of Community antitrust law thanks to the 'completion' of the common market. These changes caused new problems in the Community antitrust system, especially with respect to the vertical relationship between the Commission and the competition bodies of the Member States.

The vertical relationship between the Commission and the national authorities and courts began to assume importance at the beginning of the 1990s as a result of the number of antitrust cases (Article 81(3) notifications, complaints and *ex officio* cases) dealt with by the Commission. Given the limited number of staff working for DG Competition, there were simply too many cases for the Commission to deal with.

The increase in the number of complaints made to the Commission was also mirrored in the United States and is a reflection of the growth in the number of cases having an effect on interstate trade. On the other hand, the number of notifications seeking exemption under Article 81(3) EC was a characteristic peculiar to the European antitrust system which it is worth examining briefly (regarding notification pursuant to Article 81(3) under Regulation 17/62, see *supra*).

The large number of notifications was attributable to the restrictive way in which Article 81(1) was interpreted. At an early stage, undertakings frequently notified agreements because they were unsure what attitude the Commission would have towards the interpretation of Article 81(1). Later on, they notified because it had transpired that the Commission's attitude was in fact restrictive. Non-notified agreements could be unlawful *ex tunc*, whereas if they were notified no penalties would be imposed even if the request for the exemption for an agreement infringing Article 81(1) were subsequently to be rejected. This factor made it advisable for undertakings to notify agreements.

The high number of notifications was also attributable to the restrictive interpretation of Article 4(2) of Regulation 17/62. This was a provision which aimed to reduce the number of cases in which a notification had to be made in respect of agreements implemented by undertakings which were active in the same Member State.[2]

Initially, the Commission had tackled the problem posed by the large number of notifications by means of stop-gap solutions.

In the 1960s, the first solution to be tried was the adoption of a number of block exemption regulations. Undertakings were thus relieved of the need to notify specified categories of agreement.

The second device to which the Commission had recourse in order to stem the increase in its workload was 'comfort letters'. These were used to inform companies which had notified agreements that they did (or did not) appear to fulfil the conditions for obtaining an exemption or that they fell within the scope of a block exemption regulation. However, the non-binding nature of comfort letters and consequent lack of legal certainty obviously limited their utility for the notifying undertakings.[3]

By the beginning of the 1990s, the workload that notifications and the enforcement of Articles 81 and 82 represented for the Commission became impossible to manage. The extra increase in the Commission's activity is largely attributable to the completion of the internal market at the end of 1992. This, in turn, increased the importance of Community antitrust law at the time when the legal barriers between Member States had gradually been abolished. The elimination of legal barriers encouraged Community-wide investments and economic activity that had at least a potential effect on trade between Member States and to which Community antitrust law was thus applicable. The increased workload, allied to the limited number of Commission staff, led to the Commission handling requests for exemption extremely slowly. This slowness was recognised by the Court of Justice[4] and it even had an influence on the definition of the scope of Italian antitrust law (Pace, 2000b).

The Commission thus needed to find a way to reduce its workload in this area, quite independently of the question of amending Regulation 17/62.

In this period, the issue of the Commission's inability to cope with its workload assumed importance in the context of the vertical relationship

---

[2] See *Brauerei Bilger v. Heinrich Jehle*, Case 43-69, E.C.R. 1970, p. 127.

[3] See, for example, judgment in *Anne Marty SA v Estée Lauder*, Case 37/79 E.C.R. 1980, p. 2481.

[4] See judgment in *Brasserie de Haecht v Wilkin-Janssen*, Case 48/72, E.C.R. 1973, p. 77.

between the Commission and the national authorities. The Commission attempted to solve the problem through its strategy of decentralising Community antitrust law.

33.3. THE POLICY OF DECENTRALISATION IN THE 1990S AND THE AMENDMENT OF REGULATION 17/62

The policy of decentralising Community antitrust law in the 1990s was implemented in two ways.

The first way was to limit the Commission's direct enforcement activities. This was done:

- by initiating investigations applying Articles 81 and 82 only in cases of 'Community interest'; and
- by 'prioritising' the assessment of the complaints made to it.

This allowed the Commission both to close the file on complaints which were of no interest for Community competition policy and to defer the examination of cases which were not considered important for the protection of the common market.[5]

The second way was to decentralise the application of Articles 81(1) and 82 in order to maintain the same level of antitrust enforcement through enforcement by national bodies. This policy was implemented following two guidelines:

- with respect to the national authorities, the Commission's aim was to ensure that they always applied Community antitrust law or at least that if they applied national law, they reached the same results as if they had applied Community law (Pace, 1999, p. 270);[6] and

[5] On this point, there were around 40 judgments in a single decade. Among the more important, see *Automec Srl v. Commission*, Case T-24/90, E.C.R. 1992, p. II–2223; *IECC v Commission*, Case C-449/98 P, E.C.R. 2001, p. I–3875; *Masterfoods Ltd v. HB Ice Cream Ltd*, Case C-344/98, E.C.R. 2000, p. I–11369; *SFEI v Commission*, Case C-119/97 P, E.C.R. 1999, p. I–1341; *IECC v Commission*, Case C-450/98 P, E.C.R. 2001, p. I–3947; *Tremblay v Commission*, Case C-91/95 P, E.C.R. 1996, p. I–5547.

[6] On this point, see Commission Notice on cooperation between national competition authorities and the Commission in handling cases falling within the scope of Articles 85 or 86 of the EC Treaty, 1997 OJ C 313, p. 3, paragraph 16.

- with regard to national courts, the Commission had explained in a notice how decentralised application of Articles 81 and 82 was possible.[7]

We can therefore see that the policy of decentralisation, as developed in the 1990s, had two objectives:

- the first was to ensure that the national authorities and courts applied Community antitrust law rather than national law; and
- the second was to absorb the national authorities into the Community antitrust system.

However, without reform of Regulation 17/62, there were no tailor-made procedures to ensure that the measures by which national bodies applied national law came to the same conclusions which the Commission itself would have reached.

33.4. THE POLICY OF DECENTRALISATION IN THE PROPOSAL FOR A REGULATION OF 2000

The unsatisfactory results of that form of decentralisation of Community antitrust law made reform of Regulation 17/62 necessary. The Commission outlined how it envisaged revision of the Regulation in the 'White Paper on the modernisation of the rules implementing Articles 85 and 86 of the EC Treaty' of 1999. Reform would entail the following:

- All national authorities or courts before which the applicability of Article 81(1) of the Treaty was invoked would also consider the applicability of Article 81(3) (White Paper, paragraph 69). Reform would entail repeal of Article 9(1) of Regulation 17/62, which conferred exclusive competence to apply Article 81(3) EC on the Commission. This repeal would mean that national authorities and courts would also be able to apply that provision (White Paper, paragraph 69).
- The proposal also envisaged the establishment of a coordinated Network to facilitate collaboration between Commission and national authorities in the application of Articles 81 and 82 (White Paper, paragraph 91).

---

[7] Notice on cooperation between national courts and the Commission in applying Articles 85 and 86 of the EEC Treaty, 1993 OJ C 39, p. 6.

In 2000, following the White Paper, the Commission adopted a proposal for a regulation based on Article 83 EC.[8] In the proposal, the strategy for implementing decentralisation had been slightly amended and comprised three distinct strands:

1. The reduction of the Commission's direct enforcement activities so as to allow it to concentrate on the most important cases.
2. In line with the policy that the Commission had pursued during the 1990s, the proposal envisaged that Community antitrust law alone would be applied to cases having Community relevance (Article 3 of the proposal). National authorities and courts handling cases falling within the scope of Community antitrust law, which economically and politically would be the most important, would thus not be entitled to apply national law. Instead, they would be required to apply only Community antitrust law. This policy had a three-fold advantage for the Commission.

   - the failure of the national authorities to apply Community law and the failure of private parties to plead Community law before the courts would be resolved;
   - since national law would no longer be applied to cases having Community relevance, the risk of applying national antitrust law in a way which was inconsistent with Community law would be eliminated; and
   - the costs for the obligation to comply with both the antitrust law of the Community and that of the Member States entailed for undertakings would be eliminated.

3. The proposal for a regulation also provided procedures to assess whether bodies in the Member States had correctly applied Community competition policy (Proposal for a Regulation, Article 15(3), second part, paragraphs 11–16). This was the first time that such procedures had been envisaged.

33.5. THE POLICY OF DECENTRALISATION AS IMPLEMENTED IN REGULATION 1/03

The policy of antitrust decentralisation as implemented by Regulation 1/03 is

[8] Proposal for a Council Regulation on the implementation of the rules on competition laid down in Articles 81 and 82 of the Treaty and amending Regulations (EEC) 1017/68, (EEC) 2988/74, (EEC) 4056/86 and (EEC) 3975/87 ('Regulation implementing Articles 81 and 82 of the Treaty'), 2000 OJ C 365 E, pp. 284–296.

made up of four components.[9] These are, once again, different from the

---

[9] Council Regulation (EC) 1/2003 of 16 December 2002 on the implementation of the rules on competition laid down in Articles 81 and 82 of the Treaty, 2003 OJ L 1, p. 1.

The rules implementing Articles 81 and 82 EC are made up of the following regulations and communications:

- Regulation 773/2004 Relating to the Conduct of Proceedings by the Commission Pursuant to Articles 81 and 82 of the EC Treaty, 2004 OJ L 123/18.
- Notice on the Handling of Complaints by the Commission under Articles 81 and 82 of the EC Treaty, 2004 OJ C 101/65.
- Notice on Informal Guidance Relating to Novel Questions concerning Articles 81 and 82 that Arise in Individual Cases (Guidance Letters), 2004 OJ 101/78.
- Guidelines on the Method of Setting Fines imposed pursuant to Article 23(2)(a) of Regulation 1/2003, 2006 OJ C 210/02.
- Commission Notice on Immunity from fines and reduction of fines in cartel cases, 2006 OJ C 298/11.
- Notice on Cooperation within the Network of Competition Authorities (European Competition Network – ECN), 2004 OJ C 101/43;
- Notice on the Cooperation between the Commission and the Courts of the EU Member States, 2004 OJ C 101/54.

As regards the sectors in respect of which special rules apply, see:

- Agriculture – Council Regulation 1184/2006 of 24 July 2006 applying certain rules of competition to the production of, and trade in, agricultural products, 2006 OJ L 214/7;
- Insurance – Commission Regulation (EC) No 358/2003 of 27 February 2003 on the application of Article 81(3) of the Treaty to certain categories of agreements, decisions and concerted practices in the insurance sector (Text with EEA relevance), in 2003 OJ L 53/8.
- Inland Transport – Regulation 1017/68 on Rail, Road and Inland Waterway Transport, 1968 OJ L 175/1.
- Maritime Transport – Council Regulation No 1419/2006 of 25 September 2006 repealing Regulation 4056/86 laying down detailed rules for the application of Articles 85 and 86 of the Treaty to maritime transport, and amending Regulation 1/2003 as regards the extension of its scope to include cabotage and international tramp services, 2006 OJ L 269/1; Regulation 823/2000 on the Application of Article 81(3) to Liner Shipping Companies, 2000 OJ L 100/24 (Amended by Regulation 463/2004, 2004 OJ L 77/23).
- Air Transport – Regulation 411/2004 of 26 February 2004 amending regulations 3976/87 and 1/2003, in connection with air transport between the community and third countries, 2004 OJ L 68/1; Regulation 847/2004 on the negotiation and implementation of air service agreements between member states and third countries, 2004 OJ L 157/7.
- Energy – Directive 2003/54/EC Concerning Common Rules for the Internal Market in Electricity, 2003 OJ L 176/37; Directive 2003/55/EC Concerning Common Rules for the Internal Market in Natural Gas, 2003 OJ L 176/57, corr. 2004 OJ L 16/74.
- Electronic Communications – Guidelines on the Application of EC Competition Rules in the Telecommunications Sector, 1991 OJ C 233/2; Directive 2002/21/EC on a Common Regulatory Framework for Electronic Communications Networks and Services (Framework Directive), 2002 OJ L 108/33; Access Interconnection Directive, 2002/19/EC, 2002 OJ L 108/7; Authorization Directive, 2002/20/EC, 2002 OJ L 108/21; Universal Service Directive, 2002/22/EC, 2002 OJ L 108/51; Directive on privacy and electronic communications, 2002/58/EC, 2002 OJ L 201/37; Decision on a regulatory framework for radio spectrum policy in the European Community (Radio Spectrum Decision), Decision 676/2002/EC, 2002 OJ L 108/1; Regulation 2887/2000 on unbundled access to the local loop, 2000 OJ L 336/4; Directive 2002/77/EC on competition in the markets for electronic communications networks and services, 2002

components of the proposal for a regulation of 2000. Nevertheless, the reduction of the Commission's workload and the involvement of the Member State bodies in Community antitrust enforcement, which were the two most general objectives of the proposal, have remained intact (see the Commission's notice on guidance letters, paragraphs 1 and 6 and the Notice on the handling of complaints, paragraph 11).

The four components of the policy of decentralisation in Regulation 1/03 are as follows:

1. Reduction of the Commission's workload.
2. Article 3(1) of the Regulation requires the national authorities and courts to apply Articles 81 and 82 to cases of Community relevance. They may also apply national antitrust law to those cases in parallel with Community antitrust law. The Regulation does not, therefore, provide for the exclusive application of Community law to cases of Community relevance.
3. The establishment of procedures:

   - to ensure that the national authorities and courts apply Articles 81 and 82 EC in line with the competition policy defined by the Commission; and
   - to facilitate mutual cooperation in the application of Community law (see *infra*).

   Those procedures are relevant for the application of Articles 81 and 82 EC. They also allow it to be ascertained whether any parallel application of national antitrust law leads to results which infringe the principle of the effectiveness of Community antitrust law (see *supra*, and Article 3(2) of Regulation 1/03).
4. The Regulation introduces a new component of the decentralisation strategy, namely the *de facto* exclusive application of Community antitrust law to agreements falling within the scope of Article 81 EC, which was assumed to be necessary in order to create 'a level playing field for agreements, decisions by associations of undertakings and concerted practices within the internal market' (Recital 8). By virtue of Article 3(2) of the Regulation, the application of any prohibition of anticompetitive agreements provided by national law must come to the same conclusion that would have been reached had Article 81 EC been applied. Article 3(2) thus purports to safeguard the internal market by reducing the number of cases in which the application of national antitrust law leads to results

---

OJ L 249/21; Decision establishing the European Regulators Group for electronic communications networks and services, Decision 627/2002/EC, 2002 OJ L 200/38.

which are at odds with Community law (albeit in conformity with the principle of effectiveness, see *supra*). In so doing, it establishes an exception to the principle of the effectiveness of Community antitrust law for agreements falling within the scope of Article 81 EC (see *supra* for discussion of the illegality of Article 3(2)). Upon closer examination, it is apparent that the aim of Article 3(2) of the Regulation is similar to that of Article 3 of the proposal of 2000, that is, to reduce the costs required for companies to align themselves with both national and Community antitrust law. (The purpose cannot be to eliminate costs entirely, since Article 3(2) only applies in respect of Article 81 EC.) The last part of Article 12(2) of the Regulation also creates an incentive for national authorities applying national laws that prohibit the abuse of a dominant position to reach the same results as if they were applying Article 82 EC. Articles 3(2) and 12(2) thus re-introduce *de facto* the principle of the exclusive application of Community antitrust law which was embodied in Article 3 of the proposal for a regulation in 2000.

The Regulation undoubtedly represents a historic achievement. We can better appreciate the scale of what has been achieved if we bear in mind the debates which took place and the difficulties which were encountered in the 1930s when attempts were made to establish an international Network of states to control cartels (*supra*).

Having said this, there are some doubts as to whether the Regulation can ensure the level of antitrust control which it aims to provide.

While the Regulation's objective is to reduce the scale of the Commission's direct enforcement activity against undertakings, it provides for a number of procedures that allow the Commission to monitor measures taken by the national authorities and courts when they apply Community antitrust law. In other words, under the Regulation, the Commission does not merely remain active on the enforcement side. In order to ensure that Community antitrust law is consistently applied in 27 Member States, the Commission's activities are actually expanded. They have now been extended from undertakings whose behaviour has an impact on the Community legal order, which was the case under Regulation 17/62, to 27 national authorities and a much greater number of national courts.

We may therefore legitimately ask how the new objectives of cooperation and control can be reconciled with the 'lack of human resources from which the institution suffers', as the Commission recently admitted.[10] The risk is that the Commission's workload – which is excessive in relation to the number of staff – will continue to be the main impediment to the effective application of

[10] See *CMA CGM v. Commission*, Case T-213/00, E.C.R. 2003, p. II–913, § 320.

the Regulation, despite the fact that this was precisely the problem which the Regulation was supposed to tackle. However, in order to eliminate that risk, it is unnecessary to amend Regulation 1/03. It would be sufficient to make a – considerable – increase in the budget and the staff of DG Competition.

Due to the number and complexity of its objectives, Regulation 1/03 is longer than Regulation 17/62. It contains 38 recitals and 45 articles, whereas Regulation 17/62 contained only 12 recitals and 24 articles. However, Regulation 1/03 treats matters in the same order as Regulation 17/62 although it deals with them in 11 separate chapters: I. Principles; II. Powers; III. Commission Decisions; IV. Cooperation; V. Powers of Investigation; VI. Penalties; VII. Limitation Periods; VIII. Hearings and Professional Secrecy; IX. Exemption Regulations; X. General Provisions; and XI. Transitional, Amending and Final Provisions.

33.6. REGULATION 1/03 SEEN FROM A HISTORICAL PERSPECTIVE

It is worthwhile examining in their historical context the difficulties which the authors of Regulation 1/03 encountered at the beginning of the 21st century when they were creating a new system for the enforcement of Community law. Albeit the historical context is very different, the significance of the result can be better appreciated if we compare the objective of the Regulation with the attempts of the 1930 International Conference to create an interstate cartel control system.

Paradoxically, the authors of Regulation 1/03 were faced with the same problems that had been encountered in the 1930s. The Regulation needed to allow national authorities and courts to exercise control over the behaviour of undertakings even when the effects of that behaviour were felt outside the relevant state's sovereign territory (*supra*). It had to allow intervention to be effective and immediate. Ways therefore had to be found to overcome the problem of slowness, which is an inherent feature of international cooperation procedures between states. Effective control of cross-border infringements would have been extremely complex if it had been carried out exclusively under the domestic laws of the different Member States. For example, it would have been virtually impossible for the officials of the various national authorities to carry out surprise inspections on the premises of undertakings in other Member States. Even if other Community Member States had been cooperative, the national authorities would not have been able rapidly to obtain relevant information from outside their own state. Quite the contrary, requests for action at the international level made by national authorities might have been held up by the Member States themselves so as not to cause harm to undertakings operating on their own territory.

In the first part of the 20th century, the issue could not be solved precisely because it was difficult to create a network between different states. In the discussions which took place in the 1930s on the control of cartels at European level,

> [S]ome argued that such control should be international, whereas others took the view that, given the limited scope of cartels, each country should take the appropriate enforcement measures against cartels. In practice, private agreement could have been policed by the state in which the agreement produced effects. In reality, it would be difficult to organize a joint control by all states. (De Novellis, 1931, p. 151)

De facto, it was accepted that individual nation states were unable to tackle the problem. Capitalistic activity carried out beyond the confines of individual states by individual undertakings or by means of agreements was so extensive that every state should have accepted that it was unable to exercise control independently. To that end, the state had had to abandon part of its own powers to international organisations, such as the ECSC and the European Community, which were capable of dealing with these questions. In other words, halfway through the 20th century, in Europe the national state had shown that 'its writ would not run' on the market. Since, on the one hand, 'the State exists in so far as it can command and its value lies in being able to enforce its command' (Orlando, 1954, p. 219) and, on the other, it was incapable of regulating all conduct taking place on its own territory, it was plainly shown that in Europe the state as such was in crisis.

For the authors of Regulation 1/03, the problems were solved more straightforwardly. The difference, in comparison with the 1930s, was the existence of the European system, a supranational legal order whose rules were applicable simultaneously in all the territories of the states belonging to the organisation. Furthermore, those rules were interpreted consistently thanks to the existence of a centralised legal body, the Court of Justice. In other words, in order to solve the problem of antitrust control, Regulation 1/03 made full use of the new features which the Community order had at its disposal.

The Regulation established the Network of competition authorities. This is a closed network of bodies belonging to different states required to apply Community antitrust law.

Its 'interorganic' functioning is regulated by Community law and the purpose of the system is to maintain competition at Community level. Through the Network, which has been established to apply Community competition law, an authority may rapidly obtain documents and information from areas which are not subject to the sovereignty of its state.

Without the existence of the Community system, the antitrust control established by Regulation 1/03 could not have been applied throughout the European Union: an antitrust system extends from the North Sea to the Mediterranean Sea, and from the Atlantic Ocean to the Black Sea.

34. The Commission: Decisions, Powers of Investigation and Penalties

34.1. DECISIONS

The first chapter of Regulation 1/03 (Articles 1 to 3) sets out the principles of the Regulation. Chapter II (Articles 4 to 6) then allocates powers to the bodies which apply Articles 81 and 82 EC.

Article 4 refers to the Commission's powers. Although the general power of the Commission is already provided for in Article 85 EC, Article 4 of Regulation 1/03 is needed because a new system of antitrust enforcement replacing the system provided for by Articles 84 and 85 EC has been adopted. Consequently the bodies constituting the new system and their respective powers have to be specified.

To a large extent, the powers conferred on the Commission are the same as those that it enjoyed by virtue of Regulation 17/62. However, Regulation 1/03 introduces three new powers:

- Article 7(1) confers power on the Commission to impose structural remedies on undertakings which have infringed Articles 81 and 82 EC;
- Article 21 confers the power to carry out inspections of premises which were formerly off limits; and
- Article 29 confers a general power on the Commission to withdraw the benefit of a block exemption regulation.

Regulation 1/03 sets out the decisions which the Commission may take and also contains rules relating to their publication. Those decisions are as follows:

- decisions finding an infringement and decisions requiring an infringement to be brought to an end (Article 7);
- interim measures (Article 8);
- commitments (Article 9);
- findings of inapplicability (Article 10); and
- decisions withdrawing the benefit of a block exemption (Article 29).

A sixth type of decision, which is not specifically mentioned in the Regulation, should be added. This is the decision rejecting a complaint, otherwise known as a decision to close the file on a case. That type of decision plays an important role in the context of the new regulation (see *infra*).

34.1.1. Decisions Finding an Infringement and Requiring it to be Terminated

The first type of decision falling under Chapter III, entitled 'Commission Decisions', is the decision finding an infringement and requiring it to be brought to an end.

Article 7(1) provides that 'where the Commission, acting on a complaint or on its own initiative, finds that there is an infringement of Article 81 or of Article 82 of the Treaty, it may by decision require the undertaking and associations of undertakings concerned to bring such infringement to an end'. By virtue of Article 7(2), 'natural or legal persons who can show a legitimate interest and Member States' are entitled to lodge a complaint.

As regards the content of the decision, the Commission may impose on the addressees of the decision 'any behavioural or structural remedies which are proportionate to the infringement committed and necessary to bring the infringement effectively to an end'. The power to impose structural remedies is new for the Commission[1] and is not conferred on the national authorities. Article 7 goes on to stipulate that 'structural remedies can only be imposed either when there is no equally effective behavioural remedy or where any equally effective behavioural remedy would be more burdensome for the undertaking concerned than the structural remedy'. Even if the infringement has already ceased, the Commission retains the power to find that there has been an infringement of Articles 81 and 82 EC 'if it has a legitimate interest in doing so'.

34.1.2. Interim Measures

Regulation 1/03 expressly confers power on the Commission to order interim measures. The Court of Justice had granted the Commission this power while Regulation 17/62 was in force, albeit it was not specifically provided for in the Regulation.[2] Article 8(1) provides that the Commission, acting on its own initiative, may decide to order interim measures 'on the basis of a *prima facie*

---

[1] The Commission did not enjoy this power prior to the entry into force of Regulation 1/03. See *Automec Srl v. Commission*, Case T-24/90, E.C.R. 1992, p. II–2223, § 52.

[2] See Order in *Camera Care*, Case 792/79 R, E.C.R. 1980, p. 119.

finding of infringement'. The exercise of this power is subject to the condition that there is 'urgency due to the risk of serious and irreparable damage to competition'.

Decisions ordering interim measures 'shall apply for a specified period of time and may be renewed in so far as this is necessary and appropriate' (Article 8(2)).

34.1.3. Decision Withdrawing the Benefit of a Block Exemption Regulation

Article 29 allows the Commission to withdraw the benefit of a block exemption regulation where it 'has declared Article 81(1) of the Treaty inapplicable to certain categories of agreements, decisions by associations of undertakings or concerted practices'.

In such a case, the Commission 'may, acting on its own initiative or on a complaint, withdraw the benefit of such an exemption Regulation when it finds that in any particular case an agreement, decision or concerted practice to which the exemption Regulation applies has certain effects which are incompatible with Article 81(3) of the Treaty'.

Article 29(2) of the Regulation confers an analogous power on the national antitrust authorities (*infra*).

34.1.4. Decisions Suspending or Terminating Proceedings

Turning now to decisions promoting the Commission's decentralisation policy, Regulation 1/03 provides for two ways of limiting the Commission's direct enforcement activity:

- first, the Commission is not required to take a decision on the substance of each complaint made to it. It may close the file on a case which has no Community interest (Article 7). It may likewise reject a complaint on the ground that a national authority is dealing with, or has already dealt with, a case. This power, which is conferred by Article 13(1) and (2), is a new feature of Regulation 1/03; and
- second, Regulation 1/03 makes provision for specific decisions which enable the Commission's direct enforcement activities to be reduced. These are decisions relating to commitments made by undertakings (Article 9) and findings of inapplicability (Article 10).

As regards the first way in which Regulation 1/03 allows the Commission's enforcement activities to be reduced, there are two cases in which the Commission may close the file on a case without adopting a decision on the substance.

The Commission's general power to close the file on complaints (Article 7)

Article 7 regulates the Commission's general power to close the file on complaints made to it. It provides that 'where the Commission ... finds that there is an infringement of Article 81 or of Article 82 of the Treaty, it may by decision require the undertakings and associations of undertakings concerned to bring such infringement to an end'. The permissive language used (that is, 'where the Commission finds ... it may ... require'), confers a power, but not an obligation, to adopt a decision on the facts of the particular case. The right not to take a decision, which was conferred on the Commission in the case law decided in the 1990s,[3] is limited to situations in which there is no Community interest. In other words, Article 7 confers power on the Commission to adopt a decision rejecting a complaint. This type of decision, which is not put on a formal basis by Regulation 1/03, is final and binding on individuals and therefore constitutes a challengeable act. When adopting such a measure, the Commission must set out the reasons which have led it to close the file on the case. This contrasts with the procedure under Article 13, which does not require the Commission to give similar reasons.

The specific power of the Commission and the national authorities to reject a complaint or close proceedings (Article 13)

Article 13 likewise grants the Commission the power not to take a decision on the substance of every complaint made to it and confers a similar power on the national authorities. Article 13 allows the Commission to reject a complaint in two cases:

1. Where the same case is being dealt with by a national authority (Article 13(1)).
2. Where the complaint has 'already been dealt with by another competition authority' (Article 13(2)). In that situation, the expression 'complaint ... which has already been dealt with by another competition authority' refers to two separate situations:

   - it concerns cases in which the national authority has reached a decision on substance (such as a prohibition decision or a decision finding that no infringement has taken place); and

---

[3] *Automec Srl v. Commission*, op. cit..

- it concerns cases in which an authority decides that there are no grounds for action because it does not have sufficient evidence to prove an infringement (Article 5 last paragraph).

The type of decision referred to in Article 13(1)–(2), whereby the Commission rejects a complaint, is not the same as a decision to reject or 'close the file on' a complaint for lack of Community interest (see *supra*). When it rejects a complaint pursuant to Article 13, the Commission is not required to give detailed reasons but may simply refer to the power granted it by that article.

The purpose of a rejection pursuant to Article 13 differs according to whether it is taken by the Commission or by a national authority:

1. Rejection by the Commission may be justified on the ground of a lack of Community interest in investigating the complaint. However, even when it has rejected a complaint, the Commission still retains the possibility of monitoring any decision which the national authority might take. This can be done in ways which are both direct (through its power under Article 11(3)) and binding (by means of its power to take over cases pursuant to Article 11(6)).
2. When a national authority rejects a complaint pursuant to Article 13, it does so not by reason of a lack of Community interest but because the case is of no particular interest for it and another national authority is in a better position to carry out investigations. In this situation, the national authority relinquishing the case, unlike the Commission, has at its disposal only an indirect means of monitoring the assessment made by the authority taking over the case (Article 14(7)). This provision allows the authority which rejected the complaint to ask for the case to be put on the agenda of the Advisory Committee (see *infra*).

Article 13 does not specify the consequences which ensue for the Commission or a national authority when a national court, as opposed to a national authority, is dealing with, or has already dealt with, a case. However, the Court of Justice has held that the fact that a competition case has been brought before a court is a factor which can be taken into account in deciding whether to close the file on a complaint brought in respect of the same facts. Article 13's silence on the point can probably be explained by the fact that the 'Commission-national courts' relationship, unlike the 'Commission-national authorities' relationship, provides no 'bridge' towards Community antitrust competence. This is so because national courts must always be entitled to apply Articles 81(1) and 82 in order to safeguard the rights which those articles confer.[4] For that reason, the national courts are not part of the administrative system for the enforcement of Community law and the principle of applying 'the Community competition rules in close cooperation' set out in Article 11(1) of the Regulation does not apply to them (*infra*).

34.1.5. Decisions Accepting Commitments Offered by Undertakings

In addition to granting the Commission the power not to take a decision on the substance of a case, Regulation 1/03 contains a second way to enable the Commission's enforcement activity to be reduced. It does this by providing for two types of decision:

- a decision making commitments binding on undertakings (Article 9); and
- a finding of inapplicability (Article 10).

Commitment decisions may be taken where the Commission has initiated an investigation against undertakings. The latter are entitled to 'offer commitments' concerning the behaviour which is the subject of the proceedings where the Commission intends to adopt a decision requiring that the infringement be brought to an end.[5] The commitments must 'meet the concerns expressed … by the Commission in its preliminary assessment'. In that case, 'the Commission may by decision make those commitments binding on the undertakings'. Such a decision 'may be adopted for a specified period' and must conclude that there are no longer grounds for action by the Commission.[6] This is without prejudice to the Commission's power to reopen the proceedings upon request or on its own initiative in certain specified cases.[7] Thanks to this power, the Commission may halt an investigation after

---

[4] *Belgische Radio en Televisie v. Sv Sabam e Nv Fonior*, Case 127/73, E.C.R. 1974, p. 51.

[5] The first decision adopted under Article 9 was a Commission decision of 17 September 2004 on the request made by the German Football League concerning the joint selling of the rights to the German Bundesliga (IP/04/1110). See also the Article 9 proceedings initiated on 18 October 2004 when Coca-Cola offered the Commission commitments relating to its distribution network (IP/04/1247).

[6] This type of decision is the result of the Commission's experience in regulating mergers. The Merger Regulation provides for a similar power (Articles 6(2) and 8(2) of Regulation 4064/89, which have now been replaced by the identically numbered articles of Regulation 139/04). The Commission also acquired a similar experience in the interminable IECC case. See *International Express Carriers Conference (IECC) v Commission*, Case T-110/95, E.C.R. 1998, p. II–3605; *IECC v Commission*, Joined Cases T-133/95 and T-204/95, E.C.R. 1998, p. II–3645 and, on appeal, *IECC v Commission*, Case C-449/98 P, E.C.R. 2001, p. I–3875. See in particular, Recital 30 of the preamble to Regulation 139/04.

[7] Article 9(2) sets out the circumstances in which the Commission may reopen proceedings. It reads as follows:

The Commission may, upon request or on its own initiative, reopen the proceedings:

making a 'preliminary assessment', and hence before adopting a decision under Article 7 requiring the undertakings to bring such infringement to an end, and instead make the commitments binding on the undertakings that offered them.

Although this is the first time that this type of decision has been placed on a formal footing, it corresponds to a practice which the Commission adopted in the *International Express Carriers Conference* (*IECC*) proceedings (see *supra*, footnote 6). In that case the Commission had attempted to conclude the investigation first by accepting commitments from the undertakings concerned and, at a later stage, by claiming that there was no Community interest in continuing it.

The decision accepting commitments is extremely interesting and merits close examination.

The transparency of the negotiation process

The issue of the transparency of the process of negotiation between the firms which offer the undertakings and the Commission (or national authority) which accepts them is an aspect of Article 9 decisions that raises concerns. There is a danger that the Commission's decision will not be taken solely in the public interest in that it may be 'captured' by the undertaking (this phenomenon is known as 'regulatory capture'). In other words, the authority may act in the interest of the undertaking rather than in the public interest.

Another danger is that, instead of risking a challenge against a decision which has not been properly prepared, the Commission may prefer to do a deal with the undertakings concerned and come to a 'benevolent' conclusion. In so doing it *ipso facto* neglects the public interest.

In this context, the US experience of consent decrees in the antitrust area provides a useful point of comparison. Consent decrees are measures taken by the federal antitrust authorities (that is, the Department of Justice and the Federal Trade Commission), with a view to terminating investigations before a decision on the substance has been taken (on the rules governing consent decrees, see Von Kalinowski et al., 2000, § 96.01). The undertakings involved in the proceedings are encouraged to agree to a consent decree in order to avoid the risk of losing the case. An incentive to do this exists since, if a decision finding an infringement were to be taken, competitors and

---

where there has been a material change in any of the facts on which the decision was based;

where the undertakings concerned act contrary to their commitments;

where the decision was based on incomplete, incorrect or misleading information provided by the parties.

After having reopened the proceedings, the Commission may subsequently take a final decision pursuant to Article 7 or, as the case may be, a fresh commitment decision under Article 9.

consumers could easily sue for compensation for the loss caused by the infringement and obtain treble damages (see ibid., § 160).

The US experience with consent decrees shows how important economic interests involved in the proceedings can 'hijack' the regulator. Initially, consent decrees became effective once they had been approved by the antitrust regulator. Towards the end of the 1960s, the *ITT* case called into question the independence of the regulator from lobbying by the parties and thus cast doubt on whether the negotiated decision was in the public interest.

Following this case, an attempt was made to solve the problem by enacting the Antitrust Procedures and Penalties Act, more generally known as the Tunney Act (15 U.S.C. 16 (b)–(h)). This act required a consent decree to be approved by an independent court which would assess whether it was compatible with the public interest (see Flynn and Bush, 2003, p. 749). In the memorandum to the Act, it is explained that: 'To bring the consent decree process into the full light of day … the Act will make our courts an independent force rather than a rubber stamp in reviewing consent decrees, and it will ensure that the courtroom rather than the back room becomes the final arbiter in antitrust enforcement' (in Von Kalinowski et al., 2000, § 96.03).

The issue of whether a commitment decision under Article 9 of Regulation 1/03 is compatible with the public interest has not been addressed in Regulation 1/03. Nor does the Regulation provide any means to ensure that 'regulatory capture' does not occur. It cannot, therefore, be guaranteed that the Commission's decision will be taken in order to safeguard the public interest. As was the case in the United States before the ITT scandal, the only safeguard against potential abuses of Article 9 decisions is the reasoning which the Commission is required to adopt to support its decisions. (The same point applies in the case of decisions of national authorities.) The reasoning of an Article 9 decision will allow individuals to assess the measure and, if appropriate, bring proceedings to have it annulled. However, they will not be able to challenge the merits (that is, the complex economic analysis which the Commission has carried out in adopting the decision, *infra*), since this cannot be evaluated by the court.

A solution at Community level is badly needed. However, a provisional solution to eliminate the risk of abuse of commitment decisions could be for the Commission and the national authorities voluntarily to insert a passage in the reasoning supporting an Article 9 decision in which they expressly examine whether the decision is consistent with the 'Community public interest'.

The issue of transparency and safeguarding of the Community interest is even more problematic as regards commitment decisions taken by the national authorities. By virtue of Article 5 of the Regulation, national authorities also have the power to issue such decisions. In the light of the role which Article 84 EC confers on them, their decisions on commitments must also be taken with the intention of safeguarding the Community public interest. National authorities can more easily be 'hijacked' by undertakings than can the Commission for the following reasons:

1. The ways in which the authorities are structured and their independence guaranteed are not uniform throughout the Member States. This means that the authorities' capacity to resist outside influences also varies from one Member State to another.[8]
2. European public opinion will pay less attention to whether national authorities' commitment decisions are compatible with the Community public interest than it will when such decisions are taken by the Commission.

However, at least a partial solution to this last problem is provided by both the system of vertical descending ('top-down') control exercised by the Commission pursuant to Article 11(3) of the Regulation and the 'peer control' carried out by the national authorities under Article 14(7) (*infra*).

The dubious legality of Articles 9 and 5 of Regulation 1/03

The question of the legality of both Articles 9 and 5 of Regulation 1/03 is also a live issue. The legitimacy of commitment decisions is closely linked with the case law on the principle of the effectiveness of Community antitrust law, in particular the effect of Articles 81 and 82 EC taken in conjunction with Article 10 EC. It is settled case law that, although Articles 81 and 82 EC are in themselves 'concerned solely with the conduct of undertakings and not with measures adopted by Member States by law or regulation, the fact remains that [Articles 81 and 82 EC], taken in conjunction with Article [10], require the Member States not to introduce or maintain in force measures, even of a legislative nature, which may render ineffective the competition rules applicable to undertakings'.[9] Referring in particular to the combined effect of Articles 10 and 81, the Court went on to say that 'such would be the case if a Member State were to require or favour the adoption of agreements, decisions or concerted practices contrary to Article 81 or to reinforce their effects, or to deprive its own rules of the character of legislation by delegating to private economic operators responsibility for taking decisions affecting the economic sphere'.[10]

[8] See *Syfait v. GlaxoSmithKline*, Case C-53/03, 2005, p. I–4609.
[9] *Commission v Italy*, Case C-35/96, E.C.R. 1998, p. I-3851, § 53.
[10] *Commission v Italy*, ibid., § 54.

Although this case law was developed with reference to national rules, the reasoning underlying it, which is that the effectiveness of Articles 81 and 82 EC must be maintained, is applicable *mutatis mutandis* to the Community institutions. There is therefore no reason why they should not also be bound by the principle deriving from the relevant case law (Mestmäcker, 1992, 277).

Article 9 decisions operate in the following way. A public authority proposes or invites private persons to put forward a proposal for an agreement within the meaning of Article 81 EC. The intention is to make the agreement obligatory through a binding measure (i.e. the Article 9 decision taken by the Commission or national Authority). Commitment decisions under Article 9 and 5 thus correspond to the type of measures referred to in *Reiff*, in that they 'deprive their own legislation of its official character by delegating to private economic operators responsibility for taking decisions affecting the economic sphere'.

The Court of Justice has, over a number of years, developed and refined its case law determining when a State measure makes binding an agreement drawn up by private individuals upon request or invitation by a public authority constitutes the reinforcement of an agreement prohibited by Article 81 EC. In particular, the Court held in the recent *Arduino*[11] judgment that State measures infringe Article 10 in conjunction with Article 81 EC in the following circumstances:

- the content of the proposal has been drawn up by bodies which are not independent from the individuals who will be subject to the final measure (i.e. absence of independent experts);
- if the proposal has not been drawn up by independent experts, and thus represents only the private interests of individuals rather than the general interest,[12] the final measure in none the less usually lawful if the Member State has not 'waived its power to make decisions of last resort or to review implementation of the' proposal adopted in the final measure.[13] The final measure would be unlawful where, for example, the public body which adopted the final measure was required simply to rubber stamp the proposal made by the individuals concerned and did not therefore have the power to refuse to accept it. In those circumstances, the proposal could be said to be simply a 'cartel subject to the condition precedent of official approval'.[14]

[11] *Criminal proceedings against Manuele Arduino,* Case C-35/99, E.C.R. 2002 p. I-1529, §§ 37-40.

[12] Ibid., § 37.

[13] Ibid., § 40.

[14] On this point, see § 105 of the Opinion of Advocate General Darmon in *Bundesanstalt für den Güterverkehr v Reiff*, Case C-185/91, E.C.R. 1993 p. I-5801.

In the light of *Arduino*, we can see that Articles 9 and 5 of Regulation 1/03 would seem to be compatible with Article 81 in conjunction with Article 10 EC. On the one hand, the content of the commitment is not drawn up by independent experts, since it is put forward by the undertakings themselves. The final measures would therefore be unlawful if the proposals contravened Article 81. On the other hand, Regulation 1/03 allows the Commission and the national authorities a general power to evaluate the commitments and thus to reject them. In particular, the commitments must 'meet the concerns expressed to them by the Commission in its preliminary assessment'.

The lawfulness of Articles 5 and 9 of the Regulation thus depend on whether the Court considers that the Commission or the national authorities have not waived their power to make decisions of last resort or to review implementation of the proposal taken over in the decision.[15] In other words, the Court's role is to decide whether the proceedings are sufficient to exclude the risk that the measures adopted under Article 5 or 9 serve the interests only of the parties to the agreement. The Court would thus have a role analogous to that of the courts in the United States since the enactment of the Tunney Act. Those powers must allow the Commission and the national authorities to safeguard the Community interest, as Article 81 EC requires. Should the Court decide otherwise, Articles 9 and 5 of Regulation would infringe Article 10 EC in conjunction with Article 81 EC (or put another way they would undermine the effectiveness of Article 81 EC) and would therefore be unlawful.

The effect of commitment decisions on the antitrust powers of the Community and the Member State

Commitment decisions are also interesting because of their relationship with the discretion that the Commission and Member States enjoy when they apply Community and national competition law.

As well as being binding on the undertakings to which they are addressed, commitment decisions are also decisions within the meaning of Article 16 of the Regulation. This means that commitment decisions taken by the Commission are binding on national courts and authorities when those bodies apply Community antitrust law to the same facts. Within certain limits, the same principle applies even where they apply national law:

1. The commitment decision taken by the Commission may have an impact on any later decision of the national authorities or courts. Since the commitment decision will have concluded that there are no longer grounds for action by the Commission in respect of the conduct which is covered

[15] *Arduino*, ibid., § 40.

by the commitment, it will prevent the conduct referred to in the decision from infringing Articles 81 and 82 EC. When faced with a commitment decision, national authorities and national courts must close the file on all cases covered by the decision in respect of the period after the decision has been taken. However, this does not prevent the national authorities and courts applying EC antitrust law from finding that an infringement has occurred with respect to the period before the adoption of the Article 9 decision.

2. By virtue of Article 3(2) of Regulation 1/03, a commitment decision adopted by the Commission also has direct consequences on the Member States' powers to apply national law. Article 3(2) establishes a relationship between national and Community antitrust law (in the author's view, that relationship is unlawful, on Article 3(2), see *infra*). One consequence of Article 3(2) is that an Article 9 decision does not permit a Member State applying national antitrust law on anticompetitive agreements to the facts assessed in the commitment decision to adopt a stricter decision with respect to the period after the adoption of the commitment decision. However, decisions taken pursuant to national laws prohibiting the abuse of a dominant position may be stricter than Article 82 EC even with respect to periods after the commitment decision has been adopted.

In any event, with respect to periods preceding the Commission's commitment decision, the application of either the rules on agreements or the abuse of a dominant position of national law may lead to a prohibition decision.

Commitment decisions adopted by a national authority pursuant to Article 5 of the Regulation pose different problems. Such decisions do not fetter the Commission, other national authorities or national courts. There is thus a risk of different national authorities taking conflicting decisions, which would undermine the principle of legal certainty. This risk exists not only for the undertakings involved in the proceedings but also for competitors and consumers harmed by the alleged anticompetitive conduct. In order to eliminate the danger of such conflicting decisions, Regulation 1/03 aims to concentrate the exercise of Community antitrust competence. It has therefore established procedures for cooperation and monitoring which are equally applicable to commitment decisions.

The consequences of commitment decisions on individuals

It is also interesting to consider the effect that commitment decisions have on individuals. While commitment decisions may reduce the Commission's workload, they also reduce the level of protection conferred on consumers (who, it should not be forgotten, are also beneficiaries of the rights conferred by Articles 81 and 82 EC). This is the case because a commitment decision entails the termination of proceedings before any decision finding an infringement of antitrust law has been taken. The lack of any such decision deprives individuals, who may have suffered economic harm because of the alleged infringement, of the possibility of going before the courts with what is effectively an enforceable order in support of a claim for damages. Consequently, if an Article 9 decision has been taken, individuals may have difficulty in finding another way to vindicate rights conferred by Articles 81 and 82 EC which have been infringed by the conduct which is the subject of the decision. As we shall see (*infra*), national courts are often not in the best position to assess whether antitrust law has been infringed (for example, because they lack the appropriate investigative powers or sufficient information to enforce the prohibitions).

34.1.6. Finding of Inapplicability

In addition to commitment decisions, Regulation 1/03 provides for another type of decision which will reduce the Commission's enforcement activity and prevent it from taking a decision on the substance of a case, namely the 'finding of inapplicability' provided for by Article 10.

By virtue of that Article, the Commission alone has power 'where the Community public interest ... so requires ... acting on its own initiative' to find 'by decision' that Articles 81 and 82 EC are not applicable to particular agreements or unilateral conduct.

This type of decision is declaratory in nature.[16] When the Commission is confronted with new factual situations in respect of which it has not yet adopted any decisions, a finding of inapplicability will allow it to clarify the orientation of Community competition policy. This, in turn, will increase clarity and foreseeability in the application of Community antitrust law.

Furthermore, once an Article 10 decision has been taken, it will be liable to eliminate the Community interest in dealing with complaints relating to similar facts. Once it has clarified its policy through a finding of inapplicability, the Commission has effectively eliminated any Community interest in examining such cases. Acting under Article 7, it may, therefore, close the file on cases which fall within the scope of the 'finding of inapplicability'.

---

[16] The declaratory nature of a finding of inapplicability flows from the principle of prohibition subject to statutory exemptions which Regulation 1/03 establishes for Article 81 EC. Since Article 81 (including paragraph 3) and Article 82 EC apply without any prior decision to that effect being required, a decision finding that there has been an infringement or that there has not been an infringement of Article 81 or 82 can only be declaratory.

34.1.7. Guidance Letters

Guidance letters are a new type of measure which the Commission has deemed that it can issue although no provision to that effect was made in Regulation 1/03. According to paragraph 22 of the relevant Commission Notice, guidance letters, 'are in the first place intended to help undertakings carry out themselves an informed assessment of their agreements and practices'.

One of the reasons which led the Commission to provide for guidance letters is the unlawful direct effect of Article 81(3) EC created by Article 6 of Regulation 1/03 (*infra*). This reason is confirmed by the Commission itself, which has stated that its review of the block exemption regulations and guidelines 'allows undertakings in the vast majority of cases to reliably assess their agreements with regard to Article 81' (paragraph 4 of the Notice on guidance letters). The content of Article 81(3) is indeterminate and its application requires the exercise of discretion. The Commission has therefore taken the view that, where its own practice or the case law does not provide sufficient guidance, it must clarify, for the benefit of undertakings and national courts, what types of behaviour are compatible with Community antitrust law.

Undertakings are now required to (self-)assess Article 81(3), as a consequence of the direct effect conferred unlawfully on that provision. The obvious difficulties which they will encounter are also highlighted by the remarkable concept of 'self-assessment'. (This is an expression coined by the Commission in the Notice on guidance letters.) The Commission states, at paragraph 4 of the Notice that 'alongside the reform of rules implementing Articles 81 and 82 brought about by Regulation 1/2003, the Commission has conducted a review of block exemption regulations, Commission notices and guidelines, with a view to further assist self-assessment by economic operators'. It is clear that the concept of *self*-assessment relates to an action (that is, the assessment) which should be done by the bodies having the lawful authority to do so (that is, the Commission and the national authorities). To make the task of *self*-assessment by undertakings less complex, the Commission has had recourse to guidance letters.

Characteristics of guidance letters

Although guidance letters are issued in respect of specific cases, they are linked to the orientation of Community competition policy and thus cannot be issued by the national authorities. Only the Commission, which by virtue of Article 85 EC has the exclusive power to define Community antitrust policy, may issue guidance letters. According to paragraph 12 of the Notice on guidance letters, a request for such a letter 'can be presented by an undertaking or undertakings which have entered into or intend to enter into an agreement or practice that could fall within the scope of Articles 81 and/or 82 of the Treaty'.

Paragraph 14 makes it clear that the request should be presented informally. There is no form to be filled in and undertakings should simply present a memorandum containing certain information which is indicated in paragraph 14 of the Notice.

The questions asked of the Commission should have practical relevance rather than being merely hypothetical. The Commission makes it clear at paragraph 10 of the Notice that it 'will not issue guidance letters on agreements or practices that are no longer being implemented by the parties'.

The Notice explains the procedure which the Commission follows when a request for a guidance letter is made:

- first, 'where no guidance letter is issued, the Commission shall inform the applicant accordingly' (paragraph 17); and
- second, 'the normal rules on professional secrecy apply to the information supplied by the applicant(s)' (paragraph 15). If the request for a guidance letter is withdrawn, any information supplied will not be returned by the Commission. It may then use it in any subsequent investigations even against the undertakings which supplied it (paragraph 18).

The Commission sets out three cumulative conditions which must be met before a guidance letter can be issued:

- There must be no clarification of the question posed 'in the existing EC legal framework including the case law of the Community courts, nor publicly available general guidance or precedent in decision-making practice or previous guidance letters' (paragraph 8 (a)).
- Clarification of the questions raised must be useful, taking into account various factors which are listed in paragraph 8(b).
- It must be possible for the Commission to issue a guidance letter on the basis of the information provided (that is, without any further fact finding being required) (paragraph 8(c)).

In paragraph 9 of the Notice, the Commission explains the two sets of circumstances in which it will not issue a guidance letter:

- when the questions raised in the request 'are identical or similar to issues raised in a case pending before the European Court of First Instance or the European Court of Justice'; and

- when the agreement or practice to which the request refers is subject to proceedings pending with the Commission, a Member State court or Member State competition authority.

In other words, a request for a guidance letter may not be used as a means for the parties involved in an antitrust proceeding before a national authority or court to obtain from the Commission an indication as to how the national body should decide the case. Regulation 1/03 contains other provisions (Articles 11(5) and 15) allowing national bodies, acting on their own initiative and without the intervention of the parties, to request guidance with respect to specific situations directly from the Commission (*infra*).

In any event, the Commission reserves the right to answer only some of the questions asked in the request and, if need be, to raise questions of its own motion. Moreover, the Commission indicates no time limits for supplying a guidance letter. It specifies, at paragraph 7 of the Notice, that it may 'only provide informal guidance to individual undertakings in so far as this is compatible with its enforcement priorities'. This is because a guidance letter is an exceptional measure which is applicable only when no guidance can be gleaned from existing practice or case law.

Lastly, paragraph 19 of the Notice provides that the guidance letter will follow a standard two-part pattern. One part will set out a summary description of the facts; the other will set out the Commission's legal reasoning.

The non-binding nature of guidance letters and the absence of judicial review

The Commission acknowledges that by issuing guidance letters it fetters its own discretion. This is an indirect effect which is typical of communications and notices.[17] The Commission states that, when it examines a complaint regarding facts which have already been the subject of a guidance letter, it 'will take the previous guidance letter into account, subject in particular to changes in the underlying facts, to any new aspects raised by a complaint, to developments in the case law of the European Courts or wider changes of the Commission's policy' (paragraph 24 of the Notice; see also paragraph 25 of the Draft Notice).

Neither the Treaty nor Regulation 1/03 provide for guidance letters, although the Regulation did, in a sense, anticipate them. Recital 38 of the preamble to the Regulation specifies that 'this Regulation is without prejudice to the ability of the Commission to issue informal guidance'. Since the source of guidance letters is merely a Notice, which is a non-binding, anomalous act,

[17] *Het Vlaamse Gewest v Commission*, Case T-214/95, E.C.R. 1998, p. II–717, §§ 79–89.

the letters themselves are of an informal nature. This, in turn, means that guidance letters, like comfort letters under the Regulation 17/62 regime, are not legally binding. Nor do they bind national competition authorities or the national courts that have the power to apply Articles 81 and 82. However, paragraph 25 of the Notice makes clear that those bodies may 'take account of guidance letters issued by the Commission as they see fit in the context of a case'. Similarly, guidance letters do not prejudge the assessment of the same question by the Community Courts (paragraph 23 of the Notice).

Since they are not binding, guidance letters are not acts which are subject to judicial review. This was also the case with regard to other informal measures taken by the Commission, such as comfort letters pursuant to Regulation 17/62.

In the Notice, the Commission does not rule out examining in a formal procedure an agreement or practice which has formed the basis for a guidance letter (paragraph 24). Furthermore, the mere fact that a request for a guidance letter has been made does not have any effect on the Commission's power to open proceedings with regard to the agreement or practice which is the subject of the request (paragraph 11).

The difference between guidance letters and other measures

In order to grasp the characteristics of guidance letters, it is worthwhile showing how they differ from other measures provided for by Regulation 1/03 and Regulation 17/62.

Guidance letters differ from findings of inapplicability Guidance letters differ from findings of inapplicability (Article 10 of Regulation 1/03) in that their purpose is to provide clarification in real cases raised directly by undertakings. They may therefore be issued even in the absence of any Community public interest. By contrast, a finding of inapplicability is made by the Commission acting on its own initiative and only where the Community public interest so requires.

Findings of inapplicability will be of general value since the public interest which caused them to be adopted will in turn lead to their publication. However, despite their different nature, even guidance letters will be of general value to the extent that their non-binding nature allows. The Commission has announced (paragraph 21 of the Notice) that guidance letters will be published on the Commission's web-site. They will thus supply guidelines that will be applicable in subsequent cases.

Guidance letters and comfort letters A comparison of guidance letters with the measures provided for in Regulation 17/62 shows that guidance letters are similar in some respects to comfort letters and, in other respects, to the negative clearances provided for by Article 2 of Regulation 17/62.

Guidance letters, like comfort letters (*supra*), are non-binding. However, the scope of guidance letters is broader. The purpose of comfort letters was to give the undertakings concerned an indication as to whether an agreement would fall within the exemption established by a block exemption Regulation and hence related only to Article 81(3). Guidance letters, on the other hand, may be issued with reference to Articles 81(1), 81(3) or 82. A further difference is that comfort letters were issued irrespective of whether the facts revealed by the notification had already been the subject of an earlier proceeding for authorisation by virtue of Article 81(3). By contrast, guidance letters can be issued only in cases which have not previously been assessed in the Commission's practice or in the case law.

The difference between the two measures can be best identified by looking at their respective *raisons d'être*. Comfort letters developed as a consequence of the obligation to notify agreements which Regulation 17/62 imposed. Their purpose was to give undertakings a rapid, albeit non-binding, indication as to whether an agreement would fall within the exemption under Article 81(3) set out in a block exemption Regulation. By contrast, guidance letters are issued by the Commission primarily, although not solely, by reason of the direct effect of Article 81(3) EC conferred by Article 6 of Regulation 1/03, which allows national courts to apply Article 81(3) directly.

Guidance letters and negative clearances Unlike negative clearances under Article 2 of Regulation 17/62, guidance letters are not limited to Articles 81(1) and 82 EC but also apply to Article 81(3). Furthermore, negative clearances were binding on the parties as regards the individual agreement or practice which was the subject of the application. Guidance letters are not binding, except in so far as they fetter the Commission's own discretion (*supra*).

34.1.8. Procedural Aspects Connected with the Adoption of Decisions

Chapter VIII of Regulation 1/03 contains rules relating to hearings and professional secrecy.

Professional secrecy, which is the subject of Article 28, will be dealt with *infra*. Article 27, entitled 'Hearing of the parties, complainants and others', deals with the procedural aspects of two groups of decisions:

- the first group comprises decisions under Articles 7, 8, 23 and 24(2) of the Regulation and is covered by Article 27 paragraphs (1) to (3); and
- the second group comprises decisions under Articles 9 and 10 of the Regulation and is the subject of Article 27(4).

Procedural aspects related to decisions taken under Articles 7, 8, 23 and 24(2)

The matters falling under Article 27(1)–(3) relate to the following:

1. First, to the right of the undertakings which are the subject of proceedings to be heard on the matters to which the Commission has taken objection. Before taking a decision under Article 7 (Finding of infringement and a decision requiring an infringement to be brought to an end), Article 8 (Interim measures), Article 23 (Fines) and Article 24(2) (Reduction of penalty payments), the Commission must 'give the undertakings or associations of undertakings which are the subject of the proceedings conducted by the Commission the opportunity of being heard on the matters to which the Commission has taken objection'. In order to protect the rights of such undertakings, the Commission is required to 'base its decision only on objections on which the parties concerned have been able to comment'. In addition to protecting the undertakings which are the subject of the proceedings, Regulation 1/03 confers a formal status on the complainants by providing in Article 27(1) that 'complainants shall be closely associated with the proceedings'.
2. Second, to ensuring the parties' right of defence and entitlement to access to the file. Article 27(2) enunciates the principle that 'the rights of defence of the parties concerned shall be fully respected in the proceedings'. The 'right of access to the Commission's file' is recognised as an integral part of the rights of the defence, but it is subject to 'the legitimate interest of undertakings in the protection of their business secrets'. The right of access to the file is further limited as it does not extend to 'confidential information and internal documents of the Commission' and the national authorities. Article 27 provides that 'the right of access shall not extend to correspondence between the Commission and the competition authorities of the Member States, or between the latter, including documents drawn up pursuant to Articles 11 and 14'. Article 27(2) also provides that 'nothing in this paragraph shall prevent the Commission from disclosing and using information necessary to prove an infringement'.
3. Third, the rights of other parties to be heard. As regards the third point, in proceedings likely to culminate in one of the decisions referred to in Article 27(1), 'if the Commission considers it necessary, it may also hear other natural or legal persons'. On the other hand, when such persons ask to be heard, the Commission must grant their application 'where they show a sufficient interest'. By virtue of Article 27(3), the national authorities are also entitled to ask the Commission to hear other natural or legal persons.

Procedural aspects related to decisions taken pursuant to Articles 9 and 10 of Regulation 1/03

Article 27(4) deals with the procedural requirements connected with the publication of decisions adopted pursuant to Article 9 or Article 10 of the Regulation.

Article 27(4) provides that where the Commission intends to adopt a decision pursuant to Article 9 (a commitment decision) or Article 10 (a finding of inapplicability) 'it shall publish a concise summary of the case and the main content of the commitments or of the proposed course of action'. Following this, 'interested third parties may submit their observations within a time limit which is fixed by the Commission in its publication and which may not be less than one month'.

Publication must have regard to the legitimate interest of undertakings in the protection of their business secrets.

34.2. POWERS OF INVESTIGATION

34.2.1. The Commission's Powers of Investigation

As regards the Commission's powers of investigation, Regulation 1/03 deals with the following types of situation:

- investigations into sectors of the economy and into types of agreement (Article 17);
- requests for information (Article 18);
- the power to take statements (Article 19);
- the Commission's powers of inspection (Article 20); and
- inspections carried out by national authorities at the request of the Commission (Article 22(2)).

When examining these powers of investigation point by point, we shall also give consideration to how they are formulated. They represent a *sui generis* category that combines features of both cooperation and (with the exception of Article 17), the 'vertical ascending' control carried out by the Member States when the Commission exercises its powers of inspection. The procedures carried out by the Member States to monitor the exercise of the Commission's powers of investigation have a twofold role:

- they allow the Member States to control how the Commission exercises its powers of investigation on their territory; and
- they provide an indirect means for national authorities and courts to

protect individuals when the Commission exercises its powers of investigation.

34.2.2. Investigations into Sectors of the Economy and into Types of Agreement

The first article of Chapter V, entitled 'Powers of investigation', is Article 17 which pertains to 'Investigations into sectors of the economy and into types of agreements'.[18] It establishes a procedure which enables the Commission to discover whether anticompetitive behaviour exists even if no complaint has been made.

Article 17(1) provides that:

> Where the trend of trade between Member States, the rigidity of prices or other circumstances suggest that competition may be restricted or distorted within the common market, the Commission may conduct an inquiry into a particular sector of the economy or into a particular type of agreements across various sectors. In the course of that inquiry, the Commission may request the undertakings or associations of undertakings concerned to supply the information necessary for giving effect to Articles 81 and 82 of the Treaty and may carry out any inspections necessary for that purpose. It may request the undertakings or associations of undertakings concerned to communicate to it all agreements, decisions and concerted practices.

The third sub-paragraph of Article 17(1) authorises the Commission to 'publish a report on the results of its inquiry into particular sectors of the economy or particular types of agreements across various sectors and invite comments from interested parties'. This is clearly in order to encourage the participation of undertakings and interested parties.

Article 17(2) lists the powers of investigation which are at the Commission's disposal for this purpose.

34.2.3. Requests for Information

Article 18(1) of Regulation 1/03 entitles the Commission, in order to carry out the duties assigned to it by this Regulation, to require undertakings and associations of undertakings to provide all necessary information. Three types of request for information are envisaged by Article 18:

---

[18] The following sector inquiries have been conducted pursuant to Article 17 of Regulation 1/03: in 2004, a sector inquiry into the provision of sports content over third generation mobile networks (3G) and, in 2005, inquiries into retail banking and business insurance and gas and electricity markets.

- 'simple requests' for information to an undertaking or association of undertakings (Article 18(2));
- requests for information to an undertaking or association of undertakings made by decision (Article 18(3)); and
- requests for information to the governments and competition authorities of the Member States (Article 18(6)).

Article 18(5) has a role to play in the system of *sui generis* control exercised by the Member States. It requires the Commission to 'without delay forward a copy of the simple request or of the decision to the competition authority of the Member State in whose territory the seat of the undertaking or association of undertakings is situated and the competition authority of the Member state whose territory is affected'.

34.2.4. The Power to Take Statements

The procedures relating to the power to take statements (Article 19) and the inspection of other premises (Article 21) give the Commission greater powers of investigation than did Regulation 17/62.

Article 19(1) provides that 'in order to carry out the duties assigned to it by this Regulation, the Commission may interview any natural or legal person who consents to be interviewed for the purpose of collecting information relating to the subject matter of an investigation'. Article 19(1) does not require either the intervention of the relevant national authority or even notification of the interview to it. Nevertheless, Article 19(2) goes on to stipulate that when an interview 'is conducted in the premises of an undertaking, the Commission shall inform the competition authority of the Member State in whose territory the interview takes place'. (It should be noted that this provision differs from Article 18(5), which, when applicable, requires notice to the authority of the Member State in which the undertaking has its seat.) In the situation covered by Article 19(2), the Regulation allows the national authorities (but not the Commission) to request that their officials assist the officials and other accompanying persons authorised by the Commission to conduct the interview.

34.2.5. The Commission's Powers of Inspection

Article 20(1) of the Regulation confers on the Commission the power to conduct all inspections of undertakings and associations of undertakings necessary to fulfil the duties assigned to it by the Regulation.

Paragraphs (2) and (3) of Article 18 set out in detail the powers which the 'officials and other agents authorised by the Commission to conduct an inspection' have[19] and specify the conditions in which those powers can be exercised.[20]

Regarding the relationship between the Commission and the national authorities, the last sentence of Article 20(3) also requires the Commission to 'give notice of the inspection to the competition authority of the Member State in whose territory it is to be conducted', in good time before the inspection takes place.

As in the case of requests for information, inspections may be ordered by decision of the Commission. In that case, Article 20(4) provides that 'undertakings and associations of undertakings are required to submit to inspections ordered by decision of the Commission'.

As regards the control which the national authorities exercise over the Commission, Article 20(4) provides expressly that 'the Commission shall take such decisions after consulting the competition authority of the Member State in whose territory the inspection is to be conducted'.

Paragraphs (5) and (6) of Article 20 set out the ways in which 'the officials as well as those authorised or appointed by the competition authority of the Member State in whose territory the inspection is to be conducted' are to participate in the inspection. Such persons are required, upon request by that authority or by the Commission, to afford active assistance to 'the officials and other accompanying persons authorised by the Commission'. To that end, they enjoy the powers specified in Article 20(2).

Article 20 also provides that, where the officials and other accompanying persons authorised by the Commission find that an undertaking opposes an inspection ordered pursuant to this Article, the Member State concerned shall afford them the necessary assistance, requesting where appropriate the assistance of the police or of an equivalent enforcement authority, so as to

---

[19] Article 20(2) provides that those persons have the following powers:

'a) to enter any premises, land and means of transport of undertakings and associations of undertakings;

b) to examine the books and other records related to the business, irrespective of the medium on which they are stored;

c) to take or obtain in any form copies of or extracts from such books or records;

d) to seal any business premises and books or records for the period and to the extent necessary for the inspection;

e) to ask any representative or member of staff of the undertaking or association of undertakings for explanations on facts or documents relating to the subject-matter and purpose of the inspection and to record the answers'.

[20] Article 20(3) reads as follows:

'The officials and other accompanying persons authorised by the *Commission* to conduct an inspection shall exercise their powers upon production of a written authorisation specifying the subject-matter and purpose of the inspection and the penalties provided for in Article 23 in case the production of the required books or other records related to the business is incomplete or where the answers to questions asked under paragraph 2 of the present Article are misleading.'

enable them to conduct their inspection (Article 20(6)).

Article 20(7) provides for new and specific rules applicable 'if the assistance provided for in paragraph 6 requires authorisation from a judicial authority according to national rules'. In such cases, the 'authorisation shall be applied for. Such authorisation may also be applied for as a precautionary measure'. Article 20(8) goes on to define the extent of the national courts' powers to control the Commission's decision. It may:

- control that the Commission decision is authentic; and
- control that the coercive measures envisaged are neither arbitrary nor excessive having regard to the subject matter of the inspection.[21]

As regards review of the proportionality of the coercive measures, Article 20(8) provides for an interesting procedure which involves the relevant national court and Commission and, in certain cases, also the relevant national authority. The appropriate passage reads:

> the national judicial authority may ask the Commission, directly or through the Member State competition authority, for detailed explanations in particular on the grounds the Commission has for suspecting infringement of Articles 81 and 82 of the Treaty, as well as on the seriousness of the suspected infringement and on the nature of the involvement of the undertaking concerned. However, the national judicial authority may not call into question the necessity for the inspection nor demand that it be provided with the information in the Commission's file.

Only the Court of Justice may review whether the Commission's decision complies with general principles of Community law[22] and is hence lawful.

34.2.6. The Commission's Powers to Carry Out an 'Inspection of other Premises'

Regulation 1/03 confers powers on the Commission to carry out inspections on premises which do not belong to the undertaking which is being investigated. Such premises may be 'land and means of transport, including the homes of directors, managers and other members of staff of the undertakings and associations of undertakings concerned'. Those powers are regulated by Article 21, paragraph (1) of which provides that:

---

[21] In substance, these rules follow the judgment of the Court of Justice in *Roquette Frères v. Directeur Général de la Concurrence*, Case C-94/00, E.C.R. 2002, p. I–9011.

[22] See *Foto-Frost v. Hauptzollamt Luebeck-Ost*, Case 314/85, E.C.R. 1987, p. 4199.

> if a reasonable suspicion exists that books or other records related to the business and to the subject-matter of the inspection, which may be relevant to prove a serious violation of Article 81 or Article 82 of the Treaty, are being kept in other premises ... the Commission can by decision order an inspection to be conducted in such other premises, land and means of transport.

When this new power was conferred it was necessary to determine the categories of employees on whose premises inspections could be conducted. It was debated in particular whether inspections could be carried out on the premises of an undertaking's in-house lawyers. This would not have been possible if in-house lawyers had been recognised as being the undertaking's legal representatives. Article 21(1) resolves the issue by referring to the premises of 'directors, managers and other members of staff'.

Article 21(2) requires the Commission to consult 'the competition authority of the Member State in whose territory the inspection is to be conducted' before it takes the decision ordering the inspection.

In cases falling under Article 20, authorisation from a national judicial authority need be sought only if such authorisation is required by national law. However, in cases falling under Article 21, paragraph (3) of that Article provides that the decision 'cannot be executed without prior authorisation from the national judicial authority of the Member State concerned'. Even in this case, the national court exercises only a power of review over the Commission's decision and thus, as when Article 20(7) of the Regulation applies, it is restricted to ensuring:

1. that the Commission decision is authentic; and
2. that the coercive measures envisaged are neither arbitrary nor excessive having regard to the seriousness of the suspected infringement, to the importance of the evidence sought, to the involvement of the undertaking concerned and to the reasonable likelihood that business books and records relating to the subject matter of the inspection are kept in the premises for which authorisation is required.

As in the case of Article 20, Article 21 provides for a procedure whereby the national authority may contact the Commission 'directly or through the Member State competition authority' in order to obtain 'detailed explanations on those elements which are necessary to allow its control of the proportionality of the coercive measures envisaged'. The limits to the national court's review powers that Article 20(8) establishes apply equally to cases falling under Article 21. The second sub-paragraph of Article 21(3) of that provides that 'the national judicial authority may not call into question the necessity for the inspection nor demand that it be provided with information in the Commission's file'. In this case, too, only the Court of Justice may review the lawfulness of the Commission's decision.

Article 21(4) sets out the powers which the Commission has when it carries out inspections falling under Article 21.

34.2.7. Investigations by the Competition Authorities of Member States

Article 22 determines the powers conferred on national authorities when they carry out inspections at the request of the Commission or the authorities of another Member State.

This question will be dealt with in conjunction with the powers of investigation conferred on the national authorities by Regulation 1/03 (*infra*).

34.3. PENALTIES

34.3.1. Fines and Penalty Payments

Chapter VI of Regulation 1/03, entitled 'Penalties', empowers the Commission to impose fines (Article 23) and periodic penalty payments (Article 24).[23]

Fines

Regulation 1/03 permits two types of fine to be imposed:

1. The first category of fines can be imposed for breach of obligations connected with the powers of investigation conferred on the Commission and national authorities by Article 17 of the Regulation. When such infringements are committed intentionally or negligently, 'the Commission may by decision impose … fines not exceeding 1% of the total turnover in the preceding business year' (Article 23(1)).
2. The second category of fines may be imposed by decisions which fall under Chapter III of the Regulation. Article 23(2) provides that 'the Commission may by decision impose fines on undertakings where, intentionally or negligently':

   - they infringe Article 81 or Article 82 of the Treaty; or

[23] For an indication of how fines are determined, see Guidelines on the method of setting fines imposed pursuant to Article 23(2)(a) of Regulation No. 1/2003 (2006), which replaces the earlier Guidelines on the Method of Setting Fines, 2003 OJ C 10/16.

- they contravene a decision ordering interim measures under Article 8; or
- they fail to comply with a commitment made binding by a decision pursuant to Article 9.

Article 23(2) goes on to provide that infringements are penalised 'for each undertaking and association of undertakings participating in the infringement' by a fine which may 'not exceed 10% of the sum of its total turnover in the preceding business year'. Article 23(3) specifies that 'in fixing the amount of the fine, regard shall be had both to the gravity and to the duration of the infringement'.

Paragraphs (2) to (4) of Article 23 set out in some detail how fines are to be imposed on and paid by associations of undertakings.

Article 23(5) specifies that 'decisions taken pursuant to paragraphs 1 and 2 shall not be of a criminal law nature'.

Periodic penalty payments

Article 24 provides for a system of periodic penalty payments. The purpose of penalty payments is to compel undertakings to comply with specific obligations provided for by the Regulation. They may be obligations imposed pursuant to Articles 7, 8 or 9, or they may have been imposed in connection with the Commission's powers of investigation (Articles 17, 18(3) or 20(4)). Periodic penalty payments are imposed by Commission decisions.

Article 24(1) stipulates that the amount of the penalty payments may not exceed '5% of the average daily turnover in the preceding business year per day and calculated from the date appointed by the decision'. Article 24(2) allows the Commission to fix the amount of the periodic penalty payment at a figure lower than that which would arise under the original decision where the undertakings or associations of undertakings have satisfied the obligation which the periodic penalty payment was intended to enforce. Article 23(4) applies *mutatis mutandis* as regards the settlement of penalty payments by associations of undertakings.

Article 31 provides, in conformity with Articles 83(2) EC and 229 EC, that 'the Court of Justice shall have unlimited jurisdiction to review decisions whereby the Commission has fixed a fine or periodic penalty payment. It may cancel, reduce or increase the fine or periodic penalty payment imposed'.

34.3.2. Limitation Periods Relating to the Imposition and Enforcement of Sanctions and the Principle that Proceedings Should Last a Reasonable Time

Article 25 of Regulation 1/03 establishes limitation periods relating to the imposition of penalties and Article 26 does the same as regards the enforcement thereof. The regime which those articles establish is taken over almost *verbatim* from Regulation 2988/74. It refers only to the prescription of the Commission's powers, not those of the national authorities. Consequently, subject to the operation of the general principles of Community law (that is, equal treatment, effectiveness) the powers of the national authorities are regulated by the relevant provisions of national law.

Article 25 deals with the limitation period relating to the imposition of penalties.

Article 25(1) sets forth that the powers conferred on the Commission by Articles 23 and 24 shall be subject to the following limitation periods:

- Three years in the case of infringements of provisions concerning requests for information or the conduct of inspections;
- Five years in the case of all other infringements.

Article 25(2) goes on to specify that:

> Time shall start to run on the day on which the infringement is committed. However, in the case of continuing or repeated infringements, time shall begin to run on the day on which the infringement ceases.

Article 25 also establishes rules determining when the limitation period is deemed to be interrupted. Article 25(3) provides that:

> Any action taken by the Commission or by the competition authority of a Member State for the purpose of the investigation of proceedings in respect of an infringement shall interrupt the limitation period for the imposition of fines or periodic penalty payments. The limitation period shall be interrupted with effect from the date on which the action is notified to at least one undertaking or association of undertakings which has participated in the infringement.

Article 25(4) goes on to provide that 'the interruption of the limitation period shall apply for all the undertakings or associations of undertakings which have participated in the infringement'.

Article 25(5) establishes a maximum period within which the Commission's power may be exercised. It provides that:

> each interruption of the limitation period shall start time running afresh. However, the limitation period shall expire at the latest on the day on which a period equal to twice the limitation period has elapsed without the Commission having imposed a

fine or a periodic penalty payment. That period shall be extended by the time during which limitation is suspended pursuant to paragraph 6.

Article 25(6) deals with suspension of the limitation period. It provides that 'the limitation period for the imposition of fines or periodic penalty payments shall be suspended for as long as the decision of the Commission is the subject of proceedings pending before the Court of Justice'.

Article 26 deals with the limitation period for the enforcement of penalties. With regard to the Commission's power 'to enforce decisions taken pursuant to Articles 23 and 24' which is 'subject to a limitation of five years' (Article 26(1)), 'time shall begin to run on the date on which the decision becomes final' (Article 26(2)).

The limitation period for the enforcement of penalties is interrupted:

- by notification of a decision varying the original amount of the fine or periodic penalty payment or refusing an application for variation; and
- by any action of the Commission or of a Member State, acting at the request of the Commission, designed to enforce payment of the fine or periodic penalty payment.

Each interruption starts time running afresh (Article 26(4)).

As regards suspension of the limitation period, Article 26(5) provides that the limitation period for the enforcement of penalties shall be suspended for so long as:

- time to pay is allowed; and
- enforcement of payment is suspended pursuant to a decision of the Court of Justice.

Limitation periods relating to the imposition and enforcement of fines and periodic penalty payment should not be confused with the principle 'that the Commission must act within a reasonable time when it adopts decisions following administrative proceedings relating to competition policy'.[24] That principle is a general principle of Community law and is related to the principle of sound administration. On this point, the Court has held that 'the Commission may not defer defining its position indefinitely and that, in the interests of legal certainty and of ensuring adequate judicial protection, the Commission is required to adopt a decision or send a formal letter, if such a letter has been requested, within a reasonable time'.[25]

---

[24] See *CMA CGM v Commission*, Case T-213/00, E.C.R. 2003, p. II–913, § 317.

[25] See ibid.

35. National Antitrust Authorities: Decisions, Powers of Investigation and Penalties

The national authorities play an important role in the operation of the system established by Regulation 1/03 and are therefore the subject of detailed rules which not only define the powers conferred on them, but also stipulate which bodies may exercise these powers and the ways in which they are to be exercised.

35.1. THE NATIONAL BODIES

Unlike Regulation 17/62, Regulation 1/03 requires the Member States to designate the bodies which will apply Articles 81 and 82 of the Treaty (Article 35(1) of the Regulation; see Recital 8 of the Preamble to the Regulation).

The Member States are simply required to identify the bodies which will carry out the role of national competition authorities for the purposes of Regulation 1/03. The Member States' power to determine the structure and the characteristics of the authorities or their independence from other bodies or the influence of private individuals is not thereby affected. It is nevertheless subject to certain constraints. Article 35 of the Regulation provides that 'the Member States shall designate the competition authority or authorities responsible for the application of Articles 81 and 82 of the Treaty in such a way that the provisions of this Regulation are effectively complied with'. In so doing, the Regulation imposes an obligation to attain a particular result and this requires the Member States to devote adequate financial resources and staff to the national authorities.

The national authorities designated under Article 35 are not merely empowered to apply Community antitrust law. They also participate in the Advisory Committee (Article 14(2) and have the power to present observations in cases in which Articles 81 and 82 EC are being applied (Article 15(3)).

35.2. POWERS

Consistently with its aim and purpose, Regulation 1/03 confers certain powers on the national authorities and defines how these powers are to be exercised.

35.2.1. Powers Conferred on the National Authorities

Article 5 stipulates that the competition authorities have 'the power to apply Articles 81 and 82 of the Treaty in individual cases'.

Allocation of power
Article 5 of Regulation 1/03 confers on national authorities the power to apply Articles 81(1) and 82 EC. This provision simply confirms a power which already existed by virtue of Article 9(3) of Regulation 17/62. Regulation 1/03 also confers the power to apply Article 81(3) EC. This new power is a consequence of the amendment of two specific aspects of the regime established by Regulation 17/62:

- The abolition of the Commission's exclusive power to apply Article 81(3) and the conferral of a general power to apply Community antitrust law (that is, Articles 81(1), 81(3) and 82 EC) on the actors within the antitrust system. This is accomplished by virtue of Article 4 of the Regulation, which confers this power on the Commission, and Article 5, which confers the same power on the national authorities.
- The abolition of the system of prior notification of agreements to the Commission established by Regulation 17/62. Under the new system, the application of Article 81(3) no longer requires notification of the agreement. By virtue of Regulation 1/03, Article 81(3) may be directly applied, assuming that the conditions for its application are satisfied, at the time when Article 81(1) is examined.

Cases in which power is lost
Regulation 1/03 does not merely define the powers conferred on the national authorities. It also determines when that power is lost. Article 11(6) provides that the competition authorities are relieved of their power once the Commission opens proceedings. In particular, the power conferred by Article 5 is lost in respect of any case in which the Commission has initiated proceedings.

Article 11(6) does not apply to national courts,[1] save in cases where a

---

[1] On this point, see *Belgische Radio en Televisıe v. Sv Sabam e Nv Fonıor*, Case 127/73, E.C.R. 1974, p. 51.

court has been designated as the national competition authority (Article 35(3)). When the Commission assumes the power to apply Community antitrust law, it does not thereby remove the power of the national authorities to apply national antitrust law. (This point is relevant only where national law is applicable to situations having Community relevance, which, by virtue of Article 1(1) of Law 287/90 on the protection of competition, is not the case in Italy.)

Considerations of procedural economy prevent the parallel application of Community antitrust law being permitted. To allow two separate bodies (that is the Commission and the national authority) to assess the same facts in the light of the same provisions of the same legal system, thereby duplicating proceedings, would not be a worthwhile exercise. The main result of such duplication would be the risk of the same factual situation leading to conflicting decisions. Since it is the Commission which has the exclusive power to determine Community antitrust policy, it was obvious that it, rather than the national authorities, should have the power to take over cases. Consequently, should the Commission and the national authorities come to conflicting decisions, the Commission's decisions must be regarded as legitimate and hence prevail.

The power to take over cases, which was already provided for by Article 9(3) of Regulation 17/62 (in the article entitled 'Powers'), is dealt with in Regulation 1/03 in Chapter IV, entitled 'Cooperation'. This power is regulated in the article entitled 'Cooperation between the Commission and the national authorities'. Although the power is not classified in the same way as in Regulation 17/62, Article 11(6) of Regulation 1/03 nevertheless has a direct effect on the powers of the national authorities. The difference in classification is explicable because under Regulation 1/03 the national authorities carry out the functions of the lower-level body within a two-tier antitrust system. This role is characterised by the principle of close collaboration between the Commission and the national authorities (on this point, see *infra*). In other words, when the Commission takes over the national authorities' powers, this is regarded by the draftsmen of Regulation 1/03 as being part and parcel of the 'cooperation' between the Commission and the national authorities. The case is taken over only when the Commission adopts a formal act initiating proceedings (see the Notice on cooperation within the Network, paragraph 52).

It is evident that the Member States are uneasy about the Commission's power to take over cases which are already being investigated by the national authorities pursuant to Community antitrust law, in particular in the light of the national authorities' obligation to apply EC law. If the Commission takes over a case, this obviously has consequences on the national authorities' power even to apply national antitrust law (see *infra*). The Joint Declaration of the Council and the Commission adopted during the adoption of Regulation 1/03 by the Council illustrates this point. It indicates the cases in which the Commission may exercise the power conferred by Article 11(6) (see the Joint Declaration of the Council and Commission of 10 December 2003 on the functioning of the Network of Competition Authorities. These cases were later integrated into the Commission Notice on cooperation within the network).

National proceedings in which Community antitrust law is applied

The fact that Article 5 of Regulation 1/03 grants national authorities the power to apply Community antitrust law does not automatically mean that those authorities can apply Articles 81 and 82. The Regulation requires the Member States to establish and designate national competition authorities (Article 35) and to provide them with the means to exercise the powers conferred on them (this requirement flows from Article 3(1) of the Regulation).

National rules enabling the national authorities to apply Community antitrust law in its entirety are required because, once a Member State has identified which bodies are national authorities within the meaning of Article 5 (see Article 35), it must then establish the proceedings in which Articles 81 and 82 are to be applied. Even if the national authorities are courts rather than administrative bodies, Member States must still determine which procedures they should apply (for example, the general or special rules of civil procedure). This conclusion is confirmed by case law of courts in Germany.[2]

The point that there is a need to identify the proceedings in which Articles 81 and 82 can be applied must be distinguished from the fact that Community rules having direct effect (including these articles) are binding on all bodies within the Member States. The *Costanzo* judgment[3] illustrates that the national authorities are bound by the direct effect of Articles 81 and 82 (either standing alone or in conjunction with Article 10 EC), irrespective of whether procedures to apply those articles have been established at national level. However, national bodies can apply Articles 81 and 82 only if national procedures determining how they are to be applied have been adopted.

The decisions that the national authorities may issue by virtue of Regulation 1/03

In addition to conferring power on the national competition authorities, Regulation 1/03 determines what types of decisions those authorities may

---

[2] See Beschluss des Kammergerichtes, 4 November 1988, Kart. 11188 (Landegebühr) in *WuW-Entscheidungssammlung*, 1989, OLG 4291.

[3] *Fratelli Costanzo SpA v Comune di Molano*, Case 103/88, E.C.R. 1989, p. 1839, § 33.

take. Member States may need to establish appropriate implementing rules to this end. Article 5 provides that the national authorities, acting on their own initiative or on a complaint may take the following decisions:

- requiring that an infringement be brought to an end;
- ordering interim measures;[4]
- accepting commitments; and
- imposing fines, periodic penalty payments or any other penalty provided for in their national law.

Providing a list of the decisions that the national authorities, acting pursuant to Article 5, may take when applying Community antitrust law brings about a kind of harmonisation of their powers. Consequently, if the Commission declines to open proceedings or closes the file on a particular complaint, it can be confident that the national authorities have sufficient powers to apply Community antitrust law effectively. This is also an important safeguard for the national authorities when they suspend proceedings or reject a complaint under Article 13 in order to allow the authorities of another Member State to deal with the case.

The national authorities are also empowered by Article 29(2) of the Regulation to withdraw the benefit of exemption regulations applying Article 81(3) EC. Article 29(2) provides that a national authority may

> where, in any particular case, agreements ... have effects which are incompatible with Article 81(3) of the Treaty in the territory of a Member State, or in a part thereof, which has all the characteristics of a distinct geographic market ... withdraw the benefit of the Regulation in question in respect of that territory.

As paragraph 51 of the Notice on complaints points out, this is the first time that a general power to withdraw the benefit of a block exemption regulation has been conferred.

A similar power had been conferred on the Commission by Article 8(3) of Regulation 17/62. That power was limited to situations in which a decision applying Article 81(3) was based on incorrect information or had been induced by deceit. A similar power had also been conferred on the national competition authorities in the specific case of the block exemption on vertical

---

[4] See the use made by the Italian antitrust authority of this power. In a press release of 21 June 2005 entitled 'Pharmaceuticals: antitrust obliges Merck to license manufacture of the antibiotic Impenem Cilastatina', the Authority stated that: 'The Italian Competition Authority has decided to order an interim measure on Merck & Co. Inc, a company of the pharmaceuticals group Merck. This decision, based on EU competition law, is the first case where an interim measure has been applied by the Italian Competition Authority'.

restrictions (see Article 7 of Regulation 2790/99, see *infra*). This power was modelled on an analogous power conferred in the Merger Regulation (see Article 9 of Regulation 4068/89, now Article 9 of Regulation 139/04).

35.2.2. The Exercise of Antitrust Powers

In addition to conferring powers on the national competition authorities, Regulation 1/03 determines how those powers should be exercised.

The obligation for the Commission and the national authorities to initiate proceedings

The second paragraph of Article 5 of Regulation 1/03 provides that where on the basis of the information in their possession the conditions for prohibition are not met, the national authorities may likewise decide that there are no grounds for action on their part. This rule has been adopted to 'harmonise' the obligations of the national authorities when dealing with a complaint. Some Member States require their competition authorities to determine on the merits every complaint made to them on the basis of national antitrust law.

The second paragraph of Article 5 fulfils an additional function in the system of Regulation 1/03. It requires the national authorities to initiate proceedings if certain conditions are met. Paraphrasing that provision, that requirement applies when an infringement of Community antitrust law is proved on the basis simply of the information in the possession of the national authorities. In clearly casting an obligation on the national authorities, the second paragraph of Article 5 confers a right on the persons for whose benefit the obligation has been imposed. Those persons are entitled to require the national authorities to take action and, hence, to open an investigation.

The purpose of this right (and the correlative obligation for national authority) is to limit the risk, inherent in the 'flexibilisation' of the enforcement of Community antitrust law, that once the Commission has decided not to deal with a case because it lacks Community interest the national authorities will, likewise, subsequently decide, pursuant to Article 5, not to deal with a complaint made to them (see paragraph 22 of the Notice on cooperation within the Network). The power of the Commission and the national authorities to reject complaints, and thus not reach a decision on the merits, entails the risk that companies may be unable to vindicate Community law rights before the national courts. This situation is particularly liable to arise where the infringement of Community antitrust law is clear but it has none the less caused insufficient economic harm to warrant an individual seeking legal redress. This may be the case where the antitrust infringement has only a minor impact on the cost of goods or services.

There are few situations in which the national authorities must apply

Articles 81 and 82 EC on this basis.[5] Paraphrasing Article 5, the national authorities have 'grounds for action' where on the basis of the information in their possession the conditions for prohibition are met. It is nevertheless the case that the second paragraph of Article 5 enunciates an important principle, that is, that the national authorities must safeguard the rights conferred by Articles 81 and 82 when those rights could not otherwise be protected.

Interpreted in this way, the second paragraph of Article 5 is the key provision relating to the exercise of Community antitrust competence by national authorities. It determines the cases where national authorities must apply Community antitrust law.

In particular, it represents a compromise between two requirements:

- first, the decentralised bodies participating in the Community antitrust system safeguard the rights conferred by Articles 81(1) and 82 (since this requirement flows from Regulation 1/03, it does not extend to national antitrust law); and
- second, when the facts do not disclose an obvious breach of Community antitrust law, the obligation incumbent on national authorities to initiate proceedings applying Articles 81 and 82 EC must be limited as much as possible.

Like the national authorities, the Commission may also be required to initiate proceedings. However, its obligation comes into play in different circumstances, namely where there is a case with Community interest. In such a situation, the Commission must initiate proceedings and thus may not close the file on a complaint or refuse to deal with a case brought to its attention.

The difference between the Commission's obligation to initiate proceedings, which is based on 'Community interest', and that of the national authorities, which flows from the second paragraph of Article 5, is that where there is a Community interest, the Commission must initiate proceedings even if the outcome of the case is not clear. For example, it may be uncertain

---

[5] It could be argued that such an approach would entail an excessive workload for the national authorities. For example, a complaint to the competition authority of a Member State relating to a single contract which, on the face of it, patently did not satisfy all the conditions necessary to benefit from Article 81(3) EC would, by virtue of the second paragraph of Article 5 of Regulation 1/03, require the authority to initiate proceedings. This argument does not, however, hold water. In such a case, it is clear from the case law that 'it must be possible to foresee ... that the agreement in question may have an influence on the pattern of trade between Member States' in addition to the requirement that the agreement is capable of having an effect on competition within the common market (judgment in *STM v Maschinenbau Ulm*, Case 56/65, E.C.R. 1996, p. 262). Furthermore, 'it is for the national court to determine, on the basis of all the evidence at its disposal and in the light of the economic and legal context surrounding the agreement, whether in the case pending before it those conditions are satisfied' (judgment in *Cabour SA v Arnor 'SOCO' Sarl*, Case C-230/96, E.C.R. 1998, p. I–2055).

whether the outcome will be a finding of infringement (or that no infringement has been committed, Article 7), a commitment decision (Article 9) or a finding of inapplicability (Article 10). By contrast, the national authorities are required to open proceedings only when the information submitted by the complainant or already in the authorities' possession suffices to prove an infringement of Community antitrust law. In other words, the investigation will commence with the certainty that the result will be a finding that Community antitrust law has been infringed.

The exercise of the powers conferred by Article 13 of Regulation 1/03, which constitutes another important aspect of the exercise of the national authorities' Community antitrust powers, is dealt with *infra.*

The uniform application of Community antitrust law

As regards the exercise of Community antitrust powers by the national authorities, the Regulation sets out the authorities' obligations to apply Articles 81 and 82 EC uniformly.

Article 16(2) provides that 'when competition authorities of the Member States rule on agreements, decisions or practices under Article 81 or Article 82 of the Treaty which are already the subject of a Commission decision, they cannot take decisions which would run counter to the decision adopted by the Commission'. This provision relates to the situation in which a national authority is concluding proceedings (Article 11(6)) in a case which has already been the subject of a Commission decision. Regulation 1/03 does not preclude this possibility because the power of the national authorities to rule on the case, which is lost when the Commission opens proceedings, revives once the Commission has concluded its proceedings. In reality, the obligation incumbent on the national authorities (and also the national courts, see *infra*) not to 'take decisions which would run counter to the decision adopted by the Commission' flows from two distinct principles:

1. The exclusive power conferred on the Commission by Article 85 EC to determine Community antitrust policy.
2. The direct effect of Articles 81(1) and 82 EC. The national authorities are bound by the 'principles of Articles 81(1) and 82 EC' not because of their power to apply Community antitrust law but by reason of the direct effect of those provisions or, strictly speaking, those provisions in conjunction with Article 10 EC. The *Fratelli Costanzo* case law (cited *supra*) makes it clear that the direct effect imposes obligations on all bodies in the Member States, including national authorities and courts.

Article 16(2) simply expresses the corollary of these two principles. It states that in applying Articles 81 and 82 EC the national authorities may not come to conclusions different from those which the Commission has reached. This principle also applies to decisions which the national authorities might reach in the future.

Unlike Article 16(1), which deals with the relationship between judgments of national courts and Commission decisions, Article 16(2) regulates exclusively the situation in which a national authority takes a decision in a case after the Commission has adopted measures. It does not deal with proceedings being conducted in parallel by the Commission and the national authorities. This is so because the initiation of proceedings by the Commission in respect of a case which is already being investigated by a national authority pursuant to Community antitrust law 'shall relieve the competition authorities of the Member States of their competence to apply Articles 81 and 82 of the Treaty' (see Article 11(6)).

On the other hand, Article 16(2) does not govern the obligations of the national authorities where they take a decision before the Commission has done so. Nor does it apply if no Commission decision is contemplated. In such cases, the uniform application of Community law is ensured by the monitoring procedure provided for by Article 11(3) of the Regulation (*infra*).

Lastly, it is useful to explain the distinction between Article 16(2) and Article 3(2) and (3), analysed *supra*. Article 16(2) differs from Article 3(2) and (3) in that it prohibits the national authorities from applying Community antitrust law in a way which is inconsistent with Community antitrust policy. On the other hand, Articles 3(2) and 3(3) are provisions, adopted by virtue of Article 83(2)(e) EC, which limit the application of national antitrust law in relation to Community antitrust law.

35.2.3. The Relations Between the Powers Conferred by Article 5 of Regulation 1/03 and National Antitrust Law

Let us now consider the limits which the power granted to national authorities by Article 5 entails for the parallel application of national antitrust law. To this end, we should bear in mind that Article 3(1) of the Regulation requires Articles 81 and 82 EC to be applied in cases of Community relevance. In considering the relationship between Community and national antitrust law, we need to draw a distinction between national antitrust laws which may be applied even in cases of Community relevance (that is, cases 'which may affect trade between Member States') and laws whose scope is limited to cases which do not have Community relevance:

1. When national law is applicable even in cases of Community relevance, Articles 5 and 3(1) of the Regulation allow the national authorities (and national courts, *infra*) to apply it in parallel with Community antitrust law.

Article 3(2) (which in the author's view is illegal, see *supra*) prevents any national law prohibition on anticompetitive agreements from reaching a conclusion different from that which would be reached by the application of Article 81 EC. This rule is an exception to the general principle of effectiveness of Community antitrust law (see *supra*). Neither Article 3(2) nor Article 5 of Regulation 1/03 forbids national law from conferring on a national authority the power, by analogy with Article 81(3) EC, to exempt anticompetitive agreements from the operation of the national prohibition. The national authorities may therefore always exempt anticompetitive agreements by virtue of national antitrust law. However, in order for the national exemption measures not to infringe Article 3(2) of the Regulation, they must reach the result that would have been reached by applying Article 81 EC. In other words, the anticompetitive agreement which is to be exempt from the prohibition imposed by national antitrust law must be an agreement which, by virtue of Community antitrust law, is either exempted or not prohibited by Article 81 EC.

2. Where the scope of national antitrust law is limited to cases which do not have Community relevance (as in Italy),[6] national authorities and courts dealing, pursuant to Article 3(1), with a case having Community relevance will apply Community antitrust law only. National antitrust law will be inapplicable simply because of its restricted scope. Where national rules provide for an exemption from the domestic law prohibition on anticompetitive agreements (in Italy, this is the case with Article 4(1) of Law 287/90), Articles 3(1) of Regulation 1/03 allows that exemption to be applied only to cases which do not have Community relevance because they do not 'affect trade between Member States'. The limitation of the scope of the exemption is attributable to the self-limiting scope of national law and not to Articles 3(1) or 5 of Regulation 1/03. However, since, *ex hypothesi*, the national rules do not fall within the scope of Articles 81 and 82 EC, the exemption from the national prohibition of anticompetitive agreements is not required to conform to either the general principle of effectiveness of Community law or the (unlawful) requirements established b Article 3(2) of Regulation 1/03.

35.3. POWERS OF INVESTIGATION

Regulation 1/03 is virtually silent as regards the national authorities' powers

---

[6] Article 1(1) of Law 287/90 provides as follows: 'The provisions of this Law … apply to agreements … which do not fall within the scope … of Article 81 and/or Article 82 of the Treaty establishing the European Economic Community (EEC)'.

to investigate infringements of Articles 81 and 82 EC. The reason for this silence is that, subject to the requirement to comply with the general principles of Community law and not to frustrate the objectives of Regulation 1/03, those powers are exclusively a matter for the Member States.

The Regulation merely confers power on the national authorities to carry out inspections on their own territory on behalf of the Commission or of the competition authority of other Member States:

1. By virtue of Article 22(2) of the Regulation, the Commission may delegate inspections to national authorities. This may be done by simple request (Article 20(1) of the Regulation) or by means of a decision (Article 20(4) of the Regulation). Article 22(2) provides that national law regulates the powers of 'the officials of the competition authorities of the Member States who are responsible for conducting those inspections as well as those authorised or appointed by them'. The second sub-paragraph of Article 22(2) regulates another facet of the inspections which are carried out by the national authorities at the request of the Commission. It provides that during the inspections conducted by a particular authority, 'officials and other accompanying persons authorised by the Commission may assist the officials of the authority concerned', if 'so requested by the Commission or by the competition authority of the Member State in whose territory the inspection is to be conducted'.
2. Article 22(1) contemplates the situation which arises when a national competition authority carries out inspections 'on behalf of and for the account of' the authority of another Member State. It provides that:

   > the competition authority of a Member State may in its own territory carry out any inspection or other fact-finding measure under its own national law on behalf of and for the account of the competition authority of another Member State in order to establish whether there has been an infringement of Article 81 or Article 82 of the Treaty. Any exchange and use of the information collected shall be carried out in accordance with Article 12.

   Articles 22(1) and 22(2) of the Regulation constitute exceptions to the principle that the Regulation 1/03 does not interfere with the national rules for the application of Articles 81 and 82 EC. Moreover, Article 22(1) plays a role in the third stage of horizontal cooperation (*infra*) and is relevant in the context of the principle of the concentration of Community antitrust powers (*infra).*

35.4. PENALTIES

Regulation 1/03 does not deal with the national authorities' powers to impose penalties for the breach of Articles 81 and 82 EC, the issue of limitation periods or the circumstances in which those powers are lost:

1. So far as powers to impose penalties is concerned, Article 5 of the Regulation provides that the competition authorities of the Member States 'acting on their own initiative or on a complaint … may … impose fines, periodic penalty payments or any other penalty provided for in their national law'. The Regulation's silence as to the national law consequences of a breach of Community antitrust law allows the Member States to decide independently what kind of sanctions to impose on undertakings. Such sanctions may, for example, take the form of civil or criminal penalties or compensation. However, despite the absence of any specific provisions on the point in Regulation 1/03, the rules of the Member States relating to penalties for infringements of Articles 81 and 82 EC must nevertheless comply with the relevant general principles of Community law (that is, the principle of equivalence[7] or the principle of effectiveness of Community law).[8]
2. Regulation 1/03 is also silent as regards limitation periods and the loss of the national authorities' powers to investigate and penalise infringements of Articles 81 and 82 EC. Article 25 (entitled 'Limitation periods for the imposition of penalties') and Article 26 (entitled 'Limitation period for the enforcement of penalties') relate only to the Commission's powers. Given the absence of specific Community rules, it is for the Member States to determine the periods within which the national authorities may investigate infringements of Community antitrust law and impose and enforce any penalties.

35.5. THE COOPERATION AND CONTROL MECHANISMS IN THE ADMINISTRATIVE ANTITRUST SYSTEM

Article 3(1) plays an essential role in the antitrust system established by Regulation 1/03. It requires the national authorities and courts to apply Articles 81 and 82 EC when they initiate proceedings in a case having Community relevance. Recital 8 of the preamble to the Regulation makes it

---

[7] *Sante Pasquini v INPS*, Case C-34/02, E.C.R. 2003, p. 6515, § 57.
[8] Ibid., § 58.

clear that the objective of Article 3(1) is to 'ensure the effective enforcement of the Community competition rules and the proper functioning of the cooperation mechanisms contained in this Regulation'.

Article 3(1) is important as regards the relations between the Commission and the national authorities. It establishes an obligation for national bodies to apply the same prohibitions (that is, Articles 81 and 82 EC) pursuant to the same set of procedural rules (that is, Regulation 1/03) which are directly applicable throughout the Community. This allows interoperability between antitrust systems, in much the same way as a single operative system allows different computers to be linked up. The link between the Community system and the national systems was at least partially provided for by Regulation 17/62. The novel aspect of the system is thus 'horizontal interoperability' between the national systems *inter se*, which creates a Network of authorities applying Community antitrust law consistently.

The fact that the national authorities are established and regulated by national law and operate in a domestic context inevitably imposes limitations. However, this interoperability projects the authorities into a system regulated entirely by Community law, the so-called Network of antitrust authorities, and thus enables those limitations to be overcome. In so doing, the Regulation succeeds where the 1930 Intergovernmental Conference failed (*supra*).

To allow this interoperability to function, the Regulation has established rules for two types of proceedings.

35.5.1. Proceedings to Facilitate Cooperation between the Commission and the National Authorities

Such proceedings are activated, according to the context, either by the Commission or by the national authorities. Regulation 1/03 establishes the following sets of rules:

- 'vertical ascending' cooperation procedures, which were already provided for by Articles 84 and 85 EC and by Regulation 17/62;
- 'vertical descending' procedures, which are a new feature introduced by Regulation 17/62; and
- 'horizontal' cooperation (peer control) procedures between the authorities of different Member States. Such 'horizontal' proceedings, which contribute to the implementation of the general principle of 'concentration of Community antitrust powers' (see *infra*), have a number of functions:

    - they help to determine which nodal point in the system is in the best position to act in individual cases;

- they also allow information acquired pursuant to Regulation 1/03 to circulate among the authorities and the Commission; and
- they allow the national authorities to carry out investigations on behalf of other authorities of the network on their own territory.

35.5.2. Proceedings to Monitor the Decisions Which These Bodies Take

Regulation 1/03 provides as follows:

- Article 11(3) provides for vertical descending control. These proceedings help to prevent the interoperability of the national antitrust systems causing anarchy within the network. Looked at from a hierarchical angle, it is the Commission which, pursuant to Article 85 EC, requires the national authorities to follow a specific orientation of Community competition policy when they apply Articles 81 and 82 EC. Furthermore, via Article 11(3) proceedings, the Commission has the power of last instance to monitor whether the decisions of the national authorities and courts are consistent with the Commission's competition policy (*infra*);
- 'peer control', as embodied by Article 14(7) of the Regulation, and which acts as an incentive to the concentration of Community antitrust competence; and
- 'vertical ascending' control in Article 14(1) of the Regulation. This gives the national authorities (or, to express it more accurately, the Member States) a means of controlling the way in which the Commission applies Community antitrust law.

36. Mechanisms Allowing Cooperation between the Commission and National Antitrust Authorities: Vertical and Horizontal Cooperation

36.1. VERTICAL COOPERATION

Although Article 11 of the Regulation is entitled 'Cooperation between the Commission and the competition authorities of the Member States', paragraph 5 is in fact the only provision of the Article which establishes a form of cooperation between the Commission and the national authorities (we can classify the cooperation concerned as 'vertical descending'). The other paragraphs of Article 11 concern the ways in which the Commission monitors the application of Community competition law by the national authorities. It also relates to the first stage of the control which those authorities can exercise over the Commission (Article 11(2)).

As already stated, the Regulation provides, as between Commission and national authorities, for both 'vertical descending cooperation' and 'vertical ascending cooperation'.

36.1.1. 'Vertical Descending Cooperation'

'Vertical descending cooperation' is regulated by Article 11(5). It provides that 'the competition authorities of the Member States may consult the Commission on any case involving the application of Community law'. This form of cooperation, which is provided in order to assist the smooth application of Articles 81 and 82 EC by the national authorities, was developed in the *Automec II* and *BEMIM* case law. It was subsequently put on a more formal footing in the 1997 Notice on cooperation between the Commission and the national authorities (*supra*).

It is interesting to note how Article 11(5) differs from Article 15(1), which deals with the relations between the Commission and the national courts. Article 15(1) allows the national courts to consult the Commission only 'concerning the application of the Community competition rules'. By contrast, the facility which Article 11(5) grants to the competition authorities extends to 'any case involving the application of Community law'. This difference can be explained by the fact that, within the Community antitrust system, the national courts' role is different from that of the national authorities. It is therefore logical to endeavour to confer on the national authorities all the powers which will enable them to replace the Commission when they enforce Articles 81 and 82 EC.

A further reason for the difference between the two provisions is the wish to avoid conferring on national courts applying Community antitrust law a general power to consult the Commission on matters of Community law. Had that power been conferred, it would have obliged the Commission to respond to consultations from the national courts going beyond the area covered by competition law.

36.1.2. 'Vertical Ascending Cooperation'

'Vertical ascending cooperation' takes place when the Commission's powers of investigation are delegated to the national authorities. The powers may be delegated either by simple request or by formal decision. Article 22(2) of the Regulation makes it clear that, when such powers are delegated, national law regulates the powers of the 'officials of the competition authorities of the Member States who are responsible for conducting these inspections as well as those authorised or appointed by them'. This provision concerning the delegated powers of investigation of the national authorities constitutes an exception since, in every other respect, the individual Member States remain exclusively competent to determine how the national authorities' powers of investigation are to be carried out.

36.2. HORIZONTAL COOPERATION

In addition to the two forms of vertical cooperation outlined above, the Regulation provides for three forms of horizontal cooperation between the national authorities. These are governed by Article 13(1), the last sentence of Article 11(4) and Article 22(1), respectively. These forms of cooperation can be seen as components of the broader principle of concentration of Community antitrust powers, which also involves the Commission (see paragraph 7 of the Notice on the Network).

The 'principle of concentration of Community antitrust competence' means that every case in which Community antitrust law is applied should be handled by only one authority, which may be the Commission or a national authority. This principle is implemented through a number of procedures established by Regulation 1/03. They are as follows:

- the three stages of 'horizontal cooperation' between the national authorities (Article 13(1), the last sentence of Article 11(4) and Article 22(1) of Regulation 1/03);
- the power granted to the Commission to close the file on a complaint (Article 13 of the Regulation); and
- 'peer control' exercised by the Advisory Committee (Article 14(7) of the Regulation).

Via these three horizontal cooperation procedures, Regulation 1/03 determines which nodal point of the Network is best placed to apply Articles 81 and 82 EC to a particular case. This process is necessary because every single national authority is empowered to apply Community antitrust law and thus, in the event of more than one national authority applying Community antitrust law in parallel proceedings, there would be a risk of conflicting decisions.

36.2.1. The First Stage of Horizontal Cooperation: Exchanging Information

A more detailed analysis of the three forms of horizontal cooperation identified above shows that the first form (established by the last sentence of Article 11(4) of the Regulation) involves an important new possibility; namely that 'national competition authorities may also exchange between themselves information necessary for the assessment of a case that they are dealing with under Article 81 or Article 82 of the Treaty'.

Article 11(4) encourages contacts between the national authorities with a view to deciding which authority is in the best position to evaluate the particular behaviour at issue. Such contacts will also allow the authorities to exchange information at a later stage should there be parallel proceedings.

The last sentence of Article 11(4) relates to a procedure which is different from that envisaged by the remainder of paragraph 4. It allows the national authorities to exchange between themselves information relevant to 'a case that they are dealing with under Article 81 or Article 82 of the Treaty' and thus to bypass the Commission. This part of Article 11(4) thus introduces a horizontal relation between the national authorities that is different from the characteristic vertical 'Commission–national authorities' relationship.

This does not necessarily mean that antitrust decisions applying Articles 81 and 82 which national authorities take as a result of such exchanges of information and assessments escape the Commission's control. The system established by Regulation 1/03 provides that, irrespective of any horizontal cooperation, the national authorities must be subject to control exercised by the Commission pursuant to Article 11(4) (*infra*).

Criteria for the allocation of cases within the Network

The last sentence of Article 11(4) of Regulation 1/03 simply sets out a general rule relating to the exchange of information between national authorities. This is also relevant to determining which authority is best placed to decide an antitrust case. The Commission has also drawn up precise criteria to determine how, *in concreto*, cases should be allocated within the Network. In the Commission's view, as expressed in paragraph 8 of the Notice on cooperation within the Network, an authority is well placed to deal with a case if the following three cumulative conditions are met:

1. the agreement or practice has substantial direct actual or foreseeable effects on competition within its territory, is implemented within or originates from its territory;
2. the authority is able to effectively bring to an end the entire infringement, i.e. it can adopt a cease-and-desist order the effect of which will be sufficient to bring an end to the infringement and it can, where appropriate, sanction the infringement adequately;
3. it can gather, possibly with the assistance of other authorities, the evidence required to prove the infringement.

Depending on which of these conditions is satisfied, a single authority, two or three authorities acting in parallel or the Commission will be in the best position to decide a case. These situations are addressed in paragraphs 10 and 11, paragraphs 12 and 13 and paragraphs 14 and 15 of the Notice, respectively.

The start of the procedure and the re-allocation period

Once the criteria for the allocation of antitrust cases have been defined, the application of those criteria requires close cooperation both between the Commission and the national authorities and between the national authorities *inter se*. In the Commission's view, the first stage at which that cooperation should occur is when a national authority announces that it has opened proceedings applying Community antitrust law. Article 11(3) of the Regulation requires the national authorities to 'inform the Commission in writing' that they have opened proceedings applying Articles 81 or 82 EC 'before or without delay after commencing the first formal investigative measure'. (This step will also indirectly inform the Commission of the initiation of any national antitrust proceedings, *infra*.)

Once that information has been passed on, a period during which what the

Commission terms 're-allocation' commences. This is a period during which the Commission and the other national authorities decide whether the national authority which has initiated the procedure is better placed than the other nodal points of the Network (that is, the other authorities) to handle the case. They may use the Advisory Committee as a forum for this purpose (see the Notice on cooperation within the Network, paragraph 62). According to paragraph 23 of the Notice on the handling of complaints, the re-allocation period should not normally exceed two months. Once this period has expired, the authority or authorities should be able to continue the investigation and conclude it, unless any of the five exceptions defined by the Commission in paragraph 54 of the Notice on cooperation within the Network apply (*infra*).

Horizontal cooperation and the allocation of antitrust cases

Before the notification to the Commission pursuant to Article 11(3) has been made (and thus before the Commission has had any opportunity to intervene) the national authorities enjoy considerable independence to decide among themselves how cases should be allocated. They may do this by applying the principles of horizontal cooperation set out in Article 13(1), the last sentence of Article 11(4) and Article 22(1) of the Regulation (*supra*).

Those forms of horizontal cooperation create opportunities for national authorities to have discussions among themselves. In some cases, this may allow them to decide how the assessment of a specific case may be concentrated in the decision of a single authority, thereby complying with the principle of 'concentration of Community antitrust competence' (see *supra*). This is all done without any direct Commission intervention or, to put it another way, without the need for the Commission to commit any of its limited human resources. As mentioned *supra*, this does not prevent the Commission from carrying out its own control powers under Article 11(4) where there has been horizontal cooperation between the national authorities. Article 11(4) 'reactivates' the Commission's powers of control before the national authority takes its own decision. It stipulates that the national authority must provide the Commission with a summary of the case in respect of which a decision will be taken and 'the envisaged decision or, in the absence thereof, any other document indicating the proposed course of action'.

The effects of re-allocation on the complainants

The re-allocation of a case within the Network entails consequences for the complainant. Once it has been re-allocated, a case is no longer handled by the authority to which the complaint has been submitted. In that light, the Commission has established certain means of safeguarding the position of complainants in cases where an alleged antitrust infringement has subsequently been re-allocated to another national authority. The basic principle underlying the re-allocation procedure is expressed in paragraph 31 of the Notice on cooperation within the Network, which provides that Regulation 1/03:

> has created a system of parallel competences, the allocation of cases between members of the network constitutes a mere division of labour where some authorities abstain from acting. The allocation of cases does not therefore confer any individual rights on the companies involved in or affected by an infringement to have the case dealt with by a particular authority.

As regards the protection of complainants, 'if a case is re-allocated within the network, the undertakings concerned and the complainant(s) are informed as soon as possible by the competition authorities involved' (paragraph 34 of the Notice). In addition, as paragraph 35 of the Notice goes on to explain, 'if a complaint is lodged with the Commission pursuant to Article 7 of the ... Regulation and if the Commission does not investigate the complaint or practice complained of, the complainant has a right to obtain a decision rejecting his complaint', except where Article 7(3) of Commission Regulation 773/2004[1] applies.[2] The rights of complainants who lodge a complaint with a national authority are governed by the relevant national law.

36.2.2. The Second Stage of Horizontal Cooperation: The Suspension or Termination of Proceedings

Article 13 of Regulation 1/03 establishes the second stage of horizontal cooperation between the national authorities. This stage takes place after the authorities have exchanged information on 'a case that they are dealing with under Article 81 or Article 82 of the Treaty' (see Article 11(4) of the Regulation). Article 13 also provides certain other tools which enable the Commission to ensure that an antitrust case is handled by a single body, thereby complying with the principle of concentration of Community antitrust competence (*supra*).

Article 13(1) provides that the national authorities and the Commission may (*ex hypothesi* after exchanging information pursuant to the last sentence of Article 11(4)) suspend or reject a complaint, thereby remitting the decision in the case to another authority.

---

[1] Regulation 773/2004 Relating to the Conduct of Proceedings by the Commission Pursuant to Articles 81 and 82 of the EC Treaty, 2004 OJ L 123/18.

[2] Article 7(3) of Regulation 773/2004 provides that: 'if the complainant fails to make known its views within the time-limit set by the Commission, the complaint shall be deemed to have been withdrawn'.

This may happen:

- where more than one authority has received the same complaint;
- where more than one authority is acting *ex officio* in respect of the same case; or
- where a complaint has been made to the Commission when a national authority is already dealing with the case.

By contrast, Article 13(2) confers power on the national authorities and the Commission to reject a complaint 'which has already been dealt with by another competition authority'.

The novelty of both paragraphs of Article 13 is that they confer on the national authorities and the Commission the power to close the file on cases without being required to give reasons (this is a situation similar to that falling within the last part of Article 5 of the Regulation, *supra*). As paragraph 22 of the Notice makes clear, a national authority has the option of closing its proceedings but is not obliged to do so. Any decision suspending or closing proceedings will be taken by the individual authorities in the light of the interest which they attribute to a particular case.

The Commission has also noted that suspension or closure may be only partial, in other words it may concern only part of any proceedings opened by the national authority. Article 13 allows complaints to be closed, in so far as this is consistent with the obligation imposed by the last sentence of Article 5 of the Regulation (*supra*), where individual authorities do not consider them to be of any particular interest for the part of the Community territory affected by the alleged infringement (that is, the territory of the Member State to which the authority in question belongs).

Suspension or rejection of complaints by one national authority in cases dealt with by another national authority

Article 13(1) of the Regulation provides that 'the fact that one authority is dealing with the case shall be sufficient grounds for the others to suspend the proceedings before them or reject the complaint' concerning the same antitrust case. By the expression 'dealing with the case', Article 13 is referring both to the pre-investigation stage and the formal stage of the proceedings. The first point in time at which the Commission, and possibly the other national authorities, may be aware that the authority in question is 'acting under Article 81 or Article 82 of the Treaty' is either 'before' or 'without delay after commencing the first formal investigative measure' (see Article 11(3) of the Regulation). The Commission must receive this information 'in writing' and it 'may also be made available to the competition authorities of the other Member States'.

Article 13(1) permits an authority which has initiated investigative proceedings and completed the various activities connected with the preparation and carrying out of the investigation (such as notifications, inspections and so forth) to close the file on the case. However, closing the file will not have any negative impact on the investigations that have already been carried out. Any active steps, such as inspections will not have been carried out in vain since any information thereby acquired by the relevant authority can, pursuant to Article 12 of the Regulation, be transferred to the authority which has been designated to conclude the antitrust proceedings. The possibility of using Article 12 to 'concentrate' information and documents within a single authority, rather than allowing them to remain dispersed among several authorities allows proceedings to be opened in cases which, otherwise, would never be handled.

Where a national authority suspends proceedings pursuant to Article 13(1) of the Regulation in order to allow another authority to investigate the case and the second authority has come to a decision, the first authority has two options. Where the two proceedings relate to precisely the same factual situation, it may either 'ratify' the decision or close the file on the complaint. This course of action is permissible in the light of the *Walt Wilhelm* case law. If the first authority ratifies the decision of the second, the principle of *non bis in idem* precludes it from imposing further monetary penalties on the undertakings concerned. However, a double penalty in respect of the same facts is lawful when the first penalty is imposed under Community law and the second by virtue of national law[3] (for the effects of the decision of a national authority applying Community law on the antitrust powers of the other Member States see *supra*).

Rejection of a complaint by the Commission where a national authority is dealing with the case

Article 13(1) of the Regulation also refers to the exercise of antitrust power by the Commission. While the national authorities may either suspend proceedings or reject the complaint, the last sentence of Article 13(1) stipulates that the Commission may only reject the complaint 'on the ground that a competition authority of a Member State is dealing with the case'. This is because Article 11(6) makes it impossible for there to be parallel proceedings in which both the Commission and a national authority are applying Community antitrust law to the same case. Nevertheless, should the Commission initiate proceedings applying Articles 81 and/or 82 EC (thereby relieving the national authorities of the powers conferred on them by Article 5 of the Regulation), the national authorities may still apply national antitrust

[3] *Sotralentz v. Commission*, Case T-149/89, E.C.R. 1995, p. II–1127, § 78.

law, in so far as this is consistent with Article 3 of the Regulation.

The reasons on which the Commission and the national authorities may rely when they close the file pursuant to Article 13 still differ. When the Commission rejects a complaint, its intention is to reduce its workload by delegating to the national authorities the assessment of a case that is not of Community interest. It is then for the authorities to decide whether or not proceedings should be initiated. On the other hand, for cases which are not of Community interest, the purpose of one national authority rejecting a complaint is to concentrate the exercise of Community antitrust competence in the hands of a single national authority.

Rejection by the Commission or by the national authorities of a complaint where the case has already been dealt with

Article 13(2) of the Regulation confers power on the national authorities and the Commission to reject a complaint that has already been 'dealt with' by another competition authority. The expression 'complaint ... which has already been dealt with by another authority' refers to two different types of case:

- to cases in which the relevant national authority has reached a decision on the substance (such as finding whether or not there has been an infringement); and
- to cases covered by the second part of Article 5, in which the file has been closed on the case because the evidence adduced by the complainant is insufficient to prove the existence of an infringement.

The Commission may reject a complaint on the basis of the reasons set out in Article 13(2). It may also do so because of lack of Community interest (*supra*) or because of the nature of the complaint itself (see Article 7(3) of Regulation 773/2004, paragraph 41 of the Commission Notice on the handling of complaints).

Although the objective of Article 13 of the Regulation is to facilitate and rationalise the activity of the Commission and the national authorities, it may nevertheless have negative consequences for individuals. The possibility for the national authorities to close the file on a complaint may surreptitiously develop into a means whereby they are able to get rid of justified complaints. This can happen if none of the authorities which have received a complaint initiates a proceeding or if they close cases without giving reasons. For example, if the first authorities dealing with the case decline to open an investigation, they may rely on Article 13(1) because the case is the subject of proceedings before other authorities. For their part, the authorities that initially keep the proceedings open may subsequently be able to refuse to take further action in reliance on the second paragraph of Article 5. To avoid this happening, the safeguard provided by the second paragraph of Article 5, described *supra*, applies. If there is evidence which proves an infringement of Community antitrust law, at least one national authority (and if the case has Community interest the Commission too) must open an investigation. This obligation exists in order to safeguard the rights which Articles 81 and 82 EC confer on individuals (*supra*).

36.2.3. The Third Stage of Horizontal Cooperation: Carrying Out Investigations on Behalf of Other National Authorities

Article 22(1) of the Regulation deals with a potential third stage during which the principle of horizontal cooperation may be put into practice. That stage arises after the national authorities, acting pursuant to Article 14(3), have assessed the information on antitrust cases among themselves (first stage). After a national authority has suspended or rejected a complaint pursuant to Article 13 in order to allow another authority to investigate it (second stage). In the third stage, Article 22(1) provides for the possibility that the national authorities (including that or those which have suspended proceedings or rejected a complaint) may carry out investigations 'on behalf of and for the account of' the national authority chosen to conclude the assessment of the case.

The matter dealt with by Article 22(1) is particularly important. Article 3(1) requires the national authorities to apply Articles 81 and 82 EC on a constant basis. They are therefore obliged to deal with cases which may have effects in more than one Member State (that is, cases which affect trade between Member States). For that reason, it is essential for the national authorities to have information on the effects which the behaviour under investigation (for example, any price increase in a particular sector) has had in other Member States. Furthermore, the authorities need to have documents which may not be available in their own Member State and which might have been concealed on premises of the undertakings concerned in another Member State. Had the powers contained in Article 22(1) not been provided, the national authorities would have been in a less than ideal situation as regards obtaining and evaluating any information in reliance on the powers granted to them. Whether an authority is best placed to deal with a case depends not only on its hierarchical position (that is, as the Commission), but also on whether it has information at its disposal which allows it to assess a particular case.

Article 22(1) therefore allows a national antitrust body to carry out antitrust investigations on the territory of another Member State through the latter's antitrust authority. It may thus obtain information from all the authorities in a way similar to the Commission. By virtue of Article 22(1), an antitrust authority becomes the 'executive arm' of another antitrust authority.[4]

Article 22(1) is of great importance both conceptually and from a practical point of view. It provides the means to reconcile the contradiction between:

- the coercive powers of the Member States, which are territorially circumscribed; and
- the objective of providing the means to deal rapidly and effectively with antitrust infringements having effects on the territory of more than one Member State.

In other words, it represents a way of overcoming the difficulties, which were brought to light as early as the 1930s (*supra*), faced by European nation states in tackling the internationalisation of competition. These problems and the concomitant inability of European states to control independently the international dimension of the 'concentration of capital' also contributed to the establishment of the EEC (*supra*).

Detailed rules are required to ensure the smooth functioning of the investigative collaboration provided for by Article 22(1). The same remark applies for every stage of horizontal cooperation and, indeed, of the very 'principle of concentration of Community antitrust competence'. Rules are required to regulate:

- the exchange of information both between the national authorities and the Commission and between the national authorities *inter se*; and
- the utilisation and protection of confidential information.

That is why the final sentence of Article 22(1) stipulates that any exchange and use of the information collected shall be carried out in accordance with Article 12. (That article deals with the exchange of information circulation within the Network.)

---

[4] The Italian Competition Authority has already availed itself of this possibility. In a press release dated 15 July 2004 on an investigation into baby milk manufacturers, it is stated as follows: 'The Authority has deemed it appropriate to enlist the cooperation of the Competition Authorities of the other member countries of the European Union under Community Regulation 1/2003 (which came into force on 1 May 2004). New investigations have therefore been conducted simultaneously on the premises of the companies concerned not only in Italy, but also in France, Germany and Spain'.

36.3. OTHER TYPES OF COOPERATION

The system established by Regulation 1/03 enables information in the possession of national authorities to circulate within the Network and thus to be available to all 27 national authorities as well as the Commission. This, in turn, has required the drafting of detailed rules to determine how the information should be managed. To this end, Article 1/03 radically reforms the system established by Regulation 17/62 dealing with the use of information obtained in the context of the enforcement of Articles 81 and 82 EC:

- first, Article 12 of Regulation 1/03 relates to the circulation of information within the Network and its use as evidence;
- second, Article 28(1) deals with the principle that information can be used only for the purpose for which it was acquired. This principle applies to the Commission, the national authorities and the national courts; and
- third, the Regulation prohibits certain information from being divulged outside the Network (Article 28(2) deals with professional secrecy and Article 27(2) with the limits on the circulation of internal documents).

36.3.1. The Circulation and Use of Information within the Network

The first reform of the system of managing information established by Regulation 17/62 relates to the circulation and use of information which is to be used as evidence. Article 12 of Regulation 1/03 deals with three different aspects of this issue.

The circulation and use of information between the Commission and the national authorities and among the national authorities *inter se*
Article 12 of the Regulation provides that 'for the purpose of applying Articles 81 and 82 of the Treaty the Commission and the competition authorities of the Member States shall have the power to provide one another with and use in evidence any matter of fact and law, including confidential information' (see Recital 16 of the preamble to the Regulation). This allows the national authorities and the Commission to obtain information in the possession of other bodies within the Network. Such information may be used either as evidence of the undertakings' wrongdoing or, more generally, in order to initiate investigations (as opposed to being used in evidence *stricto sensu*).

One of the golden threads of antitrust decentralisation policy is the obligation incumbent on the national authorities and courts to apply Articles

81 and 82 EC to a case of Community relevance. Fulfilment of this obligation requires the unrestricted circulation of information between the Commission and the national authorities for the purpose of enforcing Community antitrust law. Since Article 3(1) of the Regulation requires the national authorities to apply Community antitrust law to cases which 'may affect trade between Member States', the authorities need to be able to obtain information on the effects which those cases have on the territory of other Member States, just as they do in those cases to which Article 22(1) applies (*supra*). National authorities also need to be able to obtain documents taken to or hidden in the offices of undertakings which are the subject of proceedings in the other Member States. Article 12 therefore constitutes an indispensable tool for the effective decentralised application of Community antitrust law.

The purpose and the use of information in the possession of the Network of authorities (Article 12(2) of Regulation 1/03)

Article 12(1) of the Regulation provides for the unrestricted circulation of information between the Commission and the national authorities, but Article 12(2) limits the extent to which such information can be used as evidence.

On the one hand, the information may be used for the sole purpose of applying Community antitrust law. On the other, in order to protect undertakings, the information may be used only 'in respect of the subject-matter for which it was collected by the transmitting authority' (see Recital 16 in the preamble to the Regulation).

In this way, Article 12 constitutes an express exception to the general principle, in Article 28(1), that, without prejudice to Articles 12 and 15, information collected pursuant to the powers of investigation provided for by the Regulation shall be used only for the purpose for which it was acquired (see *infra*). That is because, by virtue of Article 12(2), information may be used not merely for the purpose for which it was acquired but also in respect of the subject-matter for which it was collected by the transmitting authority.

Limiting the use of information acquired by virtue of the Regulation to the enforcement of Articles 81 and 82 means that it may not be used for the application of the law of the Member States. This rule is subject to one exception, set out in the last sentence of Article 12(2), which allows information exchanged to be used in evidence for the application of national competition law if three cumulative conditions are met. Those conditions are as follows:

1. national competition law is being applied in the same case (that is, the subject matter of the proceedings is the same);
2. national competition law is being applied in parallel to Community antitrust law (the parallel application may be carried out by one or more

national authorities or by the Commission and national authorities); and
3. the application of national law does not lead to a different outcome from the result which would be reached by applying Community law.

This provision is consistent with the objective of Article 3(2) of the Regulation, which is to prevent national antitrust law from reaching a result different from that which would be attained if Article 81 was applied (*supra*). The final sentence of Article 12(2) gives national authorities applying national law to cases of Community relevance an incentive to reach the same result as if they were applying Community antitrust law. Furthermore, unlike Article 3(2), Article 12(2) applies even where the abuse of a dominant position is in issue (*infra*). That provision gives the national authorities two options:

- it may apply any domestic law prohibiting the abuse of a dominant position which is stricter than Article 82; and
- it may use information already in its possession and obtained by virtue of the Regulation to enforce the national law prohibiting the abuse of a dominant position. If it does so, it may not apply national antitrust law differently from Article 82.

Furthermore, although the last sentence of Article 12(2) allows information obtained by virtue of Regulation 1/03 to be used for applying national antitrust law, this possibility does not have any negative impact on the operation of the Community system. The principle that information obtained pursuant to Regulation 1/03 may be used only for the application of EC law only is displaced on condition that Community law and national law are applied in parallel (and reach the same result). In other words, Article 12(2) does not give any incentive to apply national antitrust law more frequently than Community law. Quite the contrary, unlike the unlawful Article 3(2) (*infra*), it represents a legitimate incentive for the Member States to ensure that national antitrust law reaches the same conclusions as Community law.

Limitations on the use of information to impose penalties on natural persons (Article 12(3) of Regulation 1/03)

Article 12(3) limits the extent to which information exchanged pursuant to Article 12(1) may be used in evidence to impose sanctions for breach of Community antitrust law on natural persons. Generally speaking, in order that such information may be used in evidence against natural persons, Article 12(3) requires a third condition to be met in addition to the conditions imposed by Article 12(2) (*supra*). That condition is that 'the law of the transmitting authority foresees sanctions of a similar kind in relation to an infringement of Article 81 or Article 82 of the Treaty' (in that case, the information may be used even for the purpose of imposing even custodial sentences if both the Member States in question provide for that penalty). Even if that is not the case, the third condition is still satisfied where 'the information has been collected in a way which respects the same level of protection of the rights of defence of natural persons as provided for under the national rules of the receiving authority'. However, in the latter case 'the information exchanged cannot be used by the receiving authority to impose custodial sanctions'.

The reasons for these rules are set out in Recital 16 in the preamble to the Regulation. It is stated that:

> as regards natural persons, they may be subject to substantially different types of sanctions across the various systems. Where that is the case, it is necessary to ensure that information can only be used if it has been collected in a way which respects the same level of protection of the rights of defence of natural persons as provided for under the national rules of the receiving authority.

Use as evidence of information supplied in a request for leniency

The circulation and use within the Network of information supplied by undertakings to the members is also relevant to the issue of requests for leniency. The Commission has drawn attention to this problem.[5] An application for favourable treatment (leniency) has effects only in relation to the national authority to which it is made. At paragraph 38 of the Notice on cooperation within the Network, the Commission notes that an application for leniency to one authority does not have any consequences for other authorities in the Network. Taking into account the importance of timing in leniency applications, the Commission advises applicants to consider whether 'it would be appropriate to file leniency applications with the relevant authorities simultaneously'.

The uncertainty which the Commission is endeavouring to resolve in the Notice relates to the legitimate use of information that is supplied by the leniency applicant and thereby introduced into the Network. The Commission has developed two principles on the point:

---

[5] By its use of the expression 'leniency' the Commission is referring to Community and national leniency programmes the aim of which is 'to facilitate the detection by competition authorities of cartel activity and also thereby to act as a deterrent to participation in unlawful cartels' (see paragraph 37 of the Notice on cooperation within the Network). In the same paragraph, the Commission indicates that 'it is in the Community interest to grant favourable treatment to undertakings which cooperate with it in the investigation of cartel infringements. A number of Member States have also adopted leniency programmes relating to cartel investigations'.

1. *Information supplied by an undertaking and introduced into the Network by virtue of Article 11(2) and 11(3).* On this issue,

> as for all cases where Articles 81 and 82 of the Treaty are applied, where an NCA (national competition authority) deals with a case which has been initiated as a result of a leniency application, it must inform the Commission and may make the information available to other members of the network pursuant to Article 11(3) of the Council Regulation. The Commission has accepted an equivalent obligation to inform NCAs under Article 11(2) of the Council Regulation. In such cases, however, information submitted to the network pursuant to Article 11 will not be used by other members of the network as the basis for starting an investigation on their own behalf whether under the competition rules of the Treaty or, in the case of NCAs, under their national competition laws or other laws. This is without prejudice to any power of the authority to open an investigation on the basis of information received from other sources or, subject to paragraphs 40 and 41 below, to request, be provided with and use information pursuant to Article 12 from any member of the network, including the network member to whom the leniency application was submitted. (paragraph 39 of the Notice on cooperation within the Network)

2. *Information supplied by an undertaking and introduced into the Network pursuant to Article 12 of the Regulation.* According to paragraph 40 of the Notice,

> save as provided under paragraph 41, information voluntarily submitted by a leniency applicant will only be transmitted to another member of the network pursuant to Article 12 of the Council Regulation with the consent of the applicant. Similarly other information that has been obtained during or following an inspection or by means of or following any other fact-finding measures which, in each case, could not have been carried out except as a result of the leniency application will only be transmitted to another authority pursuant to Article 12 of the Council Regulation if the applicant has consented to the transmission to that authority of information it has voluntarily submitted in its application for leniency.

The principle that information may not be transmitted to any other authority pursuant to Article 12 is departed from 'if the applicant has consented to the transmission to that authority of information it has voluntarily submitted in its application for leniency'. In the same paragraph it is made clear that once consent to the transmission of information has been given, it may not be withdrawn. In paragraph 41 of the Notice, the Commission has identified certain circumstances in which the consent of the applicant undertaking is not required, namely:

- where the receiving authority has also received a leniency application relating to the same infringement (paragraph 41.1);
- where the receiving authority has provided a written commitment that the information received will not be used to impose sanctions on any persons covered by the leniency application (paragraph 41.2); and
- where the sending authority, acting pursuant to Article 22(1), has collected information on behalf of and for the account of the receiving authority which is another network member to which a leniency application has been made (paragraph 41.3).

These principles have been set out by the Commission in a Notice, which is a non-binding measure. This has led the Commission to state in paragraph 41 of the Notice that:

> information relating to cases initiated as a result of a leniency application and which has been submitted to the Commission under Article 11(3) of the Council Regulation will only be made available to those NCAs that have committed themselves to respecting the principles set out above … . The same principle applies where a case has been initiated by the Commission as a result of a leniency application made to the Commission. This does not affect the power of any authority to be provided with information under Article 12 of the Council Regulation, provided however that the provisions of paragraphs 40 and 41 are respected.

Leniency programmes raise the question of the extent to which information received by the national authorities may be relied on to initiate investigations (as opposed to being used in evidence *stricto sensu*) under Community or national antitrust law. The Commission's approach is that such information cannot be used for that purpose. In paragraph 39 of the Notice, the Commission maintains that: 'In such cases, however, information submitted to the network members pursuant to Article 11 will not be used by other members of the network as the basis for starting an investigation on their own behalf whether under the competition rules of the Treaty or, in the case of NCAs, under their national competition law or other laws'. In reality, it is difficult to prevent this happening. As the Court of Justice put it in *Spanish Banks*, national authorities which have received information which they cannot use in evidence cannot reasonably be required to ignore that information completely and thus suffer 'acute amnesia'.[6]

---

[6] *Direccion General de Defensa de la Competencia v. Asociacion Espanola de Banca privada*, Case C-67/91, E.C.R. 1992, p. I–4785, § 39.

36.3.2. The Purpose for which Information May Be Used by the Commission, the National Authorities and the National Courts

The second result of the reform of the system of handling of information introduced by Regulation 1/03 is that information may be used only for the purpose for which it was acquired (Article 28(1) of the Regulation). This is a general principle and thus not restricted to use within the Network.

Article 28(1), which is to be found in Title VIII ('Hearings and Professional Secrecy'), defines the purposes for which information collected thanks to the use of the powers contained in the Regulation may be used. It provides that 'information collected pursuant to Articles 17 to 22 shall be used only for the purpose for which it was acquired'. However, in providing that it is without prejudice to Articles 12 and 15, Article 28(1) admits exceptions to the principle which it enunciates:

- the first exception, relating to the national authorities and falling under Article 15, has already been considered *supra*; and
- the second exception falls under Article 15(1) (*infra*) and relates to the powers of the national courts. Article 15(1) provides that 'in proceedings for the application of Article 81 or Article 82 of the Treaty, courts of the Member States may ask the Commission to transmit to them information in its possession or its opinion on questions concerning the application of the Community competition rules'. This exception to the general principle expressed in Article 28(1) is required since the information requested or the questions asked may have 'a purpose' different from that for which the information was originally acquired. However, this type of circulation of information requires (not merely to protect business secrets) rules on professional secrecy (*infra*).

36.3.3. The Prohibition on Divulging Information Outside the Network

The third reform of the system of handling information which existed under Regulation 17/62 relates to the prohibition on divulging information in the possession of Network members outside the Network. The most relevant provisions in this context are Articles 27(2) and 28(2) of Regulation 1/03.

First category of information which may not be disclosed

The first category of information which may not be disclosed is information covered by professional secrecy.

Article 28(2) provides that the Commission, the national authorities and their servants 'shall not disclose information acquired or exchanged by them pursuant to this Regulation and of the kind covered by the obligation of professional secrecy'. In this context it should be noted that the Commission has made it clear in paragraph 23 of the Notice on cooperation with the national courts that the expression 'professional secrecy' in the Regulation bears the same meaning as in Article 287 EC. In particular, 'the information covered by professional secrecy may be both confidential information and business secrets'.

The Commission has stated at paragraph 28a of the Notice on cooperation within the Network that the term professional secrecy 'used in Article 28 of the Council Regulation is a Community law concept and includes in particular business secrets and other confidential information'. In its definition of 'business secrets', which is a concept which features several times in Regulation 1/03 (Articles 14(6), 27(4) and 30), the Commission maintains that 'business secrets are information of which not only disclosure to the public but also mere transmission to a person other than the one that provided the information might seriously harm the latter's interests' (paragraph 23 of the Notice on cooperation with the national courts).

Article 28(2) lists several provisions of the Regulation, noting that they constitute exceptions to the principle that information may not be disclosed outside the Network. Those provisions are as follows:

- Article 11 (Cooperation between the Commission and the competition authorities of the Member States);
- Article 12 (Exchange of information);
- Article 14 (Advisory Committee);
- Article 15 (Cooperation with national courts); and
- Article 27 (Hearing of the parties, complainants and others).

Those exceptions relate to the situations in which information 'covered by the obligation of professional secrecy' may be exchanged and used both among national authorities *inter se* and between the Commission and the national authorities. (In addition to the national courts and in cases of hearings of the parties.) Strictly speaking, permitting exchange of information in the first three cases does not require a derogation since this facility is expressly provided for.

Second category of information which may not be disclosed

The second category of information which may not be disclosed outside the Network is composed of 'internal documents of the Commission and the competition authorities of the Member States', referred to in Article 27(2) and in Recital 32 of the preamble to the Regulation.

The reason underlying this prohibition is not the same as in the case of information covered by business secrecy. Business secrets are protected in order to safeguard undertakings' right of economic initiative. They are also protected because undertakings would not be sufficiently cooperative if such safeguards were not provided for. On the other hand, the prohibition on disclosing internal documents is a way of protecting the Community antitrust administrative system, albeit this operates to the detriment of judicial protection (*infra*). The effectiveness of the network's enforcement activity would be seriously jeopardised if individuals could obtain access to the Commission's internal deliberations or contacts between the Commission and the national authorities concerning ongoing or envisaged investigations. This would not allow independent investigations to take place. It would also prejudice the effectiveness of the proceedings themselves, for example by removing the element of surprise from an inspection.

Third category of information which may not be disclosed

As regards the third category of information which may not be disclosed outside the Network, it was pointed out *supra* that the protection of the Community system entails restrictions even for national courts. The Commission may refuse to transmit documents in order to 'safeguard the interests of the Community or to avoid any interference with its functioning and independence, in particular by jeopardising the accomplishment of the tasks entrusted to it' (see paragraphs 19 and 26 of the Notice on cooperation with the national courts). Articles 20(8) and 21(1) of Regulation 1/03 (*infra)* have the same objective.

37. Control Mechanisms Allowing the Commission and National Antitrust Authorities to Control Each Other: Vertical Descending, Peer and Vertical Ascending Control

Regulation 1/03 introduces quite substantial amendments to the system established by Article 85 EC and Article 10 of Regulation 17/62 for the monitoring of the application of Articles 81 and 82 EC. The establishment of innovative monitoring procedures is a consequence of the deliberate decentralisation policy that Regulation 1/03 pursues (*supra*). The objective of this policy is to restrict the Commission's direct enforcement activities to the most important antitrust cases, thereby promoting more frequent application of Community antitrust law by the national authorities and courts. This requires detailed rules which allow it to be assessed whether a particular case should be dealt with by a national authority or the Commission (this is the 'principle of concentration of Community antitrust competence', see *supra*).

The decentralised application of Community law, which involves national bodies, rather than the Commission, applying Articles 81 and 82 EC, is regulated by three types of control which may be categorised as follows:

- 'vertical descending' control, which means that the Commission must be able to verify that national bodies are not applying Community antitrust law in a way which conflicts with EC law. This is regulated by Article 11(3) of the Regulation;
- 'vertical ascending' control, which entails an increase in the Member States' powers to control the Commission's application of Community antitrust law. This is regulated by Article 11(2) of the Regulation; and
- peer control between the national authorities *inter se*. This is a consequence of the principle of the concentration of Community antitrust law (Article 14(7) of Regulation 1/03).

Regulation 1/03 also institutes a specific forum in which general competition problems can be discussed, namely the enlarged composition of the Advisory Committee (see Article 14, paragraphs (2) and (7) of the Regulation).

37.1. VERTICAL DESCENDING CONTROL

As regards the ways in which the Commission may exercise vertical descending control, Article 11 of Regulation 1/03 stipulates for the first time the principle that 'the Commission and the competition authorities of the Member States shall apply the Community competition rules in close cooperation'. At first sight, this expression might be assumed to refer simply to the general principle of cooperation articulated in Article 10 EC. However, a comparison of the new system with the arrangements established by Article 85 EC and Article 10(3) of Regulation 17/62 shows that its effects on the relations between the Commission and the national authorities are nothing short of revolutionary. The principle of close cooperation goes beyond simple cooperation. Underlying it is more the notion of *mutual control* of the application of Community antitrust law within the Community antitrust system, which takes it beyond and distinguishes it from the obligation established by Article 10 EC. The principle of close cooperation embraces more than the old vertical ascending control which the national authorities exercised over the Commission in the context of the former principle of close and constant cooperation between the Commission and the national authorities (see Article 85 EC and Article 10(1) of Regulation 17/62). It adds the new binding 'vertical descending' control exercised by the Commission over the national authorities' application of Community law. For its part, thc Commission, at paragraph 10 of the Notice on the handling of complaints, simply states that 'in addition, Articles 11 and 15 of the Regulation create a range of mechanisms by which the Member States' courts and competition authorities cooperate with the Commission in the enforcement of Articles 81 and 82'.

By virtue of the particular role which Article 84 EC confers on the national authorities and the consequent obligations incumbent on them, the principle of close cooperation in the enforcement of Articles 81 and 82 refers exclusively to the relation between the Commission and the national authorities. It does not extend to the relation between the Commission and the national courts.

The new vertical descending control mechanism has been inserted in the new decentralisation policy in order to allow the Commission to monitor how national authorities are applying Articles 81 and 82. In other words, this principle, and Article 11(3) and (4) which implements it, aim to remedy a defect which had been revealed in the operation of the system established by Regulation 17/62. That system lacked a mechanism enabling the Commission to ensure that the Member States did not apply Community law in a way which conflicted with Community antitrust policy or Community law. In 1962 this aspect was certainly not a priority.

37.1.1. The Principles of 'Vertical Descending' Control

The monitoring of the national authorities by the Commission constitutes the means by which the principle of cooperation enunciated in Article 11(1) of the Regulation is put into practice. This control mechanism is regulated by Articles 11(3) and 11(4).

By virtue of Article 11(3), the factor triggering off the control proceedings is the national authorities' obligation to 'inform the Commission in writing' that proceedings applying Articles 81 or 82 EC have been opened 'before or without delay after commencing the first formal investigative measure'. The Commission also maintains, at paragraph 45 of the Notice on the Network, that 'under Article 11(3) of the Council Regulation, the obligation is to inform the Commission, but the information may be shared by the NCA informing the Commission with the other members of the network'.

It is worth noting that, where a national authority opens proceedings applying Articles 81 or 82 EC and subsequently closes those proceedings without finding that there has been an infringement, the notice that it gives to the Commission pursuant to Article 11(3) is the only information pertaining to those proceedings that the Commission will receive. This is so because the authority's obligation under Article 11(4) to inform the Commission of the forthcoming closure of proceedings applies only to 'a decision requiring that an infringement be brought to an end, accepting commitments or withdrawing the benefit of a block exemption Regulation'. It does not apply when the national authority simply closes the file on a case.

It is also worth noting that the notice given pursuant to Article 11(3) will also incidentally notify the Commission of the initiation of the majority of ancillary proceedings applying national law because most cases which raise questions of national antitrust law will, thanks to the broad concept of 'effect on trade between Member States' (*infra*), also fall within the scope of Articles 81 and 82. Thus, when national authorities act under national law, Article 3(1) will normally require them to apply Articles 81 and 82 as well.

One of the objectives of Article 11(3) is to avoid overlapping proceedings. As well as avoiding such overlapping, the notice given pursuant to that provision also triggers off the exercise by the Commission of its new activity of descending vertical control on national authorities applying Community antitrust law.

37.1.2. How the Commission Exercises Control

Article 11(4) of the Regulation is the linchpin of the system of Commission control. It allows the Commission to monitor the way in which the national authorities apply Articles 81 and 82 EC. It requires them to inform the Commission 'no later than 30 days before the adoption of a decision requiring that an infringement be brought to an end, accepting commitments or withdrawing the benefit of a block exemption Regulation'. According to paragraph 47 of the Notice on cooperation within the Network, the authority concerned may ask 'for a swifter reaction', in which case 'the Commission will endeavour to react as swiftly as possible'.

The national authorities are also required to 'provide the Commission with a summary of the case, the envisaged decision or, in the absence thereof, any other document indicating the proposed course of action'. This does not prevent the national authorities from giving information on any other decision that they take applying Articles 81 or 82 EC. In the Commission's view, all members of the network should inform each other about the closure of their procedures which have been notified to the network pursuant to Article 11(2) and (3) of the Council Regulation (paragraph 49 of the Notice on cooperation within the Network).

Thanks to the summary provided by the national authorities, the Commission is automatically informed not only about the decisions which those authorities intend to adopt, but also about the reasoning on which those decisions are based. If it has doubts as to the lawfulness of a draft decision, the Commission can try to persuade the national authority concerned to amend it. If the national authority nevertheless refuses to amend the draft decision, the Commission may open proceedings in respect of the same case. By virtue of Article 11(6), that course of action will automatically relieve the national authority of its power to apply Community law to the situation. In the alternative, the Commission could wait until the national authority has concluded its proceedings and subsequently open infringement proceedings against the authority's Member State if it takes the view that the decision infringes Community antitrust law. Furthermore, should there be an appeal against the decision which allegedly infringes Community law, the Commission may, pursuant to Article 15 of the Regulation, submit observations to the national court with a view to having the decision quashed (*infra*).

37.1.3. The Commission's Power to Take Over Cases

Article 11(6) of Regulation 1/03 allows the Commission to relieve the national authorities of their power to apply Community antitrust law to a particular case. This provision operates in much the same way as did Article 9(3) of Regulation 17/62. However, whereas the power conferred by Regulation 17/62 was to be found in the Article entitled 'Powers', the same power conferred by Regulation 1/03 is located in the Article entitled 'Cooperation' (for an explanation, see *supra*).

The exercise of the power to take over cases safeguards the Commission's exclusive power to determine Community antitrust policy within the Network and the European Community (Article 85 EC). Recourse to this power requires the adoption of a formal Commission act initiating proceedings (see paragraph 52 of the Notice on cooperation within the Network).

In paragraph 54 of the Notice, the Commission identifies two situations in which the power under Article 11(6) may be exercised (these are obviously in addition to the situation mentioned in paragraph 53 where the Commission has initiated proceedings before any national authority has done so):

1. Where a national authority has initiated proceedings first, the Commission may, during the initial re-allocation period of two months, initiate proceedings and thus relieve the national authority of its power to handle the case. Before doing this, the Commission will consult the authority concerned. (The same principle applies, *mutatis mutandis* if more than one authority has initiated proceedings).
2. Where a national authority has initiated proceedings before the Commission and the initial allocation period of two months has already expired, the Commission can exercise its power under Article 11(6) in five cases only. They are as follows:
   (a) Network members envisage conflicting decisions in the same case;
   (b) Network members envisage a decision which is obviously in conflict with consolidated case law; the standards defined in the judgments of the Community courts and in previous decisions and regulations of the Commission should serve as a yardstick; concerning the assessment of the facts (e.g. market definition), only a significant divergence will trigger an intervention of the Commission;
   (c) Network members are unduly drawing out proceedings in the case;
   (d) There is a need to adopt a Community decision to develop Community competition policy in particular when a similar competition issue arises in several Member States or to ensure effective enforcement;
   (e) The NCAs concerned do not object.

In addition, the Commission itself has indicated that 'where the Commission intends to apply Article 11(6) of the Council Regulation after the initial allocation period, the case can be discussed in the Advisory Committee before the Commission initiates proceedings'. The Advisory Committee may issue 'an informal statement on the matter' (see paragraph 62 of the Notice). In any event, the Commission must explain the reasons for acting under Article 11(6) to both the authority concerned and to the other members of the

Network (see paragraph 55 of the Network).

As regards the power to take over cases, the Commission points out that making the notifications under Article 11(3) and (4) will *de facto* limit the possibility of recourse to Article 11(6). This is so because the information conveyed pursuant to Article 11(3) and (4) gives the Commission the possibility to put forward its own observations on a national authority's draft decision. This in turn will reduce the risk of a national authority coming to a different conclusion from the Commission (see paragraph 57 of the Notice on the Network).

37.1.4. Requests by the Commission Asking the National Authorities to Make Information Available and Circulation of that Information

The Commission is entitled, pursuant to Article 11(4), to ask a national authority to 'make available to the Commission other documents it holds which are necessary for the assessment of the case'. This power is in some respects the mirror image of the power which Article 11(2) confers on the national authorities. Article 11(4) confers this power on the Commission so that it can be in possession of all the information which it needs to assess the draft decision that the national authority intends to take. Both the information initially supplied to the Commission and the information subsequently applied upon request 'may be made available to the competition authorities of the other Member States'.

Article 11(4), like some other provisions of the Regulation, recognises that information sent to the Commission may also be made available to the competition authorities of the other Member States. Since it is not specified who may decide whether information is circulated within the Network, the point will need to be clarified through subsequent practice. However, the Commission already appears to have taken a position on this point by providing for automatic transmission of information to all members of the Network. In paragraph 23 of the Notice on the handling of complaints, the Commission, referring to Articles 11(2) and 11(3) of the Regulation, claims that, within the network, 'information on cases that are being investigated following a complaint will be made available to the other members of the network before or without delay after commencing the first formal investigative measure'. In so doing, the Commission appears to consider that making available the information is compulsory. However, Article 11(3), referred to in footnote 22 of the Notice on the cooperation in the Network as the legal basis of this obligation, says nothing about the information to be circulated among the national authorities and the obligation to ensure circulation. Article 11(3) provides simply that 'the competition authorities of the Member States shall, when acting under Article 81 or Article 82 of the Treaty, inform the Commission in writing before or without delay after commencing the first formal investigative measure. This information may also be made available to the competition authorities of the other Member States'.

37.1.5. The Influence of Vertical Descending Control on European Antitrust Federalism

Vertical descending control plays an influential role within the system of European antitrust federalism (*supra*). It prevents the antitrust powers of the Member States from being applied in a way which does not take account of the relationship between Community and national antitrust law, either in general terms or with regard more specifically to Article 83(2)(b) of the Treaty. In the specific case of Regulation 1/03, the control proceedings avoid the adoption of decisions which conflict with Articles 3(2) and 3(3).

37.2. PEER CONTROL

By virtue of Article 11(4) of the Regulation, the Commission alone carries out the control of the measures adopted by the national authorities. However, Article 14(7) allows 'cases that are being dealt with by a competition authority of a Member State' to be put on the agenda of the Advisory Committee. This may be done by the Commission 'on its own initiative' or 'at the request of a competition authority of a Member State'. In this respect, 'a request may be made … by a competition authority of a Member State in respect of a case where the Commission intends to initiate proceedings' pursuant to Article 11(6).

37.2.1. Discussion Proposed by the National Authorities

The *ratio legis* of the power conferred on the national authorities by Article 14(7) is linked to the principle of the concentration of Community antitrust competence (on this concept, see *supra*). Article 14(7) gives the national authorities an incentive to let the investigation applying Articles 81 and 82 to be concentrated in a single national authority. Thanks to this provision, the authorities can be certain that, even when they suspend proceedings or reject a complaint pursuant to Article 13 of the Regulation, they will still be entitled to request a discussion on the way in which the selected authority is carrying out the investigation. The possibility of requesting a discussion ensures that:

- first, should another authority clearly decide the case wrongly, it will be put on the agenda of the Advisory Committee; and
- second, the Commission could take over the case pursuant to Article 11(6) and decide it itself.

For the authority which has divested itself of the power to take a decision in a case by suspending or rejecting a complaint in order to allow another national authority to deal with the case, this mechanism is important on two counts:

- There is a welcome reduction of its own enforcement activities. It can therefore use the human resources which have been freed up in order to investigate cases which are not currently being dealt with by any other authorities.
- The authority which divests itself of a case puts the decision in the hands of the authority of another Member State. Since any case falling within the scope of Articles 81 and 82 'affects trade between Member States, this decision will inevitably have a direct influence *inter alia* on competition in the state which has suspended or terminated proceedings'. Furthermore, the relationship between national and Community law governed by Article 3(2) means that the decision of the second authority applying Community antitrust law will directly have an impact on the discretion which the authority suspending or terminating the proceedings has to apply its own domestic antitrust law.

The guarantee supplied by Article 14(7) is particularly important since it is the only way in which the national authorities can intervene in proceedings initiated by other antitrust authorities applying Community antitrust law. The Advisory Committee is not consulted before formal decisions are taken in cases investigated by national authorities (this is in contrast to the situation pertaining to decisions taken by the Commission to which Article 14(1) applies). There are several reasons for this:

- it is not feasible for every decision of the national authorities to be subjected to an extremely complex control procedure involving a body composed of representatives of 27 competition authorities.
- member States are reluctant to submit to control exercised by other member States, even when the control relates to the application of Community law; and
- the limitation is a consequence of the Commission's prerogative, conferred by Article 85 EC, of determining the direction of Community competition policy.

37.2.2. Discussion Proposed by the Commission

Article 14(7) also allows the Commission, acting on its own initiative, to put a case being dealt with by a national authority under Articles 81 or 82 EC on the agenda of the Advisory Committee. It would do this in a case in which it took the view that a national authority risked reaching a conclusion inconsistent with Community competition policy or contrary to Community law. Putting the case on the agenda would draw the attention of the relevant authority (and, through the forum of the Advisory Committee, all the other authorities) to this fact. This might culminate in the Commission taking over the case pursuant to Article 11(6). As regards any decision taking over the case under Article 11(6), the Commission will only make use of this possibility if one of the situations referred to in paragraph 54 of the Notice on the Network arises (*supra*).

37.2.3. Discussion Proposed by the Competition Authority Whose Case is Being Taken Over

By virtue of Article 14(7) of the Regulation, a national authority whose case the Commission is about to take over pursuant to Article 11(6) may propose that the Advisory Committee discuss the Commission's impending decision. This course of action allows the Committee to adopt a position, albeit it does not formally issue an opinion in such a case (see the third sub-paragraph of Article 14(7)). In such a case, the intervention of the Committee can be understood as being that of the body representing the member authority. The possibility of discussing the case has several functions:

- it acts as a kind of brake against hasty decisions by the Commission or against decisions which do not fall within the five situations in which the Commission may exercise its power (*supra*);
- it is a form of peer control, exercised by the national authorities on behalf of another national authority which has requested a discussion by the Committee. The Commission's proposed decision inevitably constitutes an implicit criticism of the requesting authority; and
- the discussion, and any unpublished opinion of the Committee (*supra*), gives all the national authorities some kind of protection in respect of any decision of the Commission which might constitute a precedent.

37.2.4. The Influence of Peer Control on European Antitrust Federalism

The peer control exercised by the Advisory Committee over the national authorities has no impact on the system of Community antitrust federalism (*supra*). The purpose of peer control is to protect the individual Member States from conclusions of other national authorities which are not consistent with Community law. It also helps to safeguard the Member States from unjustified Commission decisions relieving a national authority of its power to handle a case.

In that sense, peer control can be categorised as part of Community antitrust federalism. It represents another means of ensuring that the exercise of the Member States' antitrust power, in particular their obligation to apply Community antitrust law in cases of Community relevance, is not applied in such a way as to infringe Articles 3(2) and 3(3) of Regulation 1/03.

37.3. VERTICAL ASCENDING CONTROL

Regulation 1/03 has extended the Commission's powers of control over national authorities' application of Articles 81 and 82. This, in turn, has entailed granting the Member States a greater degree of power to control the Commission than did Regulation 17/62. With regard to the Commission's power of control, reference will be made, *inter alia*, to the power of direct and binding control over national authorities and the restriction of the Member States' power to apply national antitrust law imposed by Article 3(2) which, in the author's view, is unlawful, *supra*.

The Member States' vertical ascending powers to influence Commission antitrust decisions have increased considerably.

The Member States exercise their control over the Commission pursuant to Regulation 1/03 exclusively through the Advisory Committee (Articles 11(2) and 14(1)(6)) and no longer through the individual national authorities, which was the case under Regulation 17/62 (Article 10(1) and (2)).

37.3.1. The Composition and the Functions of the Advisory Committee

As mentioned above, under Regulation 1/03 control is exercised by the Advisory Committee. It is the 'forum where experts from the various competition authorities discuss individual cases and general issues of Community law' (paragraph 58 of the Notice on cooperation within the Network).

Article 14(2) stipulates that 'the Advisory Committee shall be composed of representatives of the competition authorities of the Member States'. The composition of the Committee is interesting from two angles:

- it is made up of representatives who all have the same professional background. This helps to create a cohesive body; and

- the Committee is in principle limited to representatives of the national authorities and, by virtue of the second sentence of Article 14(2), may not discuss individual cases when representatives who are not from the national authorities are present. This should not lead us to think that the representatives on the Committee are immune to influence (which may be legitimate) from the Member States. The character and the independence of the national authorities from outside influences is a matter for the individual Member states[1] (*supra*).

Apart from its powers mentioned *supra*, the Committee carries out certain other minor functions. As well as being consulted before the Commission or the national authorities take decisions, Article 33(2) of the Regulation requires it to be consulted before the adoption of certain measures, that is, measures implementing the Regulation, block exemption regulations and guidelines. In addition, it may be the forum for discussing the allocation of cases among the national authorities.

37.3.2. Consultation of the Committee by the Commission

As regards the Committee's control functions *stricto sensu*, Article 14(1) provides that 'the Commission shall consult an Advisory Committee on restrictive practices and Dominant Positions prior to the taking of any decision' under:

- Article 7 (Findings of infringement);
- Article 8 (Interim measures);
- Article 9 (Commitments);
- Article 10 (Findings of inapplicability);
- Article 23 (Fines);
- Article 24(2) (Fixing the definitive amount of a penalty payment at a lower level); and
- Article 29(1) (Withdrawal of the benefit of a block exemption regulation).

Article 14(3) provides that 'the consultation may take place at a meeting convened and chaired by the Commission, held not earlier than 14 days after dispatch of the notice convening it'. (This period may be shortened in certain circumstances pursuant to this provision.) The notice convening the meeting must be sent 'together with a summary of the case, an indication of the most

---

[1] See *Syfait v. GlaxoSmithKline*, Case C-53/03, p. I-4609.

important documents and a preliminary draft decision'.

By contrast, the Commission is not required to notify the national authorities, through the Committee, of the opening of a procedure. It is only required to 'consult an Advisory Committee ... prior to' taking certain decisions.

37.3.3. Sending of Documents by the Commission

In order to ensure that the national authorities have all the documents necessary to enable them to take a position on decisions of the Commission in the Advisory Committee, Article 11(2) imposes certain obligations on the Commission. It provides that 'the Commission shall transmit to the competition authorities of the Member States copies of the most important documents it has collected with a view to applying' Article 7 (finding and termination of infringement), Article 8 (interim measures), Article 9 (commitments), Article 10 (finding of inapplicability) and Article 29(1) (withdrawal of the benefit of a block exemption regulation by the Commission).

By virtue of Article 12 of Regulation 1/03, documents sent or requested by the national authorities may clearly be used by them for the purpose of further proceedings, albeit within the limits imposed by Article 12(2).

In addition, the second sentence of Article 11(2) provides further that 'at the request of the competition authority of a Member State, the Commission shall provide it with a copy of other existing documents necessary for the assessment of the case'. After the documents requested by an individual authority have been received, the control over the Commission takes place within the Advisory Committee.

37.3.4. Preparing the Committee's Opinion

Article 14(3) regulates the drafting of the opinion. It provides that 'the Advisory Committee shall deliver a written opinion on the Commission's draft opinion'. This power, which remains 'even if some members are absent and are not represented', is an important aspect of the control which the Committee exercises.

The delivery of an opinion by the Committee is the main difference between the outcome of discussions of the Committee under Article 14(7) (that is, cases dealt with by national authorities applying Articles 81 and 82), and of the consultation of the Committee under Articles 14(3) to 14(6) (that is, cases investigated by the Commission). Article 14(7) provides that 'the Advisory Committee shall not issue opinions on cases dealt with by competition authorities of the Member States'. That provision has two objectives:

- It protects the national authorities from the risk of being 'judged publicly' in respect of their own proceedings. It is not a coincidence that that rule was not present in the Commission's proposal for a regulation (see Article 14(6) of the proposal).
- The risk of constantly being judged publicly would act as a disincentive for national authorities to initiate proceedings in which they would be required to apply Articles 81 and 82. These are precisely the cases in which the Commission is trying to decentralise the enforcement of Articles 81 and 82. For that reason, Article 14(6) reserves the public control of proceedings applying Articles 81 and 82 to the Commission as the body responsible for defining the direction of Community competition policy.

A significant change in comparison to Regulation 17/62 concerns the possibility, established by the last sentence of Article 14(3) Regulation 1/03, for one or more national authorities to request that 'the positions stated in the opinion ... be reasoned'. This is an interesting provision, which obliges authorities to justify their position. It can be explained by the need for transparency regarding the positions which the authorities adopt in individual cases since these may conflict with the positions of other members of the Committee.

In any case, the Committee is consulted only as regards the decisions bringing investigations to an end, which are referred to in Article 14(1). The Member States, through the national authorities, do not therefore have the opportunity to influence the Commission decisions by which investigative proceedings are initiated. Such decisions are, in reality, measures identifying the cases which should be assessed by the Commission.

Article 14(4) of Regulation 1/03 also provides for the possibility of carrying out consultations by written procedure. It does not specify when the written procedure should be used or when a meeting should be convened. It provides only that 'if a Member State so requests, the Commission shall convene a meeting'. The written procedure would appear to become the standard procedure for the consultation.

37.3.5. The Powers of the National Authorities to Control and Influence the Commission

Articles 14(5) and (6) establish the most interesting components of the national authorities' powers of control and influence over the Commission.

These two paragraphs, which form part of the broader system of Community antitrust federalism (*supra*), provide for a welcome (see Pace, 1999, § 9), albeit indirect, increase of the Member States' power to control the Commission. This goes some way to counter the erosion of the significance of the Member States' antitrust systems which has been taking place since the beginning of the 1990s.

Article 14(5) requires the Commission to 'take the utmost account of the opinion of the Advisory Committee'. Thus formulated, that obligation could have remained a dead letter. However, Article 14(5) goes on to require the Commission to 'inform the Committee of the manner in which its opinion has been taken into account' although it does not spell out how the Commission should explain in what way it has taken account of the Committee's views.

If the opinion is in writing, Article 14(6) requires that it be appended to the draft decision, as did Regulation 17/62. In addition, it is stipulated that 'if the Advisory Committee recommends publication of the opinion, the Commission shall carry out such publication taking into account the legitimate interest of undertakings in the protection of their business secrets'. This new requirement is important. Publication by the Commission of the Committee's opinion presupposes that the Committee has been unable to make effective use of the means at its disposal to influence the Commission. As a Parthian shot, the Committee then requires the Commission to publish its opinion. This requirement will assume considerable significance if the legality of the Commission's decision is subsequently challenged and reviewed by the Community courts. If the Commission's decision conflicts with the Committee's opinion and the latter has been published, either in conjunction with the decision or separately, the Commission will be required to explain why it has not followed the opinion. This requirement is reinforced by the obligation imposed on the Commission by Article 14(5) to 'take the utmost account of the opinion delivered by the Advisory Committee'. The obligation to publish is thus a spur to greater transparency of the Commission's decision.

The Commission is thus required to give reasons explaining why it has come to a different conclusion from the Advisory Committee. If it does not do so, the decision risks being annulled. Looked at from the angle of Community antitrust federalism and the ways in which the Member States have an influence on Community antitrust competence, this requirement is quite significant.

This obligation to give reasons confers added protection on the individual. It makes it easier to identify any errors in the assessment which the Commission has carried out before adopting the final decision. Protecting the individual from unlawful exercise of the Commission's power should not be restricted to the context of judicial protection. It can also be exercised in other ways which prevent the act from being unlawful before it becomes final.

Leaving aside its jurisdiction over penalties, the Court has no power to review the substance of a decision. Consequently, when it assesses whether or not the Commission has complied with its obligation under Article 14(5) of the Regulation to take the 'utmost account' of the Committee's opinion, the Court may not examine the decision on the merits. It merely examines the reasoning on which the Commission's decision is based and verifies that this reasoning is adequate and not manifestly unreasonable. If, in the decision, the Commission has failed to take the opinion into account or has omitted to explain why it has not followed the opinion the decision will consequently be annulled.

37.4. THE EXTENDED COMPOSITION OF THE ADVISORY COMMITTEE

The third sub-paragraph of Article 14(7) of the Regulation provides that 'the Advisory Committee may also discuss general issues of Community competition law'. Although this possibility has no effect on the Commission's exclusive power to define Community competition policy, it is nevertheless very important since it confers on the Member States an – admittedly indirect – power to influence the Commission's antitrust policy through their representation in the Committee. This power could potentially be developed to the point that the Committee becomes the co-pilot in the determination of Community competition policy (albeit without prejudice to the Commission's independence in this respect). In other words, this aspect, taken together with the procedures allowing the national authorities to control the Commission, forms part of the system of European antitrust federalism.

As regards the composition of the Committee for the purposes of discussing 'general issues of Community competition law', Article 14 provides that persons other than representatives of the national competition authorities may be present. Article 14(2) envisages two different situations:

- for 'the discussion of individual cases' the Committee is 'composed of representatives of the competition authorities of the Member States'; and
- for the discussion of issues other than individual cases, an additional Member State representative competent in competition matters may be appointed. The additional representatives on the Committee are also bound by the obligation under Article 28(2) of the Regulation not to disclose information covered by the obligation of professional secrecy.

The extended composition of the Advisory Committee did not feature in the proposal that the Commission put forward in 2000. It was evidently introduced by the Member States in the Council. It can be seen as a means of giving the national authorities a greater role within the Advisory Committee and thus conferring greater influence on the Member States in their dealings with the Commission.

37.5. CONTROL CARRIED OUT BY INDIVIDUAL NATIONAL AUTHORITIES

As regards the influence that individual Member States may have within the Community antitrust system, Article 14(3)–(6) of Regulation 1/03 provides that the national authorities may have a collective influence on the Commission through the Advisory Committee. Furthermore, Article 29(2) of the Regulation also confers a certain degree of autonomy on the national authorities as regards the withdrawal of the benefit of a block exemption regulation.

Although the control carried out by the national authorities is exercised through a collegiate body, individual authorities have nevertheless not lost all individual influence within the Community antitrust system. Their influence is, however, solely dependent on the extent to which their activities and decisions command respect. Respect can be achieved through their capacity to adopt their own individual approach to general questions or a specific case which they may be able to discuss or compare with the Commission or the other national authorities within the forum of the Advisory Committee.

The *Airtours* and *Carnival* merger cases prove that there is a demonstrable relationship between the quality of the work of the national authorities and the influence that they may have on Community competition policy. In *Airtours*, the Commission's decision was annulled by the European Court of First Instance on the basis of studies which had previously been carried out by the UK antitrust authority. In *Carnival*, parallel measures taken by that national authority prompted the Commission to amend its approach before it adopted its final decision.

For individual national authorities to be able to exercise influence within the Community system as a whole, it is absolutely essential that they are adequately financed and staffed. On this point, there are considerable discrepancies between the different European authorities.

38. Judicial Enforcement of Antitrust Law

38.1. JURISDICTION

Regulation 1/03 confers jurisdiction on national courts to apply Articles 81 and 82 EC. It also regulates certain aspects of the exercise of that jurisdiction to the extent that this is necessary to implement the decentralisation policy of the Regulation.

38.1.1. The Antitrust Jurisdiction of the National Courts

Unlike Regulation 17/62, Regulation 1/03 specifically confers jurisdiction in the field of Community antitrust on national courts. More precisely, Article 6 provides that 'national courts shall have the power to apply Articles 81 and 82 of the Treaty'. Regulation 17/62 did not specifically confer this jurisdiction on national courts but this did not prevent them from being able to apply Articles 81(1) and 82. As early as 1974, the European Court of Justice (ECJ) had held that 'as the prohibitions of Articles 81(1) and 82 tend by their very nature to produce direct effects in relations between individuals, these articles create direct rights in respect of the individuals concerned which the national courts must safeguard'.[1]

It is obvious that the purpose of inserting Article 6 of Regulation 1/03 was not to confer powers which already existed. Its primary (albeit unlawful) purpose is to confer jurisdiction on the national courts to apply 'also' Article 81(3) of the Treaty (Article 6 of the 2000 proposal for a regulation, Recital 4 of the preamble to Regulation 1/03). However, according to consistent case law, Article 81(3) EC, unlike Articles 81(1) and 82, does not have direct effect and as such cannot be applied by national courts. If Article 81(3) had had direct effect by virtue of Regulation 17/62, the national courts would have been able to apply it notwithstanding the exclusive power conferred on

[1] *Belgische Radio en Televisie v. Sv Sabam and Nv Fonior*, Case 127/73, E.C.R. 1974, p. 51, § 16; *Courage Ltd v. Bernard Crehan*, Case C-453/99, E.C.R. 2001, p. I–6297; see also *Manfredi v. Lloyd Adriatico Assicurazıoni*, Case C-295/04, E.C.R. 2006, not yet reported.

the Commission by Article 9(1) of that Regulation. However, such a position was never supported by the Commission's practice and was specifically rejected by the ECJ in *Delimitis*.

In conclusion, the fact that a provision like Article 6 of Regulation 1/03 was necessary to allow Article 81(3) EC to be applied by the national courts confirms the *Delimitis* line of case law. Article 81(3) EC cannot be applied directly by national courts without the insertion of a further (and unlawful) legislative provision (see section *infra*, which demonstrates that Article 6 of Regulation 1/03 is unlawful since it infringes both Article 83 EC and the principle of direct effect). Furthermore, the Commission itself had acknowledged at paragraph 69 of the White Paper on modernisation that it was only through a regulation adopted pursuant to Article 83 EC that 'the whole of Article 81 would then become a directly applicable provision which individuals could invoke in court or before any authority empowered to deal with such matters'.

The premises on which the Commission based the need to confer jurisdiction to apply Article 81(3) are unsound

Before tackling the issue of the unlawfulness of Article 6 of Regulation 1/03, we need to consider the premise on which the Commission bases its assertion that national courts must be able to apply Article 81(3) EC. This is quite simply that this power is necessary to ensure the effective decentralisation of Regulation 1/03. Allegedly, the purpose of Article 6 is to avoid a repetition of the negative consequences of 'the centralised scheme set up by Regulation No. 17'. Those consequences are, it is claimed, the hampering of the 'application of the Community competition rules by the courts and competition authorities of the Member States' (Recital 3 of the preamble to Regulation 1/03; paragraph 2 of the Notice on guidance letters). On that point, it suffices to note that over a period of almost 45 years, from 1962 to 2005, approximately 60 proceedings were commenced before national courts in the whole of the European Community. By contrast, there were 752 proceedings in the United States in 2004 alone.

In the Commission's view, the failure of the national courts to apply the Community antitrust rules in the 1990s made it necessary to enact a provision which allowed (and required) national courts to apply Article 81(3) EC.

A brief comparison with the United States shows us that an effective policy of decentralisation of antitrust law does not in fact require national courts to assess cases falling under Article 81(3) EC. In the United States, proceedings for the private enforcement of both state and federal antitrust law before state and federal courts significantly exceed the number of proceedings concluded each year by the federal and state antitrust authorities. This phenomenon is partly attributable to specific procedural rules relating to private suits

(Wamser, 1994, p. 42). In the USA, the majority of private suits relating to agreements are brought in respect of behaviour which is prohibited *per se*, such as horizontal price agreements, in respect of which there is no possibility of justification based on the rule of reason (Von Kalinowski et al., 2000, § 160). This tendency can also be explained by the difficulties, the cost and the risks attached to proving behaviour which is not manifestly anticompetitive and which has not been the subject of a decision by the federal antitrust authorities. The cases which are usually brought before the courts in the USA would, if brought in Europe, be caught by Article 81(1) and could not be exempted by virtue of Article 81(3). These are precisely the types of case in which courts in Member States already had jurisdiction under Regulation 17/62.

For this reason, the Commission's opinion that the national courts' lack of jurisdiction to apply Article 81(3) EC was behind the failure of attempts to decentralise the application of Community antitrust law does not hold water.

The general lack of success of the efforts to decentralise the application of Community antitrust law can be attributed to other reasons. One very significant reason is the lack of any incentives for companies to commence proceedings before a national court rather than having recourse to the much simpler, quicker and cheaper expedient of making a complaint to the Commission or to a national authority. Should the complaint result in a decision finding an infringement, the complainant can then sue the infringing party for damages. During the civil proceedings, the decision of the Commission or the national authority can be relied on as a kind of enforcement order.

Regulation 1/03, however, has not provided any incentives for individuals to enforce Articles 81 and 82 before national courts. Obvious incentives would be the award of exemplary or punitive damages for breach of antitrust law, or some other kind of consequences to be determined by the court. Three years after the enactment of Regulation 1/2003, in the Green Paper entitled 'Damages actions for breach of the EC antitrust rules' published on 19 December 2005, the Commission appears to have finally recognised that this type of incentive needs to be provided.

In paragraph 18 of the Notice on the handling of complaints, the Commission states baldly that 'the new enforcement system established by Regulation 1/03 strengthens the possibilities for national courts to seek and obtain effective relief before national courts'. This approach tries to put a positive spin on the national courts' obligation to apply Article 81(3). However, this is merely a peremptory assertion which does not take into account the risks and costs which must be incurred before an individual can obtain damages.

Given the lack of specific incentives, it is unlikely, even under the new regime established by Regulation 1/03, that undertakings will invoke Article 81 before national courts unless the behaviour complained of is patently contrary to Articles 81(1) or 82. In any event, the numbers of such cases are unlikely to be much greater than they were under the Regulation 17/62 system.

It is likely that, as before, individuals and companies will prefer to make complaints to the Commission or national authorities.

The risks attached to interpretation by national courts

Conferring jurisdiction to apply Article 81(3) presents more risks than advantages. Even leaving aside the fact that Article 6 of the Regulation is unlawful (*infra*), the potentially negative results of national courts applying Article 81(3) would still militate against conferring that power on them.

The application of Article 81(3) by a national court has three disadvantages:

1. Even when confronted with agreements which are patently forbidden by Article 81(1) and not exemptable according to the Commission's practice, national courts might still grant exemption under Article 81(3) in order to avoid the unwelcome social consequences of declaring the agreement void.
2. There is a danger that extraneous factors which should play no part in antitrust decisions, such as environmental, policy or industrial policy, will intrude into the application of Article 81(3). The Commission itself was concerned about this risk and referred to it in the Draft Guidelines on the Application of Article 81(3) which show that the Commission had some misgivings on the point. At § 38 of the draft, the Commission maintained: 'It is not ... the role of Article 81 and the authorities applying (Article 81(3)) to allow undertakings to restrict competition in pursuit of general interest aims'. This assertion was not supported by any reasoning and it is not grounded in any Community case law. It was changed in the final version and now reads: '42 ... Goals pursued by other Treaty provisions can be taken into account to the extent that they can be subsumed under the four conditions of Article 81(3)'. Within the Community, discretion to take account of such different interests may be conferred on the bodies competent to enforce Article 81(3), including national authorities. This is quite understandable because the Commission and the national authorities are bodies which exercise 'discretion' and are hence capable of making such an assessment. This is not the case with national courts, whose role is simply to 'interpret' the law (On the distinction between 'interpretation' and 'discretion', see Betti, 1949, p. 64).
3. Article 81(3) will not be applied consistently throughout the Community by the national courts. Such a result would conflict with the notion of

Community law as law applied uniformly throughout the entire common market. These dangers are not eliminated by the requirement imposed by Article 15(2) of the Regulation that Member States forward a copy of any judgment applying Community antitrust law to the Commission so that it may assess whether the judgment is correct:

- first, given the large number of national courts applying Community antitrust law in the 27 Member States, it would be difficult for the Commission to monitor individual judgments; and
- second, that type of monitoring activity would represent a heavy commitment for the comparatively small number of officials working for DG COMP. It could only be carried out at the expense of direct antitrust enforcement, which is the Commission's main activity.

For these reasons, even leaving aside the unlawfulness of Article 6 of the Regulation, it would be preferable to limit the application of Article 81(3) EC to the Commission and the national authorities. Moreover, those bodies have the discretion needed to apply a provision such as Article 81(3) which does not have direct effect (*infra*). That approach would, *inter alia*, allow the Commission to make effective use of the tools provided for by Article 11(3) and (4) of the Regulation in order to monitor the decisions taken by national authorities applying Article 81(3).

38.1.2. Article 6 of Regulation 1/03 Infringes Article 83(2)(b)

Article 6 of Regulation 1/03 is unlawful for two separate reasons:

- first, it is submitted that Article 83(2)(b) EC does not allow jurisdiction to apply Article 81(3) to be conferred on courts of Member States; and
- second, it is submitted that Article 81(3) neither is nor can be transformed into a provision having a direct effect that is capable of being applied directly by national courts.

As regards the first point, under the antitrust system established by Articles 84 and 85 EC and Regulation 17/62, national courts could not apply Article 81(3) since it did not have the characteristics of a directly effective provision. The national courts could apply that provision only after a competent body had taken a decision to that effect. By virtue of Articles 84 and 85 EC, both the Commission and the national authorities were designated, whereas under Article 9(1) of Regulation 17/62 the power was conferred on the Commission alone.

In stark contrast to the past situation, Regulation 1/03 is based on the premise that national courts may apply Article 81(3) provided that a legal norm adopted on the basis of Article 83(2)(b) EC expressly confers this power on them (see Recital 2 of the preamble to Regulation 1/03). Article 6 of the Regulation operates on the basis that it is the Regulation itself which, by virtue of Article 83(2)(b) EC, confers jurisdiction on national courts to apply Article 81(3) EC. However, on a correct analysis, if Article 81(3) had been applicable as a provision having direct effect, it would have been unnecessary to enact Article 6 of the Regulation to allow it to be applied by national courts (*supra*).

Moreover, Article 83(2)(b) EC deals not with this question but with something entirely different. It provides that regulations adopted on the basis of Article 83 are designed 'to lay down detailed rules for the application of Article 81(3), taking into account the need to ensure effective supervision on the one hand and to simplify administration to the greatest possible extent on the other'. It seems clear from the text of Article 83(2)(b) itself that a regulation adopted on the basis of Article 83 cannot confer jurisdiction to apply Article 81(3) on national courts because that provision is not addressed to them:

1. The purpose of a regulation adopted on the basis of Article 83 cannot be to allow national courts to exercise 'effective supervision' with regard to Article 81(3). This stems from the nature of Article 81(3) (as explained *supra* and analysed in more detail *infra*) since it is not a provision having direct effect. As such it cannot be applied by national courts. Pursuant to the 'principle of cooperation laid down by Article 10 of the Treaty, it is for national courts to ensure the legal protection' (not the administrative supervision) 'which persons derive from the direct effect of provisions of Community law'.[2] As the Commission itself acknowledged at paragraph 27 of the draft Notice on Complaints, 'the Commission, *unlike national courts, whose task is to safeguard individual rights*, is an administrative authority which must act in the public interest' (emphasis added).
2. The purpose of a regulation adopted on the basis of Article 83 cannot be to allow national courts to carry out 'administration' of Article 81(3). National courts do not 'administer', they 'protect rights which [Community law] confers on individuals'.[3] Furthermore, the cases in which the EC Treaty identifies the tasks of national courts are extremely rare. It does so

[2] *Aannemersbedrijf P. K. Kraaijeveld B.*See *v Commission*, Case C-72/95, E.C.R. 1996, p. I–5403, § 58; see also *Jeroen van Schijndel v. Stichting Pensioenfonds voor Fysiotherapeuten*, Joined Cases C-430/93 and C-431/93, E.C.R. 1995, p. I–4705, § 14.

[3] *Molkerei – Zentrale Westfalen/Lippe GmbH v. Hauptzollamt Paderborn*, Case 28/67, E.C.R. 1968, pp. 192, 206; *Solred SA v. Administración General del Estado*, Case C-347/96, E.C.R. 1998, p. I–937, § 30.

only in the case of Article 193 (which refers to 'facts being examined by a court') and Articles 234 and 68 (which define the obligations of national courts to make a reference for a preliminary ruling).[4] On the other hand, it is the bodies foreseen by the EC Treaty (that is, the Commission and in some cases the national authorities) which have the function of ensuring general and uniform compliance with Community law through administrative action[5] (see also paragraph 4 of the Notice on cooperation with national courts);

3. The drafting history of Article 83(2)(e) EC further confirms that it is not addressed to national courts. It is the result of the compromise proposed at the time of the drafting of the Treaty of Rome by Hans von der Groeben, the Chairman of the sub-group on competition rules (*supra*). Article 83(2)(e) postpones the decision on the 'detailed rules for the application of Article 81(3)' to a later regulation. However, pending the adoption of a regulation adopted pursuant to Article 83, the Community antitrust rules were to be applied by national authorities, on the basis of Article 84 EC, or by the Commission, on the basis of Article 85 EC. In other words, they were to be applied, alongside national law, where this existed, by the administrative system for the enforcement of Community antitrust law (consisting of the Commission and national authorities).

For the bodies that participate in the administrative system for the enforcement of Community antitrust law, the purpose of Article 83(2)(e) is thus to decide how they should apply Article 81(3) (for example, according to the principle of abuse or the principle of prohibition), and whether or not there should be a system of prior notification. This means that the Community legislature does not have the power to confer jurisdiction on national courts to apply Article 81(3). This is the case not merely because Article 81(3) does not have direct effect but also because Article 83(2)(b) only lays down detailed rules for its application with relation to the administrative system for the enforcement of Community antitrust law. National courts are not able to carry out the functions for which Regulations under Article 83 can be adopted, that is, the 'effective supervision' and 'administration' of Article 81(3). Consequently, Regulations adopted pursuant to Article 83(2)(b) can only lay down detailed rules for the application of Article 81(3). They may do this by determining, for the purpose of evaluation by the national courts, whether contracts may be deemed void only after the Commission and the national authorities have carried out an investigation (as provided by the

---

[4] For consideration of the expression 'National court', see *Syfait v. GlaxoSmithKline*, Case C-53/03, p. I-4609.

[5] *Molkerei – Zentrale Westfalen/Lippe GmbH v. Hauptzollamt Paderborn*, op. cit., p. 206.

system established by Articles 84 and 85 EC) or once the agreement has been notified by the Commission alone or by the Commission and the national authorities (as provided for by Articles 1(1) and 1(2) and Articles 4 and 5 of Regulation 1/03).

To resume the first reason for the illegality of Article 6 of Regulation 1/03, we can see that the text and the drafting history of Article 83(2)(b) as well as the Community case law, in particular the *Delimitis* judgment,[6] preclude national courts from being able to apply Article 81(3).[7] Article 83(2)(b) confers the power to apply Article 81(3) exclusively on the bodies within the system administering Community antitrust law, namely the Commission and, as the case may be, the national authorities. In adopting Article 6 of Regulation 1/03, the Council has enacted a rule which it had no power to adopt and has thus infringed Article 83(2)(b) EC.

Consequently, Article 81(3) should be applied exclusively by the Commission and the national authorities.

38.1.3. Article 6 of Regulation 1/03 Infringes the Principle of Direct Effect

In the second place, Article 6 of Regulation 1/03 is unlawful because it requires national courts to apply a provision which does not have direct effect (on the difference between direct applicability and direct effect, see Pace, 2005, p. 453).

Article 81 (3) as a provision which does not have direct effect

The reasoning underlying Regulation 1/03 does not address the issue of whether Article 81(3) EC has direct effect. Article 6 purports to solve the problem of the applicability of Article 81(3) by deeming that national courts have jurisdiction to apply that provision. That approach ignores the reasoning in *Delimitis* (see *supra*) and presupposes that under Regulation 17/62 the only reason why national courts could not apply Article 81(3) was because of the competition policy choice made by the Commission and by the Council when

---

[6] In *Delimitis*, the ECJ held that even under the system established by Regulation 17/62, national courts had no power to apply Article 81(3) EC because that provision did not have direct effect and because the Commission had exclusive competence to apply it pursuant to Article 9(3) of the Regulation. In one limb of its reasoning, the ECJ explained that the Commission enjoyed this exclusive power on the basis of Article 91(1) of Regulation 17/62. In the other limb, the ECJ attributed the Commission's exclusive competence to the fact that Article 81(3) did not have direct effect or, as the Court expressed it, to the necessity for the Commission to make 'complex economic assessments, in particular in order to assess whether an agreement falls under Article 81(3)' (*Stergios Delimitis v. Henninger Bräu AG*, Case C-234/89, E.C.R. 1991, p. I-935, § 44).

[7] On the irrelevance of the *Ahmed Saeed* case law to this particular point, see Pace, 2005, p. 451.

they enacted that regulation. In reality, the application of Article 81(3) by national courts was not feasible 'simply' because Article 81(3) cannot be applied by national courts since it does not have direct effect. This point applies irrespective of whether Regulation 17/62 or Regulation 1/03 is applicable.

Not only Article 6 itself, but also recent case law, confirms that Article 81(3) does not have direct effect (*infra*). Using the formulation adopted in the Community case law, the implementation of Article 81(3) depends 'on the adoption of subsequent measures which either the Community institutions or the Member States may take in the exercise of a discretionary power'.[8] Even the way in which the Guidelines on the application of Article 81(3) are formulated shows that it is hard to imagine, in the light of current case law, that courts and individuals could apply Article 81(3) as a provision having direct effect (see in particular the kind of evaluation that national courts should carry out according to paragraphs 75, 85, 86, 87, 88, 94 and 103 of the Guidelines on the application of Article 81(3)).

In three distinct lines of case law, the Community courts have confirmed that Article 81(3) does not have direct effect:

- The ECJ has stated that one of the aims of Article 81(3) is to promote, albeit indirectly, 'a harmonious development of economic activities within the whole Community'.[9] The Court expressly recognises that the bodies applying Article 81(3) (that is the Commission and, as the case may be, the national authorities) must have a certain discretionary power when applying that provision. This is inconsistent with its having direct effect and being applied by national courts.
- The Court has stated that the content of Article 81(3) is not precise in that its function is to allow 'the requirements for the maintenance of workable competition to be reconciled with the safeguarding of objectives of a different nature'.[10] This too entails recognising a discretion which is inconsistent with the provision having direct effect.
- The ECJ has consistently held that complex economic assessments are necessary to apply Article 81(3).[11] It is precisely because of these assessments that the Court has refused to examine the substance of

---

[8] *David Petrie v. Commission*, Case T-191/99, E.C.R. 2001, p. II–3677, § 34.

[9] *Walt Wilhelm v. Bundeskartellamt*, Case 14/68, E.C.R. 1969, p. 1, § 5; *Ahmed Saeed Flugreisen v. Zentrale Zur Bekaempfung Unlauteren Wettbewerbs*, Case 66/86, E.C.R. 1989, p. 803, § 63.

[10] *Metro SB – Grossmaerkte GmbH et Co. KG v. Commission*, Case 26/76, E.C.R. 1977, p. 1875, § 21.

[11] See, *inter alia*, *Consten and Grundig v. Commission*, Joined cases 56 and 58–64, E.C.R. English special edition 1966, pp. 299, 501; *Stergios Delimitis v. Henninger Bräu AG*, Case C-234/89, E.C.R. 1991, p. I–935, § 44.

Commission decisions[12] applying Article 81(3). It shows once again that that provision lacks sufficient precision to be directly effective (on the inapplicability on to Article 81(3) of the case law relating to the interpretation of Article 86(2) EC, see Pace, 2004, p. 466).

Article 6 of Regulation 1/03 and the prevalence of the interest in allowing the Community antitrust system to function correctly over the protection of the individual

The Commission has argued that the application of Article 81(3) by national courts will help to enhance 'the protection of individual rights' conferred by that provision (see section II, Part C of the proposal for a regulation).

Correctly analysed, Article 6 of the Regulation has the effect of making individuals bound by a provision (that is, the combined effect of Articles 81(1) and 81(3)) as if it had direct effect despite the fact that it is not sufficiently precise.

Applying Article 81(3) as if it had direct effect admittedly allows individuals to challenge an infringement of the combined provisions of Articles 81(1) and 81(3) before a national court. At the same time it infringes the principle of direct effect, which is a fundamental principle of Community law. On the one hand, Article 6 unlawfully allows individuals, as beneficiaries of the rights conferred by Article 81 EC, to invoke Article 81(3) before national courts. This allows them to rely on an individual Community law right, which is unnecessary in the context of the present policy of decentralising Community antitrust policy (*supra*). On the other hand, individuals, as persons bound to comply with the prohibition established by Article 81 EC, are prevented by Article 6 of the Regulation from relying on the principle of direct effect and they have to make good any harm flowing from infringing Article 81,[13] even if they cannot independently assess the scope of the exemption from the prohibition.

This shows further that the aim of the reform of Article 81(3) was not, as the Commission claimed, to 'enhance the protection of individual rights' conferred by that provision. On the contrary, the reform clearly has a negative effect on the position of individuals. Its purpose is to decentralise the

---

[12] See, *inter alia*, *Asia Motor France SA v. Commission*, Case T-154/98, E.C.R. 2000, p. II–3453; *British American Tobacco Company v. Commission*, Joined Cases 142 and 156/84, E.C.R. 1987, p. 4487, § 62; *John Deere Ltd v. Commission*, Case C-7/95 P, E.C.R. 1998, p. I–3111; *Stichting Certificatie Kraanverhuurbedrijf (SCK) e Federatie van Nederlandse Kraanbedrijven (FNK) v. Commission*, Joined Cases T-213/95 and T-18/96, E.C.R. 1997, p. II–1739.

[13] *Courage Ltd v. Bernard Crehan*, Case C-453/99, E.C.R. 2001, p. I–6297, §§ 26 and 27; see also *Manfredi v. Lloyd Adriatico Assicurazioni*, Case C-295/04, E.C.R. 2006, not yet reported.

application of Article 81(3) EC to the national courts, thereby ostensibly improving the Community legal system.

That said, the Court of Justice in the *CIF* case has recently taken a diametrically opposed approach. In the *CIF* case the Court gave greater weight to safeguarding the position of the individual than to the efficient functioning of the Community legal system.[14]

The principle of '*ego te baptizo piscem*' and the consequences of attributing direct effect to Article 81(3) EC

Despite the considerations set out above, it is obviously not entirely beyond the bounds of possibility that the Court of Justice might overrule the earlier case law establishing that Article 81(3) does not have direct effect. The change of the title of Article 1 of Regulation 1/03 and the fact that Article 6 is formulated on the premise that Article 81(3) does have direct effect might make this easier for the Court of Justice.

In the proposal for a regulation of 2000, Article 1 was entitled 'Direct applicability'. In the final version of the Regulation, Article 1 received the more general title 'Application of Articles 81 and 82 of the Treaty'. In contrast, Article 6 of the proposal provided that 'national courts ... shall have jurisdiction to apply Article 81(3) EC'. This wording would have made it difficult for the Court to overrule its earlier case law without attributing the change of approach to the Regulation. Such a change of interpretation would not be legitimate since it is settled law that the direct effect of a provision flows from the way in which the provision itself is worded.[15] However,

---

[14] *CIF v. AGCM*, op. cit.. In that case, the ECJ rejected the argument that individuals faced with a national rule which was unlawful because it infringed Article 10 in conjunction with Article 81 EC should be required to disapply the rule irrespective of whether a court or other national authority had taken a position on it. The ECJ held that individuals were required to disapply a national rule which was unlawful in the light of the *Reiff* case law only once a public body, in that case, a national antitrust authority, had declared that the rule was illegal (paragraphs 53 and 54). By contrast, in *Commission v. Ladbroke Racing Ltd*, Joined Cases C-359/95 P and C-379/95 P, E.C.R. 1997, p. I-6265, the Commission had maintained that: 'Article 81 remains applicable to undertakings' conduct despite the existence of national statutory obligations and irrespective of the possible application of Articles 3(g), 10 and 81 of the treaty with regard to those state measures. In fact, the Commission argues that an undertaking can and, by virtue of the primacy of Community law and the direct effect of Articles 81(1) and 82 of the Treaty, must refuse to comply with a state measure that requires conduct contrary to those provisions' (ibid., § 20). Had it not been rejected by the ECJ in *CIF*, the Commission's approach would, as a consequence of the principle of the primacy of Community law, have placed the burden of disapplying on their own initiative a law that is allegedly unlawful not as a consequence of the behaviour of the individual but as a result of the member State having infringed Community law.

Similarly, Article 6 of Regulation 1/03 places on individuals the risk of wrongfully complying with a undetermined obligation (Article 81(3), thereby requiring individuals to behave as if Article 81(3) was a determined obligation.

[15] See *Van Gend & Loos v. Netherlands Inland Revenue Administration*, Case 26-62,

Article 6 of the Regulation provides that 'national courts shall have the power to apply Articles 81 and 82 of the Treaty'. If the Court were to overrule its earlier case law on the direct effect of Article 81(3), this would not require any amendment of Article 6 and would also rule out any suggestion that the change of approach had been dictated by the Regulation.

However, if the Court were to alter its interpretation of Article 81(3), it would need to modify no fewer than three distinct lines of consistent case law holding that Article 81(3) does not have direct effect (*supra*). It would also need to overrule a fourth line of case law (the *Ahmed Saeed* case law) which holds that national courts are not bodies that formulate competition policy and even a fifth line (the *Delimitis* case law) expressly holding that courts cannot apply Article 81(3) because that provision does not have direct effect. Even this would not solve the problem that Article 6 of the Regulation is unlawful because it conflicts with Article 83 EC.

Furthermore, if the case law on Article 81(3) were to be changed, thereby conferring jurisdiction on national courts to apply that provision, this would do away with one of the basic principles of the doctrine of direct effect. As was pointed out above, direct effect flows from the way in which the provision itself is worded.[16] But Regulation 1/03 provides that the direct effect of Article 81(3) is a direct (see paragraph 14 of the Notice on the handling of complaints) or indirect[17] result of the wishes of the Council (that is, the Member States) expressed in a Regulation. Article 6 is capable of seriously undermining the cardinal principle of the Community legal system that 'the Member States are the masters of the Treaty when it comes to changing the constitutional fundamentals of the Community, but they are not the masters as regards the interpretation and application of Community law in force' (Mestmäcker, 2003, p. 5). Article 6 of the Regulation, itself unlawful, would extend the power of the Member States to modify the way in which a Treaty provision, *in casu* Article 81(3) EC, has been consistently interpreted by the Court of Justice in over 40 years of case law. This would restrict the independence from Member State intervention which the Court enjoys when interpreting Community law.

This infringement cannot be justified by the fact that the Member States

---

E.C.R. English special edition 1963, p. 1; *David Petrie v. Commission*, Case T-191/99, E.C.R. 2001, p. II–3677, § 34.

[16] See *Van Gend & Loos v. Netherlands Inland Revenue Administration*, op. cit. p. 1; *David Petrie v. Commission*, op. cit..

[17] This is the case even if the Court should overrule its existing case law. It is clear from Recital 4 of the preamble to Regulation 1/03 that the applicability of Article 81(3) is not a consequence of the Court's case law but stems from the Regulation. Recital 4 reads as follows: 'courts of the Member States have the power to apply not only Articles 81(1) and 82 of the Treaty, which have direct applicability by virtue of the case law of the Court of Justice of the European Communities, but also Article 81(3) of the Treaty'.

unanimously voted for the adoption of Regulation 1/03. Quite the contrary, this factor merely aggravates the violation which Article 6 of the regulation represents. It means that, for the reasons identified *supra*, all of the Member States unanimously and without any scruples voted to accept a provision despite the fact that it would have a deleterious effect on the protection of individuals.

With regard to Article 6 of the Regulation, the Court can thus reassert its role as guardian of Community legality for the benefit of individuals when confronted with unlawful behaviour of the Community institutions, as it did in the *CIF* judgment.

Adding a humour note, the behaviour of the Community institutions in wanting to attribute direct effect to a provision which does not have that quality is reminiscent of the old story of a Cardinal who wanted to eat meat on Good Friday and ordered a steak. When reminded that this was forbidden, he blessed the steak and uttered the words '*Ego te baptizo piscem*' ('I baptise you as a fish') and ate it!

In deciding to deem that a provision has direct effect despite the fact that Community law precludes it from having that quality, the Community institutions have acted in a way which is not very different from the Cardinal.

In conclusion, by requiring national courts to apply Article 81(3) EC, Article 6 opens Pandora's box as regards the principle of direct effect and the independence of the Court of Justice. It is an unlawful choice, the reasons for which may now be understandable. However, it is not yet possible to estimate the long-term impact of that choice on the Community legal order and the protection of the individual.

In any event, the consequence of the illegality of Article 6 of Regulation 1/03 is, as we have already stated, that Article 81(3) should only be applied by the Commission and the national competition authorities.

38.1.4. The Exercise of Jurisdiction

Regulation 1/03 deals with certain aspects of the way in which national courts are to exercise their antitrust jurisdiction, as it also does with respect to the national authorities.

Article 16(1) of the Regulation contains a rule on the 'uniform application of Community competition law'. Article 16(1) is based on the same principles as Article 16(2), which applies to national competition authorities. The two provisions put flesh on the bones of the same general principles of Community competition law.

Article 16(1) applies in two types of situation: the first is where the Commission has taken a decision before the national court gives its ruling; the second is where the national court has given judgment before the Commission takes its decision:

1. If the national court gives judgment after the Commission, it is bound by the Commission's decision. A national measure, in this case the judgment of a national court, may not come to a result different from the Commission. Even if the Commission has not taken a decision, the national court may not come to a conclusion in conflict with Community antitrust policy. By virtue of its exclusive power to define Community competition policy (Article 85), the Commission determines the correct interpretation of Articles 81 and 82 EC. If the national court considers that the Commission's decision is itself unlawful, it may not simply set it aside. However, as pointed out in paragraph 13 of the Notice on cooperation with the national courts, a national court may make a reference for a preliminary ruling to test the validity of the decision.[18]
2. If the national court gives judgment in a case which is pending before the Commission but in respect of which no decision has yet been taken, it 'must avoid giving decisions which would conflict with a decision contemplated by the Commission in proceedings it has initiated' (Article 16(1)). In this way, Article 16(1) gives directions to the national court as to the judgment which should lawfully be given in the national proceedings.

There is no equivalent provision in Article 16(2). That is because, if the Commission initiates proceedings in a case in which a national authority is applying Community antitrust law, the national authority loses its power to apply Articles 81 and 82 EC in that case.

However, Article 16(1) does not empower the Commission to take over cases before national courts because that would preclude judicial protection of the individual rights conferred by Articles 81 and 82 EC (see the *Sabam* judgment).

Article 16(1) also provides an express legal basis allowing national courts to stay proceedings so that they do not make a ruling which conflicts with the later decision of the Commission. The relevant sentence reads: 'the national court may assess whether it is necessary to stay its proceedings'.

It has been argued that Article 16(1) is unconstitutional in certain Member States because it provides that national courts are bound by the decision of an administrative body, *in casu* the Commission. That would, it is argued, be in breach of the principle of the independence of the judiciary. However, that view is incorrect for two reasons:

---

[18] See *Foto-Frost v. Hauptzollamt Luebeck-Ost*, Case 314/85, E.C.R. 1987, p. 4199, § 12 ff.

1. The principle that measures taken by the Commission can bind national courts was not introduced for the first time by Regulation 1/03. It has been a characteristic of Community law since 1957. This point was clarified while Regulation 17/62 was in force by *Delimitis* in 1992[19] and it was subsequently confirmed by *Masterfoods* in 2000.[20]
2. The argument that Article 16(1) is unconstitutional can be rebutted. Since 1957, Article 85 of the EC Treaty has conferred power on the Commission to define 'the principles laid down in Articles 81 and 82'. This power was conferred on the Commission precisely in order to allow it to have an appropriate degree of independence from the Member States. The fact that national courts are bound by the Commission's competition policy as expressed, *inter alia*, through decisions is simply the other side of the same coin. There is thus an indissoluble link between the content of Articles 81 and 82 EC, the Commission's exclusive power to define Community competition policy and its supranational character (that is, its independence). If national courts had the power to define Community competition policy in order to safeguard their own independence, this would weaken the supranational character required by the Community legal order, especially by the Commission.

   Furthermore, the concept of the independence of the judiciary does not imply that it is completely autonomous. To illustrate the point, we can examine how the expression 'an independent and impartial tribunal' within the meaning of Article 6 of the European Convention on Human Rights has been interpreted. Under the ECHR, the independence of the judiciary does not entitle judges to interpret the rules enacted by their own legal system entirely as they wish. It means that courts 'must be free to apply their own rules of procedure concerning the powers of the judge, the conduct of the proceedings in general and the confidentiality of the documents on the file in particular'.[21] This concept of the independence of the judiciary is not inconsistent with the fact that since 1957 the Community has conferred the power to define competition policy on a particular body and that national courts must respect this when they make their own rulings.

We should not forget that in order to safeguard 'this concept' of the independence of national courts, Regulation 1/03 provides for specific mechanisms of cooperation and control as between national courts and the

---

[19] See the practice of the Commission referred to in *Stergios Delimitis v. Henninger Bräu AG*, Case C-234/89, E.C.R. 1991, p. I–935.

[20] *Masterfoods Ltd v. HB Ice Cream Ltd*, Case C-344/98, E.C.R. 2000, p. I–11369.

[21] *Kingdom of the Netherlands v. Commission*, Joined Cases C-174/98 P and C-189/98 P, E.C.R. 2000, p. I–1.

Commission. Those mechanisms differ from what is established for the national competition authorities (for other ways of ensuring the independence of the national courts, see *infra*).

38.1.5. The Relations Between Jurisdiction under Article 6 of Regulation 1/03 and National Antitrust Law

With regard to the power to apply Community antitrust law conferred on national courts by Article 6 of the Regulation, and any restrictions which this may entail for the parallel application of national antitrust law, we have to distinguish between two situations:

1. Where domestic law allows national antitrust rules to be applied even to cases of Community relevance. In that case, Article 6 and Article 3(1) of the Regulation allow national courts to apply national law in parallel with Community law (see *supra* for a discussion on the point that it is impossible for national courts to apply Article 81(3) EC, unless they are administrative national competition authorities, because it does not have direct effect).
2. Where national law so defines the scope of national competition law that it applies only to cases which are not of Community relevance. In that case, when examining a case of Community relevance, the national courts may apply Community law only. Its application is compulsory by virtue of Article 3(1) of Regulation 1/03 and national antitrust law cannot be applied because its scope has been defined in a way that automatically excludes any overlap with Community law (see *supra*).

38.2. PENALTIES

Regulation 1/03 is silent as to the private or public law consequences of an infringement of Article 81 or 82 EC. Equally it says nothing relating to the time barring of actions related to those articles. The Regulation thus leaves these issues to the discretion of the Member States.

There are none the less certain fetters which Community law imposes in this respect:

1. Community law provides for a right to compensation for harm flowing from the breach of Articles 81 and 82 EC, irrespective of what national law provides.[22]

[22] See *Courage Ltd v. Bernard Crehan*, Case C-453/99, E.C.R. 2001, p. I–6297; see also

2. The Member States' right to attach different public or private law consequences (for example exemplary damages or criminal law sanctions) to infringements of Articles 81 and 82 EC is circumscribed by certain general principles of Community law such as equivalence[23] or effectiveness.[24]
3. Regulation 1/03 contains no provisions on the limitation of actions based on Articles 81 and 82. This question is thus left up to the Member States,[25] on condition that they comply with the general principles of Community law.

38.3. COOPERATION AND CONTROL MECHANISMS

Article 3(1) of Regulation 1/03 requires not only national authorities but also national courts to apply Community antitrust law to cases of Community relevance. This requirement is a consequence of the 'expected failure' of the Commission's attempt in the 1990s to persuade individuals to rely on Community antitrust law instead of domestic antitrust law. In the absence of any incentives to prefer Community antitrust law, individuals naturally continued to rely on national law. It was not reasonable to expect them to stop behaving as rational individuals and, instead, act 'spontaneously' to safeguard the common market.

In its attempts to 'encourage' individuals to rely on Community antitrust law, Regulation 1/03 has not created incentives for them to choose the legal system which is most advantageous. It has, instead, illiberally coerced them into relying on Community antitrust law in cases of Community relevance.

The role of Article 3(1) differs depending on whether it is applicable to the network of authorities or the national courts:

- With reference to the network, it aims to establish interoperability between the antitrust enforcement systems part of the network. This is aimed at 'the proper functioning of the cooperation mechanisms contained in this Regulation' (Recital 8 of the Preamble to the Regulation).
- With reference to national courts, the aim is to decentralise the enforcement of Community antitrust law (or, more accurately, as Recital 8 of the preamble to the Regulation expresses it, to 'ensure the effective enforcement of the Community competition rules'). When individuals

---

Manfredi v. Lloyd Adriatico Assicurazioni, Case C-295/04, E.C.R. 2006, not yet reported.

[23] See *Sante Pasquini v INPS*, Case C-34/02, E.C.R. 2003, p. 6515, § 95.

[24] See *Sante Pasquini*, ibid., § 58.

[25] See *Sante Pasquini*, ibid., § 95.

allege that national antitrust law has been infringed in a case of Community relevance, they are equally obliged to claim that Community antitrust law has been breached.

The consequence of the need to safeguard judicial independence is that there is no 'interoperability' between national courts. Nevertheless, Chapter IV of Regulation 1/03, entitled 'Cooperation', does not merely regulate the relations between the Commission and the national authorities (bodies of the Community antitrust administrative enforcement system). It also governs relations between the Commission and national courts and, to a lesser extent, between national courts and national authorities. As regards the relations between the Commission and the national courts, it provides for two types of proceedings (as in the case of the relations between the Commission and the national authorities):

1. The first category of proceedings comprises types of cooperation with the Commission which the national courts can activate independently. The cooperation proceedings are all 'vertical descending', in particular those which allow the Commission to act as *amicus curiae* and the other powers open to the national courts, such as staying their proceedings or making a reference for a preliminary ruling referred to in Article 1/03. In particular, the purpose of the proceedings linked with the Commission's role as *amicus curiae* is to facilitate the national courts' task of applying Articles 81 and 82 EC. This should make it more likely for individuals to have resort to national courts rather than to the Commission or the national authorities. Those proceedings also allow the national courts to avoid taking decisions which infringe Community antitrust law. When they apply Community antitrust law they are under the same obligation as the national authorities to come to the same conclusions that the Commission itself would have reached. So far as the national courts are concerned, that obligation is put on a statutory footing by Article 16(1) of Regulation 1/03.
2. The second category concerns direct control mechanisms which the Commission (and the national authorities) can exercise ex officio. The control proceedings, unlike those within the administrative antitrust system, are all 'vertical descending' (Commission – national courts and national authorities – national courts). Their purpose is to prevent courts from giving judgments which infringe Community law. In the light of the protection of national courts' independence, those proceedings of cooperation and control are structured differently from the proceedings of the Community administrative antitrust system.

39. Mechanisms Allowing Cooperation between the Commission and the National Courts

The cooperation mechanisms which the national courts themselves can use are a new feature within the Community legal order. As pointed out in paragraph 15 of the Notice on cooperation with the national courts, 'other than the co-operation mechanism between the national courts and the Court of Justice under Article 234 EC, the EC Treaty does not explicitly provide for co-operation between the national courts and the Commission'.

39.1. THE COMMISSION'S *AMICUS CURIAE* ROLE

The first way in which the national courts and the Commission may cooperate pursuant to Regulation 1/03 is through the Commission's role as *amicus curiae*. This should not be confused with the cooperation which underlies the relationship between the Commission and the national authorities and which is regulated by Article 11(1).

The principle contained in Article 11(1) applies only to the relationship between the Commission and the national authorities (*supra*). It is thus limited to the relations existing between the bodies making up the Community administrative antitrust enforcement system. The principle is implemented through the mutual control which the Commission and the national authorities exercise, albeit with different levels of intensity, and, indirectly, through the control exercised by the national authorities *inter se* (*supra*).

By contrast, the cooperation between the national courts and the Commission is not based on the 'principle of cooperation' in the sense in which that expression is used in Article 11(1). This feature is a consequence of the independence which the national courts enjoy even within the Community antitrust system. It is not by chance that the Commission has the power to relieve the national authorities of their power to apply Articles 81 and 82 (under Article 11(6)), whereas it lacks this power with respect to national courts. This allows the national courts to fulfil their role of safeguarding individual rights conferred by Articles 81 and 82 EC and, indirectly, to maintain their independence.[1]

By virtue of Article 15(1), entitled 'Cooperation with national courts', national courts may, when applying Community antitrust law, ask the Commission to transmit to them:

- information in its possession; and
- its opinion on questions concerning the application of the Community competition rules.

Article 15(1) establishes a way for the Commission to facilitate the application of Articles 81 and 82 EC by the national courts. The system is similar, but not identical, to what is provided in respect of the national authorities.

Article 15 enables the national courts to apply Articles 81 and 82 directly and independently and to resolve any doubts which they may entertain when applying Community law. In this way, Article 15(1) should also help to reduce the number of complaints with which the Commission or the national authorities will have to deal directly, thereby allowing the workload of the Commission and the national authorities to be reduced.

The Commission affords assistance to national courts in order to ensure that Community antitrust law is applied consistently. It thus has an *amicus curiae* role. In paragraphs 19 and 20 of the Notice on cooperation with the national courts, the Commission gave notice that in this context it will not hear any of the parties directly and, if it is contacted by any of the parties, it will inform the national court of this as a way of ensuring the court's independence.

The Commission carries out its *amicus curiae* role in two ways:

- by transmitting information; and
- by giving its opinion on the application of the competition rules.

39.1.1. Transmission of Information by the Commission

One aspect of the Commission's *amicus curiae* function is the transmission of any information in its possession to the national courts. The laconic wording of Article 15(1) gives the Commission considerable discretion in this respect.

In the Notice on cooperation with the national courts, the Commission itself has given some indication as to how it will apply Article 15(1). In the

---

[1] *Belgische Radio en Televisie v. Sv Sabam e Nv Fonior*, Case 127/73, E.C.R. 1974, p. 51, § 16.

Notice, the Commission concentrates on the information which the national courts may request and on the maintenance of professional secrecy.

Procedures applicable to information on ongoing proceedings

With regard to information on ongoing proceedings, a national court may for example ask the Commission for documents in its possession or for information of a procedural nature to enable it to discover whether a particular case is pending before the Commission, whether the Commission has initiated a procedure or whether it has already taken a position. A national court may also ask the Commission when a decision is likely to be taken, so that it can determine whether it should stay its proceedings or adopt interim measures (see paragraph 21of the Notice). (This reflects what was already the position by virtue of *Delimitis* and the 1993 Notice on cooperation with the national courts.[2]) When it receives a request for information or documents, the Commission will endeavour to provide them within one month from the date on which it receives the request (paragraph 22). In addition to what is indicated by the Commission, the national courts may also request specific information on 'economic or legal data'.[3]

Procedures applicable to information covered by the obligation of professional secrecy

Particular procedures applicable to information covered by the obligation of professional secrecy (that is, confidential information and business secrets) are established.

By its use of the expression 'business secrets', the Commission means 'information of which not only disclosure to the public but also mere transmission to a person other than the one that provided the information might seriously harm the latter's interests' (paragraph 23 of the Notice).

On this point, it is worth recalling that, pursuant to Article 28(1) and (2) of the Regulation, courts may receive from the Commission information covered by professional secrecy which may not otherwise be disclosed by the Commission and the national authorities. Such information may be used by the national courts for purposes other than those for which it was acquired (*supra*).

The Commission is in any event amenable to exchanging even information covered by professional secrecy with the national courts, provided that this does not water down the guarantees laid down in Article 287 EC. At paragraph 24 of the Notice, the Commission points out that the case law of

---

[2] The information to which the 1993 Notice on cooperation with the national courts referred concerned 'factual data, such as statistics, market studies and economic analyses' (ibid., § 40).

[3] *Stergios Delimitis v. Henninger Bräu AG*, Case C-234/89, E.C.R. 1991, p. I–935, § 53.

the Community courts[4] confirms that the duty of loyal cooperation requires the Commission to provide the national court with whatever information the latter asks for, even information covered by professional secrecy. However, in offering its cooperation to the national courts, the Commission may not in any circumstances undermine the guarantees established by Article 287 EC. For this reason, 'in transmitting information to national courts, the Commission has to uphold the guarantees given to natural and legal persons by Article 287 EC. Article 287 EC prevents members, officials and other servants of the Commission from disclosing information covered by the obligation of professional secrecy'.

To this end, the Commission has established a procedure whereby the national court commits itself to complying with certain standards of confidentiality in the way in which it uses the information. Before transmitting information covered by professional secrecy to a national court,

> the Commission will remind the court of its obligation under Community law to uphold the rights which Article 287 EC confers on natural and legal persons and it will ask the court whether it can and will guarantee protection of confidential information and business secrets. If the national court cannot offer such guarantee, the Commission shall not transmit the information covered by professional secrecy to the national court. Only when the national court has offered a guarantee that it will protect the confidential information and business secrets, will the Commission transmit the information requested, indicating those parts which are covered by professional secrecy and which parts are not and can therefore be disclosed'. (paragraph 25 of the Notice)

Notwithstanding this system, there are cases in which the Commission may legitimately refuse to transmit the information requested by the national courts (*supra*). The Commission specified at paragraph 26 of the Notice that it will refuse to send such information

> for overriding reasons relating to the need to safeguard the interests of the Community or to avoid any interference with its functioning and independence, in particular by jeopardising the accomplishment of the tasks entrusted to it. Therefore, the Commission will not transmit to national courts information voluntarily submitted by a leniency applicant without the consent of the applicant.

It may be inferred from the wording of Article 15(1) that the national courts may not ask 'the Commission to transmit to them information in its

[4] *Postbank NV v. Commission*, Case T-353/94, E.C.R. 1996, p. II–921, §§ 86 and 87; *Stanley George Adams v. Commission*, Case 145/83, E.C.R. 1985, p. 3539, § 34.

possession' in proceedings for the application of the antitrust law of the Member State concerned. The sole exception to this principle is to be found in Article 12(2) which, in any event, applies only to 'exchange of information' between the Commission and the national authorities. Article 28, on professional secrecy, does not provide for any further exception apart from the derogations provided for by Articles 11, 12, 14, 15 and 27. Such an exception would also have allowed the national courts to have obtained information from the Commission for that purpose.

39.1.2. Commission Opinions on the Application of the Competition Rules

Article 15(1) also allows national courts to ask the Commission for 'its opinion on questions concerning the application of the Community competition rules'; in particular, specific questions relating to the economic or legal analysis of issues which have arisen in the course of a national proceeding. The purpose is to avoid the situation whereby national courts take decisions which conflict with Community law.

In paragraph 27 of the Notice, the Commission stresses that the national courts should make use of this facility only if they cannot deal with the case before them, *inter alia*, in the light of the practice of the Commission.

When such a request is made, the Commission will endeavour to reply within four months from the date on which it receives the request (paragraph 28 of the Notice).

In order to respect the independence of the national court, the Commission, when giving its opinion, will limit itself to providing the national court with the factual information or the economic or legal clarification asked for, without considering the merits of the case pending before the national court. Moreover, unlike the authoritative interpretation of Community law by the Community courts, the opinion of the Commission does not legally bind the national court (paragraph 29 of the Notice).

Article 15(1)'s scope differs from that of Article 11(5) which relates to the national authorities' power to consult the Commission. Under Article 15(1), the scope of the questions that the national courts may ask the Commission is limited to 'questions concerning the application of the Community competition rules'. Article 11(5), however, allows the national authorities to 'consult the Commission on any case involving the application of Community law'. The fact that the scope of the questions which the national courts may ask is more limited is attributable to the desire to limit the Commission's direct intervention as far as possible, which is the main principle underlying the Regulation. None the less, it can be deduced from the wording of Article 15(1) that, provided that the request is made 'in proceedings for the application of Articles 81 or 82 of the Treaty', the national court may in any event ask questions on the application of any of the Community competition rules, not merely the antitrust rules.

In the words of the Court of First Instance, although they have no binding force, the opinions of the Commission show that 'the voluntary compliance with the non-binding acts of the institutions is an essential factor in the achievement of the goals of the Treaty'.[5] However, such opinions, which are non-binding acts addressed to the national courts, offer only limited judicial protection to the parties to the national proceedings because the Court of Justice refuses to review them even if the national court has complied with them.[6] Consequently, if the national court requests the Commission to give 'its opinion on questions concerning the application of the Community competition rules', either of its own motion or at the request of the parties, the Commission's opinion cannot be the subject of judicial review. It is thus up to the national court to decide whether to follow the Commission's opinion or whether it should make a reference for a preliminary ruling pursuant to Article 234 EC.

39.2. STAYING PROCEEDINGS BEFORE NATIONAL COURTS IN ORDER TO AVOID JUDGMENTS CONFLICTING WITH COMMISSION DECISIONS

In addition to providing for the transmission of information and opinions pursuant to Article 15(1) of the Regulation (that is the Commission's *amicus curiae* role), the Regulation establishes a second method of cooperation through Article 16(1) which provides that 'the national courts may assess whether it is necessary to stay its proceedings' pending a final decision by the Commission. In this way, the national courts have the opportunity to avoid taking decisions which might conflict with the Commission's decision if there are parallel proceedings.[7]

At paragraph 12 of the Notice, the Commission explains that, if a national court stays its proceedings when the Commission is conducting a parallel investigation into the same case, it 'will endeavour to give priority to cases for which it has decided to initiate proceedings within the meaning of Article 2(1) of Commission Regulation (EC) No 773/2004 and that are the subject of national proceedings stayed in this way, in particular when the outcome of a civil dispute depends on them'.

---

[5] *Nefarma v. Commission*, Case T-113/89, E.C.R. 1990, p. II–797, § 79.

[6] See ibid., §§ 79–97.

[7] See *Brasserie de Haecht v. Wilkin-Janssen*, Case 48/72, E.C.R. 1973, p. 77, § 13.

39.3. PRELIMINARY REFERENCES PURSUANT TO ARTICLE 234 EC

A third method of cooperation to assist national courts to give judgments which are not in conflict with Community antitrust law is referred to in Article 16(1), last sentence. It recalls that, if they are doubtful as to how to apply Articles 81 or 82 EC, national courts may make a reference for a preliminary ruling pursuant to Article 234 EC.

40. Mechanisms Allowing the Commission and National Antitrust Authorities to Monitor the Decisions of the National Courts

40.1. THE ROLE OF THE COMMISSION IN MONITORING THE NATIONAL COURTS

Article 15(3) provides for another set of mechanisms to facilitate the correct application of Community antitrust law. These differ from the mechanisms which we have just examined in that they are activated by the Commission or the national authorities *ex officio* rather than by the national court of its own motion. Article 15(3) allows the Commission to submit written, and on occasions oral, observations to courts of Member States 'where the coherent application of Article 81 or Article 82 of the Treaty so requires'.

Since Regulation 1/03 contains no provisions specifying the procedure for submitting observations, 'Member States' procedural rules and practices determine the relevant procedural framework. Where a Member State has not yet established the appropriate procedures, the national court has to determine which procedural rules are appropriate for the submission of observations in the case pending before it' (paragraph 34 of the Notice). When enacting the relevant provisions, the Member States are, however, bound to comply with general principles of Community law, such as effectiveness and equivalence, as indeed are the national courts when they apply them.

Article 15(3) is preceded by a provision which requires Member States to forward to the Commission a copy of any written judgment of national courts ruling on the application of the provisions of Community antitrust law. This information enables the Commission to be formally kept up to date with the judgments given by the national courts and the requirement to forward it can thus be seen to be connected with the proceedings falling under Article 15(3).

Article 15(3) is based on the Commission's role as the body which determines the orientation of Community competition policy and thus the only body which is entitled to clarify the content of the 'principles of Articles 81 and 82'.

In common with all the provisions of Chapter IV, entitled 'Cooperation', the mechanism established by Article 15(3) of the Regulation constitutes one component of the overall strategy pursued by the Regulation, which is to allow greater decentralisation of the enforcement of Articles 81 and 82 while, at the same time, establishing mechanisms allowing the decisions of the Member State bodies to be monitored.

Article 15(3) establishes a procedure which is quite different from the *amicus curiae* role conferred on the Commission by Article 15(1).

Article 15(1) establishes a form of cooperation between the Commission and the national courts. By contrast, Article 15(3) establishes a comparatively intrusive means by which the Commission can monitor judgments of the national courts. (The function of Article 15(3) is thus analogous to that of Article 11(3), with the obvious difference that the one provision applies with respect to national courts while the other applies to the national authorities.) Monitoring judgments allows the Commission to assess and, if need be, challenge decisions of the national courts. This can be done before a final judgment is given or even after any judgment has become unappealable. In any event the Commission will always respect the independence of the national courts (Notice on cooperation with national courts, paragraph 19).

Control may be exercised in two types of situation:

1. The Commission is entitled, by virtue of Article 15(3), to submit written observations to courts of the Member States 'where the coherent application of Article 81 or 82 of the Treaty so requires'. This possibility undoubtedly applies if national court proceedings are pending at first instance (this may have been brought to the Commission's attention through information communicated by the national authorities or from media reports). It could also apply if a judgment is appealed (in which case the Commission should have received a copy of the judgment at first instance pursuant to Article 15(2)). The written observations allow the Commission to explain to the national court how it should apply Articles 81 and 82 EC correctly to the case at issue. The Commission 'will limit its observations to an economic and legal analysis of the facts underlying the case pending before the national courts' (paragraph 32 of the Notice). In terms of its aim, this mechanism has effects on the relations between the Commission and the national courts analogous to those which Article 11(4) has on the relations between the Commission and the national authorities. However, one difference is that opinions expressed by the Commission in the context of Article 15(3) are not subjected to an examination by the Advisory Committee. Moreover, in order to permit the

national courts to fulfil their function of providing judicial protection of the rights conferred by those articles under the *SABAM–Fornior* case law, the Commission does not have the power to relieve national courts of their jurisdiction to apply Articles 81 and 82 EC.[1]

2. The Commission may even carry out an *ex post* control of judgments which have become unappealable if it considers that the national courts have wrongly applied Articles 81 and 82 EC. It may do this by commencing infringement proceedings against the relevant Member State pursuant to Article 226 EC.[2] Article 15(3) of the Regulation does not specify what weight the national court must give to the Commission's observations. These observations are not contained in a binding act within the meaning of Article 249 EC, nor are they dealt with by the Regulation. This raises the question already discussed with regard to opinions of the Commission issued pursuant to Article 15(1) (*supra*). Since 'observations', like an 'opinion', are not subject to review by the Court of Justice, the national court is entitled not to follow them and, instead, to make a reference for a preliminary ruling.

Nevertheless, the national court should bear in mind, first, that the Commission submitted its observations in order to avoid the Member State breaching its Community law obligations through a decision of a national court and, second, that the judgment may have consequences for individuals (*supra*). Consequently, if there is no judgment of the Court of Justice replying to a question referred for a preliminary ruling relevant to the case before it, the national court should give due weight to the Commission's observations.

40.2. THE ROLE OF THE NATIONAL AUTHORITIES IN MONITORING THE NATIONAL COURTS

Article 15(3) also gives national antitrust authorities the power to submit observations to the national courts on antitrust issues. They may, acting on their own initiative, submit written and, with the permission of the court, oral observations 'on issues relating to the application of Article 81 or Article 82 of the Treaty'.

It is apparent from the wording of Article 15(3) that it confers on the national authorities a role that is different from that of the Commission. The national authorities submit written observations 'on issues relating to the

[1] See *Belgische Radio en Televisie v. Sv Sabam e Nv Fonior*, Case 127/73, E.C.R. 1974, p. 51.

[2] See *Gerhard Köbler v. Republik Österreich*, Case C-224/01, E.C.R. 2003, p. I–10239.

application of Articles 81 and 82 of the Treaty'. However, the Commission, taking account of its exclusive powers to determine Community competition policy, intervenes only 'where the coherent application of Article 81 or Article 82 of the Treaty so requires'.

The national authorities' concern is thus not to ensure the 'coherent application' of competition policy, but rather to avoid a situation in which their own Member States infringe Community law through a judgment handed down by their own courts. In other words, the Regulation has delegated to the national authorities a power to help ensure that Community antitrust law is correctly applied in the judgments handed down by their own courts. The objective of Article 15(3) is to limit the Commission's enforcement activity, which is the overall objective of the Regulation. Its aim is particularly to ensure that the Commission intervenes only to guarantee the coherent application of Community antitrust law, which is one of its prerogatives.

The fact that Article 15(3) serves a different purpose explains why it does not specify how a national authority is to be informed of judgments applying Community antitrust law given by 'its' courts. This is a question of purely national relevance. The Member States themselves will enact specific provisions on this point (as is also suggested by the wording of Article 15(4)). Such provisions might require the national competition authorities to be informed, by whatever means, not only of individual judgments, but also of Community competition law cases initiated before the courts of the Member State in question.

Since Regulation 1/03 concerns the 'implementation of the rules on competition laid down in Articles 81 and 82 of the Treaty', the Commission and national authorities are not entitled by virtue of Article 15(3) to 'submit written observations to the national courts' on issues relating to the application of national antitrust law. However, since Article 15(3) gives the national authorities the means to prevent their Member State from infringing Community law through judgments of their courts (see *supra*), national authorities may *ex officio* submit observations on Articles 81 and 82 EC in cases where Community and national law are being applied in parallel. The purpose of this would be to avoid the national courts which are applying Community and national law in parallel from coming to conclusions which are in conflict, *inter alia*, with Article 3(2) of the Regulation.

40.3. INFORMATION RELEVANT TO THE PREPARATION OF THE OBSERVATIONS

The second sub-paragraph of Article 15(3) allows the Commission and the national authorities to 'request the relevant court of the Member State to transmit or ensure the transmission to them of any documents necessary for the assessment of the case'. They can thus have the information which they require to prepare their observations. That provision precludes the documents which are transmitted being used pursuant to Article 12 of the Regulation, which concerns the exchange and use of documents as between bodies of the Network (*supra*). Similarly, the information may not be used as evidence in other proceedings before the Commission or national authorities.

Although information communicated pursuant to the second sub-paragraph of Article 15(3) may not be used as evidence in antitrust proceedings, the documents lodged during proceedings (even by the plaintiff) may later be used to initiate a separate antitrust proceeding. As the Court stated in *Spanish Banks*, the national authorities are not required to suffer from 'acute amnesia' and thus pretend that they have never seen particular documents,[3] even if those documents may not be used as evidence. This means that if a proceeding is opened on the basis of documents communicated pursuant to Article 15(3), the Commission and the national authorities may exercise their own investigative powers against infringements of both Community and national antitrust law.

---

[3] *Direccıon General de Defensa de la Competencia v. Asociacion Espanola de Banca prıvada*, Case C-67/91, E.C.R. 1992, p. I–4785, § 39.

PART X

EUROPEAN MERGER CONTROL

41. The Role of Merger Control in the EC Treaty

A concentration takes place when two or more undertakings are absorbed by, or merge into, a single undertaking. Concentrations among firms assume significance for competition law when the process of concentration reduces the number of undertakings in a specific sector, thereby creating a situation capable of distorting the market. This may happen where particular undertakings acquire or reinforce a dominant position on the market. A regulation aiming at avoiding concentrations having a negative impact on competition then has to be devised.

In Europe, Article 66 of the ECSC Treaty provided for a system of merger control. This system was, however, limited to the coal and steel sector (see *supra*).

In 1957 the draftsmen of the Treaty of Rome debated whether it would be appropriate to include merger control provisions in the EEC Treaty. In the end nothing came of these discussions (see *supra*).

In 1965, the risk of excessive concentration in certain sectors of the common market prompted the Commission to issue its first memorandum in this field.[1] In the memorandum, the Commission analysed whether direct reliance on the antitrust rules, in particular Article 82 EC, could provide safeguards against an excessive level of concentration on the market. Article 82 would prohibit concentrations implemented by an undertaking enjoying a dominant position. However, the idea of merger control by means of Article 82 EC encountered three sizeable hurdles:

- it was capable of controlling only concentrations put into effect by undertakings which were already in a dominant position;
- control of the operation could take place only *ex post*, that is, after the concentration had been implemented. This caused considerable problems if the merger turned out to be anticompetitive. In particular, it

[1] Memorandum of the Commission to the Governments of the Member State, *Concentration of Enterprises in the Common Market*, EEC Competition Series, Study No. 3, Brussels, 1966.

could be difficult to re-establish the situation on the market as it existed before the merger; and

- the application of Article 82 EC did not permit the control of the anticompetitive effects of concentrations carried out in oligopolistic markets.

In 1973, the first proposal for a merger control instrument was put on the table. The discussions among the Member States led to a large number of amendments being tabled, but no agreement on a final text was reached. Given the lack of a tailor-made system, the Commission began to examine concentrations in the light of Article 82,[2] and at a later stage under Article 81.[3]

New life was breathed into the process of enacting a merger control procedure by the process that culminated in the Single European Act (1986) (Monopolkommission, 1989, p. 36). The objective of this process was to create the internal market by 31 December 1992. The Community Merger Regulation (Regulation 4064/89)[4] was ultimately enacted in 1989 and entered into force in 1990.

The Regulation provided as follows:

- there was an obligation to notify concentrations to the Commission before implementing the transaction;
- the concentrations which had to be notified to the Commission were determined by reference to the turnover thresholds of the undertakings involved;
- concentrations were prohibited where the operation would create or

---

[2] *Europemballage Corportazion and Continentale Can v. Commission*, Case 6/72, E.C.R. 1973, p. 215.

Other concentrations assessed by the Commission under Article 82 EC are as follows: *Mannesmann/Demag*, Third Competition Report (1973), No. 73; *VEBA/Gelsenberg*, Fourth Competition Report (1974), No. 128 f; *Fiat/Kloeckner-Humboldt-Deutz*, Fifth Competition Report (1975), No. 83; *GKN/Sachs*, Sixth Competition Report (1976), No. 181 f.; *Michelin/Actor*, Eighth Competition Report (1978), No. 146; *AVEBE/KSH*, ibid., No. 147; *Citroen-Peugot/Chrysler*, ibid., No. 149; *Kaiser/Estel*, Ninth Competition Report (1979), No. 131; *Coats Patons/Gueterrmann*, ibid., No. 132; *Fichtel & Sachs/Hurek*, ibid., No. 133; *Pilkington/BSN-Gervais-Danone*, Tenth Competition Report (1980), No. 152; *Michelin/Kleber-Colombes*, ibid., No. 156; *Baxter Travenol Laboratories/Smith Kline RIT*, ibid., No. 157; *Amicon/Fortia and Wright Scientific*, Eleventh Competition Report (1981), No. 112; *Eagle Star/Allianz Versicherung*, Twelfth Competition Report (1982), No. 103; *Berisford Napier Brown*, Thirteenth Competition Report (1983), No. 166; *Kloeckner/Krupp*, Fourteenth Competition Report (1984), No. 106, 108; *Ashland Oil Inc./Cabot Co.*, ibid., No. 109; *Pont-à-Mousson/Stanton & Staveley*, ibid., No. 110.

[3] *British American Tobacco and R.J. Reynolds industries v. Commission*, Joined Cases 142 and 156/84, E.C.R. 1987, p. 4487.

[4] Council Regulation 4064/89 of 21 December 1989 on the control of concentrations between undertakings, OJ L 395 of 30 December 1989, p. 1.

reinforce a dominant position; and

- the Regulation established proceedings to allow the referral of concentrations as between the Commission and the Member States when the initial forum (which might be either the Commission or national authorities) was not the most appropriate.

Some aspects of Regulation 4064/89 were later modified by Regulation 1310/97, in particular:

- the turnover threshold determining whether the concentration needed to be notified to the Commission was amended. The new criteria extended the scope of Regulation 4064/89 to concentrations which, previously, did not need to be notified;
- the proceedings for referral of concentrations between the Commission and the Member States were also amended in order to take account of the changes to the turnover thresholds; and
- merger control was extended to the creation of joint ventures and to concentrations. Moreover, control pursuant to Article 81 EC was required for joint ventures whose parent companies remained active in the field of the joint venture and could therefore coordinate their behaviour contrary to Article 81.

In 2004 a new merger control Regulation was enacted (Regulation 139/04)[5]. This Regulation has:

- re-organised the structure of Regulation 4064/89 taking into account the amendments brought about by Regulation 1310/97; and
- brought about further changes to merger control procedures, in particular to:
    - o the test used to determine whether concentrations are incompatible with the common market; and
    - o the proceedings for the referral of concentrations between the Commission and the national authorities.

[5] Council Regulation 139/04 of 20 January 2004 on the control of concentrations between undertakings (the EC Merger Regulation).

42. Competence in the Field of Merger Control in the EC Treaty

The Treaty of Rome does not expressly regulate the competence to control mergers. In order to adopt the Merger Regulation, an appropriate legal basis in the Treaty had to be found. The legal basis was expressly identified in Regulation 4064/89 as Articles 83 and 308 (formerly 87 and 235) EC. Recital 6 of the preamble to that Regulation recognises that Articles 81 and 82 EC are applicable 'according to the case law of the Court of Justice, to certain operations' but goes on to state that they 'are not, however, sufficient to control all operations which may prove to be incompatible with the system of undistorted competition envisaged in the Treaty' (Bos, 1992, p. 395).

In the Council's view, as set out in Recital 7 of the preamble to Regulation 4064/89, that situation meant that 'a new legal instrument should ... be created in the form of a Regulation to permit effective control of all concentrations from the point of view of their effect on the structure of competition in the Community and to be the only instrument applicable to such concentrations'. Consequently, the Council chose as legal basis 'not only ... Article 83 but, principally, ... Article 308 of the Treaty, under which the Community may give itself the additional powers of action necessary for the attainment of its objectives' (see Recital 8 of the preamble).

Thus, it appears that, in the Council's view, there were two reasons why the merger control regime had to be based not merely on Article 83 EC but also on Article 308:

- first, rules had to be enacted which would apply even to mergers which did not fall under Articles 81 and 82 EC; and
- second, an instrument had to be adopted which, from an antitrust point of view, would be the only one to be applied to such situations.

The legal basis selected was confirmed in Regulation 139/04, Recital 7 of the Preamble to which reproduces practically word for word Recitals 7 and 8 of the preamble to Regulation 4064/89.

43. Basic Concepts of European Merger Control: The Concept of Merger, Merger Subject to Notification and Prohibited Merger

As the legal basis of the regulation indicates, merger control is but one facet of the general Community power to control competition. As such, merger control has to be examined against the more general background of the purpose and objectives of the European Community and Union. For that reason, a concentration must be appraised 'within the general framework of the achievement of the fundamental objectives referred to in Article 2 of the Treaty establishing the European Union and Article 2 of the Treaty on European Union' (see Recital 23 of the preamble to Regulation 139/04).

In order to understand merger control, we must first define certain basic concepts, namely:

- the concept of a 'concentration' (Article 3 of Regulation 139/04);
- the concentrations subject to the control provided for by the Regulation (Article 1); and
- the circumstances in which a concentration is to be prohibited.[1]

[1] For the various Commission Communications, see: Notice on the concept of concentration, 1998 OJ C 66/5; Notice on the concept of undertakings concerned, 1998 OJ C 66/14; Notice on the calculation of turnover, 1998 OJ C 66/25; Notice on the concept of full-function joint ventures, 1998 OJ C66/1; Guidelines on the Assessment of Horizontal Mergers, 2004 OJ C 31/5; Commission Notice on restrictions directly related and necessary to concentrations, 2001 OJ C 56/24; and Notice on remedies acceptable under the Merger Control Regulation, 2001 OJ C 68/3.

On the various procedural aspects relating to merger control, see: Commission Regulation 802/2004 Implementing Council Regulation 139/2004 on the Control of Concentrations between Undertakings, 2004 OJ L 133/1; Commission Notice on a simplified procedure for treatment of certain concentrations under Council Regulation n. 139/2004, 2004 OJ C 56/32; and Commission Notice on Case Referral in respect of concentrations, 2004 OJ C 56/2.

43.1. THE DEFINITION OF A CONCENTRATION

Regulation 139/04 (hereafter the 'Merger Regulation') applies to concentrations 'bringing about a lasting change in the control of the undertakings concerned and therefore in the structure of the market' (Recital 20).

According to Article 3(1), a lasting change can be brought about in one of the following was:

- through the merger of two or more previously independent undertakings or parts of undertakings; or
- through the acquisition of direct or indirect control of the whole or parts of one or more other undertakings by the means indicated in Article 3(2). Furthermore, Article 3(3) identifies the person who is deemed to acquire control. This is important for the purpose of determining who is required to notify (*infra*).

For the purposes of Regulation 139/04, the creation of a joint venture performing on a lasting basis all the functions of an autonomous economic entity and which results in 'a change of control on a lasting basis' is deemed to constitute a concentration (Article 3(4)).

43.2. THE CONCENTRATIONS WHICH ARE SUBJECT TO THE CONTROL PROVIDED FOR BY THE MERGER REGULATION

Recital 8 of the preamble to the Merger Regulation shows that the Council intended the provisions of the Regulation to 'apply to significant structural changes, the impact of which on the market goes beyond the national borders of any one Member State'. Consequently, the Merger Regulation applies only to concentrations having a 'Community dimension'. These are concentrations falling under Article 3 where the aggregate turnover of all the undertakings concerned exceeds thresholds set out in Article 1. That is so 'irrespective of whether or not the undertakings effecting the concentration have their seat or their principal fields of activity in the Community, provided they have substantial operations there' (Recital 10).

The Merger Regulation sets out two types of threshold relevant to determining whether a concentration has a Community dimension.

In the first threshold, defined in Article 1(2), there is a concentration having a Community dimension where:

- the combined aggregate worldwide turnover of all the undertakings concerned is more than €5000 million; and
- the aggregate Community-wide turnover of each of at least two of the undertakings concerned is more than €250 million.

Even if those two conditions are satisfied, the concentration does not have a Community dimension where 'each of the undertakings concerned achieves more than two-thirds of its aggregate Community-wide turnover within one and the same Member State'.

In the second threshold, a concentration that does not meet the thresholds laid down in Article 1(2) nevertheless has a Community dimension where:

- the combined aggregate worldwide turnover of all the undertakings concerned is more than €2500 million;
- in each of at least three Member States, the combined aggregate turnover of all the undertakings concerned is more than €100 million;
- in each of at least three Member States included for the purpose of the second point, the aggregate turnover of each of at least two of the undertakings is more than €25 million; and
- the aggregate Community-wide turnover of each of at least two of the undertakings concerned is more than €100 million.

A concentration which satisfies those conditions is nevertheless deemed not to have a Community dimension where 'each of the undertakings concerned achieves more than two thirds of its aggregate Community wide turnover within one and the same Member State' (Article 1(3) Reg. 139/04).

Article 5 indicates specifically how the turnover of the undertakings concerned is to be calculated. Those criteria are also supplemented by a Commission Notice.

Article 21(1) makes it clear that Regulation 139/04 is the only Community instrument applying to the control of concentrations having a Community dimension. The only exception is 'in relation to joint ventures that do not have a Community dimension and which have as their object or effect the coordination of the competitive behaviour of undertakings that remain independent'. Article 21(1) goes on to stipulate that, in that case, Council Regulations 1/2003, 1017/68, 4056/86 (now Regulation 1419/2006) also apply.

The Regulation provides for two exceptions to the principle that concentrations having Community relevance are assessed exclusively by the Commission pursuant to EC law. Those exceptions are:

- a concentration referred to a Member State before the notification has

been made (Article 4(5)); and
- a concentration referred to a Member State after the notification has been made (Article 22).

43.3. WHEN A CONCENTRATION IS PROHIBITED

One of the most important modifications introduced by the new Merger Regulation relates to the tests used to assess whether or not a specific operation is compatible with the common market. In this regard, we have to make a distinction between:

- mergers or the acquisition of companies; and
- the creation of a joint venture that is an autonomous economic entity.

43.3.1. Mergers or the Acquisition of Companies

As stated in Recital 14 to its preamble, Regulation 4064/89 prohibited concentrations 'with a Community dimension which created or strengthened a position as a result of which effective competition in the common market or in a substantial part of it [was] impeded'.

Regulation 139/04 amplifies this test in order to be able to assess the 'consequences that concentrations in oligopolistic market structures may have'. This is because, in oligopolistic markets 'it is all the more necessary to maintain effective competition' (Recital 25). The Merger Regulation has therefore partially modified the test for determining when concentrations are prohibited. In this regard, Regulation 139/04 operates on the basis that, although there is lively competition in many oligopolistic markets,

> under certain circumstances, concentrations involving the elimination of important competitive constraints that the merging parties had exerted upon each other, as well as a reduction of competitive pressure on the remaining competitors, may, even in the absence of a likelihood of coordination between the members of the oligopoly, result in a significant impediment to effective competition.

That criterion did not feature in Regulation 4064/89. Nor had the case law 'expressly interpreted Regulation 4064/89 as requiring concentrations giving rise to such non-coordinated effects to be declared incompatible with the common market' (Recital 25). For that reason 'in the interests of legal certainty', the Community legislature provided for the amended Regulation to 'permit effective control of all such concentrations by providing that any concentration which would significantly impede effective competition, in the common market or a substantial part of it, should be declared incompatible with the common market'. The notion of 'significant impediment to effective competition', which partially modifies the test set out in Regulation 4064/89, 'should be interpreted as extending, beyond the concept of dominance, only to the anticompetitive effects of a concentration resulting from the non-coordinated behaviour of undertakings which would not have a dominant position on the market concerned' (Recital 25).

In the last analysis, as the Commission pointed out, 'a significant impediment to effective competition generally results from the creation or strengthening of a dominant position. With a view to preserving the guidance that may be drawn from past judgments of the European courts and Commission decisions pursuant to Regulation (EEC) 4064/89, while at the same time maintaining consistency with the standards of competitive harm which have been applied by the Commission and the Community courts regarding the compatibility of a concentration with the common market, the Regulation should accordingly establish the principle that a concentration with a Community dimension which would significantly impede effective competition, in the common market or in a substantial part thereof, in particular as a result of the creation or strengthening of a dominant position, is to be declared incompatible with the common market' (Recital 26).

It is on the basis of that objective that Regulation 139/04 determines when a concentration is or is not compatible with the common market. In particular:

- Concentrations which 'would not significantly impede effective competition in the common market or in a substantial part, in particular as a result of the creation of a dominant position' are, by virtue of Article 2(2), compatible with the common market. Without prejudice to Articles 81 and 82 of the Treaty, concentrations are presumed to be compatible with the common market 'where the market share of the undertakings concerned does not exceed 25% either in the common market or in a substantial part of it' (Recital 32).
- By virtue of Article 2(3), concentrations 'which would significantly impede effective competition, in the common market or in a substantial part of it, in particular as a result of the creation or strengthening of a dominant position', are deemed incompatible with the common market.

43.3.2. The Creation of a Joint Venture that is an Autonomous Economic Entity

Full function joint ventures have to be assessed differently. The creation of a joint venture which performs on a lasting basis the functions of an autonomous economic entity is a concentration within the meaning of

Regulation 139/04 (Article 3(4)). It must therefore be notified to the Commission if it exceeds the thresholds set out in Article 1. However, the creation of the joint venture can also have repercussions on competition if the parent companies of the joint venture are active on the same market as the joint venture. To that end, Regulation 139/04 provides that such an operation must be assessed in accordance with Article 81 EC. In particular, 'to the extent that their creation has as its consequence an appreciable restriction of competition between undertakings that remain independent' (Recital 27). Article 2(4) provides that 'such coordination shall be appraised in accordance with the criteria of Articles 81(1) and 81(3) of the Treaty, with a view to establishing whether or not the operation is compatible with the common market'.

In such a case, Article 2(5) of Regulation 139/04 requires the Commission to take into account:

- whether 'two or more parent companies retain, to a significant extent, activities in the same market as the joint venture or in a market which is downstream or upstream from that of the joint venture or in a neighbouring market closely related to this market';
- whether 'the coordination which is the direct consequence of the creation of the joint venture affords the undertakings concerned the possibility of eliminating competition in respect of a substantial part of the products or services in question'.

44. Allocation of European Merger Control Powers as between the Community and the Member States

As in the case of antitrust law, the allocation of Community powers has certain 'vertical' characteristics.

The special feature of the Community merger control system is that concentrations having a Community dimension fall exclusively within Regulation 139/04, Article 21(3) of which provides that 'no Member State shall apply its national legislation on competition to any concentration that has a Community dimension'.

The exclusive application of the Regulation serves to provide for a single set of control proceedings (see *supra*). This, in its turn, accelerates the process of prior notification for concentrations falling within the scope of the Regulation. For the firms involved this should give a clearer view of their obligations.

There are, however, two exceptions to the general principle that national law may not be applied to concentrations that have a Community dimension.

44.1. THE EXERCISE OF THE POWERS OF INVESTIGATION PROVIDED FOR BY NATIONAL LAW

Although the Member States may not exercise their own powers to appraise concentrations that have a Community dimension, they may nevertheless, in certain cases, exercise their powers of investigation. Article 21(3), second sub-paragraph, provides that where the Commission is appraising a concentration, the Member States may 'carry out any enquiries necessary' or, 'after referral, pursuant to Article 9(3), first subparagraph, indent b), or Article 9(5), to take the measures strictly necessary for the application of Article 9(8)'.

44.2. THE PROTECTION OF LEGITIMATE INTERESTS OTHER THAN THOSE PROTECTED BY REGULATION 139/04

The exclusive application of the Merger Regulation does not prohibit the application of national rules which protect legitimate interests other than those relevant under the Merger Regulation. This right is already granted by Article 296 EC which provides that 'the provisions of this Treaty shall not preclude the application of the following rules: no Member State shall be obliged to supply information the disclosure of which it considers contrary to the essential interests of its security'.[1] By virtue of Article 21(4) of the Merger Regulation, national measures must nevertheless be 'compatible with the general principles and other provisions of Community law'.

Article 21(4), second sub-paragraph, of the Merger Regulation itself mentions public security, plurality of the media and prudential rule as interests which may be considered 'legitimate'. However, the list is not exhaustive and the Merger Regulation does not rule out the possibility that other legitimate interests may exist. In order to identify what interests are legitimate, Article 21(4), third sub-paragraph, of the Regulation has introduced a procedure enabling the Commission to assess whether a given public interest is compatible with the 'general principles and other provisions of Community law'. That provision stipulates that 'any other public interest' (that is, any interest not listed in the second sub-paragraph) 'must be communicated to the Commission by the Member State concerned and shall be recognised by the Commission after an assessment of its compatibility'. This procedure must be carried out before the measures referred to in the first sub-paragraph of Article 21(4) may be taken. The Commission is required to 'inform the Member State concerned of its decision within 25 working days of that communication'.

---

[1] As regards decisions pursuant to Article 21, see M.1346 – *EDF/London Electricity*, Decision of 27 January 1999 (decision taken pursuant to Regulation 4064/89; M.1724 – *BSCH/Champalimaud*, Decision of 30 June 1999. As regards judgments of the Court of Justice interpreting Article 21(3) reg. 4064/89 see, *Portuguese Republic v. Commission*, Case C-42/01, E.C.R.2004. p. I–6079.

PART XI

THE MERGER CONTROL SYSTEM ESTABLISHED BY REGULATION 139/04

45. The Commission: Powers, Proceedings Assessing the Merger and Penalties

The system of merger control established by Regulation 139/04 requires undertakings to notify concentrations having a Community dimension to the Commission. The notification triggers off proceedings characterised by deadlines within which the Commission must assess the effects of the operation on the market. The purpose of binding deadlines is to allow the undertakings involved to be able to predict accurately how long the proceedings will last.

The proceedings fall into two stages:

- The first and obligatory stage is the so-called Phase I. During Phase I, the Commission assesses whether the concentration may represent a threat to competition. If such a risk is present, it may initiate the second phase.
- There may be a second stage, known as Phase II. During Phase II, the Commission assesses more thoroughly the threats to competition which a concentration represents. Phase II may culminate in a Commission decision prohibiting the concentration.

45.1. POWERS

Within the system of merger control established by the Merger Regulation, it is the Commission that has sole power to take the decisions provided for in the Regulation. As Recital 8 of the preamble to the Regulation points out, according to the one-stop shop system, the Commission is the only body that can take decisions concerning concentrations with a Community dimension (exceptions to this rule will be examined *infra*). Article 21(2) provides that the Commission's exclusive power is subject to review by the Court of Justice.

45.1.1. Decisions

Regulation 139/04 establishes the decisions that the Commission is empowered to take and Article 20 determines how they are to be published. Those decisions are as follows:

- finding that the concentration does not fall within the scope of the Regulation;
- declaration, before or after the initiation of Phase II, that a concentration is compatible with the common market;
- declaration that a concentration is incompatible with the common market;
- revocation of a decision which it has previously taken declaring a concentration compatible with the common market;
- dissolution of the concentration and restoration of the situation prevailing before the concentration;
- firms' undertakings; and
- interim measures.

Decisions finding that that a concentration does not fall within the scope of the Regulation (Article 6(1)(a))[1]

This type of decision is taken by the Commission after the concentration has been notified. Article 6(1) provides that: 'the Commission shall examine the notification as soon as it is received and where it concludes that the concentration does not fall within the scope of this Regulation, it shall record that finding by means of a decision'.

Decisions declaring that a concentration is compatible with the common market before or after the initiation of Phase II (Article 6(1)(b)[2]

The Commission has the power to declare that a concentration is compatible with the common market:

- at the end of Phase I; or
- at the end of Phase II.

---

[1] With reference to decisions taken pursuant to Article 6(1)(a), see M.3003 – *Electrabel/Energia italiana/Interpower*, Decision of 23 December 2002 (decision taken pursuant to Regulation 4064/89).

[2] With reference to decisions taken under Article 6(1)(a), see M.4151 – *Orıca/Dyno*, Decision of 23 May 2006; M.4150 – *Abbott/Guıdant*, Decision of 23 May 2006; M.4141 – *Linde/BOC*, Decision of 6 June 2006; M.4137 – *Mittal/ARCELOR*, Decision of 2 June 2006; M.4066 – *CVC/SLEC*, Decision of 20 March 2006.

As regards decisions taken at the end of Phase I, Article 6(1)(b) provides that where the Commission

> finds that the concentration notified ... does not raise serious doubts as to its compatibility with the common market, it shall decide not to oppose it and shall declare it compatible with the common market. A decision declaring a concentration compatible shall be deemed to cover restrictions directly related and necessary to the implementation of the concentration.

As regards decision taken during Phase II, the Commission may be confronted with two different tests:

1. The Commission examines whether 'a notified concentration fulfils the criterion laid down in Article 2(2)'. It provides that 'a concentration which would not significantly impede effective competition in the common market or a substantial part of it, in particular as a result of the creation or strengthening of a dominant position, shall be declared incompatible with the common market';
2. Where the concentration notified takes the form of a joint venture, the Commission must also examine whether the concentration fulfils 'the criteria laid down in Article 81(3) of the Treaty'.

By virtue of both Articles 6(1)(b) and 8(1)[3] of the Merger Regulation, a decision declaring a concentration compatible, irrespective of whether it is taken during Phase I or Phase II, 'shall be deemed to cover restrictions directly related and necessary to the implementation of the concentration'.

Decisions finding that a concentration is incompatible with the common market (Article 8(3))[4]

Such a decision may only be taken at the end of Phase II. Article 8(3) of the

---

[3] With reference to decisions taken pursuant to Article. 8(1), see M.3975 – *Cargill/Degissa Food Ingredients*, Decision of 29 March 2006; M.3625 – *Blackstone/ACETEX*, Decision of 13 July 2005; M.3178 – *Bertelsmann/Springer*, Decision of 3 May 2005.

[4] With reference to decisions taken pursuant to Article 8(3), see M.3440 – *ENI/EDP/GDP*, Decision of 9 December 2004 (under Regulation. 4064/89); M.2416 – *Tetra Laval/SIDEL*, Decision of 30 October 2001(under Regulation 4064/89), decision annulled by the CFI in *Tetra Laval v. Commission*, Case T-5/02, in E.C.R. 2002, p. II–4381, confirmed on appeal by the ECJ in *Commission v. Tetra Laval*, Case C-12/03 P, in *E.C.R. 2005*, p. I–987; M.2283 – *Schneider/Legrand*, Decision 10 October 2001 (pursuant to Regulation), decision annulled by the CFI in *Schneider Electric v. Commission*, Case T-310/01, E.C.R. 2002, p. II–4071; M.2220 – *General Electric/Honeywell*, Decision of 3 July 2001 (pursuant to Regulation 4064/89, decision upheld by the CFI in *Honeywell International v. Commission*, Case T-209/01, not yet reported, and in *General Electric Company v. Commission*, Case T-210/01, not yet published; M.2187 – CVC/Lenzing, Decision of 17 October 2001 (pursuant to Regulation 4064/89).

Merger Regulation provides that the Commission must declare that a concentration is incompatible with the common market when:

- It 'fulfils the criterion laid down in Article 2(3)' (that is, it would significantly impede effective competition in the common market or in a substantial part of it, in particular as a result of the creation or strengthening of a dominant position); or
- In the cases referred to in Article 2(4) (that is, when the concentration is a joint venture) a concentration is incompatible when 'the coordination of the competitive behaviour of undertakings that remain independent' (Article 2(4)) 'does not fulfil the criteria laid down in Article 81(3) of the Treaty' (Article 8(3)).

Decisions revoking a previously taken decision declaring a concentration compatible with the common market (Articles 6(3) and 8(6))

The Commission has the power to revoke decisions that it has previously taken. Revocation may take place:

- in the case of a decision taken during Phase I, by virtue of Article 6(3)(a), 'where the decision is based on incorrect information for which one of the undertakings is responsible or where it has been obtained by deceit';
- in the case of a decision taken during Phase I or Phase II, 'where the undertakings concerned commit a breach of an obligation attached to the decision' (Articles 6(3)(b) and 8(6)); or
- in the case of a decision taken during Phase II, where the declaration of compatibility 'is based on incorrect information for which one of the undertakings is responsible or where it has been obtained by deceit' (Article 8(6)).

Decisions requiring dissolution of a concentration and restorative measures (Article 8(4))[5]

By virtue of Article 8(4) of the Merger Regulation, the Commission has the power to require undertakings to make structural changes. This may be done to restore the competitive situation where a concentration has been implemented:

- despite its having 'been declared incompatible with the common market'; or

---

[5] With reference to decisions pursuant to Article 8(4), see M.2416 – *Tetra Laval/SIDEL*, Decision of 30 January 2002 (pursuant to Regulation 4064/89).

- in contravention of 'a condition attached to a decision taken under paragraph 2, which has found that, in the absence of the condition, the concentration would' be incompatible with the common market by virtue of Article 2(3) or 2(4).

In order to re-establish the status quo, the Commission may exercise one of two distinct powers:

- it may 'require the undertakings concerned to dissolve the concentration, in particular through the dissolution of the merger or the disposal of all the shares or assets acquired, so as to restore the situation prevailing before the implementation of the concentration; in circumstances where restoration of the situation prevailing before the implementation of the concentration is not possible through dissolution of the concentration, the Commission may take any other measure appropriate to achieve such restoration as far as possible'; or
- it may 'order any other appropriate measure to ensure that the undertakings concerned dissolve the concentration or take other restorative measures as required in its decision' (Article 8(4)).

Decisions incorporating undertakings (Articles 6(2)[6] and 8(2)[7])

Like Regulation 1/03, Regulation 139/04 allows undertakings to make commitments in order to meet any competition concerns that the Commission may have. Undertakings may be presented before or after the initiation of Phase II.

Undertakings accepted during Phase I are not incorporated in an independent decision. They are part of the decision declaring the concentration compatible with the common market. Article 6(2) provides that 'the Commission may attach to its decision ... conditions and obligations intended to ensure that the undertakings concerned comply with the commitments they have entered into *vis-à-vis* the Commission with a view to rendering the concentration compatible with the common market'. According to Recital 30, commitments made during Phase I should be accepted only

[6] With reference to decisions pursuant to Article 6(2) subject to conditions, see M.3420 – *GIMD/Socpresse*, Decision of 16 June 2004 (pursuant to Regulation 4064/89).

[7] With reference to decisions pursuant to Article 8(2), see M.3333 – *SONY/BMG*, Decision of 19 July 2004 (pursuant to Regulation 4064/89), annulled by judgment of the Court of First Instance in Case T-464/04, *Impala v. Commission*, not yet reported.

With reference to decisions under Article 8(2) subject to conditions, see M.4000 – *INCO/Falconbridge*, Decision of 4 July 2006; M.3916 – *T-Mobile Austria/Tele.Ring*, Decision of 26 April 2006; M.3868 – *Dong/Elasm/Energie E2*, Decision of 14 March 2006, M.3796 – *Omya/J.M. Huber Pcc*, Decision of 19 July 2006; M.3696 – *E.ON/MOL*, Decision of 21 December 2005.

'where the competition problem is readily identifiable and can easily be remedied'.

Undertakings made in Phase II are recorded as an autonomous decision taken pursuant to Article 8(2) of the Merger Regulation, which provides that 'where the Commission finds that, following modification by the undertakings concerned, a notified concentration fulfils the criterion laid down in Article 2(2) and, in the cases referred to in Article 2(4), the criteria laid down in Article 81(3) of the Treaty, it shall issue a decision declaring the concentration compatible with the common market'. Article 8(2) of the Merger Regulation goes on to provide that 'the Commission may attach to its decision conditions and obligations intended to ensure that the undertakings comply with the commitments they have entered into *vis-à-vis* the Commission with a view to rendering the concentration compatible with the common market'.

Interim measures (Article 8(5))

Article 8(5) allows the Commission to take interim measures to restore or maintain competition where there has been a contravention of Regulation 139/04. It may do this in three types of case, namely:

- the concentration has been implemented in contravention of Article 7 (the standstill obligation) and no decision as to its compatibility has yet been taken;
- the concentration has been implemented in contravention of a condition attached to a decision in Phase I or Phase II; or
- the concentration 'has already been implemented and is declared incompatible with the common market'.

45.1.2. The Proceedings Assessing the Concentration

Regulation 139/04 sets out in considerable detail the proceedings for the review of concentrations. The procedure contains the following steps:

- notification of the concentration;
- Phase I (initial appraisal); and
- Phase II (thorough appraisal of the concentration).

The Commission has issued several notices and prepared documentation to help the undertakings involved in the merger appraisal. In addition, it has adopted a regulation implementing Regulation 139/04 (Commission Regulation 802/04).[8]

Notification of concentration

Merger notification is effected by filling in and lodging the required number of copies of the appropriate Commission standard form (CO or RM)[9] and any annexes which the relevant form may require. The purpose served by notification is to require all concentrations with a Community dimension to be submitted to the Commission, thereby ensuring 'effective control' (Recital 34).

In principle, a concentration should be notified to the Commission 'following the conclusion of the agreement, the announcement of the public bid or the acquisition of a controlling interest'. In any event, pursuant to the first sub-paragraph of Article 4(1), concentrations must be notified 'prior to their implementation'. By virtue of the second sub-paragraph of Article 4(1), notification is also allowed 'where the undertakings concerned demonstrate to the Commission a good faith intention to conclude an agreement or, in the case of a public bid, where they have publicly announced an intention to make such a bid, provided that the intended agreement or bid would result in a concentration with a Community dimension'.

Furthermore, Article 4(2) identifies the undertakings which are required to effect the notification. This is particularly important since it is relevant to determining the persons who are liable to penalties if they do not comply with their obligation (see *infra*).

Once a concentration has been notified it may not be implemented forthwith (this is known as the standstill obligation). This obligation is imposed in order to avoid the Commission being confronted with the difficult task of having to restore the competition *status quo ante* should it transpire that the concentration is in fact incompatible with the common market (*supra*). Except in cases covered by Article 7(2), a concentration with a Community dimension as defined in Article 1 or which is to be examined by the Commission under the pre-notification procedure under Article 4(5) may not be implemented:

1. Before it has been notified;
2. Until it has been declared compatible with the common market by:

---

[8] Commission Regulation 802/04 of 7 April 2004 implementing Council Regulation 139/04 on the control of concentrations between undertakings, OJ L 133 of 30 April 2004, p. 1.

[9] Short Form CO is used for concentrations which are presumed not to raise competition problems. The Commission issued a Notice dealing specifically with this type of concentration; see Notice on a simplified procedure for treatment of certain concentrations under Council Regulation (EC) 139/2004, 2006 OJ C 56/32.

- a decision pursuant to Article 6(1)(b) finding that the concentration does not raise serious doubts as to its compatibility;
- a decision pursuant to Article 8(1) or 8(2) finding that the concentration is compatible with the common market, if necessary following modification; and
- the Commission not having taken a decision within the time limits set by Article 10(6), in which case the concentration is deemed to have been declared compatible with the common market (Article 7(1)).

However, by virtue of Article 7(3), the Commission may, on a reasoned request by the undertakings concerned, grant a dispensation from the obligation to suspend implementation of the concentration.

Regulation 139/04 also establishes the consequences of failure to comply with the standstill obligation on the legal validity of the transaction. In principle, 'in the interest of legal certainty, the validity of transactions must ... be protected as much as necessary' (Recital 34). However, Article 7(4) of the Regulation provides that the validity of any transaction carried out in contravention of the obligation to suspend implementation is dependent on a decision on the specific concentration. The decisions referred to are:

- a decision pursuant to Article 6(1)(b) finding that the concentration does not raise any problems of competition;
- a decision taken after an investigation (Articles 8(1) to 8(3)); and
- a failure by the Commission to take a decision within the appropriate time limits whereby the Commission is deemed to have given its agreement to a notified concentration (Article 10(6)).

However, Article 7(4) goes on to provide that a failure to comply with Article 7(1) is not to have an effect on the validity of transactions in securities unless the buyer and seller were or should have been aware of the failure to comply with Article 7(1).

The Commission is subject to certain procedural obligations once notification has been effected. Article 4(3) requires it to 'publish the fact of the notification, at the same time indicating the names of the undertakings concerned, their country of origin, the nature of the concentration and the economic sectors involved'. When carrying out this obligation, it is required to 'take account of the legitimate interest of undertakings in the protection of their business secrets'.

Phase I

Once the concentration has been notified, the first stage of the appraisal of the concentration begins. Article 6(1) requires the Commission to 'examine the notification as soon as it is received'. Once it has carried out this examination it may take one of three types of decision relating to the concentration:

1. A decision pursuant to Article 6(1)(a) where the Commission 'concludes that the concentration notified does not fall within the scope of the Regulation'.
2. A decision pursuant to Article 6(1)(b) that the concentration is compatible with the common market. Such a decision must be taken where the Commission 'finds that the concentration notified, although falling within the scope of this regulation, does not raise serious doubts as to its compatibility with the common market'. In such a case, the Commission must 'decide not to oppose it and shall declare that it is compatible with the common market'. This type of decision also covers 'restrictions directly related and necessary to the implementation of the concentration'. Article 6(2) provides that a decision under Article 6(1)(b) may also be taken 'where the Commission finds that, following modification by the undertakings concerned, a notified concentration no longer raises serious doubts'. This is so even where, had the modifications not been made, the Commission would have had to initiate Phase II. In order to 'ensure that the undertakings concerned comply with the commitments they have entered into *vis-à-vis* the Commission with a view to rendering the concentration compatible with the common market', 'the Commission may attach to its decision under Article 6(1)(b) conditions and obligations'.
3. Where the Commission 'finds that the concentration notified falls within the scope of the regulation and raises serious doubts as to its compatibility with the common market, it shall decide to initiate proceedings'. By virtue of Article 6(5), should it decide to initiate proceedings, the Commission must notify 'the undertakings concerned and the competent authorities without delay'.

In any event, with the exception of referral proceedings falling under Article 9, any proceedings initiated by virtue of Article 6(2) must be concluded by a decision taken pursuant to Article 8, paragraphs 1 to 4.

Phase I time limits As regards time limits applicable within Phase I, Article 10(1) of the Merger Regulation provides that the three decisions referred to in Article 6(1) must be taken within 25 days. Time starts to run 'on the working day following that of the receipt of a notification or, if the information to be supplied with the notification is incomplete, on the working day following that of the receipt of the complete information'.

By virtue of the second sub-paragraph of Article 10(1), that period is 35 days in two cases:

1. where the Commission receives a request from a Member State in accordance with Article 9(2) (*infra*); and
2. where the undertakings concerned offer commitments pursuant to Article 6(2) with a view to rendering the concentration compatible with the common market.

The time limits do not need to be complied with where the Commission, acting pursuant to Article 6(3), revokes a decision taken under Article 6(1)(a) or (b). In that case, Article 6(4) provides that 'the Commission may take a decision under paragraph 1, without being bound by the time limits referred to in Article 10(1)'.

In any event, Article 10(4) provides that the time limit of 25 or 35 days set by Article 10(1) shall exceptionally be suspended where, owing to circumstances for which one of the undertakings involved in the decision is responsible, the Commission has had to request information pursuant to Article 11 or to order an inspection pursuant to Article 13.

Article 10(6) stipulates that 'where the Commission has not taken a decision in accordance with Article 6(1)(b), (c), ... within the time limits set in paragraphs 1 and 3 respectively, the concentration shall be deemed to have been declared compatible with the common market'. This rule is without prejudice to Article 9, which applies in the case of a referral.

Phase II

If the Commission considers that 'the concentration notified falls within the scope of this Regulation and raises serious doubts as to its compatibility with the common market, it shall decide to initiate proceedings' (Article 6(1)(c)) [10]. During those proceedings, the Commission may examine thoroughly whether a concentration is compatible with the common market.

At the end of the proceedings, the Commission may issue three types of decision:

1. *Decisions pursuant to Article 8(1) declaring a concentration compatible with the common market.* The Commission may issue this type of decision in two situations:

   - where the concentration fulfils the criterion laid down in Article 2(2) (that is, it is compatible with the common market); and

[10] With reference to decisions under Article 6(1), see M.4180 – *Gaz de France/Suez*, Deicision of 19 June 2006; M.4094 – *INEOS/BP Dormagen*, Decision 28 February 2006; M.4009 – *CIMC/BURG*, Decision of 13 March 2006; M.4000 – *INCO/Falconbridge*, Decision of 24 February 2006; M.3923 – *AMI/Eurotecnica*, Decision of 18 October 2005.

- if the concentration is a joint venture falling under Article 2(4), where it fulfils the criteria laid down in Article 81(3) of the Treaty.

A decision which declares 'a concentration compatible shall be deemed to cover restrictions directly and necessary to the implementation of the concentration' (Article 8(1) second paragraph). This is the same rule which applies in the case of a decision pursuant to Article 6(1)(b).

2. *Decisions pursuant to Article 8(2) declaring a concentration compatible with the common market following modification.* This type of decision, like a decision taken under Article 8(1), declares that the concentration is compatible with the common market since it 'fulfils the criterion laid down in Article 2(2) and, in the cases referred to in Article 2(4), the criteria laid down in Article 81(3) of the Treaty' (Article 8(2)).
   Unlike decisions taken pursuant to Article 8(1), a decision under Article 8(2) is taken following the modification of the notified concentration by the undertakings concerned. As in the case of a decision under Article 6(1)(b), the Commission may in this case too attach to its decision conditions and obligations intended to ensure that the undertakings concerned comply with the commitments they have entered into vis-à-vis the Commission with a view to rendering the concentration compatible with the common market (Article 8(2), second sub-paragraph).
   Similarly, as in the case of Articles 6(1)(b) and 8(1), second sub-paragraph, 'a decision declaring a concentration compatible shall be deemed to cover restrictions directly related and necessary to the implementation of the concentration' (Article 8(2), third sub-paragraph).
3. *Decisions pursuant to Article 8(3) declaring a concentration incompatible with the common market.* Article 8(3) provides that where the concentration 'fulfils the criterion defined in Article 2(3) (that is, concentration that significantly impedes competition) or, in the cases referred to in Article 2(4) (that is, joint ventures with coordination between the parent companies), does not fulfil the criteria laid down in Article 81(3) of the Treaty, it shall issue a decision declaring that the concentration is incompatible with the common market'.

Phase II time limits As regards time limits under Phase II, the Regulation also establishes binding time limits applicable to decisions taken under Article 8.

Article 10(2) establishes the general principle that decisions pursuant to Article 8(1) or (2) declaring a concentration compatible with the common market must be taken as soon as it appears that the serious doubts as to compatibility have been removed. This rule is not applicable to decisions taken under Article 8(3). Article 8(8) requires the Commission to 'notify its decision to the undertakings concerned and the competent authorities of the Member States without delay' (this same rule is provided for by Article 6(5)).

In any event, Article 10(3) provides that decisions pursuant to Article 8(1) to (3) 'concerning notified concentrations' must be taken within 'not more than 90 working days of the date on which the proceedings are initiated'.

The period of 90 days becomes '105 working days where the undertakings concerned offer commitments ... with a view to rendering the concentration compatible with the common market'. However, there is no extension if the commitments 'have been offered less than 55 working days after the initiation of proceedings'. In that case, it is presumed that the Commission has had sufficient time to assess the impact of the commitments on the concentration notified.

Furthermore, Article 10(3), second sub-paragraph, goes on to provide that the periods set by the first sub-paragraph of that provision 'shall likewise be extended if the notifying parties make a request to that effect not later than 15 working days after the initiation' of Phase II. The notifying parties may only make one such request. Likewise, 'at any time following the initiation of proceedings, the periods set by the first sub-paragraph may be extended by the Commission with the agreement of the notifying parties' (Article 10(3), second part).

However, the total duration of any time extension or extensions effected pursuant to Article 10(3), second paragraph, may not exceed twenty days.

Article 8(7) provides in two cases for an exception allowing the Commission to take a Phase II decision without being bound by the time limits described above:

- where 'it finds that a concentration has been implemented':
    - in contravention of a condition imposed in a decision taken at the end of Phase I; or
    - in contravention of a condition imposed in a decision taken during Phase II finding that, in the absence of the condition, the concentration would raise serious doubts as to its compatibility with the common market;
- where a decision has been revoked pursuant to Article 8(6).

Article 10(4) grants the Commission an exceptional power to suspend the period of 90 or 105 days where, 'owing to circumstances for which one of the undertakings involved in the concentration is responsible, the Commission has had to request information by decision ... or to order an inspection by decision'.

As in the case of decisions adopted in accordance with Article 6(1)(b), Article 10(6) stipulates that where the Commission has not taken a decision under Article 8(1), (2) or (3) (that is, a Phase II decision) within the time limits set out above, 'the concentration shall be deemed to have been declared compatible with the common market', without prejudice to cases of referral to a national authority.

The effects of a decision annulling a Commission decision
Article 10 also establishes the consequences of the annulment of a decision taken by the Commission pursuant to the Regulation:

- with regard to the examination of the concentration concerned; and
- with regard to the obligations of the notifying parties.

Article 10(5) provides that if the Court annuls 'the whole or part of a Commission decision which is subject to a time limit set by this article, the concentration shall be re-examined by the Commission with a view to adopting' a Phase I decision. The concentration 'shall be re-examined in the light of current market conditions'.

If, in the meantime, the original notification has become incomplete (for example, because of intervening changes in market conditions or with respect to the information provided), Article 10(5) provides that 'the notifying parties shall submit a new notification or supplement the original notification without delay'. The same paragraph goes on to provide that 'where there are no such changes, the parties shall certify this fact without delay'.

The second and third sub-paragraphs of Article 10(5) also apply in the cases referred to in Articles 6(4) and 8(7).

Lastly, Article 10(5) goes on to provide that the periods within which the Commission must take a decision in Phase I shall start on the working day following that of the receipt of complete information sent in:

- a new notification;
- a supplemented notification; or
- a certification within the meaning of Article 10(3).

45.1.3. Procedural Aspects of the Application

Like Regulation 1/03, Regulation 139/04 provides for specific rules ensuring the rights of defence of the parties to the proceedings.

Article 18(1) establishes, subject to the specific exception envisaged by Article 18(2), a specific right to be heard before any of the following decisions are adopted:

- decision taken pursuant to Article 6(3) (that is, a decision revoking an earlier decision that the concentration does not fall within the scope of the Regulation or that it does not raise serious doubts as to its compatibility);
- a decision pursuant to Article 7(3) (that is, decision granting a derogation from the standstill obligation);
- a decision provided for in Article 8(2) to (6) (i.e. decision taken during Phase II); or
- decisions under Articles 14[11] and 15 (that is, decision related to fines and to periodic penalty payments).

Article 18(1) provides in particular that the 'Commission shall give the persons, undertakings and associations of undertakings concerned the opportunity, at every stage of the procedure up to the consultation of the Advisory Committee, of making known their views on the objections against them'.

With reference to the parties to the proceedings, Article 18(3) goes on to provide that 'the Commission shall base its decision only on objections on which the parties have been able to submit their observations'.

A further aspect of the rights of the defence, which is referred to in Recital 42, is the right of access to the file. Article 18(3) provides that this must be granted 'subject to the legitimate interest of undertakings in the protection of their business secrets'. This does not prevent the Commission or the competent national authorities from hearing other natural or legal persons where they deem this necessary. Furthermore, 'natural or legal persons showing sufficient interest … shall be entitled, upon application, to be heard'.

45.2. POWERS OF INVESTIGATION

The Merger Regulation entitles the Commission to request all necessary information and to conduct all necessary inspections throughout the Community so that it may properly appraise concentrations (see Recital 38). The Regulation in particular makes provision for:

- requests for information (Article 11);
- inspections carried out by the authorities of the Member States (Article 12); and
- the Commission's powers of inspection (Article 13).

---

[11] With reference to decisions pursuant to Article 14(1), see M.3255 – *Tetra Laval/SIDEL*, Decision of 7 July 2004 (under Regulation 4064/89).

With certain exceptions (for example, Article 11(5) and (7)), the content of the powers of investigation which the Merger Regulation confers on the Commission, and the way in which they are to be exercised, are *mutatis mutandis* the same as those conferred by Regulation 1/03.

In particular, Article 11 of the Merger Regulation (requests for information) corresponds to Articles 18(1) to (6) and 19 of Regulation 1/03.

Article 12 of the Merger Regulation (inspections by the authorities of the Member States) corresponds to Article 22(2) of Regulation 1/03.

Article 13 of the Merger Regulation (the Commission's powers of inspection) corresponds to Article 20 of Regulation 1/03.

Reference is therefore made to the appropriate parts of this book for further detail on these aspects (*supra*).

45.3. PROFESSIONAL SECRECY

Like Regulation 1/03, the Merger Regulation sets out rules relating to the purposes for which information acquired pursuant to the Regulation may be used and to professional secrecy:

1. Article 17(1) provides that 'information acquired as a result of the application of this Regulation shall be used only for the purposes of the relevant request, investigation or hearing';
2. Article 17(2) provides that without prejudice to Article 4(3), Articles 18 and 20, the Commission and the competent authorities of the Member States, their officials ... shall not disclose information they have acquired through the application of the Regulation of the kind covered by the obligation of professional secrecy.
3. Article 17(3) provides that the rules on professional secrecy described above do not 'prevent publication of general information or of surveys which do not contain information relating to particular undertakings or associations of undertakings'.

45.4. PENALTIES

In order to enforce compliance with the Merger Regulation, the Commission is given power to impose fines and periodic penalty payments (Recital 43). Pursuant to Article 229 EC, the Court of Justice is given unlimited jurisdiction to review such penalties, as is also the case under Regulation 1/03. The Court may therefore cancel, reduce or increase a fine or periodic penalty payment (Article 16).

45.4.1. Fines

Depending on the seriousness of the infringement committed, the Commission may impose one of two types of fine.

First, By virtue of Article 14(1) of the Merger Regulation, the Commission may by decision impose on the relevant undertakings or associations of undertakings fines not exceeding 1% of the aggregate turnover of the relevant body. This power may be exercised only where the infringement was committed 'intentionally or negligently'. With the exception of the infringement relating to the breaking of seals affixed during an inspection (Article 13(1) (f)), the infringements listed in Article 14(1) relate to the supply of incorrect, incomplete or misleading information:

- in a notification (Articles 4 and 22);
- in reply to a request for information (Article 11); or
- during an inspection (Article 13).

Second, by virtue of Article 14(2) of the Merger Regulation, the Commission may by decision impose fines not exceeding 10% of annual turnover when the relevant infringement is committed intentionally or negligently. This second category of fine can be imposed in the case of:

- failure to notify a concentration (Articles 4 and 22);
- implementation of a concentration in breach of the standstill obligation (Article 7);
- implementation of a concentration declared incompatible with the common market pursuant to Article 8; or
- failure to comply with a condition or obligation imposed by Articles 6, 7 or 8.

In the case of both types of fines, account must be taken of 'the nature, gravity and duration of the infringement' when the amount of the fine is fixed (Article 14(3)). Decisions imposing fines 'shall not be of a criminal law nature' (Article 14(4)).

45.4.2. Periodic Penalty Payments

In order to ensure the enforcement of decisions taken by the Commission, Article 15(1) empowers the Commission, by decision, to impose periodic penalty payments on the undertakings or associations concerned. The penalty payment may not exceed 5% of the average daily aggregate turnover of the undertaking or association of undertakings concerned for each working day of delay, calculated from the date set in the decision. This type of penalty may be imposed in order to compel the addressees to:

- supply information requested by a decision taken pursuant to Article 11;
- submit to an inspection which the Commission has ordered by a decision pursuant to Article 13;
- comply with an obligation imposed by a decision taken pursuant to Articles 6, 7 or 8;
- comply with any measures taken by a decision pursuant to Article 8(4) or (5) (that is, where a concentration has been implemented despite being incompatible with the common market or in breach of a condition).

If the addressees have complied with the obligation which the penalty payment was intended to enforce, Article 15(2) allows the Commission to 'fix the definitive amount of the periodic penalty payment at a figure lower than that which would arise under the original decision'.

46. National Antitrust Authorities: Powers

The role of the national authorities under Regulation 139/04 is very limited in comparison with the role conferred on them by Regulation 1/03. This is a consequence of the exclusive competence enjoyed by the Commission over concentrations having a Community dimension (or which have been referred to it pursuant to the Regulation). It follows that there is no possibility of parallel national and Community proceedings.

Despite this, the Merger Regulation refers to the Commission and the national authorities as a network of authorities (Recitals 12 and 42 of the preamble).

The participation of the national authorities in the system of Community merger control is therefore limited to:

- the assessment carried out by the Advisory Committee pursuant to Article 19[1] (*infra*). This is linked to European antitrust federalism discussed above (*supra*); and
- exercising the investigative powers conferred by the Merger Regulation.

In particular, by virtue of Article 12, at the request of the Commission national authorities must carry out inspections:

- which the latter considers necessary (Article 13(1)); or
- which it has ordered (Article 13(4)).

In substance, this corresponds to the powers conferred by Article 22(2) of Regulation 1/03. However, one important difference is that, under Regulation 139/04, a national authority may carry out this type of activity only on behalf of the Commission, and not on behalf of the authorities of other Member States.

[1] With reference to decisions pursuant to Article 19, see, M.3083 – *GE/Instrumentarium*, Decision of 4 July 2003 (under Regulation 4064/89).

47. Mechanisms Allowing Cooperation between the Commission and National Antitrust Authorities

Turnover thresholds determine whether a concentration will be assessed by the Commission or a national authority. Furthermore, Regulation 139/04 does not allow the parallel application of Community and national law to the same concentration (*supra*). In some cases, this black and white system of allocating power system may not be capable of identifying which body is best placed to appraise a specific concentration.

In order to overcome these potential problems, Regulation 139/04, building upon a process which began while Regulation 4064/89 was in force, establishes certain cooperation procedures applying as between the Commission and the national authorities. It addresses the relations between:

- using turnover to identify when the Commission is competent;
- the need for a concentration with a Community dimension but having effects restricted to one Member State to be appraised by the authorities of that state; and
- the need for concentrations notified to a number of Member States to be appraised by the Commission.

Recital 11 of the preamble to the Merger Regulation makes the point that 'the rules governing the referral of concentrations from the Commission to Member States and from Member States to the Commission should operate as an effective corrective mechanism in the light of the principle of subsidiarity'. In particular, these rules protect the competition interests of the Member States in an adequate manner and take due account of legal certainty and the 'one-stop shop' principle.

The Regulation provides for two types of referral proceeding (from the Commission to the national authorities or vice versa); namely referral proceedings:

- before the notification has been made (Article 4); and
- after the notification has been made (Articles 9 and 22).

The Commission has issued a notice[1] in order to explain the cases and the ways in which referrals are made.

47.1. REFERRAL BEFORE NOTIFICATION

Regulation 139/04 introduces for the first time the possibility of referring a concentration to either the Commission or the Member States before it has been notified. This has been done, as Recital 16 of the preamble expresses it, 'so as to further improve the efficiency of the system for the control of concentrations within the Community'.

In order to avoid the referral upsetting the operation of national and Community time limits, 'the Commission and national competition authorities should decide within short, clearly defined time limits whether a referral to or from the Commission ought to be made, thereby ensuring the efficiency of the system' (Recital 16).

Regulation 802/04 stipulates that an application for a referral before notification (either to a Member State or the Commission) must be made using a special form (RS). This allows the Commission to receive sufficient information to begin its assessment of the application for referral.

47.1.1. Referral to a Member State (Article 4(4))

Article 4(4) establishes a procedure to determine whether a concentration which has a Community dimension, but which 'may significantly affect competition in a market within a Member State', may be notified to the national authority on whose territory the concentration may have a significant effect.

Article 4(4) allows the undertakings required to notify the concentration to inform the Commission, prior to making the notification, 'by means of a reasoned submission, that the concentration may significantly affect competition in a market within a Member State which presents all the characteristics of a distinct market and should therefore be examined, in whole or in part, by that Member State'.

The Commission must then transmit this request to all the Member States without delay.

The Member State referred to in the reasoned submission must give its view within 15 working days of receiving the submission. If it has not made

[1] Commission Notice on Case Referral in respect of concentrations, 2005 OJ C 56, 5 March 2005, p. 2.

its views known within that period, it is deemed to have agreed to have the case referred to it.

The Commission must assess whether 'such a distinct market exists and whether competition in that market may be significantly affected by the concentration'. If that is the case, the Commission may, unless the Member State disagrees, 'decide to refer the whole or part of the case ... with a view to the application of that state's national competition law'.

The decision as to whether or not to refer the case must be taken within 25 working days from the day on which the Commission receives the reasoned submission. If the Commission does not take a decision within that period, it is deemed to have decided to refer the case in accordance with the submission made by the persons or undertakings concerned. In any event, the Commission is required to inform the other Member States and the persons or undertakings concerned of what it has decided. Should the Commission decide to refer the concentration to a Member State, the undertakings concerned may not make a notification to the Commission and national competition law applies to it (Article 4(4)).

47.1.2. Referral to the Commission (Article 4(5))

Article 4(5) allows concentrations not having a Community dimension and required to be notified to at least three national authorities to be referred to the Commission. This possibility is granted for two separate reasons:

1. because such a concentration clearly has Community relevance since it is capable of being reviewed under the merger control laws of at least three Member States; and
2. in order to avoid conflicting decisions by different national authorities deciding on the same concentration.

If there is a concentration 'which is capable of being reviewed under the national competition laws of at least three Member States', the persons required to make the notifications 'may, before any notification to the competent authorities, inform the Commission by means of a reasoned submission that the concentration should be examined by the Commission' (Article 4(5)). The Commission must transmit this submission to all Member States without delay. Any Member State which is competent to examine the concentration may, within 15 working days of receiving the written submission, express its disagreement with referring the case. If no Member State expresses its disagreement within 15 working days, 'the concentration shall be deemed to have a Community dimension and shall be notified to the Commission' as provided for by Regulation 139/04. In such situations, no

Member State may apply its own competition law to the concentration. On the other hand, if a Member State expresses its opposition to a referral, the case may not be referred and the Commission must inform all Member States and persons concerned without delay (Article 4(5)).

47.2. REFERRAL AFTER NOTIFICATION

Like Regulation 4064/89, Regulation 139/04 provides for the possibility of referring a concentration from the Commission to the Member States and vice versa.

47.2.1. Referral to the Competent Authorities of the Member States (Article 9)

Article 9 allows a national authority to request the referral to it of a concentration which 'threatens to affect significantly competition in a market within that Member State which presents all the characteristics of a distinct market'. In particular, Article 9(1) provides that 'the Commission may ... refer a notified concentration to the competent authorities of the Member State concerned'. This must be done 'by means of a decision notified without delay to the undertakings concerned and the competent authorities of the other Member States'.

Pursuant to the procedure established by Article 9, a Member State may, within 15 working days of the receipt of the notification, inform the Commission of competition problems that the concentration may have on its national market. The Member State may give this information on its own initiative or upon the invitation of the Commission. The concentration must have one of the following features, defined by Article 9(2):

- it must threaten to affect significantly competition in a market within that Member State, which presents all the characteristics of a distinct market; or
- it must 'affect competition in a market within that Member State, which presents all the characteristics of a distinct market and which does not constitute a substantial part of the common market'.

By virtue of Article 9(4), the Commission must decide whether or not to refer within 35 days of receipt of the notification.

Where the Commission has already initiated Phase II, it must take a decision on referral within 65 working days of the notification of the concentration concerned. By virtue of Article 9(5), 'if the Commission despite a reminder from the Member State concerned' has not taken a decision on referral or any preparatory steps under Article 8(2), (3) or (4) within 65 working days, 'it is deemed to have taken a decision to refer the case to the Member State concerned'.

By virtue of Article 9(3),[2] if the Commission considers that there is such a market and that such a threat exists, it may either:

- deal with the case in accordance with this Regulation; or
- refer the whole or part of the case to the competent authorities of the Member States concerned with a view to the application of that state's competition law.

On the contrary, the Commission considers that 'such a distinct market or threat does not exist, it shall adopt a decision to that effect which it shall address to the Member State concerned, and shall itself deal with the case' in accordance with Regulation 139/04 (Article 9(3), second sub-paragraph).

In the different case 'where a Member State informs the Commission pursuant to paragraph 2(b) that a concentration affects competition in a distinct market within its territory that does not form a substantial part of the common market, the Commission shall refer the whole or part of the case referring to the distinct market concerned if it considers that such a distinct market is affected' (Article 9(3), third sub-paragraph).

Where the concentration has been referred to a Member State, Article 9(6) provides that 'the competent authority of the Member State concerned shall decide upon the case without undue delay'. Furthermore, within 45 working days from the referral by the Commission, the competent authority must inform the parties of 'the result of the preliminary competition assessment and what further action, if any, it proposes to take'. The time limit may exceptionally be suspended if the notifying parties have omitted to provide required information. Where a notification is requested by virtue of national law, 'the period of 45 working days shall begin on the working day following that of the receipt of a complete notification by the competent authority of that Member State'. In this way, Regulation 139/04 gains a foothold in national merger control law. For that purpose, Article 9(7) establishes the criteria which the national authority must use to determine the relevant market. In addition, Article 9(8) stipulates that 'in applying the provisions of this Article, the Member State concerned may take only the measures strictly

[2] With reference to decisions pursuant to Article 9(3), see M.3905 – *Tesco/Carrefour*, Decision of 22 December 2005 concerning a partial referral; M.3864 – *FIMAG/Zueblin*, Decision of 14 October 2005 concerning a partial referral; M.3754 – *Strabag/Dywidag*, Decision of 23 June 2005, concerning a partial referral.

necessary to safeguard or restore effective competition on the market concerned'.

Article 9(9) provides that 'in accordance with the relevant provisions of the Treaty, any Member State may appeal to the Court of Justice, and in particular request the application of Article 243 of the Treaty, for the purpose of applying its national competition law'.

47.2.2. Referral to the Commission (Article 22)[3]

Article 22 concerns concentrations that do not have a Community dimension but nevertheless 'affect trade between Member States and threaten to significantly affect competition within the territory of the Member State or States making the request'.

Member States may request the Commission to examine the concentration within 15 days from the date on which the concentration was notified. If no notification is required, time starts to run on the day on which the concentration was made known to the Member State concerned.

Article 22(2) provides that the Commission must, without delay, inform the competent authorities of the Member States and the undertakings concerned of the request.

Any other Member State has the right to join the initial request within a period of 15 working days of being informed by the Commission of the initial request. In that case, all national time limits relating to the concentration are suspended until it has been decided where the concentration is to be examined. In this type of case, as in cases falling under Article 9, the Regulation supplements national rules relating to the control of a concentration which does not have a Community dimension.

Once a Member State has informed the Commission that it does not wish to join the request, the suspension of its national time limits ends (Article 22(2)).

By virtue of Article 22(3), the Commission may, at the latest 25 days after it has passed on the information relating to the request, decide to examine the concentration 'where it considers that it affects trade between Member States and threatens to significantly affect competition within the territory of the Member State or States making the request'. If the Commission does not take a decision within this period, it is deemed to have adopted a decision to examine the concentration in accordance with the request.

If the decision is positive, the Commission must inform all Member States

---

[3] With reference to decisions pursuant to Article 22, see M.3796 – *Omya/J.M. Huber PCC*, Decision of 18 May 2005; M.3136 – *GE/AGFA NDT*, Decision of 5 December 2003 (under Regulation 4064/89).

and the undertakings concerned of its decision and may request, subject to the cases referred to in Article 22(4), the submission of a notification pursuant to Regulation 139/04. Consequently, and by analogy with Article 21, 'the Member State or States having made the request shall no longer apply their national legislation on competition to the concentration'.

48. Mechanisms Allowing the Commission and National Antitrust Authorities to Control Each Other

Like Regulation 1/03, Regulation 139/04 establishes control proceedings. However, unlike Regulation 1/03 it contains no mechanism providing for descending vertical ('top-down') control. Nor does it provide for peer control as between national authorities. It simply establishes an ascending vertical mechanism. This is effected by:

- monitoring of the Commission by individual national authorities; and
- collegiate monitoring of the Commission carried out by the Advisory Committee on concentrations.

The difference in this respect as compared with Regulation 1/03 is attributable to the exclusive powers that Regulation 139/04 has conferred on the Commission to control concentrations having a Community dimension.

48.1. CONTROL CARRIED OUT BY INDIVIDUAL NATIONAL AUTHORITIES

With the aim of allowing the individual national authorities to monitor the Commission's activity, Article 19(2) of the Regulation provides that 'the Commission shall carry out the procedures set out in this Regulation in close and constant liaison with the competent authorities of the Member States, which may express their views upon those procedures'. Article 19(1) stipulates that 'the Commission shall transmit to the competent authorities of the Member States copies of notifications and, as soon as possible, copies of the most important documents lodged with or issued by the Commission pursuant to this Regulation'.

With specific reference to referral pursuant to Article 9, the Commission shall obtain information from the competent authority of the Member State as referred to in paragraph 2 of that article and give it the opportunity to make known in its views at every stage of the procedure up to the adoption of a decision. Within that procedure, 'it shall give it access to the file' (Article 19(2)).

48.2. CONTROL CARRIED OUT THROUGH THE ADVISORY COMMITTEE ON CONCENTRATIONS

Collegiate monitoring of decisions taken by the Commission is carried out by the Advisory Committee on concentrations. It consists 'of representatives of the competent authorities of the Member States'. To that end, 'each Member State shall appoint one or two representatives; if unable to attend, they may be replaced by other representatives'. Article 19(4) stipulates that 'at least one of the representatives of a Member State shall be competent in matters of restrictive practices and dominant positions'.

The Advisory Committee must be consulted before the Commission takes any decision:

- pursuant to Article 8(1) (that is, declaring the concentration compatible with the common market);
- pursuant to Article 8(2) (that is, declaring the concentration compatible with the common market following modifications);
- pursuant to Article 8(3) (that is, declaring that the concentration is incompatible with the common market);
- pursuant to Article 8(4) (that is, requiring restoration of the situation prevailing before the implementation of a prohibited concentration);
- pursuant to Article 8(5) (that is, taking interim measures);
- pursuant to Article 8(6) (that is, revoking a decision declaring a concentration compatible with the common market);
- pursuant to Article 14 (that is, imposing a fine); and
- pursuant to Article 15 (that is, imposing a periodic penalty payment).

Article 19(5) provides that consultation of the Committee 'shall take place at a joint meeting convened at the invitation of and chaired by the Commission'. The invitation must be sent with 'a summary of the case, together with an indication of the most important documents and a preliminary draft of the decision to be taken for each case considered'. The meeting may not take place before ten days from the sending of the invitation. In exceptional cases, the Commission may shorten that period as appropriate in order to avoid serious harm to one or more of the undertakings concerned by a concentration (Article 19(5)).

At the end of the consultation, the Committee delivers 'an opinion on the

Commission's draft decision, if necessary by taking a vote', even if any members are absent and unrepresented. The opinion must be delivered in writing and appended to the draft decision.

By virtue of article 19(6) of Regulation 139/04, the Commission is required, as it is by the corresponding provision of Regulation 1/03, to 'take the utmost account of the opinion delivered by the Committee' and to 'inform the Committee of the manner in which its opinion has been taken into account'.

Article 19(7) requires the Commission to communicate the opinion of the Committee, together with the decision, to the addressees of the decision. The decision is subsequently made public, having regard to the legitimate interests of the undertakings in the protection of their business secrets (Article 19(7)).

Bibliography

Albonetti, A. (1960), *Preistoria degli Stati Uniti d'Europa*, Giuffrè, Milan.

Alexiadis, P. and Sullivan, P. (2004), 'Vertical restraints: new directions in EU policy', *The European Antitrust Review, A Global Competition Review Special Report*, pp. 68–72.

Allan, B. (2006), *Article 82: A Commentary on DG Competition's Discussion Paper, Competition Policy International*, v.2, no. 1, pp. 43–82.

Amato, G. (1998), *Il potere e l'antitrust*, Il Mulino, Bologna.

Arias, G. (1931), 'Paneuropa e i cartelli', *Il Popolo D'Italia*, 22 September, p. 1.

Balladore Pallieri, G. (1959), 'Il mercato comune europeo e la legislazione italiana antimonopolistica', *Diritto Internazionale*, p. 407.

Ballarino, T. (2001), *Manuale di Diritto delle Comunità Europee*, Cedam, Padua.

Barbagallo, C. (1929), *Le origini della grande industria contemporanea*, La nuova Italia, Venice.

Barbagallo, C. (1930), 'Le grandi cause del progresso dell'industria Europea ed Americana dal 1815 al 1850', in *Economia politica contemporanea – saggi di economia e finanza in onore del prof. Camillo Supino*, vol. II, Cedam, Padua, p. 283.

Barbier de la Serre E. (2006), 'Le contrôle des concentrations et la procédure accélérée: bref retour sur un franc succès', *Revue Lamy de la Concurrence*, no. 6, p. 56–61.

Basedow, J. (2001a), 'La renationalisation du droit communautaire de la concurrence', *Revue des Affaires Européennes*, p. 92.

Basedow, J. (2001b), 'Who will protect competition in Europe? From central enforcement to authority networks and private litigation', *European Business Organization Law Review* (Liber Amicorum E.-J. Mestmäcker), p. 443.

Bauer, J.P. and Page, W.H. (2002), 'Practices prohibited by the Sherman Act', *Federal Antitrust Law – A Treatise on the Antitrust Laws of the United States*, Anderson Pub. Co., Cincinnati, **2**.

Baumgarten, F. and Meszlény, A. (1906), *Kartelle und Trusts – Ihre Stellung im Wirtschafts – und Rechtssystem der wichtigsten Kulturstaaten*, Verlag von Otto Liebmann, Berlin.

Baxter S. and Dethmers, F. (2006), 'Collective dominance Under EC merger control: after Airtours and the introduction of unilateral effects is there still a future for collective dominance?', *European Competition Law Review*, p. 148.

Beaud, M. (2000), *Storia del capitalismo: Dal Rinascimento alla New Economy*, 5th edn, Mondadori, Milan (original title: *Histoire du capitalisme*, 2000).

Benisch, W. (1955), 'Zur Problematik eines gesetzlichen Schutzes des Leistungswettbewerbs', *Wirtschaft und Wettbewerb*, p. 421.

Benisch, W. (1956), 'Ist das Kartellverbot Grundgesetzwidrig?', *Der Betrieb*, p. 37.

Betti, E. (1949), *Interpretazione della legge e degli atti giuridici*, Giuffrè, Milan.

Blake S. and Schnichels, D. (2004), 'Leniency following modernisation: safeguarding Europe's leniency programmes', *European Competition Law Review*, p. 765 ss.

Blum, A. (1932), 'The law of trade combinations (trusts and *konzerns*) in Germany', in Scott, L. et al., *Trade combinations in U.S.A., France, Germany, Poland*, Librairie du Recueil Sirey, Paris.

Bos, P., Stuyck, J. and Wytinck, P. (1992), *Concentration Control in the European Economic Community*', Graham & Trotman, London.

Böhm, F. (1933), *Wettbewerb und Monopolkampf*, Heymann, Berlin.

Böhm, F. (1948), 'Das Reichsgericht und die Kartelle', *ORDO*, p. 197.

Böhm, F. (1956), 'Verstößt ein gesetzliches Kartellverbot gegen das Grundgesetz?', *Wirtschaft und Wettbewerb*, p. 173.

Brinker, I. (2000), 'Art. 83 EGV', in Jurgen Schwarze (ed.), *EU–Kommentar*, Nomos Verlagsgeselschaft, Baden-Baden.

Brittan, L. (1993), 'The future of competition policy', *European Business Law Review*, p. 27.

Broberg, Morten P. (2003), *The European Commission's Jurisdiction to Scrutinise Mergers*, Kluwer Law International, The Hague, London, New York.

Callies, C. (2002), *Art. 5 EGV*, in Christian Calliess, Matthias Ruffert and Hermann-Josef Blanke (eds), EUV/EGV *Kommentar*, **2**, Neuwied, Luchterhand, p. 382.

Cameron, R. and Neal, L. (2003), *A Concise Economy History of the World from Palaeolithic Times to the Present*, 4th edn, Oxford University Press, Oxford.

Canino, F. (2004), 'La cooperazione internazionale', Gian Luigi Tosato and Leonardo Bellodi (eds), *Il nuovo Diritto europeo della concorrenza – aspetti procedurali*, Giuffrè, Milan, p. 255.

Capelli, F. (2000), 'La riforma della disciplina comunitaria della concorrenza e i nuovi compiti affidati ai giudici nazionali (con particolare riferimento alla situazione italiana)', *Diritto comunitario e degli scambi internazionali*, p. 395.

Caronna, F. (2004), 'Article 81 as a tool for controlling minority cross-shareholdings between competitiors', *European Law Review*, 29, no. 4, pp. 485.

Caruso, F. and Sico, L. (2003), *Le nuove frontiere della disciplina della concorrenza e del mercato nell'Unione europea*, Giappichelli, Turin.

Cassese, S. (1998), *I garanti delle regole*, Il Mulino, Bologna.

Cassinis, P. (2004), 'La sentenza della Corte nel caso del "Consorzio industrie fiammiferi" (CIF): prevalenza del diritto comunitario e tutela della concorrenza in contesti regolamentati', *Foro Amministrativo*, p. 292.

Catalano, N. (1962), 'Relazione tra le regole di concorrenza stabilite dal Trattato istitutivo della C.E.E. e le legislazioni degli Stati membri', *Rivista di Diritto Europeo*, p. 335.

Cipolla, C. (1995), *Storia facile dell'economia italiana dal medioevo a oggi*, Mondadori, Milan.

Clarich, M. (2005), *Autorità indipendenti – Bilancio e prospettive di un modello*, Il Mulino, Bologna.

Coleman, M. and Grenfell, M. (1999), *The Competition Act 1998: Law and Practice*, Oxford, University Press, Oxford.

Cook C.J. and Kerse, C.S. (2005), *EC Merger Control*, Sweet & Maxwell, London.

Corwin, D.E. (1967), *Control of Cartels and Monopolies: An International Comparison*, Dobbs Ferry, Oceana Publications, NY.

Cseres, K.-J., Schinkel, M.-P. and Vogelaar, F.O.W. (2006), *Criminalization of Competition Law Enforcement: Economic and legal implications for the EU member states*, Edward Elgar, Cheltenham, UK, and Northampton, MA.

D'Alberti, M. (1999), 'Procedimenti "generali" e "singolari": problemi attuali e miglioramenti possibili', *Il procedimento davanti alle autorità indipendenti*, Giappichelli, Turin.

Dagnino, V. (1928), *I cartelli industriali – nazionali e internazionali*, Fratelli Bocca editori, Turin.

De Novellis, L. (1931), *L'unificazione economica dell'Europa*, Treves, Milan.

Del Marmol, C. (1959), 'Les Ententes industrielles en Droit comparé', *La Revue de la Banque*, Brussels, p. 35.

Deringer, A. (1965), 'Das Kartellrecht des EWG-Vertrages im Verhältnis zum nationalen Recht', Karlsruhe, Verlag C.F. Müller, Schriftenreihe/Juristische Studiengesellschaft Karlsruhe, **68**, p. 9 ss.

Dermot, C. and Cooke, J.D. (2004), *The Modernization of EU Competition*

Law Enforcement in the European Union: FIDE 2004 National Reports, Cambridge University Press, Cambridge.

Draetta, U. (1961a), 'Il regolamento di applicazione degli artt. 85 e 86 del Trattato di Roma', *Rivista di Diritto internazionale*, p. 144.

Draetta, U. (1961b), 'Le regole di concorrenza applicabili alle imprese della Comunità economica europea', *Diritto Internazionale*, p. 48.

Dreher, M. (2000), 'Gemeineuropäisches Kartellrecht', *Festschrift Alfred Söllner*, Beck Verlag, Munich, p. 217.

Egge, M.G., Bay, M.F. and Calzado, J.R., (2004), 'The new EC merger regulation: recipe for profound change or more of the same', *Il Diritto dell'Unione Europea*, no. 3, p. 461.

Eggmann, E. (1945), *Der Staat und die Kartelle*, Dr. H. Girsberger Verlag, Zurich.

Ehlermann, C.D. (1987), 'The internal market following the Single European Act', *Common Market Law Review*, p. 409.

Ehlermann, C.D. (1993), 'Ist die Verordnung Nr. 17 noch zeitgemäß?', *Wirtschaft und Wettbewerb*, p. 996.

Ehlermann, C.D. (1996), 'Cooperation between Competition Authorities within the European Union', in *Antitrust fra diritto nazionale e diritto comunitario*, Giuffrè, Milan, p. 472.

Ertel, E. (1930), *Internationale Kartelle und Konzerne der Industrie*, C.E. Poeschel Verlag, Stuttgart.

Eucken, W. (1949), *Die Wettbewerbsordnung und ihre Verwirklichung*, Ordo, p. 1.

Fattori, P. and Todino, M. (2004), *La disciplina della concorrenza in Italia*, Il Mulino, Bologna.

Fetter, F.A. (1931), *The Masquerade of Monopoly*, Harcourt, Brace, New York.

Flynn, J. and Bush, D. (2003), 'The misuse and abuse of the Tunney Act in the Microsoft cases: the adverse consequences of the "Microsoft Fallacies"', *Loyola University of Chicago Law Journal*, p. 749.

Fortunet, P. (1954), 'Dirigisme et libre concurrence: De la réglementation des ententes professionnelles et des conditions de vente par le décret du 9 août 1953', *Revue des Sociétés*, p. 236.

Fox, Eleanor M. and Bermann, George A. (2002), *Cases and Materials on the Competition Law of the European Union*, West Group St. Paul, MN.

Freise, H. (1994), *Wettbewerb und Politik in der Rechtsordnung des Nationalsozialismus Primat der Politik und ständischer Gedanke im Kartell-, Wettbewerbs- und Organizationsrecht 1933–36*, Nomos, Baden-Baden.

Friedländer, H. (1938), *Die Rechtspraxis der Kartelle und Konzerne in Europa*, Polygraphischer Verlag, Zürich.

Frignani, A. (1993), 'Art. 1 l. 287/90', in A. Frignani, R. Pardolesi, A. Patroni Griffi, and L.C. Ubertazzi, (eds), *Diritto antitrust italiano: Commento alla legge 10 ottobre 1990, n. 287*, **I** and **II**, Zanichelli, Bologna, p. 93.

Frignani, A. and Waelbroeck, M.A. (1997), *Concurrence (Commentaire Megret – 4)*, 2nd edn, Éditions de l'Université de Bruxelles, Brussels.

Furse, M. (1999), *Competition Law of the UK and EC*, Blackstone Press, London.

Furse, M. (2004), 'On a darkling plain: the confused alarms of Article 82 EC', *European Competition Law Review*, p. 317.

Gauer, C., Hjolbye, L., Dalheimer, D., De Smijter, E., Schnichels, D. and Laurila, M. (2004), 'Regulation 1/2003 and the Modernisation Package fully applicable since 1 May 2004', *Competition Policy Newsletter*, p. 1.

Genovese, A. (2004), *Il risarcimento del danno da illecito concorrenziale*, ESI, Naples.

Geradin, D. (2004), *Modernisation and Enlargement: Two Major Challenges for EC Competition Law*, Intersentia Publishers, Antwerp and Oxford.

Géradin D., Paulis, E., Sarrazin, E., Wachsmann, A., Wezenbeek, R. and Whish, R. (2006), 'Quelle réforme pour l'article 82 CE ?', *Concurrences*, n°4, pp. 10–17.

Gerber, D.J. (1998), *Law and Competition in Twentieth Century Europe: Protecting Prometheus*, Oxford University Press, Oxford.

Gerber, D.J. and Cassinis, P. (2006), 'The "modernisation" of European Community Competition Law: achieving consistency in enforcement', *European Competition Law Review*, Part I, p. 10; Part II, p. 51.

Ghezzi, F. (2000), 'Il libro bianco della Commissione sulla modernizzazione del diritto della concorrenza comunitario', *Concorrenza e mercato*, Giuffrè, Milan, p. 175.

Gide, P. (1953), *Le Projet Français de Loi Anti-Trust et les expériences etrangères: Etats-Unis, Angleterre, Allemagne*, Librairie du Recueil Sirey, Paris.

Ginsburg D.H. (2005), 'Comparing Antitrust Enforcement in the United States and Europe', *Journal of Competition Law and Economics*, 1, no. 3, p. 427.

González Díaz, F.E. (2004), 'The reform of European merger control: quid novi sub sole?', *World Competition*, 27, no. 2, p. 177.

Goyder, D.G. (1998), *EC Competition Law*, 3rd edn, Oxford University Press, Oxford.

Guglielmetti, G. (1970), *La concorrenza e i consorzi*, Unione tipografico-editrice torinese, Turin.

Hallstein, W. (1961), 'Wirtschaftliche Integration als Faktor politischer Einigung', in *Festgabe für Alfred Müller-Armack*, Duncker & Humbolt, Berlin, p. 267.

Hamel, J. and Lagarde, G. (1954), 'Controle des ententes industrielles', *§ 231 Traite de Droit Commercial*, Librairie Dalloz, Paris.

Haussmann, F. (1938), *Konzerne und Kartelle im Zeichen der 'Wirtschaftslenkung'*, Verlag für Recht und Gesellschaft A.G. Zurich.

Heimler, A. (1998), 'National priorities, national law and European law: the Italian experience', *European Competition Law Review*, p. 315.

Heinemann, A. (1989), *Die Freiburger Schule und ihre geistigen Wurzeln*, VVF, Munich.

Heinemann, A. (1996), 'Antitrust Law of Intellectual Property', *in TRIPs Agreement of the World Trade Organization*, Studies in Industrial Property and Copyright Law, Max Planck Institut Munich, p. 239.

Herlitzka, N. (1963), 'Bemerkungen zur historischen Entwicklung von Kartellen', in Ludwig Kastl and Max Metzner (eds), *Kartelle in der Wirklichkeit Festschrift für Max Metzner zu seinem fünfundsiebzigsten Geburstag*, Heymann, Köln, p. 117.

Hofheinz, P. and Perez, E. (2002), 'Monti changes course on carnival', *The Wall Street Journal Europe*, 22 July, p. 5.

Holmes, S. and Humpe, C. (2006), 'The CFI rules on GE/Honeywell', *Competition Law Insight*, **5**, no. 1, pp. 9–11.

Hovenkamp, H. (1994), *Federal Antitrust Policy: The Law of Competition and Its Practice*, St. Paul, MN, West Pub. Co..

Idot, L. (2004a), 'Concentrations: adoption du noveau règlement d'application', Europe, no. 6, p. 29.

Idot, L. (2004b), *Droit communautaire de la concurrence:le nouveau système communautaire de mise en oeuvre des articles 81 et 82 CE*, Série Concurrence/FEDUCI, Brussels.

Isay, R. (1955), 'Wirtschaftliche und rechtliche Konsequenzen des Böhm-Entwurfs', in *Wirtschaft und Wettbewerb*, 1955, p. 339.

Jimena Quesada L. (2005), *European Constitution and Competition Policy*, Philos Edizioni, Rome.

Jones A. and Sufrin B.E., (2004), *EC Competition Law: Text, Cases, and Materials*, 2nd edn, Oxford University Press, Oxford and New York.

Joshua, J. (2004), 'Competition Law enforcement. Criminalisation, cartels leniency and class actions: a look into the future', *Competition Law Insight*, p. 769.

Jung, C.H.A. (1995), *Subsidiarität im Recht der Wettbewerbsbeschränkungen*, C.F. Mueller, Heidelberg.

Kastl, L. and Metzner, M. (1963), *Kartelle in der Wirklichkeit Festschrift für Max Metzner zu seinem fünfundsiebzigsten Geburstag*, Heymann,

Cologne.

Katzler, C.V. (1963), 'Die Entscheidung des Reichsgerchts vom 4. 2. 1897 über die rechtliche Zulässigkeit von Kartellen und Syndikaten', in Ludwig Kastl and Max Metzner (eds), *Kartelle in der Wirklichkeit Festschrift für Max Metzner zu seinem fünfundsiebzigsten Geburstag*, Heymann, Cologne, p. 143.

Kerse, C.S. (1998), *E.C. Antitrust Procedure*, 4th edn, Sweet & Maxwell, London.

Kiersch, G. (1963), 'Die internationalen Stahlkartelle zwischen den beiden Weltkriegen', in Ludwig Kastl and Max Metzner (eds), *Kartelle in der Wirklichkeit Festschrift für Max Metzner, zu seinem fünfundsiebzigsten Geburstag*, Heymann, Cologne, p. 345.

Kjølbye, L. (2004), 'The new Commission Guidelines on the application of Article 81(3): an economic approach to Article 81', *European Law Review*, v. 29, no. 4, p. 566.

Klug, O. (1963), 'Die Problematik der amtlichen deutschen Kartellpolitik', in Ludwig Kastl and Max Metzner (eds), *Kartelle in der Wirklichkeit Festschrift für Max Metzner zu seinem fünfundsiebzigsten Geburstag*, Heymann, Cologne, p. 153.

Koch, N. (1959), 'Das Verhältnis der Kartellvorschriften des EWG Vertrages zum GWB', *Betriebsberater*, p. 241.

Korah, V. (2004), *An Introductory Guide to EC Competition Law and Practice*, Hart Publishing, Oxford.

Krämer, L. (1987), 'Unique Européen et la protection de l'environnement', *Revue Juridique de l'Environnement*, p. 79.

Kronstein, H. (1961), 'The Significance of the Provisions concerning Restraints of Competition within the total Perspective of the European Coal and Steel Community Treaty and the European Economic Community Treaty', in *Cartel and Monopoly in Modern Law*, Verlag C.F. Muller, Karlsruhe, p. 131.

Kronstein, H. (1962), 'Cartel control: a record of failure', in *Recht und Wirtschaftliche Macht*, 1946, Verlag C.F. Müller, Karlsruhe, p. 119.

Lador-Lederer, J.J. (1959), *Capitalismo mondiale e cartelli tedeschi tra le due guerre*, Giulio Einaudi editore, Florence.

Lammers, C. (1927), *Kartellgesetzgebung des Auslandes: Bericht an den Völkerbund für die internationale Wirtschaftskonferenz*, Carl Heymanns Verlag, Berlin.

Lammers, C. (1930), *Internationale Industrie – Kartelle (Völkerbunds–Denkschrift)*, Carl Heymanns Verlag, Berlin.

Lasok, K.P.E. (2004), 'When is an undertaking not an undertaking?', *European Competition Law Review*, p. 383.

Lehnich, O. (1928), *Kartelle und Staat unter Berücksichtigung der*

Gesetzgebung des In- und Auslandes, Verlag von Reimar Hobbing, Berlin.

Lenaerts, K. and Bray, R. (2006), *Procedural Law of the European Union*, Sweet & Maxwell, London.

Lenaerts, K. and Van Nuffel, P. (2005), *Constitutional Law of the European Union*, Sweet & Maxwell, London.

Libertini, M. (2002), 'Una disciplina antitrust speciale per le comunicazioni elettroniche', *Contratto e impresa: Europa*, p. 910.

Lombardo, S. (2002), *Regulatory Competition in Company Law in the European Community. Prerequisites and Limits*, Peter Lang, Frankfurt am Main.

Lowe, P. (2002), *Competition Policy in the European Union*, speech held at the *American Antitrust Institute* on July 1st 2002.

Maitland-Walker, J. (1999), 'The new U.K. competition law regime', *European Competition Law Review*, p. 51.

Maitland-Walker, J. (2003), *Competition Laws of Europe*, London.

Mangini, V. and Olivieri, G. (2005), *Diritto antitrust*, Turin.

Mastroianni, R. (2001), 'Osservazioni in merito all'effettività del sistema italiano di tutela "decentrata" del diritto comunitario della concorrenza', *Il Diritto dell'Unione europea*, p. 78.

McCurdy, G.v.S. (2004), 'The impact of modernisation of the EU competition law system on the courts and private enforcement of the competition laws: a comparative perspective', *European Competition Law Review*, p. 509.

Mengozzi, P. (2003), *Istituzioni di diritto comunitario e dell'Unione europea*, Cedam, Padua.

Mestmäcker, E.J. (1955) 'Der Böhm-Entwurf eines Gesetzes gegen Wettbewerbsbeschränkungen', *Wirtschaft und Wettbewerb*, p. 285.

Mestmäcker, E.J. (1965), 'Offene Märkte im System unverfälschten Wettbewerbs in der europäischen Wirtschaftsgemeinschaft', *Wirtschaftsordnung und Rechtsordnung: Festschrift Franz Böhm*, Verlag C.F. Müller, Karlsruhe, p. 345.

Mestmäcker, E.J. (1966), 'Die Beurteilung von Unternehmenszusammenschlüssen nach Art. 86 des Vertrages über die Europäische Wirtschaftsgemeinschaft', in *Festschrift für Walter Hallstein*, Peter Lang, Frankfurt am Main, p. 322.

Mestmäcker, E.J. (1992), 'Zur Anwendbarkeit der Wettbewerbsregeln auf die Mitgliedstaaten und die Europäischen Gemeinschaften', *Europarecht–Energierecht–Wirtschaftsrecht*, in Jürgen F. Baur, Peter-Christian Müller-Graff, Manfred Zuleeg and Carl Heymanns (eds), Verlag KG, Cologne, p. 277.

Mestmäcker, E.J. (1993), 'Die Wirtschaftsverfassung in der europäischen Union', *Vorträge und Berichte*, n. 28, Zentrum für europäisches

Wirtschaftsrecht, Rheinische Friederich-Wilhelms Universität Bonn, p. 1.

Mestmäcker, E.J. (2000), 'The EC Commission's modernization of competition policy: a challenge to the Community's constitutional order', *European Business Organization Law Review*, p. 401.

Mestmäcker, E.J. (2001), 'Die Wirtschaftsverfassung der EG zwischen Wettbewerb und Intervention', in Thomas Bruha, Joachim Jens Hesse and Carsten Nowa (eds), *Welche Verfassung für Europa?*, Nomos Verlagsgeselschaft, Baden-Baden, p. 163.

Mestmäcker, E.J. (2003), *Wirtschaft und Verfassung in der Europäischen Union*, Nomos Verlagsgesellschaft, Baden-Baden, p. 5.

Mestmäcker, E.J. and Schweitzer, H. (2004), *Europäisches Wettbewerbsrecht*, 2nd edn. Beck, Minich.

Moavero Milanesi, E. (1992), *Antitrust e concentrazioni fra imprese nel diritto comunitario*, Giuffrè, Milan.

Monopolkommission (1999), *Kartellpolitische Wende in der Europäischen Union?*, Sondergutachten **28**, no. 28, § 55, April.

Monopolkommission (2001), *Folgeprobleme der europäischen Kartellrechtsreform*, Sondergutachten, **30**, no. 32, § 20, October.

Monti, M. (2001), 'La dimensione internazionale della politica di concorrenza europea', *Mercato, Concorrenza e Regole*, p. 423.

Motta M., and Polo, M. (2005), *Antitrust: Economia e politica della concorrenza,* Il Mulino, Bologna.

Nörr, K.W. (1994), *Die Leiden des Privatrechts*, Mohr, Tübingen.

Orlando V.E. (1954), 'Sul concetto di Stato', *Diritto pubblico generale – Scritti vari (1881–1940)*, Giuffrè, Milan, p. 199, 219.

Pace, L.F. (1999), 'L'evoluzione della tutela amministrativa della concorrenza nel diritto *antitrust* comunitario e nazionale', *Diritto dell'Unione europea*, 1999, p. 355.

Pace, L.F. (2000a), 'I rapporti tra i sistemi di tutela della concorrenza federali/comunitari e i sistemi antitrust degli Stati membri nella Comunità europea e negli Stati uniti d'America', Doctoral Thesis, Facoltà di Scienze politiche, Istituto di Teoria dello Stato e Istituzioni politiche comparate, Università 'La Sapienza' – Roma.

Pace, L.F. (2000b), 'Il sistema italiano di tutela della concorrenza e il "vincolo comunitario" imposto al legislatore nazionale: l'art. 1 l. n. 287/90', *Rivista italiana di Diritto pubblico comunitario*, p. 176.

Pace, L.F. (2002), 'In tema di norme nazionali illegittime per violazione del combinato disposto degli artt. 10 e 81 TCE', *Rivista italiana di Diritto pubblico comunitario*, p. 454.

Pace, L.F. (2004), 'Die Dezentralisierungspolitik im EG-Kartellercht. Sind Art. 3 II, 6 der VO 1/2003 rechtmässig?', *Europäische Zeitschrift für Wirtschaftsrecht*, p. 301.

Pace, L.F. (2005), *I fondamenti del diritto antitrust europeo. Norme di competenza e sistema applicativo dalle origini alla Costituzione europea*, Giuffrè, Milan.

Pappalardo, A. (1962), 'Il primo regolamento di applicazione degli artt. 85 e 86 del Trattato della CEE', *Rivista delle Società*, p. 345:

Pardolesi, R. and Palmieri A. (2005), 'L'antitrust per il benessere (e il risarcimento del danno) dei consumatori', *Il Foro italiano*, p. 1014.

Pekàry, T. (2003), *Storia economica del mondo antico*, Il Mulino, Bologna, 2003, p. 195 (original title: *Die Wirtschaft der griechisch-römischen Antike*).

Pera, A. (1997), *La modernizzazione del diritto comunitario della concorrenza: rivoluzione o evoluzione?*, Acts of the Seminar 'Le nuove regole della concorrenza', held in Rome, at Associazione Bancaria Italiana (ABI), 3 July.

Picone, P. (1989), 'L'applicazione extraterritoriale delle regole sulla concorrenza e il diritto internazionale', in F. Capotorti, et al. (eds), *Il fenomeno delle concentrazioni di imprese nel diritto interno e internazionale*, Acts of a Seminar held in Naples on 29 April 1988, Cedam, Padua, p. 81.

Picone, P. and Ligustro A. (2003), *Diritto dell'organizzazione mondiale del commercio*, Cedam, Padua.

Plaisant, R. and Lassier, J. (1956), *Les Ententes Industrielles sous forme de Sociétés ou d'Associations*, Juris-Classeurs, Paris.

Rasch, H. (1955), 'Kartellverbot und Grundgesetz', *Wirtschaft und Wettbewerb*, p. 679.

Rasch, H. (1958), *Wettbewerbsbeschränkungen Kartell- und Monopolrecht; Kommentar zum Gesetz gegen Wettbewerbsbeschränkungen*, 2nd edn, Verlag Neue Wirtschafts-Briefe, Herne.

Riley, A. (2005), 'Beyond leniency: enhancing enforcement in EC antitrust law', *World Competition*, p. 327.

Ritter, L., Braun, W.D. and Rawlinson, F. (2005), *European Competition Law: A Practitioner's Guide*, 2nd edn, Kluwer Law International, The Hague, London, Boston.

Roberti, G.M. (1997), 'La tutela del denunziante in caso di inerzia della Commissione nelle procedure in materia di concorrenza', *Il Diritto dell'Unione europea*, p. 154.

Salandra V. (1934), *Il diritto delle unioni di imprese (consorzi e gruppi)*, A. Milani, Padua.

Scagnetti, G. (1933), *Cartelli industriali internazionali, con particolare riguardo al loro sviluppo nel dopoguerra*, Tipografia delle Terme.

Schanze, B. (2003), *Die europaorientierte Auslegung des Kartellverbots*, Peter Lang, Frankfurt am Main.

Schulze, R. and Hoeren, T. (eds) (2000), *Dokumente zum Europäischen Recht (Band 3) – Kartellrecht (bis 1957)*, Springer Verlag, Berlin.

Schumacher, H. (1962), 'Die Durchführung der Artikel 85 und 86 des Rom Vertrages', *Wirtschaft und Wettbewerb*, p. 475.

Scott, L. (1932), 'Introduzione', in Leslie Scott et al. (eds), *Trade Combinations in U.S.A, France, Germany, Poland*, Librairie du Recueil Sirey, Paris, p. 7.

Seitz, C. (2002), *One-stop Shop und Subsidiarität*, Carl Heymanns Verlag KG, Cologne.

Sinclair, D. (2004), 'Abuses of dominance at a crossroads. Potential effect, object and apreciability under Article 82 EC', *European Competition Law Review*, p. 491.

Siragusa, M. (1987), 'Notification of agreements in the EEC: to notify or not to notify?', *Annual Proceedings of the Fordham Corporate Law Institute*, p. 243.

Spengler, A. (1957), *Die Wettbewerbsregeln der Europäischen Wirtschaftsgemeinschaft*, Bundesverband der deutschen Industrie (BDI), Cologne.

Steindorff, E. (1961), 'The Provisions Against Restraints of Competition in the European Community Treaties and the National Law', *Kartelle und Monopole im Modernen Recht*, Verlag C.F., **I**, Muller, Karlsruhe, p. 191.

Strozzi, G. (2005), 'Il Trattato costituzionale', *Il Diritto dell'Unione Europea*, no. 3, p. 631.

Talamanca, M. (1989), *Istituzioni di Diritto romano*, **I**, Giuffrè, Milan, p. 111.

Tchernoff, J. and Lapie, P.O. (1932), 'Industrial and trade combinations under French law', in Leslic Scott et al. (eds), *Trade combinations in U.S.A., France, Germany, Poland*, Librairie du Recueil Sirey, Paris.

Temple Lang, J. (2006), 'Article 82', *Competition Law Insight*, **5**, n°1, p. 3.

Tesauro, G. (2002), 'Esiste un ruolo paragiurisdizionale dell'Antitrust nella promozione della concorrenza?', in F. Kostoris (eds), *Le Autorità indipendenti e il buon funzionamento dei mercati*, Giuffrè, Milan.

Tesauro, G. (2004), La tutela della concorrenza tra diritto comunitario e diritto italiano, *Economia e politica industriale*, p. 143.

Tesauro G. (2005), *Diritto comunitario*, Cedam, Padua.

Tizzano, A. (1981), 'Lo sviluppo delle competenze materiali delle Comunità europee', *Rivista di diritto europeo*, p. 139.

Tizzano, A. (1996), '*L'applicazione decentrata degli articoli 85 e 86 del Trattato CE in Italia. La tutela della concorrenza: regole, istituzioni e rapporti internazionali*', *Autorità garante della concorrenza e del mercato* (Temi e problemi – edizione speciale), Rome, p. 95.

Todino, M. (1997), *L'Autorità e l'applicazione decentrata degli articoli 85 e*

86 del Trattato CE, Rome, Autorità garante della concorrenza e del mercato (Temi e problemi), p. 9.
Tosato, G.L. (1965), *I regolamenti delle Comunità europee*, Giuffrè, Milan.
Tosato G.L. and Bellodi, L. (2004), *Il nuovo diritto europeo della concorrenza: Aspetti procedurali*, Giuffrè, Milan.
Toulemon, A. (1954), 'Le Décret-loi du 9 août 1953 relatif au maintien ou au rétablissement de la libre concurrence industrielle ou commerciale', *Revue trimestrielle de Droit Commercial*, p. 269.
Tridimas, T. (1999), *The General Principles of EC Law*, Oxford University Press, Oxford.
Usher, J.A. (1998), *General Principles of EC Law*, Longman, London, p. 37.
Van Bael, I. and Bellis, J.F. (2005), *Competition Law of the European Community*, Kluwer Law International, The Hague.
Van den Bergh, R. and Camesasca, P.D., (2001), *European Competition Law and Economics: a Comparative Perspective, Intersentia*, Antwerpen.
Veljanovski C. (2004), 'EC merger policy after GE/Honeywell and Airtours', *The Antitrust Bulletin*, p. 153.
Venit, J. (2003), 'Brave new world: the modernization and decentralization of enforcement under articles 81 and 82 of the EC Treaty', *European Competition Law Review*, no. 40, p. 545.
Vickers, J. (2004), 'Merger policy in Europe: retrospect and prospect', *European Competition Law Review*, p. 455.
Villani, U. (2004), 'I diritti fondamentali tra Carta di Nizza, Convenzione europea dei diritti dell'uomo e progetto di Costituzione europea', *Il Diritto dell'Unione Europea*, p. 73.
Vito, F. (1939), *I sindacati industriali – Cartelli e gruppi*, 3rd edn, Giuffrè, Milan.
Völcker, S.B. (2004), 'Mind the gap: unilateral effects analysis arrives in EC merger control', *European Competition Law Review*, p. 395.
Von der Groeben, H. (1964), 'Die Aufgaben der Wettbewerbspolitik im Gemeinsamen Markt und in der Atlantischen Partnerschaft', *Wirtschaft und Wettbewerb*, p. 1003.
Von der Groeben, H. (1996), 'Ernst Joachim Mestmäckers Beitrag zur Gestaltung einer europäischen Wettbewerbspolitik', in *Festschrift für Ernst-Joachim Mestmäcker zum siebzigsten Geburstag*, Nomos Verlagsgeselschaft, Baden-Baden, p. 29.
Von Kalinowski, J.O., Sullivan, P. and McGuirl, M. (2000), *Antitrust Laws and Trade Regulation*, 2nd edn, Lexis, New York.
von Puttkamer, E. (1965), 'Der Briand-Plan, Vorbote der europäischen Integration?', in *Zur Integration Europas: Festschrift für Carl Friedrich Ophüls*, Verlag C.F. Müller, Karlsruhe, p. 143.
Waelbroeck, D., Slater, D. and Even-Shoshan, G. (2004), 'Study on the

conditions of claims for damages in case of infringement of EC competition rules', *Comparative and Economics Reports*, Ashurst, Brussels.

Wagenführ, H. (1931a), *Kartelle in Deutschland*, Verlag der Hochschulbuchhandlung Krische & Co., Nuremberg.

Wagenführ, H. (1931b), *Kartellverträge – Deutsche ausländische und internationale Kartellverträge im Wortlaut*, Verlag der Hochschulbuchhandlung Krische & Co, Nuremberg.

Wagenführ, H. (1933), *Kartellgesetzgebung in Deutschland*, Verlag der Hochschulbuchhandlung Krische & Co, Nuremberg.

Wamser, F. (1994), *Enforcement of Antitrust law: a Comparison of the Legal and Factual Situation in Germany, the EEC, and the USA*, Peter Lang, Frankfurt am Main.

Weiler, J.H.H. (1991), 'The Transformation of Europe', *Yale Law Journal*, p. 243.

Wells, W.C. (2002), *Antitrust and the Formation of the Postwar World*, Columbia University Press, New York, p. 163.

Werr, F. (1936), *Internationale Wirtschaftszusammenschlüsse (Kartell und Konzern) und Staat als Vertragspartner*, Carl Heymanns Verlag, Berlin.

Whish, R. (2005), *Competition Law*, Oxford University Press, London.

Wiedenfeld, K. (1927), *Kartelle und Konzerne*, Walter de Gruyter & Co., Berlin.

Wils. P.J. (2005), *Principles of European Antitrust Enforcement*, Oxford and Portland OR.

Wolfgang Nörr, K. (1994), *Die Leiden des Privatrechts–Kartelle in Deutschland von der Holzstoffkartellentscheidung zum Gesetz gegen Wettbewerbsbeschränkungen*, J.C.B. Mohr, Tübingen.

Wood, D. and Seikyte, S. (2000), 'Article 82 and cost allocation', *Competition Law Insight* 2006, **5**, no. 3, p. 13.

Zacher, H.F. (1996), 'Grußwort', in Ulrich Immenga (ed.), *Festschrift für Ernst-Joachim Mestmäcker zum siebzigsten Geburstag*, Nomos Verlagsgeselschaft, Baden-Baden, p. 24.

Zanghì, C. (2000), *Istituzioni di diritto dell'Unione europea*, 3rd edn, G. Giappichelli, Turin.

Index